Service Operations
Management

Service Operations Management

Strategy, design and delivery

Christine Hope
and
Alan Mühlemann

FINANCIAL TIMES
Prentice Hall
An imprint of Pearson Education

Harlow, England · London · New York · Reading, Massachusetts · San Francisco
Toronto · Don Mills, Ontario · Sydney · Tokyo · Singapore · Hong Kong · Seoul
Taipei · Cape Town · Madrid · Mexico City · Amsterdam · Munich · Paris · Milan

Pearson Education Limited
Edinburgh Gate
Harlow CM20 2JE
Tel: +44 (0)1279 623623
Fax: +44 (0)1279 431059

and Associated Companies throughout the world

Visit us on the World Wide Web at:
http://www.pearsoned.co.uk

First published 1997 by
Prentice Hall Europe
© Prentice Hall 1997

ISBN 0 201 79523 X

Typeset in 10/12 Times
by PPS, London Road, Amesbury, Wilts.

Printed and bound by CPI Antony Rowe, Eastbourne

Library of Congress Cataloging-in-Publication Data

Available from the publisher

British Library Cataloguing in Publication Data

A catalogue record for this book is available from
the British Library

ISBN : 0–13–149915–7

Contents

Part I

Services: an overview

Chapter 1

Role of services within the economy

Chapter outline

- ☆ Definition of service
- ☆ What is operations management?
- ☆ Service classifications
- ☆ Life cycle of firms
- ☆ Importance of services
- ☆ Models of services
- ☆ Public vs private
- ☆ How the book is organized

Definition of service

In the 1978 edition of the *Pocket Oxford Dictionary*, the noun 'service industry' is defined as 'providing services, not goods'. 'Goods' are defined as 'movable property, merchandise'. From this comes the idea that manufacturing industry provides tangible goods, while service industry provides something intangible. 'Tangible' is defined as 'perceptible by touch: definite, clearly intelligible, not elusive or visionary'. The argument is then raised that even the most tangible goods like cars have an intangible element. When buying a car, the purchaser, although buying something which is very tangible – it can be touched, seen and even smelt – is looking for something in addition, which cannot be seen. Prestige, safety and reliability are all intangible aspects which cannot be touched. In particular, the image of the car is a very elusive concept. What was it that made a Peugeot 205 *the* car to own in the early 1990s by young trendy men? Of course, it had to be turbo charged with the largest engine – but even so, it had something which is indefinable, at least as far as that particular 'set' were concerned. Volvos go together with a staid, conservative type of person. Sleek red sports cars go with a fast sexy image. The fact that the performance of some of the sporty-looking cars is not as fast or responsive as some saloon cars is usually overlooked. Somehow, this tangible good called a car, the primary use of which is to transport passengers from point A to point B, conjures up all sorts of images which reflect upon the owner.

Having at this point established that there may not be such a thing as a 'pure' good, the question is, then, is there such a thing as a 'pure' service? A form of business which would typically be considered to be in the service sector is the accounting profession. What is being purchased is advice – perhaps regarding the payment (or non-payment) of tax. The client will probably receive a written report containing documents to submit to the Inland Revenue, or maybe even just a letter explaining action which has been taken on the client's behalf. Either way, the report itself is a tangible object. In this case, the piece of paper itself is not being bought for its own sake – it is simply evidence of the service performed.

In all businesses a purchaser receives something in exchange for some form of payment. That something is the output of some kind of process. It is a product of the transformation or production process. It may be a good or a service, or some kind of combination of the two. The actual balance between tangible and intangible elements of the product can be anywhere between 100 per cent tangible, 0 per cent service; and 0 per cent tangible, 100 per cent service. Consider Figure 1.1: to the left are examples of very tangible products which are hard to associate with even an image! Unleaded petrol for the car is hard to get excited about. Having said that, back in the 1960s Esso promoted its product by advising customers to 'Put a tiger in your tank'! At the far right lies counselling. Having your problems listened to by a trained psychiatrist is not supplemented by a physical product which can be taken away at the end of the session. No physical or tangible product is bought. However, even here there *is* a tangible element – the consultation will take place within a physical surrounding, the layout and decor of which will affect the experience.

The service industry could be redefined as 'providing predominantly intangible products', as opposed to the manufacturing sector which could be defined as 'providing predominantly tangible products'. There is no black and white cut-off point between the two. The argument then arises as to why anyone should discriminate between the two. Why have any distinction? Why write a book devoted to the management of *service* operations? Why not just have books on the management of operations? Lockyer (1986) was a proponent of the latter argument. The counter-argument is that services have characteristics which raise different types of problem for operations managers, which need different approaches. There are four major characteristics of service which cause such problems, i.e. ones which are not usually associated with the manufacturing sector:

- *S*imultaneity of production and consumption.
- *H*eterogeneous nature of the product.
- *I*ntangibility of the product.
- *P*erishability of the product, i.e. a service cannot be stored.

There are other characteristics of a service, but these others and the four presented here will be described in more detail, together with an examination of the implications of the characteristics for the operations manager, in the next chapter. However, just to get some idea of how the differences may pose different problems for the service operations manager, take the first characteristic, simultaneity: the product is produced and consumed at the same time. An example of this is a haircut. The customer has to be present for the operation to take place. This contrasts with the manufacture of a car which is made in a factory, perhaps in Japan. If mistakes are made in the production process in the first case, the

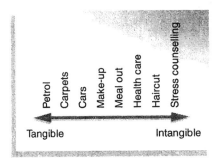

Figure 1.1 Tangibility–intangibility continuum

customer will certainly notice: for example, the hair colouring that went wrong because the hairdresser mixed up the wrong solution will hardly be missed! However, if a car spray comes out the wrong colour because the wrong 'solution' was used, it can be reworked and the customer need never know. In both cases the operations managers should be trying to 'do it right first time every time', but the importance of getting it right is much more important when the customer is present. In addition, the process is usually harder to control when the customer is present, because customers introduce an element of unpredictability that is not present in a factory. In the example of a haircut, the reason for the colour coming out wrong may have had nothing to do with the mixing of the colourant, but everything to do with an abnormal lack or surfeit of pigment in the customer's hair itself, or because the customer distracted the hairdresser.

What is operations management?

So what is operations management? In a manufacturing setting, the comparable term would be production management. In the production of any product (good, service or a combination of both), a transformation takes place of inputs of whatever kind, in form or time or place, into an output or product. This is shown diagrammatically in Figure 1.2.

A production or operations manager is responsible for managing this transformation process. In the case of a manufacturing setting, the inputs may be raw materials such as steel, together with labour and equipment; the transformation process may be the manufacture of a car, bringing together the inputs in, hopefully, the most efficient and effective manner; to produce the output, the product, in this case a car. The transformation will take place in a factory, which needs to be laid out, using the most appropriate equipment. The work will need to be scheduled to meet delivery dates. In a service setting, such as education, the inputs are the students, the lecturers, the lecture notes, etc. The transformation process may take place in a lecture theatre or in tutorial rooms. The educated students are the output or product of the process. The process has to be managed, with issues of timetabling (scheduling) and provision of infrastructure (lecture theatres with heating and lighting, etc.), in just the same way as in a factory.

Five areas of responsibility have been described for a production manager, often referred to as the five Ps of production:

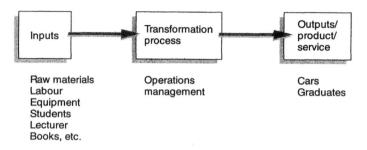

Figure 1.2 The transformation process

- Product.
- Process.
- Programmes.
- Plant.
- People.

The same areas fall under the remit of the operations manager in a service context. Examples in a service context are as follows:

- *Product.* Product design and specification: for example, the home loan package offered by a building society.
- *Process.* How are the insurance claims handled? Are they dealt with in batches, or individually as they come into the office?
- *Programmes.* In what order, and when are customers dealt with in a hospital? When are operations scheduled? How many hours of the day are the operating theatres in use? Are there priority patients who interrupt the pre-arranged schedule?
- *Plant.* At a hairdressing salon, what type of equipment is purchased – which of the heat treatment machines used when colouring or perming hair is the most effective, economical, easy to use, easy to maintain, etc?
- *People.* Selection, training, appraising, motivating, supervising and rewarding air hostesses are all concerns of the operations manager, as ill-trained or unmotivated employees will not perform well and will adversely affect the transformation process. In services, people are often *the* most critical factor in a successful operation.

All of these aspects of operations management will be dealt with later in the book.

Service classifications

Various classifications of services have been suggested. These look at different aspects of the service provided and identify similarities or differences which are used to classify the service. This is particularly useful when looking at ways of improving performance by studying comparable firms. Benchmarking has become a very topical issue in the last five

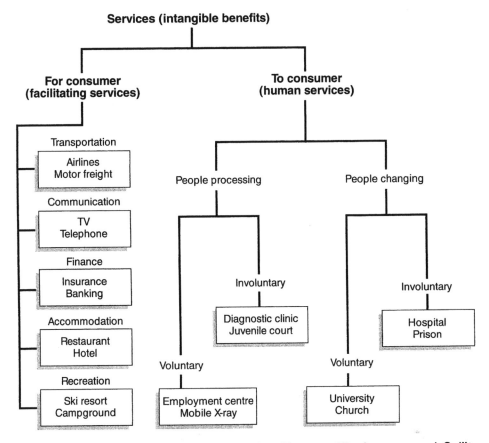

Figure 1.3 Consumer perspectives of service (Source: Fitzsimmons and Sullivan, *Service Operations Management*, McGraw-Hill, 1982, p. 17; reproduced with permission of the McGraw-Hill Companies)

years or so. How is my firm doing in comparison to Joe Bloggs' firm? If Joe Bloggs is in the same line of business, then the comparison may be meaningful and helpful, but unless the businesses are essentially similar, any comparison would be like comparing the yield rate of an apple tree with that of a tomato plant! The following classifications have different bases of comparison. The model which is most appropriate to the given situation should be the one chosen. Four models are included here:

- Customer perspective (Figure 1.3).
- Customization and judgement (Table 1.1).
- Capital vs labour intensity (Figure 1.4).
- Contact of processor with customer (Figure. 1.5).

The first question to ask yourself, with the consumer perspective, is whether the service you are providing is *for* the consumer or done *to* the consumer. If it is done *for* the consumer, the next question is: which of these areas does my firm fit into? For example, your

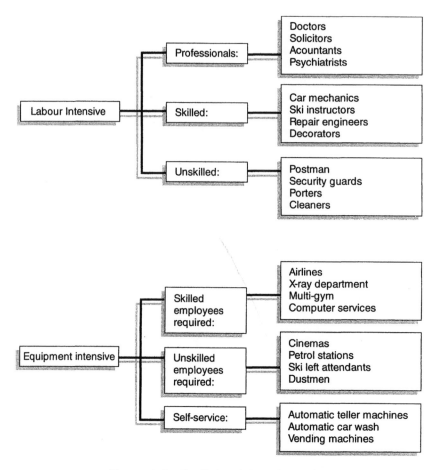

Figure 1.4   Capital vs labour intensity

organization may provide accommodation of some form. It may be a motel by a motorway. Clearly comparisons with other motels on motorways would be the ideal – how do they operate? However, direct competitors may not be willing to co-operate and will certainly not want to tell you the secret of their success! The next best thing would be to study other forms of accommodation provision – maybe city centre hotels. Differences will have to be allowed for, but there will be examples of good practice that could usefully be copied. British Rail on its Inter-City trains clearly looked to the airlines: 'British Rail welcomes you on board. We do not expect any delays and we should arrive in King's Cross at 10.04 hours. Your chief steward today is Fred, who will be only too happy to serve you with ...'.

If the service is done *to* the consumer, does it *change* or *process* the consumer? Is it *voluntary* or *involuntary*? Again, what you should be trying to do is identify the type of relationship you have with the consumer of your service, and then look for other organizations with a similar profile.

The same principle applies when using any of the classification schemes presented here.

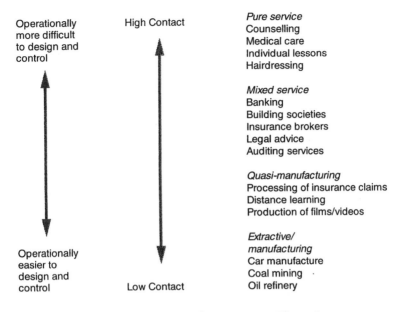

Figure 1.5 Contact of processor with customer

Table 1.1 Customization and judgement in service delivery

Degree of judgement required by contact personnel	Customization of service	
	High	Low
High	Family doctor Driving instructor Legal advice Hairdresser Piano lessons Financial advice	Lectures to large groups Guided tours
Low	Telephone service High class restaurant Personal banking Hotel services	Bus service College refectory Theatre Exhaust/tyre replacement

In Figure 1.5, some examples of quasi-manufacturing are given where customer contact is quite low. In such situations, where similarities exist between a service and a manufacturing setting, there may well be operations management techniques which can be applied equally successfully in either context. Statistical process control is a technique which has been used in the manufacturing sector for over 50 years to help ensure quality of the product. Although its use in services is limited, it has been usefully applied in a service context (Mundy *et al.*, 1986). The expression 'if the cap fits, wear it' seems to apply here. If there are techniques

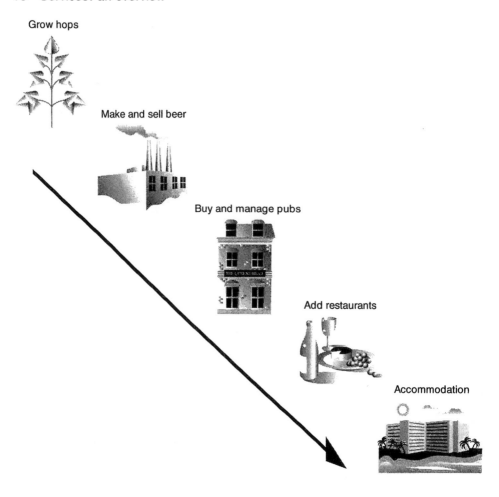

Grow hops

Make and sell beer

Buy and manage pubs

Add restaurants

Accommodation

Figure 1.6   Life cycle of a firm

which are used in one sector, be it manufacturing or service, which can sensibly be transferred to the other, then do it. But the first step must always be an analysis of the context: are the underlying situational circumstances sufficiently similar to make the transfer of the technique sensible?

Life cycle of firms

Most firms start off in a small way. Even the banking sector originally started with individual money lenders. Many firms in the service sector remain small. Hairdressers typically have only one salon. Steiners and Vidal Sassoon are exceptions to the norm. One of the reasons for this is the need for personalized service delivered near to where the customer lives.

However, often, over time, many successful organizations grow. Owners, who used to carry out all the functions required to run the business, from bookkeeping to marketing, eventually hire specialists. Over time, the firm expands its range of products. Examples of this are numerous, but a well-known firm, with stores throughout the UK is Boots. Originally a chemist's shop in Nottingham, Boots now, in addition to the chemist side of the business, sells stationery, books, CDs, computers and kitchenware, and has fairly recently opened optician's services within stores. This picture has also been mirrored outside the service sector. Firms involved in the extractive industry have expanded vertically forwards and have ended up with part of their operations extending into the service sector.

In the scenario illustrated in Figure 1.6, a farmer starts by growing hops and selling them to a brewery. He used some of the hops to brew his own beer. Then, as the homebrew tasted so good, he decided to start making it on a commercial scale, and so expanded into the brewing industry. After a few more years, he decided to expand further by buying up some of the public houses he had been supplying. These pubs served bar meals. Under the influence of his wife, the quality of these meals improved greatly, and a further opportunity was seized when restaurants were added to a selection of his pubs. His final expansion came with the move into the accommodation sector, with an upgrading of some of the pubs/restaurants to inn status. At the end of the day, farming and brewing had become very minor parts of the business. The majority of the business now lay in the service sector.

The significance of the changing nature of a business over time lies in the fact that the characteristics will also change over time with consequent implications for the operations manager.

Importance of services

The progression seen in the above example of a firm mirrors the stages of a country's development. It is generally recognized that the stages of development follow a pattern:

- Stage 1: economies based on agriculture and extractive industries.
- Stage 2: development of manufacturing industries.
- Stage 3: growing predominance of service industries.

The importance of the service sector in any one country, therefore, is partly dependent upon the current stage of economic development. (For a fuller discussion of the stages of economic development, see Fitzsimmons and Fitzsimmons, 1994, pp. 5–9.)

In post-industrial countries like the UK and the USA, the service sector is now more important than the manufacturing sector. Figure 1.7 shows the relative contributions of agriculture, construction, production (manufacturing) and services to GDP in the UK in real terms, i.e. the effects of inflation have been taken out of the figures.

GDP has been rising for most of the period since 1971. Three downturns have occurred during the period: in the mid-1970s due to the oil crisis, in the early 1980s and in the early 1990s. Only in the last downturn has the figure for services gone down, in 1991 and 1992, and then the contribution to GDP from services started to rise in 1993, even though the general downturn in GDP continued. This is not unusual. In the USA, services have proved to be equally resilient. One of the reasons for this resilience is the lack of stockholding in services.

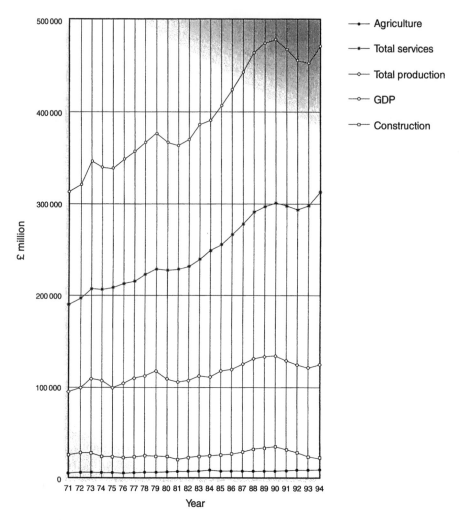

Figure 1.7 GDP at constant factor cost (Source: Based on data from HMSO, *Blue Books*, various years)

Factors which affect the importance of the service sector are as follows:

- Distribution of wealth.
- Amount of leisure time.
- Size of the dependent population.
- Number of homes where both partners work.

Taking each of these factors in turn, just how do they influence the significance of the service sector within an economy?

Distribution of wealth

If the wealth of a nation is held by a privileged few, with the majority of the population

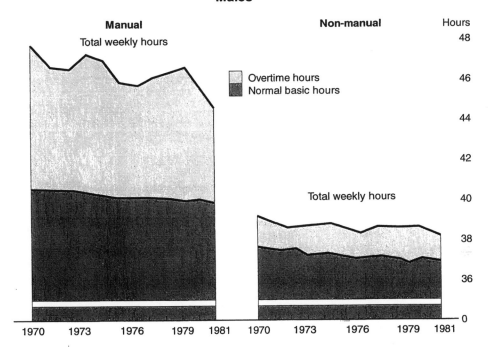

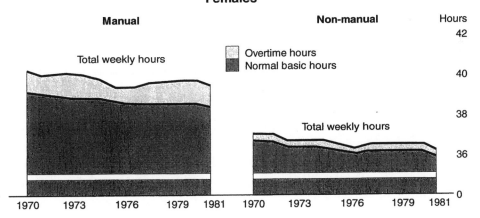

Note: Figures relate to April each year and to full-time employees – males aged 21 and over and females aged 18 and over – whose pay for the survey period was not affected by absence.

Figure 1.8 Trends in average weekly hours of UK full-time employees (Source: HMSO, *Social Trends*, 1983 p. 57)

Millions

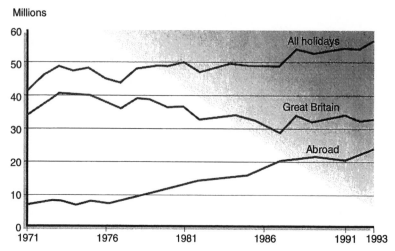

Figure 1.9   Holidays taken by British residents: by destination (Source: HMSO, *Social Trends*, 1995, p. 215)

living near the poverty line, the demand for services generally will be low. Services which facilitate industry, such as transport of goods, will still exist, but services for the population generally – personal insurance, entertainment, education, etc. – will be at a relatively low level, accessible only to a few people.

Amount of leisure time

When the amount of time spent not working increases, so too does the demand for leisure activities and facilities for entertainment. There is more time available for hobbies and special interests, such as windsurfing or health farms. Figure 1.8 shows the trends in the average weekly hours of full-time employees for the UK over the period 1970 to 1981. This shows a steady decline in the number of hours spent working, which has led to a gradual increase in spare time. In 1994 the average was 43.5 hours for males and 30.6 hours for females (HMSO, *Social Trends*, 1996).

The tourism industry in particular has been particularly positively affected by the increase in paid holidays since the Holidays with Pay Act in 1938 (see Figure 1.9). Unfortunately, in the UK, much of this growth has been in overseas holidays, but many second holidays are taken within the UK. All of these activities involve a demand for services.

Size of the dependent population

Two major service areas are health care and education. With the advances in medicine over the last century, life expectancy has increased, and the number of old people needing all kinds of support, from help with the cleaning, to fairly intensive care in a nursing home, not to mention medical treatment, has increased steadily, as can be seen in Figure 1.10.

In 1951, approximately 7 million people in the UK were over pensionable age (males aged 65 and over, females aged 60 and over). By the year 2031, the projected number of

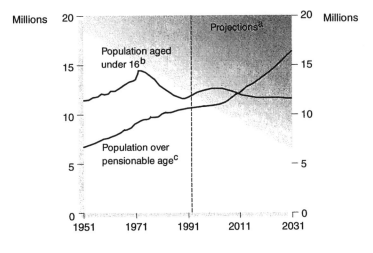

a 1991-based projections.
b Data for 1951 to 1971 relate to population under 15
   (the school-leaving age was raised in 1972).
c Males aged 65 and over, females aged 60 and over.

Figure 1.10 UK dependent population: by age (Source: HMSO, *Social Trends*, 1994, p. 23)

people over retirement age is approximately 16 million. In 1991, there were 30 people of pensionable age for every 100 of working age. This is projected to be 46 per every 100 by the year 2031.

The population aged under 16, apart from peaking at just under 15 million in the early 1970s, has remained reasonably stable at around 12 million, and is also projected to remain at approximately this level. The demand for education and health care for children has therefore not risen on the basis of numbers. However, the government has professed to encourage the raising of education standards within the UK, which in part has meant the encouragement of further and higher education. During the 1970s, the number of places at universities and polytechnics rose significantly. However, with the reduction in grants for students, access to higher education is becoming more restricted again. Also, over the period 1989/90 to 1994/5, student numbers rose by over 60 per cent, while government funding only rose by approximately 10 per cent (*Times Higher Educational Supplement*, 1996). Therefore, the future trend is unclear : although in principle the numbers in higher education should increase, the practicalities of making ends meet may inhibit this growth.

Number of homes where both partners work

The consequence of both partners in a household working are twofold:

- Higher income – greater disposable income.
- Greater demand for services due to value of time.

With two incomes coming into a household, there will be more 'spare' income left to spend on non-essentials. To begin with, when setting up home, spare income is used to buy

Producer Services (intermediate markets)
• Financial services:
    banking, insurance, leasing
• Shipping and distribution:
    ocean, rail, trucking, air freight, wholesaling, warehousing, distribution
• Professional and technical:
    licensing and sales, engineering design services, architectural design,
    construction management and contracting, other management services,
    legal services, accounting
• Other intermediate services:
    computer, data processing, communication services (including software),
    franchising, advertising, other (commercial real estate, business travel,
    security, postal services, contract maintenance, etc.)

Consumer services (final markets to private citizens)
• Retailing
• Health care
• Travel, recreation, entertainment
• Education
• Other social services, including government
• Other personal services (restaurants, home repair, laundry, etc.)

Figure 1.11 Classification scheme for service providers (Source: Office of Technology Assessment, 1985)

washing machines, tumble dryers, dish washers and so on. After a while, more income will be spent on leisure, holidays and services generally. Tied in with this is the concept of value of time. In contrast to the situation where one of the partners remains at home and does all the cooking, cleaning, gardening and general repairs, the couple who are both in full-time employment are more likely to pay others to clean, garden and do any repairs, as they can afford to pay someone else to do the job, and prefer to spend their free time enjoying themselves. They are also more likely to eat out in restaurants or buy take-away food. Increasingly, more and more fast-food outlets will deliver meals free within a certain radius, from curries to pizzas.

Models of services

Earlier in the chapter, typologies of service by inherent characteristics within the particular service were presented. Other types of model, categorized more by the sectors within which the service firms operate, or in which they provide a useful function, have been suggested by various authors. One of the simplest is the classification scheme for service providers presented by Akehurst (1989) sourced from the Office of Technology Assessment, Washington, DC, and presented here in Figure 1.11.

Murdick *et al.* (1990) present the taxonomy of services reproduced here in Figure 1.12.

Distributive services: physical and informational

Retail and wholesale trade

Non-profit services

Producer services
- Finance
- Insurance
- Real estate
- Business services
- Legal services
- Membership organizations
- Miscellaneous professional services

Consumer services
- Health care
- Education
- Personal services
- Car repair, garages, miscellaneous maintenance
- Hotel/motel/food services
- Restaurant/food services
- Leisure services
- Private households

Figure 1.12 A taxonomy of services (Source: Murdick *et al.*, *Service Operations Management*, 1990, p. 6; © Reprinted by permission of Prentice-Hall Inc., Upper Saddle River, NJ)

Riddle (1986) presents a model (Figure 1.13) showing the interactions between the different sectors of the economy, which illustrates the wide range of needs for services. Primitive societies based on subsistence farming and barter for goods have little or no need for support services. But as soon as industrialization and specialization take place, a need for, at the very least, transportation arises. Subsequently, financial services for the raising of credit and insurance are required, and so on.

Together these models provide an excellent picture of the importance and range of service industries. With technological advances, more and more primary and secondary industries will become increasingly capital intensive and less labour intensive. Services will become even more sophisticated and wide ranging.

Public vs private sector

Many services have been or still are provided by the state. The size of the public sector in the UK has been reducing, as over the last decade many of the state-owned enterprises have been sold off. This was triggered by the Thatcher government, which believed in market forces and privatization. The very fact that many once public sector enterprises are now privately owned suggests that, so far as operations management is concerned,

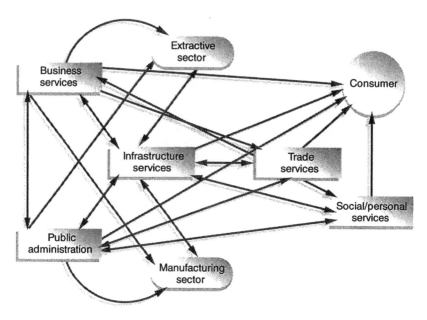

Figure 1.13   Interactive model of an economy (Source: Riddle, 1986, p. 27)

there really is no difference. Whether or not an organization is owned by the government, the requirement should still be to produce either a good or a service efficiently and effectively at a minimum cost. The operational issues will be the same. Even in charitable organizations, the goal should be to do the job in the best possible way. There are differences, however, some of which are listed below:

- Who is the customer – the end user or the government?
- Objectives – long-term survival or short-term profit?
- Uncertainty – a new government may make a U-turn (education)
- Monopolistic power.

Who is the customer?

In most private organizations, the person who pays the bill at the end of the day is the customer. In terms of success, it is generally accepted that the most successful firms will be those which most closely meet the requirements of the customer. In a state-owned enterprise, the paymaster is the government. It holds the purse strings and can 'call the tune'. But the government is not the end user. Take, for example, the case of education. The student is the end user, but has little power to take his or her business elsewhere. There is private education, and the University of Buckingham is a private establishment, but the majority of students will not be able to afford this. Ask students what they would prefer, larger or smaller classes, more or less facilities generally. The universities themselves have little discretion over the staff/student ratios, or the level of funding generally to support library facilities, etc. In health care, who is the customer? The patient, the GP, the government?

Dalrymple *et al.* (1995), in the context of local government, used a technique frequently used in the service sector to measure service quality. They found that: 'the results ... indicate that the degree and nature of payment and receipt for different types of service provision may critically affect the assessment criteria used by "customers"' (p. 4). This becomes very important when issues of strategy and service design are considered.

Objectives of the organization

This brings us on to the next issue – what are the objectives of the organization? Are they profit maximization, long-term security, maximum market share, maximum accessibility or what? Any operational strategy should be in line with the overall objectives of the organization. A general example of this will be capacity management. There will almost always be a trade-off between utilization of resources and customer satisfaction. If the aim is to provide a service whenever it is needed without delay, underutilization of resources is inevitable. This does not always mean lower profits in the private sector unless the customer is unwilling or unable to pay a higher price to receive such service. However, the organization will still be trying to provide that particular level of service at a minimum cost. In operational terms there would be no difference, given the same objectives, i.e. to serve customers without delay, whether the setting was in a private or state-owned hospital.

The problem often arises when a state-funded organization is set objectives, but is also constrained by rules and regulations. The BBC has been seen as a large, inefficient, cumbersome organization, and there has been uncertainty regarding its charter renewal unless it can operate more competitively. There may well be inefficiencies with too many layers of management, and too much bureaucracy, but at the same time, the remit to provide programmes for all sectors, including minority specialist programmes, makes comparisons with private enterprises unfair and unrealistic.

Uncertainty

One of the problems facing state-owned enterprises is uncertainty regarding the direction the paymaster (i.e. the government) will take, given changes in the controlling political party. In the UK in the 1980s and 1990s, there was a period of relative stability in the sense that the Conservative Party was in power without interruption. Even so, education has still been an area which has seen many changes of direction, which makes long-term planning impossible. Funding levels have often been changed *after* decisions have had to be taken with respect to student numbers. Managing in these circumstances adds a level of difficulty not generally faced by private organizations. On the other hand, private firms suffer changes of ownership and direction. They too have to adjust as the economy goes into or comes out of a recession.

Monopolistic power

A final, major and often significant difference is monopolistic power, i.e. no competitors. In such a situation, it is argued that the power allows waste and inefficiencies. There is no need to be competitive because no other players are allowed on to the field. Operationally, however, the issues will be the same, and the approaches taken *should* be the same: operations should be designed and managed in a way which will meet the objectives of the organization as effectively and efficiently as possible.

How the book is organized

The book is divided into four sections. Part I lays the foundation for the rest of the book, examining the characteristics of service, and presenting some frameworks for managing services generally. Part II examines the strategy, initially from a corporate perspective. Issues involved when cascading overall objectives down to functional levels are then addressed. In particular, the interdependence between functional strategies is considered. Finally in Part II, a detailed examination of operations strategy is presented. Only when the strategy has been developed should service design be considered in depth. Part III of the book is divided into three chapters, looking at the marketing interface, the procedures and issues involved when specifying the service, and finally the details which need to be considered. Part IV covers the delivery issues: location, transportation and distribution, process design and improvement, resource management, measurement and finally human resource management.

References

Akehurst, G. (1989) 'Service industries', in P. Jones (ed.), *Management in Service Industries*, Pitman, London.

Dalrymple, J.F., M. Donnelly, A.D. Curry, A.D. and M.K. Wisniewski (1995) 'Assessing the quality of local government service provision using the SERVQUAL scale' in R. Teare and C. Armistead (eds.), *Services Management: New directions, new perspectives*, Cassell, London.

Fitzsimmons, J.A. and M.J. Fitzsimmons (1994) *Service Management for Competitive Advantage*, McGraw-Hill, New York.

Fitzsimmons, J.A. and R.S. Sullivan (1982) *Service Operations Management*, McGraw-Hill, New York.

HMSO (various years) *Blue Books*.

HMSO (various years) *Social Trends*.

Lockyer, K.G. (1986) 'Service: a polemic and a proposal', *International Journal of Operations and Production Management*, vol. 6, no. 3, pp. 5–9.

Mundy, R.M., R. Passarella and J. Morse (1986) 'Applying SPC in service industries', *Survey of Business*, vol. 21, no. 3, pp. 24–9.

Murdick, R.G., B. Render and R.S. Russell (1990) *Service Operations Management*, Allyn and Bacon, Boston, MA.

Office of Technology Assessment (1985) 'International competitiveness in the service industries', unpublished report, Washington, DC.

Riddle, D.I. (1986) *Service-Led Growth*, Praeger, New York.

Times Higher Educational Supplement (1996) 23 February, p. 3.

Chapter 2

Service characteristics and models

Chapter outline

Service characteristics

As discussed in Chapter 1, certain differences exist between manufacturing industries and services. The two most highlighted differences are the degree of tangibility of the product and the degree of contact with the customer. Situations characterized by either high customer contact/involvement or intangibility of the product are classified as in the service sector. These two characteristics are in fact ways of identifying a service, just as characteristics of a car may be used to identify whether it may be classified as a sports car or a saloon car.

The two id-entifying characteristics, intangibility and high customer contact, may be thought of as the *core* characteristics of service. From these two stem many other facets of service, which all have implications for the management of operations.

In Chapter 1, four of the most commonly identified characteristics of service were presented: simultaneity, heterogeneity, intangibility and perishability. Closer consideration will reveal that perishability stems from intangibility, and simultaneity and heterogeneity stem from high customer contact. Perishability means that the output or product cannot be stored for later consumption or sale. This is because the product is intangible. Production and consumption are simultaneous when the customer needs to be present throughout the production process, i.e. there is high customer contact. Similarly, heterogeneity means that

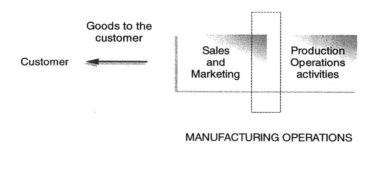

MANUFACTURING OPERATIONS

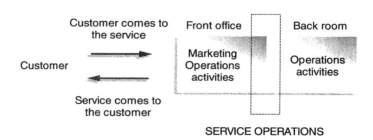

SERVICE OPERATIONS

Figure 2.1   Back room/front office

each product differs from previously produced products. This occurs when the production process differs with each customer, because each customer will react/behave in a different way, and each interaction between customer and service provider will be to some extent unique – again as a consequence of high customer contact. Thus, if a factor analysis were to be performed, only two major factors would emerge as underlying characteristics of service. It is, however, useful to break these factors or characteristics down further, as by doing so, a fuller understanding of services may be gained, together with a clearer understanding of the problems associated with the various facets of services. In this chapter, therefore, each of the many characteristics of service will be examined, together with an identification of the problems arising as a consequence. This should provide a foundation for the rest of the book, where ways in which these problems may be tackled will be presented.

High customer contact

A frequently presented illustration of the contrast between service and manufacturing is presented in Figure 2.1. This illustrates how, in a manufacturing situation, marketing provides an interface between production and the customer. Production takes place out of sight of, or contact with, the customer: for example, in a factory. This contrasts with a service context, where the customer has to be physically present in order for the service to be produced: for example, the customer has to be present in the dentist's chair for a check-up, a filling, etc. It is not possible in this example for the product to be produced without the customer! In the extreme, in services there may be hardly any 'back room' activities. Support activities such as purchasing of supplies, billing and the keeping of financial records will, however, inevitably occur, and these do not have to be done in the presence of the customer. There will therefore always be *some* 'back room' activity. The consequences of this high customer contact are numerous and vary with the degree and manner of contact. These consequences will be examined more closely under the detailed breakdown of characteristics.

Types of customer contact

In Figure 1.5, examples of types of business along the degree of contact continuum were given. As the degree of contact lessens, the freedom to design efficient production processes increases. What is not shown is the different manner in which the contact may take place. Contact may be in person, by phone or by letter. It may occur throughout the production process, intermittently or merely at the start and end of a process. Table 2.1 shows the range of types of contact possible. Customers may be served individually, in small groups or *en masse*.

Table 2.1 Types of contact

Configuration	Manner	Timing
Individuals *dental patient*	In person *visit to hairdresser*	Throughout *a massage*
Small groups *ski classes*	By phone *banking direct*	Intermittent *audit clients*
En masse *large lectures*	By letter *mail order*	Start and end *delivering and collecting clothes at dry cleaners*
	Mass media *radio/television*	

As the amount of contact reduces or the customer becomes more remote from the conversion process, the job of managing the process becomes easier. Techniques used in manufacturing which take advantage of standardization and economies of scale, for example, become available, and the differences between service and manufacture disappear. It is in these areas that a general text on operations management covers the necessary management techniques for an operations manager. This book only covers, in any depth, those techniques which can be seen to be directly of relevance in a service setting. For example, the technique of line balancing a production flow line – where the production process is broken down into elements which are then shared equally among workers in a sequence, smoothing the flow of work from start to finish, and thereby maximizing machine utilization and minimizing the time workers are idle – is rarely appropriate in a service context, where high customer contact and a high degree of heterogeneity are present. Two of the prerequisites of line balancing are a high degree of standardization (there is no scope for customization on a flow line) and a steady demand (unless it is possible to hold stocks). In a 'pure' service, neither will be possible. Consequently, this technique is only briefly covered. Where such techniques are appropriate, they will be covered in Part IV of the book. One of the first steps you must take, therefore, as a manager of operations in services, is to consider the type of contact, since the degree and type of contact will affect the types of technique available to you as a manager.

Problems arising from the characteristics

Heterogeneity

As briefly discussed earlier, in services, one characteristic is the heterogeneous nature of the product. Various factors affect the extent of diversity of design of a product. In counselling, no two patients will ever be exactly alike. The course of a session will vary according to the individual needs of the person being counselled. Even two sessions with the same person will differ, due to the moods of both counsellor and patient. Similarly, in a doctor's surgery, no two appointments will ever be the same. The product/service in the two examples given will never be repeated in exactly the same manner.

It could be argued that customers are always different. Even the most homogeneous set of people, of similar age, sex, background, education, interests, etc., will differ. In the case of a manufactured good, such as a car, each customer will have slightly different requirements, but with just one type of car, such as a red Peugeot 205, with a given set of specifications, it will be possible to meet the requirements of a large number of customers. Television programmes are a service: again it will not be necessary to provide a different programme for each and every customer.

So once again, there is a continuum along which the product/service lies, in this case the degree of heterogeneity of the customers and hence the product. This may be linked to Figure 1.3, in which services were categorized from a consumer perspective. Where services are people processing (e.g. an interview at a job centre) or people changing (e.g. a haircut), the degree of heterogeneity will be greater than where a facilitating service is being provided *for* a consumer (e.g. a telephone service).

The problems associated with this characteristic largely revolve around the inability to standardize either the product or the procedures needed to deliver the service. One of the aspects of delivering a quality product, which will be covered later in the book, is the requirement of identifying customer requirements and writing a specification for the product. The actual product produced can then be compared with the specification to judge quality and consistency of delivery. When the product specification changes every time, there is no way of ensuring that the mode of delivery is the best possible. There is no time to study, test, adapt or refine the product. Training is difficult, as each encounter with the customer will be different and will not follow a prescribed pattern. As the method of delivery will differ on subsequent occasions, the customer will not know what to expect. Mood will often play a large part in the quality of delivery of a service. When a person is preoccupied, or not feeling well, the delivery of the service may well be affected. Even during the course of a day, a receptionist who was friendly and helpful at the beginning of the day may become tired, irritable and most unhelpful by the end of a trying few hours.

Simultaneity

Quite apart from the fact that every time a service is reproduced it will be different, making standardization difficult and quality hard to define and ensure, the very fact that the customer is present throughout the production process, or during part of the process, means that factors which would not normally be an issue in a factory have to be considered.

Safety

One very important issue is customer safety. Clearly, the safety of employees is always a factor, but customers are not trained, may not be familiar with safety regulations, or may be children. As a consequence, the layout and design of facilities is very important. Nursery schools are a good example: barred gates need to be in place where there are stairs, while colouring crayons need to be non-toxic, just in case the child decides to eat the crayon! British Rail has gradually been replacing the external doors of its trains with doors which will not open until the train has stopped and the guard has flicked a switch, to protect customers from the foolish and potentially dangerous habit of opening doors before the train came to a complete halt in the station.

Signposting

Quite apart from safety, facilities need to be well signposted. Customers arriving for the first time at any facility will need to know where to go. Most organizations will have a reception, which will be the first point of contact for either new members of staff or customers. New employees will usually be told, or shown, where to report on their first day. After that, they will either be given a tour of the parts of the factory they need to know, or be told by fellow workers. A visitor to a hospital, however, will not necessarily have been given any instructions on how to find Ward 'X'. Unless there is clear signposting, visitors could inadvertently wander into isolation wards or operating theatres! Out-patients frequently have to find their way round hospitals, maybe to have an X-ray or other specialized tests. One solution has been to paint different coloured lines on the floor, so that a nurse need only tell the patient to follow the *red* line to reach the X-ray department, or maybe the *green* line for the exit.

Layout

The actual layout will need thought, not just from a safety point of view, but also from an ease of access perspective. Is there adequate car parking? Will the customer's trolley fit between the displays? How easy is it to 'drive' the trolley full of plants through the bric-à-brac sales area at the garden centre on the way to the checkout?

Décor

In some situations, the décor will affect the service. Décor influences the atmosphere of a facility. There may be a trade-off between functionality and atmosphere. In a hospital, thick carpets would be so much nicer to step out of bed on to in the morning (or at any time of day, come to that). In some private hospitals, carpets are in place. However, from a cleaner's perspective, or a hygiene perspective, easily washable floors would be much more functional.

Manner of delivery

Because the customer is present during the production process, he or she can observe how the product is produced. Maybe a new employee is serving a customer in an insurance office. A form is not filled in correctly, and a colleague, unobtrusively observing the operation, corrects the new employee. The customer will be aware that it has taken two attempts to fill the form in correctly. He or she may lose confidence in the competence of the employee and may then take their business elsewhere. This contrasts with a factory, where faulty goods may be reworked, and the customer will never know. On the other hand, this facet of service may be seen positively, from a customer's perspective. If I am present when my gardener is digging a pond, and he or she does not use enough sand underneath the liner, I can intervene in time, and may be sure that the job is done properly, to my specification. If a job is capable of being completed in a 'backroom', the customer is not in a position to intervene when necessary. If I had been away while the pond was being made, I would have been none the wiser, and may have been quite happy until problems developed later. The gardener, however, would have been much happier to work unsupervised.

I have a house alarm which needs servicing annually. One of the engineers who comes to service the system is pleasant and friendly. Another engineer does not really like the servicing side of the job and would much prefer to install systems. This has implications for the selection and training of employees who have to deal with members of the public. Technical skills alone are not enough. Interpersonal skills are necessary – and are much more difficult to acquire than technical skills in many cases. How a service is delivered is important. The second engineer may well know his job, but he does not have the patience to explain the system to the customer. When any workers actually provide a service in the home, not leaving dirty footprints through the house, being polite and helpful, and cleaning up after completing the actual task in hand, are all important factors.

No pre-test

In many cases, because production and consumption take place simultaneously, it is impossible to pre-test the service. Once a hairdresser has cut a customer's hair, there is no sticking it back on again! How many times have you heard someone say, 'the barber/hairdresser took too much off' or 'the colour hasn't come out how I wanted it to – it's too reddish'? A car may be taken out for a testrun. A suit may be tried on in the fitting room. The kettle which did not work when you got it home may be taken back. One of the problems with the hairdresser may have been poor communication skills on the part of the customer. On the other hand, the hairdresser may have lacked the necessary interpersonal skills, and was unable, or not prepared, to find out just what was required.

Unpredictability

People do not always behave as expected. Quite apart from the fact that no two customers will ever want exactly the same service, the fact that the customer is present during the conversion process leads to inevitable surprises which may lead to disruptions of the service. Customers turn up late for appointments. They get lost going from the emergency department of a hospital to the X-ray department. Students ask too many or too few questions in the lecture. A child is travel sick on the transfer bus from the airport to the hotel on a package holiday. A passenger on a long-haul flight is vegetarian and has not previously informed the carrier at the time of booking.

The effect of unpredictability can have a major impact on scheduling/capacity management. Customers take longer than expected and create bottlenecks and queues which negatively affect the experience of other customers. Customers who do not turn up on time, or who do not take as long to process as expected, lead to underutilization of resources. In the case of the students, the planned amount of ground that was to be covered in a lecture may be impossible because of too many questions. On the other hand, more ground than planned could have been covered because the students did not ask any questions.

The quality of the service may be seen to diminish in the eyes of some customers because of the disruptions caused by other customers. In some cases, plans may have taken into account the fact that something unexpected could happen. Take the example of the sick child on the bus. This kind of occurrence is not totally unexpected, and additional transfer time may be allowed. However, holidaymakers already feel unhappy about the length of time spent waiting in airport lounges. If extra time allowances are added to transfer times, to meet unexpected events, which, by their very nature, will not happen most of the time, then most of the time customers *will* have to wait longer in the airport lounges than absolutely necessary, causing dissatisfaction. There is clearly a trade-off. Plans need to be made which try and allow for the unpredictability of the customers, without causing dissatisfaction or a lowering of service standards. In some cases this may mean training the customer.

Often, customers do not act as expected because they do not know what is expected of them. Layout and signposting may both be used to help minimize problems. Procedures to try and ensure that customers are asked at an appropriate time to give necessary information, such as the fact that they are vegetarian, can prevent disruption at the point of service. Students coming to university are asked to indicate if they have any disabilities. There should then be systems in place to ensure that, at the beginning of term, this information is passed on to those who need to know that, for example, a student with some form of visual impairment will need hand-outs enlarging. The person responsible for room allocation should be made aware that a particular lecture needs to be scheduled in a lecture theatre with wheelchair access. What is more likely to happen is that the procedures will not be in place, and it is only when the first lecture is about to start that the need for access or enlarged hand-outs comes to light.

Unpredictability therefore has implications for scheduling, information gathering from the customer, design of procedures, training of the customer, layout and signposting, and, of course, training of employees who need to be able to deal with the unexpected.

Customer as unpaid employee

One aspect of the customer's presence within the system may be seen as very positive. Customers can actually be considered as unpaid employees, fulfilling tasks that would otherwise have to be done by paid employees. Any kind of self-service situation falls into this category. Self-service petrol stations mean that perhaps ten cars can be served simultaneously without the need for ten petrol pump attendants, as would have been the norm in the 1960s. Most hotels now offer a buffet breakfast. This may be marketed as a positive feature which allows more choice and customization, insofar as customers can choose exactly the right size portions from a wide variety of dishes, which they can see, and so make an informed choice. Supermarkets clearly work on the concept of customers serving themselves. However, there has been a movement back in some stores towards more actual service counters for such items as fresh fish.

Incidental to self-service is the role of quality controller. Fruit and vegetables which are of poor quality are rejected by being left on the shelves. Customers may point out to the management commodities past their sell-by date. They may act in the role of supervisor to a paid employee providing service – the new waitress assigned to serve the table where the regulars sit and who can give the odd word of advice, or the new service engineer initiated into the idiosyncrasies of the university departmental computer network by the computer officer.

The implications for an operations manager of using the customer as an unpaid employee are mainly related to the reduced need for paid employees. However, to do this successfully, as with any employee, there is a need for training. The customers will need to know what their role is. For example, guests visiting a hotel for the first time will not know whether or not, at breakfast, they are supposed to help themselves. Is it really all right to help oneself to the champagne – is it there for show?! It can be very annoying for customers to queue for five minutes to be served a drink at a bar, only to be told when they get to the front of the queue that they should have paid first at the cash desk on the other side of the room and obtained a ticket to present to the barmaid! This system operates at some motorway service stations in Italy. It does minimize the need to have multilingual servers, as only the cashier needs to be able to understand what it is that the customer requires. However, it can cause a great deal of confusion if the customers are not made aware that this type of system operates. The customer needs some training, however basic.

Labour intensive
Figure 1.4 gave a classification of service firms by capital intensity and labour skills. At one extreme, service organizations may not be labour intensive. Car washes may not involve the customer in any contact whatsoever with service personnel. The purchase of a token from a machine, which is then placed in the slot at the entrance of the car wash, may be all that is required to obtain the service. At the other extreme, counselling will usually preclude the use of equipment, and is purely people based. A tape recorder may be used to keep a record of sessions with patients, but mechanization of the actual process is impossible.

Where a service may be provided by a machine – for example, a cash point outside a bank – labour intensity may be reduced and a cheaper method of service delivery substituted. The service may then be provided on a 24 hours a day basis, with none of the additional costs for shift working, etc. The efficiency may be improved, and the customer may be perfectly happy to be served by a machine. On the other hand, automated teller machines clearly do not have the personal touch of a cashier. The little old lady who goes to the bank regularly, withdraws small amounts of cash at a time and enjoys the human contact because she is lonely, would perceive the withdrawal of cashiers as a very negative step. Not only are machines impersonal, but they may also be confusing and frightening.

The reflection from the sun makes them difficult to use. There is the risk of being mugged while using the machine. Some customers may never perceive the 'machines' as anything but a move in the wrong direction. Operations managers need to be sensitive to the needs of their customers and resist the temptation to replace less efficient and more costly humans with more efficient and less costly machines: in the long run, if service quality is perceived to fall, custom may be lost to competitors who still provide a personal service, and the machines could well prove to be very costly in terms of reduced profits.

The option to mechanize services is often, therefore, precluded by other considerations. A particular problem arising from this is the need for training employees. As services cannot be stored, fluctuations in demand are often met by adjusting the number of employees and the length of hours worked. This often results in part-time working or temporary staff being taken on to meet peaks in demand. High rates of labour turnover are also common. The investment in training necessary in such situations to ensure that standards of service delivery are satisfactory is frequently not made, because of the high recurrent costs involved. Aggravating this problem is the fact that training in interpersonal skills is not easily or rapidly achieved.

High levels of personal judgement
Employees operating machines will be trained in technical skills. They will have to make decisions regarding, for example, the best running speed of an engine given prevailing conditions, and so on. In many cases, very little thought or decision making is required when routine, repetitive tasks are involved in the production process. Routines and procedures are designed which may be followed. Guidelines are provided to meet different eventualities. It is difficult in a service setting, when there is a high level of contact with the customer, to produce procedures and guidelines to fit every situation. The front-line employee who is dealing with a customer will be making judgements about how to provide the service. A successful taxi driver will try and judge whether or not a particular customer wants to be talked to. Is a running commentary of the areas of interest *en route* appropriate? Are the passengers tourists who would welcome the information, or would the passenger prefer the time to collect his or her wits for the forthcoming job interview? A skiing instructor will have to judge whether or not this particular ski class as a whole would prefer to have intensive coaching so that they might win the race at the end of the week, or a much more leisurely set of lessons, with the instructor leading them safely to the best mountain hüttes for schnapps and glühwein. Once again, training in interpersonal skills to enable service employees to use their judgement successfully is difficult. Such skills are usually much harder to acquire than, for example, the technical skills of driving a car. Clearly all technical skills are not easily acquired, but often, as with skiing, the employee has a natural aptitude and interest in the sport, and learning is a pleasure.

Numerous outlets
Another characteristic of services is the need for outlets near to the customer. If the customer needs to be present during the transformation process, e.g. the customer has to be present to have a haircut, then usually the location of the service needs to be convenient. Some customers may travel a couple of hundred miles to London to have their hair cut at a famous (and expensive) salon. However, most will only travel to the next town, or indeed

require the service to be provided in the village. Local GPs are an excellent example of this. A doctor who set up a practice on the side of Ben Nevis might find the demand for his services somewhat limited. The effect of this is a proliferation of small units operating across the country. Another good example of this characteristic comes from the financial services sector: banks and building societies have branches all over the country. This contrasts with factories, which may be located near to supplies of raw materials to minimize transport costs, and where production may take advantage of economies of scale.

Problems associated with this dispersal of units thus include the inability to take advantage of economies of scale, difficulty in controlling widespread units, and hence difficulty in ensuring consistency and required service quality levels.

Doctors may want to purchase expensive items of equipment for use at the surgery. This could provide a higher level of service for patients, as treatment would be available conveniently near to home. However, low levels of utilization of this expensive equipment would often result, making the financial viability of such options doubtful.

Procedures may be laid down, and raw material provided from central locations, in an attempt to ensure that service is of a consistent standard across all outlets. Low standards at one outlet may have an effect on the whole chain of outlets and are potentially costly. For example, if a customer stays in a hotel which is part of a chain in one part of the country, and has a bad experience, then he or she will be very unlikely to stay in any other hotels which are part of that particular chain. The image of the whole chain may be damaged by one or two inferior outlets.

Distribution

Many services are provided on the customer's premises: for example, home helps, gardening services, and servicing of gas and electrical equipment within the home. There is an increasing trend for restaurant and fast (or semi-fast) food establishments to provide a delivery service. Distribution and routing problems and solutions are common to both the service sector and the manufacturing sector. What is different, however, is the need actually to carry out a service in the customer's home. Equipment has to be transported to the site of provision of service. Again, this is not restricted to the service sector.

However, an important consideration, which often seems to be overlooked, is the way the service is provided in the home. Quite apart from the need for interpersonal skills, which has been discussed earlier, an appreciation of the concerns of customers for their safety and the state of their home is required. Many services which are provided in the home are for old people who cannot easily get out and who need help in decorating, etc. They often feel particularly vulnerable. Housewives alone in the house may also feel vulnerable. Measures need to be taken to reassure the customer. Knowing the name of the service engineer in advance, and the time of the visit, are two very simple measures which may lead to reduced anxiety. Training service engineers to take care to protect carpets and furniture where necessary can also lead to enhanced perceptions of the quality of the service delivered. These sorts of issues do not arise when producing a product in a factory, but do characterize services provided in the home.

Quality control is limited to process control

Although in any setting, whether manufacturing or service, getting it 'right first time' and controlling the process are the preferred options for ensuring quality, in a manufacturing setting, where the customer is not present, two critical differences exist. First, if something does go wrong in the conversion process, there is the opportunity to rectify the error before the product reaches the customer, and the customer should only ever receive a 'quality' product. A haircut gone wrong cannot be rectified. The second difference has to do with the knowledge, or ignorance, of the fact that the product or service has been faulty in the first place. If the leather covering on a seat was damaged during packing, for example, there is the opportunity to recover the seat and the customer will never know. But if an actor forgets his or her lines during a play and silence ensues, the audience will know. This is because they are present during the production of the product. If the play were being recorded for broadcast on television, however, then the final audience, the viewers at home, would be unaware that the scene was a retake.

This illustrates how being able to produce out of sight in the 'backroom', as shown diagrammatically in Figure 2.1, makes the transformation process that much easier to manage. Quality control in services where the customer is present is limited to process control. This in turn is made difficult, as we have seen, by the unpredictability and heterogeneous nature of the employee–customer encounter.

Intangibility

As discussed in Chapter 1, in services, the output from the transformation process is often intangible. Figure 1.1 illustrated how there is usually a mix of intangible and tangible for any product. Where the balance swings towards intangibility, the industry may be thought of as belonging to the service sector.

This particular characteristic causes many problems, most of which are linked to the problem of measurement. As we have seen, the *Pocket Oxford Dictionary* defines 'tangible' as 'perceptible by touch: definite, clearly intelligible, not elusive or visionary'. If a product is the opposite of this and cannot be touched, seen or smelt, how can it be measured or defined?

One of the very first steps which needs to be taken to ensure reproducibility of any product is to write a product specification, giving dimensions and attributes. A vague description will not be enough to allow others to reproduce the product. Customers, buying a car, will study the specifications, which will include such things as the length, width, boot dimensions, type of breaking system, colour, weight, speed from 0 to 60 mph, and fuel consumption for different types of driving conditions. The customers will know what it is they are buying. The car manufactured in Germany should be the same as the car manufactured in a plant in Japan, if built to specification. The production process will be set up to reproduce, again and again, repeats of the product meeting the given specification.

But if customers are buying something intangible, how can they know just what it is they are buying, if it cannot be described precisely? Subjectivity is inevitable. What makes an exciting and pleasurable experience for one person may constitute a frightening and nightmarish experience for another. Take flying – for some, the take-off, when the aeroplane accelerates down the runway, is exhilarating; for others, the take-off represents the start of what seems like a lifetime of fear.

When a service involves providing an experience of any kind, whether exciting, relaxing, entertaining, romantic or exhilarating, defining the dimensions of that service is fraught with difficulties. Even if surrogate measures can be made, they tend to be of the form describing the surroundings or conditions for providing the service, rather than a definition of the service itself. In terms of what the customer perceives the service to be, that service, provided in the same manner on two different occasions, may also seem different, because of the mood of the customer. A happy customer is more likely to see an experience in a favourable light than a customer in a bad temper.

If there is no clear specification of the product, how can it be checked against specification for quality control purposes? How can conformance to a standard be established, if there is no clear specification to act as a standard? Much of the time in services, what needs to be measured is the interaction between employee and customer. How well does the counsellor perform? How effective is the doctor at reassuring the patient? If a patient is afraid and 'stressed out', recovery will take longer. When performance measurement is difficult, feedback, to enable an improvement in delivery of the service, will be of doubtful reliability and of little use. Feedback will nevertheless be needed. How to measure performance and provide the required feedback is an area which has been receiving a great deal of attention from researchers over the last decade. Some of the findings of this research will be presented in Chapters 7 and 13.

Another consequence of intangibility, which is linked to the measurement problem, is the fact that it is not easy to specify how long it will take to provide a service, thus making scheduling difficult. This is also linked with the characteristics of heterogeneity and unpredictability which were discussed earlier.

Perishability

Perishability is one of the characteristics of service most frequently presented. It is a direct consequence of the intangibility of the product. Whenever there are elements of the product which are not tangible, and which cannot therefore be stored in a warehouse for later use, the option to produce for later consumption does not exist. Services are even more perishable than fruit, which does have some storage life. Once a flight from London to Paris has taken off from Heathrow with empty seats, those seats cannot then be stored and used again. One of the major tools at a manager's disposal for the management of capacity is the ability to hold stock to meet fluctuations in demand. In Figure 2.2, demand fluctuates and production is constant. When production exceeds demand, the product may be stored to meet future demand. If demand exceeds the rate of production, customers may still be supplied from stock, or orders may be taken for goods to be supplied, sometime in the future.

The number of people employed will be constant. The raw materials purchased will be at a steady and predictable rate, and so on. The only really difficult problem is identifying the optimal level of production such that, over time, supply equals demand. Costs of holding stock do need to be weighed against the savings gained by not having to incur costs for overtime, the hiring and firing of employees, etc. However, in many situations, the ability to hold stocks makes capacity management much easier than trying to supply a product *when* demanded.

When the product is intangible, the option to produce for stock is not open to managers. What would happen if Figure 2.2 were to relate to a service is that when demand exceeded supply, customers would either have to go away dissatisfied, or have to queue. On the other hand, when the ability to supply exceeds demand, resources will be unable to provide the service, and they will be idle, which is clearly expensive. This is why, in situations where

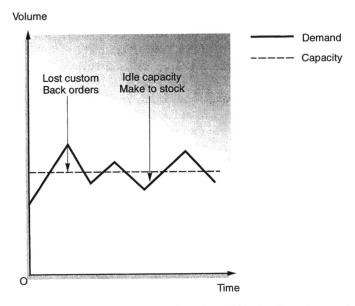

Figure 2.2 Constant output levels and fluctuating demand

the cost of providing a service is high, the main priority is usually given to ensuring that capacity is fully utilized. An example of this is the consultant's out-patient clinic. Overbooking of patients ensures that the consultant never has to wait for a patient.

Capacity management is dealt with in Chapter 12.

Easy to imitate

Service firms often differentiate themselves by the way the service is delivered. The actual core service provided may not differ substantially, but the way it is 'packaged' may give one firm a competitive edge over another. At one time, banks and building societies had relatively short opening hours. After the building societies started to provide similar services to banks in the late 1980s, they gained a competitive edge over the banks by being open for customers on a Saturday morning. The problem was that it was relatively easy for the banks to imitate the building socieities and also open on a Saturday morning. This shows that it is very difficult to gain a sustained competitive edge in services. It is not possible to obtain patents for intangible services, and as such, no long-lasting benefit can be obtained by being the first to design and introduce a new product, as can be the case with a physical product.

Accounting/pricing/charging

One final characteristic worth a mention is the nature of the pricing strategies adopted within the service sector. When buying a physical product, there may well be a number of different prices charged for the same product, depending upon the identity and status of the customer. Trade discounts, prompt payment discounts, bulk-purchase discounts, etc.

may mean that some customers are charged quite markedly higher prices for the same product than others. However, the base price will be set, the differences usually being in the form of some discount.

Services can also be offered in the same way, with a fixed price for one driving lesson, or a discounted rate for a series of ten driving lessons. However, the range of options for pricing is often much greater. Air travel is notorious for the range of prices which may be charged on just one flight. Quite apart from the difference in fares charged between first-, business- and economy-class seats, when the flight was booked, the ability to alter a booking, whether or not the return flight was within a week, but covered a Saturday night, etc. may mean that, although each price clearly related to a slightly different product, two passengers sitting next to each other on a flight from London to Paris, receiving the same service in terms of checking-in and in-flight service, could be paying fares different from each other by a factor of five or more.

Customers do not always know how much a service will cost. Solicitors charge for their time, for the number of phone calls made, and for the number of letters written. Sceptics would say that many of the letters written are unnecessary and that solicitors have little incentive to hurry a case along – after all, the longer it takes, the more they can charge. Because, in most cases, there will be a large gap in knowledge between the solicitor and client, the client is not in a position to challenge the manner in which the solicitor operates. Even the sceptics do realize, however, that it is not always possible to predict how long a matter will take to solve, and thus the estimation of a realistic price in advance is not always possible.

This situation is not totally unheard of outside the service sector. Many building projects cost more than estimated. The Channel Tunnel is a prime example of forecast costs being far outstripped. However, for most products which the average consumer will purchase, the price will have been fixed in advance. Not only that, customers will know just what it is they are going to get for their money. In the case of services, customers may often feel that they have not had value for money. If a physical product does not perform as expected, it is possible to take it back and ask for a refund, but if a massage was not relaxing, it is not possible to take it back and ask for a refund in the same way.

Conclusion

From the foregoing discussion of the characteristics of services, it should have become apparent that the situation facing a manager of service operations poses many problems not faced by an operations manager in a manufacturing setting. There are many common problems, and many techniques suitable for use in either context. Service operations managers are sometimes too quick to dismiss some of the techniques developed in the context of the factory. A survey of operations management techniques in hotels (Witt and Clark, 1990) found only limited usage of techniques which could have been advantageous. The reason for this was lack of knowledge in many cases. It is important to remember that similarities do exist, and advantage should be taken of the lessons learnt in manufacturing contexts where appropriate. Notwithstanding this fact, because of the differences, various service-specific models for the management of operations have been developed which attempt to provide an appropriate framework for service managers. Some of these will be considered in Chapter 7.

References

Witt, C.A. and B.R. Clark (1990) 'Tourism: the use of production management techniques', *Service Industries Journal*, vol. 10, no. 2, pp. 306–19.

Discussion topics/exercises

1. Choose a service which you are familiar with. Analyse the service in terms of the characteristics presented in the chapter. Identify problems which are likely to arise for the operations manager because of these characteristics.

2. Do you think it right for customers to have to serve themselves? What are the arguments for and against this practice?

3. Discuss the following statement: ' It is more difficult to ensure a quality service than a quality product'. Do you agree or disagree with this statement, and why?

4. Using Table 2.1, think of examples for each type of contact. In each situation, discuss the factors which will have to be considered when designing the service package.

Part II

Strategic aspects

Chapter 3

Strategy in services

Chapter outline

Strategy: a definition

The defintion of strategy given in the *Collins English Dictionary* (3rd edn, 1991) is: '1. the art or science of the planning and conduct of a war; generalship; 2. a long term plan for success, especially in business or politics; 3. a plan or stratagem'. Its derivation is from a French word, *stratégie*, which itself comes from a Greek word referring to the function of a general.

A picture begins to emerge of the meaning of strategy: it is about the development of long-term plans and policies within the organization which will lead to or enable it to continue its success. It should involve (but not exclusively) the most senior executives within the organization. This process or activity goes under a variety of names within the organization, including corporate strategy, corporate planning, business strategy, business policy and strategic management. Some writers attempt to make distinctions between some of these different terms. The distinction is often made relative to the level in the organization at which this long-term planning takes place, and in part therefore is dependent on the size and scope, and the organizational/functional structure, of the enterprise.

At the highest level is the corporate strategy, which is the long-term plan for the success of the enterprise. Larger organizations frequently consist of a number of (strategic)

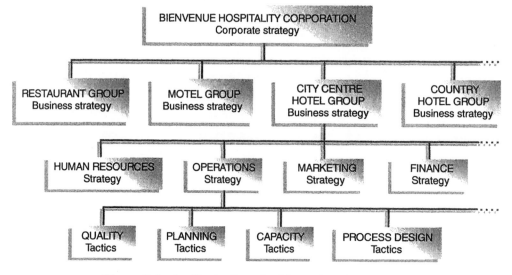

Figure 3.1   An illustration of a hierarchy of strategies

business units which are effectively self-contained, serving a particular market with a somewhat limited range of services (sometimes with a geographic dimension). Thus the corporation might be a key player in the hospitality business with business units covering (1) restaurants on major routes, (2) motel-like accommodation on major routes, (3) city centre hotels and (4) country hotels. Each business unit could have its own business strategy, which would be its own long-term plan linked to its own environment and markets, within the context of achieving the strategy of the organization as a whole.

The next level of strategy concerns the various functions within the organization or business unit. These are the so-called functional strategies which support the achievement of the corporate or business plan, and would normally include such functions as operations, human resources, marketing, finance, information technology, logistics and so on, as appropriate to the organization concerned. An example is given in Figure 3.1.

It is important not to confuse these functional strategies with the more general tactics adopted by the organization: these are the plans adopted to achieve the short- or medium-term aims, which may be the milestones as the strategy unfolds. Some of the broad areas for these are also shown in Figure 3.1. Thus the hotel group would have 'tactics' for the various aspects of planning: for example, systems and procedures to ensure effective and efficient acquisition, storage and usage of the consumable items (food, toiletries and so on) required.

The need for a strategy

An organization without a strategy is like a motorist on a long journey without a map. Moreover, given the uncertainty and complexity of the commercial environment, to continue the analogy with the motorist, at best the road signs have been removed, and at worst

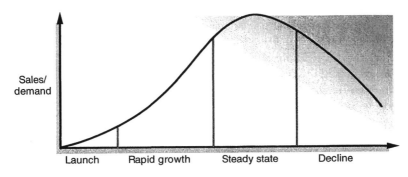

Figure 3.2 Product or service life cycle

they have been relocated again, at random! However, before starting to plan the route it is necessary to determine the destination. Thus before starting the strategic planning process, the organization must ask some fairly fundamental questions about where it is, what it is doing, what it wants to be and what it wants to do.

It is important for an organization to recognize the significance of the life cycle associated with a product or service. An example is shown in Figure 3.2. Typically, demand or sales grow from a zero base at launch through a period of rapid growth which will require significant resources, through to a steady state which comes with maturity, to a gradual decline. This 'maturity/gradual decline' can come as a result of a change in customer requirements or expectations, or because a competitor offers a 'better' service. Profits normally follow the product life cycle, with these typically being made after the launch period, growing, reaching a peak, and then falling during the decline. This introduces the need for a 'successor', which should be part of the long-term plan or strategy of the organization. Lack of planning can result in a period of stagnation for the organization with low income, low contribution and poor resource utilization. The new service development process should be such that, ideally, the new service should be launched before the existing service has fallen significantly into decline.

Often the 'new service' can involve a substantial 'overhaul' of the manner in which the existing service is delivered, perhaps exploiting some technological development. An example could be the introduction of debit cards by banks to replace cheques by an electronic means of transferring cash between accounts.

There are a number of limitations in using the product life cycle. These include the difficulty in establishing the phase a service is currently in, the variability in the shape and duration of the cycle, and the extent to which it is influenced by the actions of the organization. These are discussed in more detail in some of the references (e.g. Kotler, 1991, pp. 364–6).

Strategic management

The formalization of the process by which the organization asks, and attempts to answer, the fundamental questions about what it wants to be and to do is often referred to as establishing the organization's mission. This involves a vision (by the most senior executives) of where the organization wants to be over the next 5–10 years. It is about the overall purpose of the enterprise.

Thompson and Strickland (1992) suggest that, after establishing the organization's mission, the next step in this process is the development of a series of performance objectives which can be used to measure the organization's progress towards achieving its mission. These should be both realistic and achievable. A key step within this is the development of a strategy to achieve these performance objectives. The effectiveness of this long-term plan will have a major impact on the corporate success of the organization. Some of the issues of importance in the development of a strategy will be described later. The strategy having been developed, it must then be implemented successfully. This will inevitably involve change, and the effective management of this change process is crucial. Finally, performance must be monitored and corrective action taken as appropriate.

The strategic management process has been summarized by Craig and Grant (1993) in the acronym 'MOST': Mission (covering a description, attitude and direction), Objectives (the performance ambitions), Strategy (addressing resource deployment and competitive advantage) and Tactics (the planned actions). Some aspects, like ways of achieving competitive advantage, will be covered in more detail later in this chapter.

Mission statement

There is some controversy surrounding whereabouts in the sequence of steps involved in the strategic management development process the preparation of the mission statement should be located. It is tempting to merge it with the visionary process which drives the whole development. However, it is necessary to look rather more deeply at its role and use before determining at what point it can sensibly be articulated.

In the above there is a tacit acceptance that the mission statement is (simply?) a formalization of the vision by the senior executives of where the organization should be 'going' over the next 5–10 years. However, a substantial amount of research has been conducted on mission statements. A significant contribution is made by the Economist Special Report No. 1208, describing some of the work completed by the Ashridge Strategic Management Centre (Campbell and Yeung, 1990).

It is suggested that almost 80 per cent of the top UK companies have a mission statement. There are many reasons for companies preparing such a statement: underpinning these is perhaps the desire to communicate and publicize the organization's 'ambitions' internally and externally. However, in the research reported at Ashridge, there appeared to be no clear understanding of what mission statements are or what issues they should address, when the centre started its work in 1987. It noted that, when asked to send their mission statements, companies returned documents with a variety of titles. Some of these titles included 'purpose statement', 'corporate objectives', 'vision statement', 'company philosophy' and 'corporate principles'.

From its work, the centre came up with a model of what a mission statement should include under four broad headings:

Answer each question 0= No 1= To some degree 2= Yes

1. The purpose
a. Does the statement describe an inspiring purpose that avoids playing to the selfish interests of the stakeholders – shareholders, customers, employees, suppliers? 0 1 2
b. Does the statement describe the company's responsibility to its stakeholders? 0 1 2

2. Strategy
a. Does the statement define a business domain explaining why it is attractive? 0 1 2
b. Does the statement describe the strategic positioning that the company prefers in a way that helps to identify the sort of competitive advantage it will look for? 0 1 2

3. Values
a. Does the statement identify values that link with the organization's purpose and act as beliefs that employees can feel proud of? 0 1 2
b. Do the values 'resonate' with and reinforce the organization's strategy? 0 1 2

4. Behaviour standards
a. Does the statement describe important behaviour standards that serve as beacons of the strategy and the values? 0 1 2
b. Are the behaviour standards described in a way that enables individual employees to judge whether they have behaved correctly or not? 0 1 2

5. Character
a. Does the statement give a portrait of the company capturing the culture of the organization? 0 1 2
b. Is the statement easy to read? 0 1 2

Maximum score 20; good score 15; poor score less than 10.

Figure 3.3 Do you have a good mission statement? (Source: *Do You Need a Mission Statement?*, Special Report No. 1208, table 3. The Economist Publications)

- Purpose: the reasons for the organization's existence.
- Strategy: the nature of the business and the achievement of competitive advantage.
- Standards and behaviours: norms and rules about how things are done.
- Values: the beliefs and principles which lie behind the standards.

The centre produced a checklist which can be used to 'evaluate' a mission statement. This is shown in Figure 3.3.

> **Our mission is to make BAA the most successful airport company in the world**
>
> This means:
> * always focusing on our customers' needs and safety.
> * seeking continuous improvement in the cost and quality of our services
> * enabling all employees to give of their best
>
> In developing our core airports business, safety and security will have highest priority at all times. We will continuously improve quality and cost-effectiveness, fully develop our retail and property potential, and achieve world class standards in capital investment while remaining prudently financed. In addition we intend to build an international business which enhances the quality and growth prospects of the Group.
>
> We will ensure that customers receive excellence and value in the services BAA provides. To do this we will provide a good and safe working environment which attracts and retains committed staff. Through training and two-way communication we will help them to fulfil their potential and contribute directly to the Company's success. We will encourage shareholders to believe in our company by giving them consistent growth in earnings and dividends as well as recognizing the needs of local communities by demonstrating that the Company is a good neighbour with concern for the environment.

Figure 3.4   Mission statement: British Airports Authority (Source: Company report and accounts, 1994)

Organizations from a variety of environments are now developing mission statements. Schools and colleges, building societies, travel agents and local authorities all have mission statements, which are often 'abbreviated' as slogans. Examples of these are given in Figures 3.4 and 3.5. While it can be seen that these differ in title and content, and it could be argued that they are being quoted out of context, they were taken from the first pages of each organization's recent annual report and accounts.

The strategy development process

It is clear that the development of a coherent and consistent strategy is a key factor in the successful growth of any organization. However, there can be a significant gap between the recognition of the need and the actual delivery of an appropriate strategy. The process will be completed more effectively with the utilization of a structured approach, and an understanding of some of the key tasks involved in the process. Moreover, substantial work has been completed in this area and it is important to incorporate those ideas as appropriate to the particular organization. Figure 3.6 shows six of the key inputs into the strategy development process. They are shown broadly in the order in which they might be completed by an organization, but some might be going on in parallel, or local

The Bank of Scotland Group aims

to provide a range of distinctive financial services throughout the United Kingdom and internationally;

to maintain its reputation for stability and integrity and to show long term growth in profits and dividends

to be professional, friendly, prompt and imaginative in its dealings with its customers;

to train, develop, inform, respect and encourage staff so that they can perform an effective and fulfilling role.

Through its branch network, the clearing bank aims to make a particular contribution to the cultural and economic prosperity of Scotland.

Figure 3.5 Corporate statement: Bank of Scotland (Source: Company report and accounts, 1994)

circumstances might dictate a change of sequence. This process is not unique, and most authors on strategy have their own preferred approach (e.g. Luffman *et al.*, 1991). However, there is general agreement on some of the analyses which it is necessary to carry out and some of the models which can be of use in the process.

Internal analysis

Early on in the process, it is necessary for the organization to carry out a critical internal appraisal across a whole range of dimensions. This is frequently referred to as a 'strengths and weaknesses' audit, and when linked with an examination of the external factors impacting on the organization – the opportunities and threats – gives rise to a SWOT analysis.

Focusing on the internal aspects, the organization should identify its strengths. These are those aspects which it is good at and/or which give it advantage over its competitors. Conversely, it is equally important to identify the weaknesses: those aspects which the organization does poorly and which put it at a disadvantage when compared to its competitors. Clearly this analysis is a major task, and some structure will ensure that it is completed in a comprehensive manner. This structure can be based around the functional areas of the organization, which might include human resources, operations, sales and marketing, finance and accounting and so on. Within each there will be a whole range of dimensions which can contribute to either strengths or weaknesses. Some of these are illustrated in Figure 3.7. A comprehensive list around a similar structure is given in Argenti

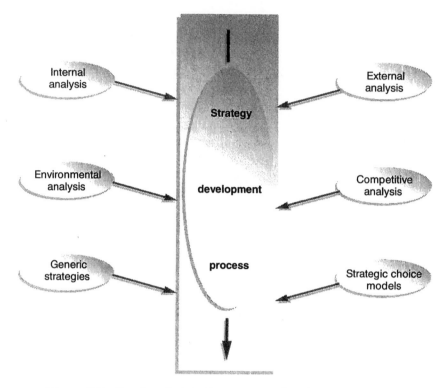

Figure 3.6　Key inputs into the strategy development process

(1980). Thus a strength of the Marriot Hotel chain might be the quality of the service which is offered, a strength of Marks and Spencer could be the motivation and commitment of staff and a strength of Lloyds Bank might be the advertising campaign linked to the 'Black Horse' image.

Developing the idea of a strength further, Prahalad and Hamel (1990) present the idea of a 'core competence': this is something a company does especially well in comparison to its competitors. A recognition of core competences and their development can give an organization significant competitive advantage.

Environmental analysis

It would be logical to move from the internal analysis to the external analysis. However, before looking at these opportunities and threats, it is necessary to examine what contributes to them. A major driving force is the environment in which the organization operates, so an environmental analysis can formalize the collection of the information to support this next step. It is often suggested that this analysis should be broken down into four key areas: political, economic, social and technological (sometimes referred to as PEST or STEP analysis).

Political factors can operate locally (e.g. planning regulations), nationally (e.g. safety legislation, such as seat belts in coaches) and internationally (e.g. in the European Union,

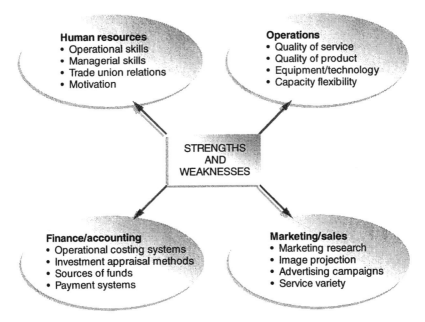

Figure 3.7 Areas of potential strengths and weaknesses

value added tax harmonization, transportation barriers). Political decisions can have an impact on a whole range of an organization's activities through tax controls and incentives, privatization/nationalization of industries, and changes in government.

Economic factors apply equally at all levels, although smaller companies are more likely to be heavily influenced by local and national factors. Factors like inflation, taxation, interest rates and exchange rates can have a major impact – take the problems faced by tour operators in setting the price of overseas holidays over a year ahead of demand, when a significant part of the cost might be in local currencies.

Social factors are coming to play an increasingly important role, and have a significant impact on a whole range of organizations, from the perspective of employees and also of 'customers'. Attitudes to work have changed dramatically over time, with a move from the 'live to work' to the 'work to live' philosophy, linked to a change in expectations and values. Environmental impact is also currently high on the agenda. With the concern about the effect of the motor car, this could result in a significant change in the requirement for public transportation systems. Home working is a development being followed by a number of organizations. This is particularly suitable for those service operations with low face-to-face personal contact, when telephone/computer links can be effective.

Finally, technological factors can influence all types of organization. Possibly the area having most impact is information technology and computer usage. In some areas this has led to a substitution for labour and a significantly 'improved service'. Consider the changes in domestic banking offered by automated teller machines (ATMs) and in retailing by bar code scanning linked to electronic point of sale systems (EPOS). Access to a whole range of banking services has been significantly improved, and customer waiting and service time in retailing has been substantially reduced.

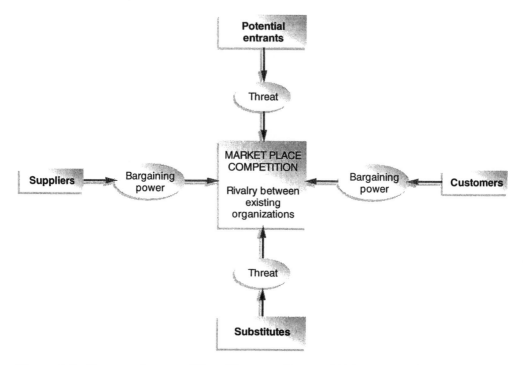

Figure 3.8 Forces of competition (Source: Porter, 1980, p. 4; adapted with the permission of The Free Press, a division of Simon & Schuster, from *Competitive Strategy: Techniques for Analysing Industries and Competitors*, by Michael E. Porter. Copyright © 1980 by The Free Press.)

However, the issues are clearly interrelated. Information technology and communication facilitate home working. Politicians react to social concern for the environment through legislation. Legislation can have an impact on inflation, interest and exchange rates. The forecaster has a challenging task in attempting to predict all of these interconnected aspects.

Competitive analysis

It is also necessary to look at the competitive forces at play, and it makes sense to do this before the formal external analysis. Porter (1980) suggests that there are five forces which drive competition. Central is the rivalry among existing organizations in that market. There are then the threats of new entrants to that market, together with the threat of substitute services. Finally, there is the power of both the buyers of the services and the providers of supplies. This is shown diagrammatically in Figure 3.8.

The threats of new entrants are dependent to a great extent on the barriers to entering the particular market. The rivalry among existing firms depends on a number of interacting features, such as high exit barriers and high fixed costs. The identification of potential substitutes can be problematic, since these may not always be apparent and can result from new technology. The bargaining power of buyers can be high when a single buyer takes a large proportion of the total service. Equally, the bargaining power of the supplier is strong if the organization's major inputs come from a single supplier. These factors are discussed in more detail in Bowman and Asch (1987).

It is possible to apply the above analysis to the operations of a national airline (e.g. British Airways, Air France). Potential entrants into airline operations are faced with significant entry barriers which can include high capital requirements. Substitutes exist on certain routes: for example, between the major European cities, in the form of high-speed city centre-to-city centre rail links. State employees are often 'encouraged' to use the national airline when travelling on official business, and when the 'purchasing' process is managed centrally this can exert significant customer pressure. Suppliers of some services at airports (e.g. fuel, catering) and indeed the airports themselves may have a virtual monopoly at any point in time, and may have significant bargaining power.

External analysis

External analysis is often summarized as the identification of opportunities and threats, which as mentioned earlier, mirror the strengths and weaknesses of the internal analysis. Clearly the environment and competitive factors also feed into this analysis. Thompson and Strickland (1992) suggest that market opportunities have a major input into the development of an organization's strategy, and that a successful strategy should capitalize on an organization's best growth opportunities and develop defences to threats to its competitive position. They go on to claim that SWOT analysis is far more than preparing four lists under these headings. It is about analyzing the strengths, weaknesses, opportunities and threats identified, and forming conclusions about the company's position and the strategic actions necessary.

Generic strategies

Porter (1985) suggested that there were three key generic competitive strategies. These have become known as cost leadership, differentiation and focus, and are shown diagrammatically in Figure 3.9.

The attraction of cost leadership is clear. It offers the organization the opportunities for superior profits, and leaves it in a strong position to take part in price wars, forcing competitors out of the market and gaining increased market share. There have been examples of this in the package tour market in the 1980s, and retail food chains in the 1990s. It could be argued that a coach company offers a low-cost transportation service in comparison to, say, rail transportation, although it is crucial to ensure that we are comparing like with like. A key to cost leadership is how this is achieved, and it should be clear that the operations area has a key role to play in this.

Differentiation has increasingly become a competitive strategy adopted by successful service organizations. A key to this is knowledge of what the customer wants and values. Differentiation strategies can be particularly effective in markets where there is traditionally a wide range of standard offerings. An example might be the package holiday market where some companies now offer packages where everything is included in the price: meals, drinks and tours. The holidaymaker need take no spending money. Marketing has an important

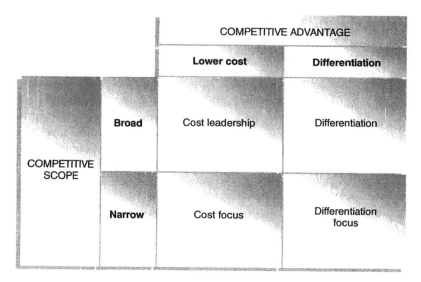

Figure 3.9 Generic strategies (Source: Porter, 1985, p. 12; adapted with the permission of The Free Press, a division of Simon & Schuster, from *Competitive Advantage: Creating and Sustaining Superior Performance*, by Michael E. Porter. Copyright © 1985 by Michael E. Porter.)

role in ensuring that sufficient customers exist and that the 'product/service' continues to meet the ever-changing requirements of customers. Operations have an equally important role in ensuring that the cost of the differentiation is less than the financial benefit to be gained from it in the competitive market place. These operational/marketing aspects will be returned to in Chapter 4. However, it is worth noting that the large element of intangibles within services offers great potential for differentiation. Factors such as the appearance of the facilities, and the attitudes and behaviour of employees, are important.

Focus involves selecting part of a market, and meeting its requirements more closely than the remaining organizations serving the entire market. It is clearly important to ensure that the market segment targeted is large enough to sustain the planned scale of operations, and to monitor its requirements so that the match continues over time, and the segment does not disappear. In the car servicing market, organizations like Kwik Fit and Associated Tyre Services (ATS) focus on the exhaust/tyre/shock absorber part of the market, competing on price and speed of provision. An organization which focuses on cost can perform better than its competitor satisfying the entire market by removing 'non-essential' parts of the service. Some airlines attempted this in the 1970s by removing complementary in-flight catering. Thompson and Strickland (1992) summarize this as follows: 'a focuser's basis for competitive advantage is either lower costs than competitors in serving the market niche or an ability to offer niche members something different from other competitors' (p. 111). They note that low-cost focus requires a segment whose requirements can be satisfied in a less costly manner, and differentiation focus needs a segment with unique requirement characteristics.

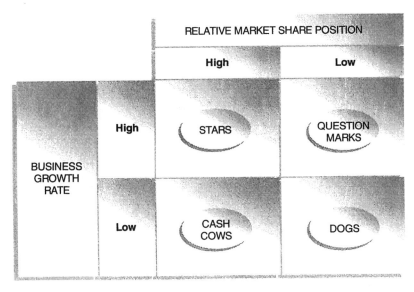

Figure 3.10 Boston Box

Strategic choice models

A number of models have been developed to assist with strategic choices. Probably one of the most widely known is that developed by the Boston Consulting Group (BCG), commonly referred to as the Boston Box (Hedley, 1977). This can be used to model the portfolio of services offered by an organization or the divisions or business units of a diversified service organization, and is presented in Figure 3.10. Sophisticated scales are sometimes used for the relative market share and growth rate dimensions, and circles are used to represent services (or divisions), with the areas of these circles proportionate to the percentage of the corporate revenue they represent. Stars are the services (or business units) which are growing rapidly, and have a relatively high market share position. They tend to be self-sustaining in terms of cash flow, and it is normally accepted that they represent the best profit and growth opportunities available. Cash cows are those which have high relative market share in low-growth sectors. As a result of this, they tend to have a strong position yet require little investment, thus generating significant cash surpluses. These provide valuable resource for the organization, which can be used to develop future stars. Cash cows may have been stars in the past.

Dogs have relatively low market share in sectors with a low growth rate. As such they are likely to be fairly unprofitable, and it is suggested that organizations should attempt to drop them, as there is no real point in retaining them. Often they are yesterday's cash cows.

Question marks are sometimes referred to as 'problem children'. Their position in a sector with a high growth rate makes them attractive, but their relatively low market share normally means that a significant cash injection is required to turn them into stars. Thus the 'question marks' with the best potential should be selected and resources from 'cash cows' used to develop them into 'stars'. The remainder should be dropped. As a business

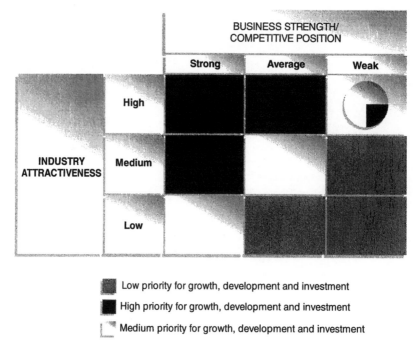

BUSINESS STRENGTH/
COMPETITIVE POSITION

Low priority for growth, development and investment

High priority for growth, development and investment

Medium priority for growth, development and investment

Figure 3.11   General Electric matrix

sector matures the stars become cash cows, and as the market matures they become dogs and should be dropped.

The focus in the Boston Consulting Group analysis is on cash flows and investment, and can lead to a strategy of 'optimizing' the organization's portfolio of services. However, a number of criticisms have been levelled at the approach. These include the fact that the classifications 'high' and 'low' are too wide, and there are other significant factors apart from relative market share and business growth rate. As with any model, it should be used to support decisions by a strategist who understands the basic assumptions, and its scope and limitations.

An alternative model is that developed by General Electric (Hofer and Schendel, 1978). This is based on a nine-cell matrix, again with two key dimensions: business strength/competitive position and industry attractiveness. Business strength/competitive position is taken to be a composite of a number of factors, including relative market share, possession of desirable core competences, relative cost position and calibre of management. Industry attractiveness includes market size and growth rate, intensity of competition, emerging opportunities and threats, and barriers to entry and exit. On each dimension, each factor is given an appropriate weight, and then each service is assessed according to each factor and a combined value calculated. Figure 3.11 shows an illustration of such a matrix.

The area of the circle is proportional to the size of the commercial sector and the pie slice within the circle represents the size of the particular service's market share. The

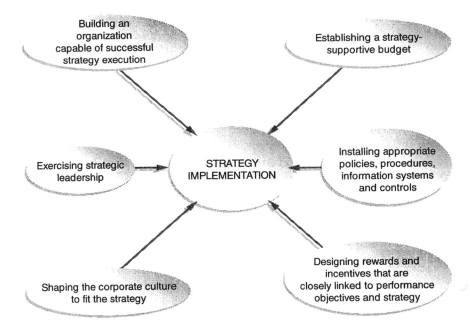

Figure 3.12 Steps in strategy implementation (Source: adapted from Thompson and Strickland, *Crafting and Implementing Strategy: Text and Reading* (6 edition) © 1995, p. 241)

advantages of this model over the BCG matrix are the use of three rather than two classifications on each dimension and the wider range of issues included within each dimension. The derived strategies, as the figure indicates, relate to priorities for growth, development and investment.

There are a number of other models, but the interested reader is referred to the references at the end of the chapter for further reading on this theme.

Strategy implementation

Effort spent on the strategy development process is wasted unless sufficient attention is paid to the implementation. Rarely does the strategy not imply a change, so the management of change can be considered a key issue.

Thompson and Strickland (1992) identify six key tasks in implementing strategy, which are shown in Figure 3.12. They suggest that, in building the organization capable of executing the strategy, key tasks involve developing the necessary skills and core competences. In establishing a strategy-supportive budget, it is necessary to ensure that each unit has an adequate budget to carry out its part of the plan and that resources are used effectively. A key element for the systems and procedures is correct and timely information. In designing rewards it is crucial that these motivate all to do their best to ensure the strategy is successful, and to instil a results orientation. Shaping the corporate culture involves establishing shared values, setting ethical standards and building high performance into the culture. Key aspects in strategic leadership are dealing with the politics of strategy, enforcing ethical standards and leading the process of shaping values.

Discussion

Clearly, for an organization to have a chance to succeed in the long term, it must spend time and resources in developing a strategy. This is clear from a study of those companies which have continued to grow and become successful. This process need not be carried out in an *ad hoc* manner, but can be systematically tackled, and some established approaches used to support the analysis. These have been described in this chapter.

References

Argenti, J. (1980) *Practical Corporate Planning*, Unwin, London.

Bowman, C. and D. Asch (1987) *Strategic Management*, Macmillan, Basingstoke.

Campbell, A. and S. Yeung (1990) *Do You Need a Mission Statement?*, Economist Special Report No. 1208, Economist Publications, London.

Craig, J. and R. Grant (1993) *Strategic Management*, Kogan Page, London.

Hedley, B. (1977) 'Strategy and the business portfolio', *Long Range Planning*, February, pp. 9–15.

Hofer, C. and D. Schendel (1978) *Strategy Formulation: Analytical Concepts*, West, New York.

Kotler, P. (1991) *Marketing Management, Analysis, Planning, Implementation and Control* (7th edn), Prentice Hall, Englewood Cliffs, NJ.

Luffman, G., S. Sanderson, E. Lea and B. Kenny (1991) *Business Policy: An analytical introduction* (2nd edn), Blackwell, Oxford.

Porter, M.E. (1980) *Competitive Strategy: Techniques for analysing industries and competitors*, Free Press, New York.

Porter, M.E. (1985) *Competitive Advantage: Creating and sustaining superior performance*, Free Press, New York.

Prahalad, C. and G. Hamel (1990) 'The core competence of the corporation', *Harvard Business Review*, vol. 69, no. 3, pp. 79–93.

Thompson, A. and A. Strickland (1995) *Crafting and Implementing Strategy: Text and Reading* (6th edn), Irwin, Homewood, IL.

Discussion topics/exercises

1. Analyze the mission-style statements given in Figures 3.4 and 3.5 using the framework of Figure 3.3.

2. Discuss the development of a mission statement for a comprehensive school offering an education for 11–18-year-olds. The school has a budget of around £4 million, 1800 pupils and over 100 teachers and support staff. It is located in a semi-rural area 15 miles from the centre of Bradford in West Yorkshire, and takes pupils from a 10 mile radius, including a range of small villages and large towns.

3. Select an organization of your choice, and describe the key features and parameters which are important in developing a corporate strategy. Identify the information necessary to support this process, and its sources. Be realistically creative where appropriate.

4. Use actual case material to explain the following concepts:
   (a) generic strategies
   (b) the Boston Box
   (c) the General Electric matrix.

Chapter 4

Functional strategies

Chapter outline

Introduction

In the previous chapter, Figure 3.1 indicated that the business strategy (or corporate strategy for a smaller organization without separate business units) would be 'cascaded down' into functional strategies. These functional strategies are the long-term plans which lay down how these individual areas are to contribute to and support the organization's achievement of its long-term goals. There is no definitive list of the 'correct' set of functions, and these will depend on the nature of the organization being considered. These would, however, normally include finance (and accounting), marketing, operations, human resources, information systems, logistics and quality. Some understanding of the factors behind the

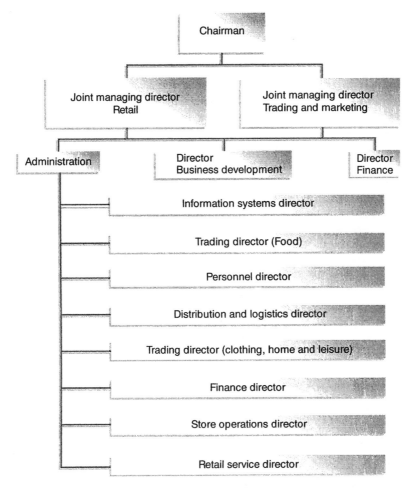

Figure 4.1 Directors and administration of a major retail chain

identification of different functions by organizations can be gained by an examination of either the responsibilities of their boards of directors or the organizational structure as given in the report and accounts. An illustration is given in Figure 4.1. Some presentational changes have been made.

Financial or accounting strategy

There is frequently confusion concerning the differences between finance and accounting, and the lay person tends to use these two words interchangeably. If both are seen as concerning information provision, a simple distinction is that generally financial data are provided for 'external consumption' while accounting data are for 'internal usage'.

A strong focus within the financial aspect concerns provision of information on the organization as a whole for the shareholder and related individuals and as such it is often seen to have some of its foundations within economic theory. This information is frequently in the 'public domain' and often forms part of the annual report and accounts prepared by public limited companies (PLCs) and deposited annually at Companies House in London. There are conventions which must be followed in the preparation and presentation of this information. This area has less importance from the strategy perspective and as a consequence will not be considered further within this section. Maher *et al.* (1991) examine an organization's information flow and identify a number of key activity areas, including financial accounting (e.g. creditors), managerial accounting (managerial decision making), operations, personnel, and sales and marketing. Clearly a number of the areas will require access to the same data, although possibly analyzing and using it for different purposes (for example, sales and marketing will be using historical data, among other factors, to predict future sales targets, which will also be used by operations to plan service delivery systems). There needs to be an overarching strategy – an information strategy – to guide the development of this information provision. This will be covered later in this chapter.

Before examining the strategic issues, it is worth briefly examining the two related aspects of managerial accounting: (1) decision making and (2) planning, control and performance evaluation.

Managerial decision making

This is generally concerned with *ad hoc* decisions at a variety of levels of significance or importance to the organization. The process will normally involve estimating the implications (primarily financial, including costs and revenues) of a range of alternatives, and using this evaluation (together with some set of criteria) to support the selection of an appropriate course of action. Thus at one level an airline may be considering replacing part of its fleet of aircraft and be looking at a range of different models from different manufacturers, together with a variety of ways of financing the replacement (lease, outright purchase and so on). The strategic implications of this decision will be linked to a series of issues which relate to how the airline is developing in the long term. Is it expanding or developing the short-haul or long-haul capability of the operations? This will have significant impact on the aircraft types being considered. How does it see the balance in carrying capacity between first, executive and tourist classes fitting with its strategy? This will influence the internal configuration and layout of the planes being purchased. The link to the strategy of the airline in both of these cases is clear.

Smaller-scale, apparently shorter-term decisions also have to be made. It is tempting to assume that these have no strategic significance. However, frequently they are contributing to an organization's overall competences, and taken together a group of these may be moving this core competence in a direction which is incompatible with the organization's overall strategy. For example, the pathology laboratory in a hospital might be replacing a worn-out and dated piece of equipment, and be generally reviewing its use of the latest technology, while the National Health Trust which runs the hospital has a strategy which ultimately involves outsourcing non-core activities, of which pathology is considered as one. Consequently, in the light of the uncertainty surrounding the future of the pathology department and its possible closure, the decision should be deferred.

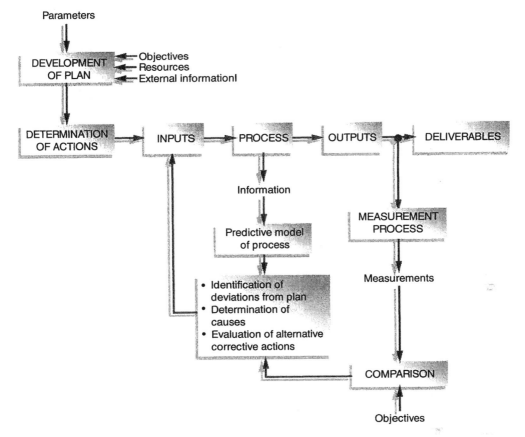

Figure 4.2 General planning and control process (Source: Adapted from Emmanuel *et al.*, 1991, p. 36; adapted with the permission of Chapman and Hall, London, from *Accounting for Management Control* (2nd edn), by C. Emmanual, D. Otley and K. Marchant. Copyright © 1991 Chapman and Hall.)

Planning, control and performance evaluation

The focus here is on the provision of financial and accounting information to support the organization's planning and control systems. A general model of a planning and control process is presented in Figure 4.2.

This process can be illustrated by continuing the example introduced in the previous section. The airline has leased a mix of different capacity aircraft to operate on a variety of short-haul routes throughout Europe. This is consistent with the mission of growing to become the number one European carrier by the year 2000, and the corporate strategy developed to achieve this. All planes carry only two classes of passenger, executive and tourist. On the planes used for the shorter flights, there is a flexible, movable partition between the classes, which allows the balance between executive and tourist seats to be changed from flight to flight if necessary. On those used on the longer flights, seat layout is different in executive class, allowing more space and comfort, but fixing the balance of seats between the two classes. In arriving at the decision to lease the particular fleet of short-haul jets with certain configurations of executive/tourist accommodation, forecasts were made of running costs, numbers of passengers, ticket prices, revenues and so on.

After making the decision, a plan can be prepared showing the best combinations of planes to individual scheduled flights on different routes, to meet the forecast numbers of passengers, costs and so on, in order to maximize the total profit. The operation of this transportation network can then be monitored on an ongoing basis. It could be that passenger revenues do not meet the budget, which might be because the forecast number of business travellers in executive class was optimistic. As a consequence the forecasts may be revised. This might result in some flights being allocated fewer executive seats (and therefore more economy class) or a reallocation of types of plane to routes. It is important to recognize as part of this process the need to optimize the entire system, not individual components. Thus as part of the process of reallocation, while one route might produce less profit, the increase in profits from other routes might more than compensate for this. At the end of the first year of operations, demand for seats on one route might have been such to justify the evaluation of whether to lease a larger plane, or a second plane, with increased frequency of flights.

Strategic management accounting

Strategic management accounting has been defined by Simmonds (1981) as

> the provision and analysis of management accounting data about a business and its competitors for use in developing and monitoring the business strategy, particularly relative levels and trends in real costs and prices, volume, market share, cash flow and the proportion demanded of a firm's total resources. (p. 26)

It is claimed that profit is determined by an entire range of internal and external factors, and the traditional approach to the analysis of this has been through an examination of the internal factors. In the increasingly competitive environment, external factors are more likely to have a significant impact. Good control of costs is no longer the key factor leading to good profits. For example, the increased profitability an airline sees from one of its routes may not be simply because it has maintained its costs on that route, but because one of its competitors has reduced its level of advertising on the route, reduced the frequency of service or withdrawn from the route altogether.

For an organization with a strategy of cost leadership, a recognition of the experience curve relationship can be advantageous if a standardized type of service is being delivered. Empirical evidence suggests that, with every doubling of accumulated experience with a service delivery process, the unit delivery cost might drop to around 80 per cent of the previous level. This gives significant advantage to the first entrant into a growth market.

Just as variance analysis can be carried out internally on a standard costing basis (the comparison of actual and predetermined standard costs), the same can be applied to the variances between an organization's costs, prices and volumes and those of the competition. These require the establishment of management accounting systems to capture this information on a continuous basis. While price data are relatively easy to obtain, externally reconstituting cost data is a more complex process. However, this is facilitated in a service environment by the nature of the process. As the presence of the customer is frequently necessary, it is at least possible to observe the major visible elements of the delivery system. Thus the tour operator can sample the holidays offered by the competition. Equally, data on volume and market share are more difficult to establish. It is also important to recognize that these data need forecasting into the future. The broader issues involved in benchmarking – obtaining comparative performance data on similar organizations – are considered in Chapter 11.

It is claimed that the existing accounting reporting mechanisms for costs, profits and so on should be extended to market share data. The absolute value of the market share is a good indication of an organization's position in the market, while increasing or decreasing values signals a weakening or a strengthening.

Another example of accounting supporting strategy is in financial performance measures, designed to indicate how well the strategy is being achieved. A particular case might be in the allocation of overhead costs (Hiromoto, 1988). Consider an environment in which the strategy is to achieve high levels of automation (e.g. banking). It could be argued that in order to cost services (and consequently arrive at a pricing structure), using labour cost is inappropriate since labour cost will be a small proportion of the total cost of provision. However, while this is true in the context of short-term costing/pricing decisions, in the longer term focus on labour cost has the effect of driving this down through the use of higher levels of automation. This promotes behaviour which supports the organization's strategy.

Generic strategies and accounting control systems

Miles and Snow (1978) developed a typology for studying organizations which is particularly useful for exploring strategic issues. This typology identifies four generic strategy perspectives: defenders, prospectors, analyzers and reactors. The principal characteristics of each are presented in Table 4.1, based on Miles and Snow's original statements, and Simons (1990).

Research studies have indicated that to pursue defender, prospector and analyzer strategies successfully, an organization needs to be strong in both general and financial management. Moreover, defenders need competences in operations, and arguably because of its emphasis on efficient service delivery, in cost management. Prospectors require skills in research and development (of new service opportunities) and market research (Miles and Snow, 1978; Snow and Hrebiniak, 1980). Clearly, organizations may move through the different types of strategy over a period of time, and do not necessarily have all of the characteristics listed. However, Café Select (selling cups of freshly ground coffee, croissants, etc.) could be regarded as a defender within the fast-food market; the Virgin organization (with interests ranging from records to air travel) might be considered a prospector; and Marks and Spencer, with its core products of food and clothes, could be thought of as an analyzer.

It has been argued (Miles and Snow, 1978) that successful firms should ensure that their control systems are designed and developed to take due account of their strategies. 'They argue that Defenders will emphasise cost control, trend monitoring and efficiency rather than scanning the environment for new opportunities. Prospectors by contrast will use comprehensive planning and measure performance more subjectively' (Simons, 1987,

Table 4.1 Four basic strategy types

Strategy type	Characteristics
Defender	Niche in relatively stable service environment More limited range of services than competitors Compete through higher quality, superior service, low cost Focus on efficient service delivery Centralized structure
Prospector	Operates in a broad service area 'First in' with new services or in new markets Uncertain environment Does not maintain market strength in all areas Flexible structure
Analyzer	Hybrid Maintains core of stable services Enters new markets when viability established Often 'second in' with more efficient service delivery systems Matrix structure
Reactor	No consistent service-market orientation Does not aggressively defend its services or markets, loses opportunities Does not take risks Structure inappropriate to purpose

p. 360). In a study, Simons looks at the relative significance of a number of attributes of control in the context of the four types of strategy. These attributes include external scanning, results monitoring, cost control and reporting frequency. His empirical results showed a number of interesting pointers. Exception reports and monthly reviews were used significantly by prospector firms to monitor deviations from budget; moreover, quarterly and monthly updates of budget targets were frequently required. Defender firms tended to use 'head office' staff to report variances, while prospectors gave this responsibility to the operations manager. External scanning activities were widely carried out by all groups, but more aggressively by prospectors. Qualitative forecast information played an important role in prospector firms, with both groups claiming to use scenarios for planning. Defender scenarios were focused, while those of prospectors tended to be less structured, of the star-gazing variety. The study suggested that defender firms provide bonuses based on achievement of predetermined budget targets to a greater extent than prospector firms. Prospector firms generally tailor their control systems to users' needs to a greater extent than defender firms. Defender firms are likely to have stability in their control systems, while prospectors need to modify theirs frequently to adapt to changing circumstances.

Marketing strategy

It is essential to have a clear picture of what is meant by 'marketing'. A variety of writers have put emphasis on different aspects of the activity. Kotler (1991) claims to like the following definition:

Marketing is a social and managerial process by which individuals and groups obtain what they need and want through creating, offering and exchanging products of value with others. (p. 4)

Jobber (1995) states that:

Modern Marketing can be expressed as:
The achievement of corporate goals through meeting and exceeding customer needs better than competition. (p. 5)

Doyle (1994) suggests that:

The fundamental idea of marketing is that organizations survive and prosper through meeting the needs of customers (p. 33).

Kotler (1991) proposes that there are four orientations under which companies carry out marketing activities:

- *Operations.* This suggests that the customer will select those services which are widely available and low cost. Managers in these companies focus on high operational efficiencies. Thus in the international travel service, offering a basic coach service between London and Budapest could fall into this category.
- *Service.* This suggests that the customer will choose the service which has the highest quality and performance. Managers here aim at delivering excellent service and constantly seeking to improve it over time. Thus an independent airline might offer first-class (as opposed to business-class or tourist-class) seats on the service between London and Budapest.
- *Selling.* This suggests that customers, if left alone, will not normally buy enough of a company's services, so there must be a sustained selling and promotion effort. Thus the state airline might have to run a service between London and Budapest, and be involved in heavy promotion to fill the seats.
- *Marketing.* This suggests that the key to achieving a company's goals consists in determining the needs of the target markets and delivering its services more effectively and efficiently than competitors.

Clearly, the link between all of these activities is the view adopted of the customer. Only in the final analysis is any real attempt made to identify the customer requirements. For the first two, some basic (unsubstantiated) assumptions are made about customer behaviour, while in the third, substantial efforts are made to alter behaviour. Also of importance is the recognition of the difference between selling (trying to persuade the customer to purchase the service which is being provided) and marketing (identifying customers' needs and satisfying these). This leads to the cynical definition of selling as 'persuading people to buy services which they do not want with money which they do not have'. Unfortunately, there have been examples of this in a variety of sectors, including insurance, timeshare property and banking.

The earlier 'definitions' of marketing could lead the reader to think that the term encompasses all aspects of management. This should not be seen as the case. However, the boundaries with other functions are rather fuzzy, and, especially with operations, multiple roles can often be combined. The front-line operations staff member is ideally

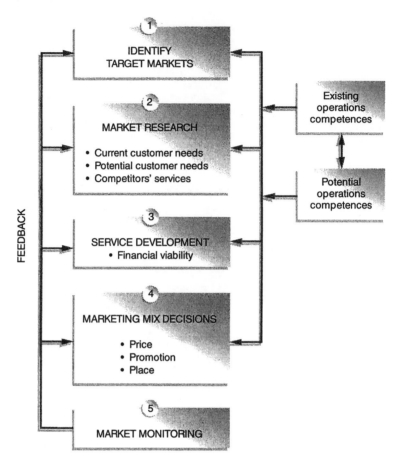

Figure 4.3   Five key marketing management tasks (Source: Doyle, 1994, p. 39)

positioned, delivering a service, to establish future needs of a customer, or to provide information about complementary services. For example, when you order the foreign currency for your holiday, the counter clerk in a bank or a building society can advise you on the availability of travellers' cheques and holiday insurance.

A number of writers have attempted to specify the roles and responsibilities of the marketing manager. An overview of the five marketing management tasks suggested by Doyle (1994) is given in Figure 4.3. The process starts with the identification of those groups with whom the organization will trade. This is followed by the collection of information about those groups' current and future needs and desires, and importantly what the competition are doing or plan to do to satisfy these. The organization must then develop its own services which can compete successfully for these groups' custom. This will involve decisions concerning price, promotion and place (distribution and delivery) of the service. Recognizing that markets are dynamic and change over time, it is necessary to monitor the situation constantly so that changes can be made to the key parameters, when necessary.

Clearly a key factor in the successful development and delivery of the service is the matching of this with the existing and potential operations competences of the organization.

The third and fourth steps are frequently amalgamated into the 'four Ps' which are the key decision areas of the marketing mix: product (or service), price, promotion and place. It has been suggested that, in services marketing, these must be joined by three further Ps: people, physical evidence and process (Booms and Bitner, 1981). However, it could be argued that many of the key issues within these three 'service' Ps are primarily under the control of the operations manager (e.g. people – training; physical evidence – layout; process – design of the delivery system). While there are inputs into the decision-making process from marketing, they are not solely marketing decisions, and hence will be dealt with elsewhere.

Kotler (1991) defines marketing strategy as:

> comprising the broad principles by which marketing management expects to achieve its business and marketing objectives in a target market. It consists of basic decisions on marketing expenditures, marketing mix and marketing allocation (p. 68).

Some of these broad issues will be discussed in the following sections.

Targeting strategies

It is generally accepted that there are three generic targeting strategies: undifferentiated, differentiated and focused. Undifferentiated involves the marketing mix aimed at the entire market, focused involves the marketing mix aimed at a single market segment, while differentiated is when each market segment has its own marketing mix.

British Airways operates differentiated marketing with its combined first-class, business-class and economy-class flights between London and Hong Kong: a different marketing mix (class of travel) for each market segment (company chairpeople, business people and tourists). Saga operates focused marketing in targeting the 50-year-plus age group.

Another example of differentiation is captured by the descriptions of the hotel chains provided by an international travel services group: haute de gamme, de confort international, économique, très économique avec sanitaires privatifs, très économique.

Choice of targeting strategy is a fundamental decision which must be consistent with the organization's corporate mission and goals. The decision has significant implications in terms of marketing resources (training sales staff, promotion and so on) and operations (economies of scale). Some of these operational issues will be dealt with elsewhere.

Service growth strategies

Ansoff (1957) developed a matrix which identified the generic strategies for growth, corresponding to examining current and new markets against current and new services.

With the market penetration strategy, the organization attempts to increase market share, possibly by encouraging existing customers to use the existing service more frequently (e.g. travel companies persuading clients to take a second holiday) or by attracting customers from competitors. The market development strategy involves looking for new markets for existing services. Some schools have adopted this approach in taking mature students

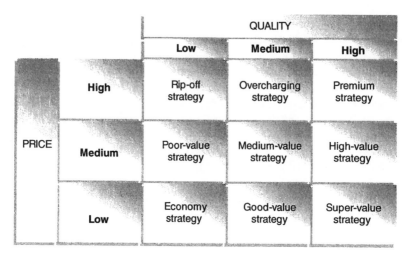

Figure 4.4   Nine price quality strategies (Source: Doyle, 1994, p. 224)

(rather than 16–18-year-olds) into their sixth forms to study on A-level courses. Building societies offering their customers personal banking is an example of a service development strategy, with the organization offering a new service to its current market. Diversification is the most complex as it involves both new services and new markets.

All of these growth strategies should be linked to the corporate-level strategy, and have implications for marketing and, more significantly, operations, particularly in terms of resources.

Pricing strategies

Pricing is one of the major decisions facing an organization, and it has a major impact on profitability. Often there is a perceived link to quality. Kotler (1991) suggests nine price/quality strategies. These are shown in Figure 4.4, following the adaptation made by Doyle (1994). The strategies along the diagonal represent the equilibrium between quality and price. Those below the diagonal represent good value to the consumer (and could be used to gain substantial competitive advantage). In contrast, above the diagonal the positions are unsustainable in the long term.

Pricing can be based on a number of considerations: cost, demand and the competition are three of these. Detailed discussion of the advantages and disadvantages of these different approaches can be found in the references. However, a number of the features of services cause further complexity here. One is the inability to hold stocks. The revenue for an empty hotel room is lost for ever. This can be seen in the prices for which it is possible to obtain a hotel room in a major city. The nightly rack rate (standard charge) could be £120. It might be possible to negotiate £60 over the phone. The corporate rate is £45, and an organization prepared to take a number of rooms on a regular rate could be charged £32. A similar situation arises for the traveller prepared to travel 'stand-by' by air, taking any empty seats at the last moment. Significant price reductions are allowed for this. Other

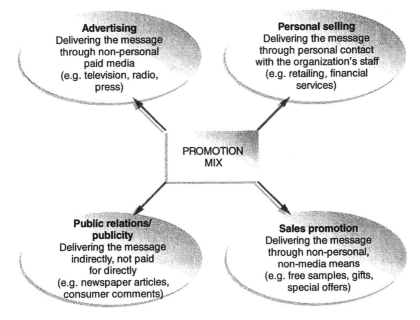

Figure 4.5 Approaches to promotion

illustrations are 'early bird' and 'happy hour' prices charged in restaurants and bars during non-peak hours.

Promotion strategies

Of key importance to any organization is communication with existing and potential customers. How do potential customers get to know about existing and new services offered by the organization? The organization decides on the message to be communicated, which is then prepared in a format for the selected media (e.g. television advertisement, poster by the road side and so on). This is then interpreted by the intended/potential customer, who reacts in some way or another. It is important to recognize that the presentation, receipt and feedback from the message are all subject to misinterpretation – frequently referred to as 'noise' – due to the 'imperfections' in the environment. An example of this might be the name given to the French chain of sports wear retailers 'Athletes Foot', which conjures up one picture in French eyes and another interpretation by English-speaking potential customers.

It is generally accepted that there are four broad approaches to promotion:

- Advertising.
- Sales promotion.
- Publicity.
- Personal selling.

Examples of each of these are given in Figure 4.5. A major strategic decision for the marketing director is the 'promotion mix' – how to spread the available resources across

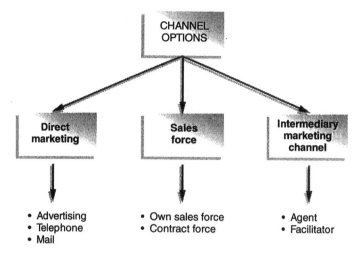

Figure 4.6 Three generic marketing channels (Source: Doyle, 1994, p. 318)

these four areas. The intangibility of services adds to the importance of this aspect. It gives a good opportunity, through advertising and also through the other approaches, to 'form' the customers' expectations. Each form of promotion has its own set of advantages and disadvantages, and a full analysis can be found in the various marketing texts in the reference section.

Marketing channel strategies

The final P of the marketing mix was place. These decisions concern how an organization will reach its target market. Doyle (1994) suggests that there are three generic marketing channels open to an organization. These are shown in Figure 4.6. Taking insurance as an example, it is possible to see all three options used. This links to issues associated with location and distribution. Frequently, the need for the customer to be present during the delivery of the service, and the impossibility of holding stocks of the service, impose significant constraints on these aspects.

Human resource management strategy

Human resource management (or HRM, as it is frequently abbreviated to) is a term which has relatively recently come into management texts. It is generally 'replacing' the somewhat outdated 'personnel management and industrial relations'. Needless to say, there is much debate over the precise differences between the two phrases. There does, however, appear to be agreement that a difference is in the emphasis in HRM on the long-term, strategic issues associated with the management of people (Cowling and James, 1994). Storey (1995) defines HRM:

Beliefs and assumptions
- That it is the human resource which gives competitive edge
- That the aim should be not mere compliance with rules, but employee commitment
- That therefore employees should be very carefully selected and developed

Strategic qualities
- Because of the above factors, human resource decisions are of strategic importance
- Top management involvement is necessary
- Human resource policies should be integrated into the business strategy, stemming from it and even contributing to it

Critical role of managers
- Because human resource practice is critical to the core activities of the business, it is too important to be left to the personnel specialists alone
- Line managers need to be closely involved both as deliverers and drivers of human resource policies
- Much greater attention is paid to the management of managers themselves

Key levers
- Managing culture is more important than managing procedures and systems
- Integrated action on selection, communication, training, reward and development
- Restructuring and job redesign to allow devolved responsibility and empowerment

Figure 4.7 The HRM model (Source: Storey, 1995, p. 6)

as a distinctive approach to employment management which seeks to achieve competitive advantage through the strategic deployment of a highly committed and capable workforce using an array of cultural, structural and personnel techniques. (p. 5)

He goes on to 'define' the HRM model as shown in Figure 4.7.

This underlines the strategic aspects of HRM, and suggests that it is possible to identify the key elements of HRM. Some of these major facets are shown in Figure 4.8. Although these are shown as emanating from HRM, they will clearly overlap. For example, personnel planning will have implications for recruitment and selection; and collective bargaining, training and development, and motivation and rewards will be linked.

The importance that organizations place on aspects of HRM is frequently reflected in their corporate or mission statements. Examples can be seen in Figures 3.4 and 3.5.

Cowling and James (1994) suggest that strategic issues which relate to people management are currently seen as organization structures, culture change, management development, performance management, reward management and the development of flexible, multiskilled teams.

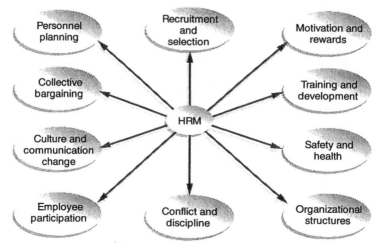

Figure 4.8 Facets of human resources management

Some of the strategic HRM decisions are outlined and discussed in more detail in the following sections.

Strategic personnel planning

This is one of the key strategic decision-making tasks in HRM. It derives more or less directly from the organization's strategic plan. In essence it involves asking the basic questions: what human resources are required to achieve the strategy and how are these to be acquired? Clearly, determining the nature of the resources requires the close co-operation of operations management who will have knowledge of key considerations like the skills and competences likely to be required.

Figure 4.9 presents in rather more detail some of the major steps involved in this process based on Bramham (1989) and Zabriskie and Huellmantel (1989).

Consider a college department which currently offers a range of courses in mainstream technology. A strategic review has been carried out and the college has agreed the department's strategy of moving from its current range of courses based solely on technology, to a portfolio which has a smaller number of technology courses with a set where the technology is taught alongside management studies. Simplifying the human resource requirements, these could be put into three broad categories: administrative/managerial, technical support and professional (teaching). The reduced technology content of the courses will reduce the need for both technical and professional staff in these areas. Depending on the profile and interests of the individuals concerned, this can be handled by transfer, retraining, retirement or possibly redundancy. It is likely that the new developments will require some new staff – an administrator and a leader for the teaching staff – but that some of the requirements might be covered by retraining. Clearly, significant detail will be required concerning the launch dates of the new courses and projected student

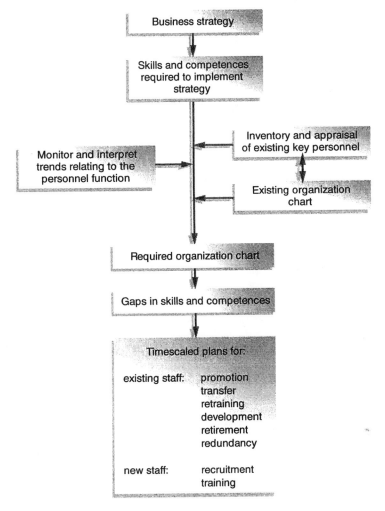

Figure 4.9 The strategic personnel planning process

numbers in order to establish the numbers of staff required and when recruitment and training will need to take place. The personnel function will also bring to this process information concerning current trends in remuneration (e.g. use of performance-related pay), contract types appropriate (e.g. fixed-term, part-time, rolling contracts) and other such issues.

As with any planning process, this needs monitoring and reviewing in the light of the various forecasts and other uncertain elements which provide inputs. For example, adjustments may be necessary to staff requirements if student numbers exceed forecasts, and revised targets are agreed.

The strategic implications of reward systems

Reward systems operated by organizations have become more and more complex, with a variety of what are sometimes regarded as fringe benefits (e.g. non-contributory pension schemes, free health insurance, company cars) and performance-related elements (ranging from purely financial to 'free holidays' and share options). These can act as a significant motivator, but it is important that they are seen to be used fairly and to encourage and promote behaviour which is consistent with the long-term strategy. They can be used as part of the process of changing the culture within an organization. However, on occasions some changes in reward systems have been driven by short-term cost considerations and the need to respond to immediate pressures from the labour market. Murphy (1989) describes the introduction of a reward system to Abbey National which was designed to support a shift in culture to meet the needs of the market place.

Other strategic issues associated with human resource management

Frequently in strategy implementation, there is reference to a 'change in the organization's culture'. So what is an 'organization's culture'? It can be simply described as 'the way we do things around here', or in more detail as 'a pattern of basic assumptions that a group has invented, discovered or developed in learning to cope with its problems of external adaptation and internal integration' (Cowling and James, 1994, p. 81). Thus an organization might say that it intends to move to a customer-focused culture. This move can be supported by a three-step process. First, there is *unfreezing*, by which individuals become receptive to new ideas, supported by discussion groups, explanations of benefits of the new approaches, challenging of attitudes of the status quo, and training in new skills required. This is followed by *movement* during which acceptance is gained for the new ideas. The final step is *freezing*, during which the new ideas become part of the culture.

Kochan and Barocci (1985) develop links between the different stages in the product life cycle (introduction, growth, maturity, decline) and aspects of the critical human resource activities (recruitment selection and staffing, compensation and benefits, employee training and development and labour/employee relations). Thus, for example, they propose that during the introduction stage there is the need to attract the best 'talent', while in the decline it is necessary to plan workforce reductions.

Historically, human resource management has been seen as an 'add-on' or 'support' function within an organization. As seen above, successful management of human resources can be much more than that. Swiercz and Spencer (1992) argue that, in the case of Delta Airlines, HRM can be seen to have actually given the airline a sustainable competitive advantage. In the case of Delta, the labour force was seen not as peripheral to the organization, but as central, and corporate decision making took into account that good staff relations and management could provide an edge over competitors which had a more combative relationship with their employees.

Information strategy

Organizations and the individuals within them generate and receive vast amounts of information, through a variety of different media. Cashmore (1991) suggests that this can be classified as follows:

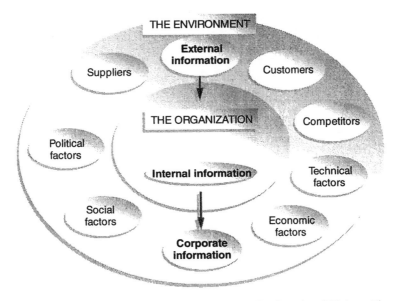

Figure 4.10 Information flows (Source: Cashmore, 1991, p. 7)

- External information flowing into the organization, on such issues as customer requirements, competitors' prices and political influences.
- Corporate information about the organization, flowing out of the organization (e.g. advertising).
- Internal information flowing within the organization (e.g. costs, skills of staff).

This information *should* contribute to improved efficiency and effectiveness through improved decision making. However, unfortunately this is not always the case.

It is important to distinguish between data and information, and where an information systems fits into this. Data comprise facts and figures which have normally been collected and stored. These become information when they have undergone some processing which enables them to be used (often to support some decision-making process). The raw data, process and information is referred to as the information system. Thus in assessing the performance of a student on a particular course of study, we would take the marks obtained in the individual examination questions attempted and the course work and combine these in the prescribed format to arrive at the overall grade. This information would be used to decide if the student had passed or failed the course.

Some writers (e.g. Ward *et al.*, 1990; Wiseman, 1985) distinguish between the roles of technology-based information systems as they have developed over time. These start with (1) data processing with an emphasis on automating existing information processes and improved efficiency; and move to (2) management information systems, satisfying requirements for decision support and improved effectiveness, and (3) strategic information systems which improve competitiveness. A hotel might start with a basic data-processing system which records occupancy, reservations and services provided for each room. This might

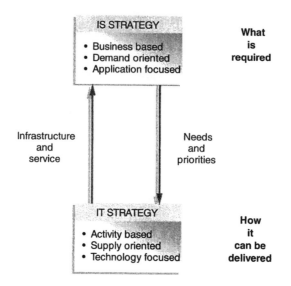

Figure 4.11   IS and IT strategies (Source: Earl, 1989, p. 63)

be developed into a management information system which would analyze the rate of consumption, profitability and so on of the various services provided. If the hotel were part of a larger chain, then the reservation systems of each could be linked to a central system whereby a series of reservations could be made across different hotels, or by which if one hotel were full, the enquirer could be presented with a range of alternative options.

In simplistic terms, the information strategy is the long-term plan for the provision of information which will support the corporate plan. This can be broken down into the *systems* aspect which covers what information is required and the *technology* aspect of how it is to be provided, resulting in a 'combined' information system/information technology (IS/IT) strategy. Earl (1989) produces a compact representation of this, as shown in Figure 4.11.

A variety of models exist for the strategic IS/IT planning process. Figure 4.12 shows the model proposed by Ward *et al.* (1990), comprising the basic inputs and outputs of the process. The internal and external business environment factors come from the basic analyses which were completed as part of the business strategy development process (see Chapter 3), and include the PEST and SWOT analyses. The internal IS/IT environment refers to the current and planned systems which support the organization, and the effectiveness of their contribution. It includes the skills and competences of those working in the IS/IT area. The external IS/IT environment refers to the broader perspective of developments in IS/IT in terms of technological trends and opportunities to use IS/IT in innovative ways. This is complemented by the various planning approaches and tools and techniques which cover both strategic analysis (e.g. the Boston Box) and IS/IT itself (e.g. use of the latest advanced programme generation tools). The outputs comprise the business IS strategy, IT strategy and IS management strategy. The requirement for information and systems is

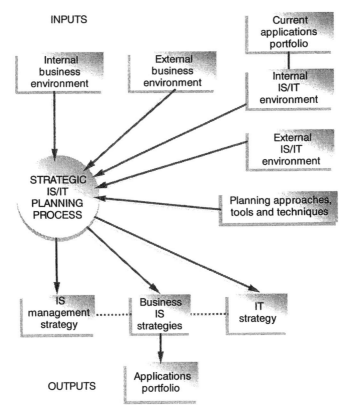

INPUTS

Current applications portfolio

Internal business environment

External business environment

Internal IS/IT environment

External IS/IT environment

STRATEGIC IS/IT PLANNING PROCESS

Planning approaches, tools and techniques

IS management strategy

Business IS strategies

IT strategy

OUTPUTS

Applications portfolio

Figure 4.12   The strategic IS/IT planning process (Source: Ward *et al.*, 1990, p. 96; copyright © 1990, Wiley, reprinted by permission of John Wiley & Sons Ltd.

contained within the business IS strategy, with as its key element the applications portfolio. The IT strategy concerns the means of delivery of the systems (including computer hardware). The IS management strategy covers the softer issues relating to the organization of the IS/IT provision. These are covered in more detail in Ward *et al.* (1990).

Gaining competitive advantage through strategic information systems

Since the 1980s there have been an increasing number of organizations claiming to have developed information systems which give them signficant competitive advantage, and the term 'strategic information system' (SIS) has been used to describe such systems. These have covered such diverse areas as airline reservation systems (SABRE – American Airlines System, and Apollo), the automated insurance environment (United Service Automobile Association, Skania International, Insurance Inc.), banking and finance (Union Bank of Finland, Nottingham Building Society), tourism (Thomson Holidays), communications (Mintel) and health care. These and other cases are described in more detail in Wiseman (1985), Ward *et al.* (1990), Hopper (1990) and Large (1986).

Discussion

The operations strategy is key for a service organization, particularly with the current emphasis on a customer focus. Clearly this must be prepared in a systematic and structured manner, taking due account of marketing implications. This interface is crucial given the blurred line between marketing and operations in this type of environment.

References

Ansoff, I. (1957) 'Strategies for diversification', *Harvard Business Review*, vol. 35, no. 5, p. 114.

Booms, B.H. and M.J. Bitner (1981) 'Marketing strategies and organizational structures for service firms', in J.H. Donnelly and W.R. George (eds.), *Marketing of Services*, American Marketing Association, Chicago, IL.

Bramham, J. (1989) *Human Resource Planning*, Institute of Personnel Management, London.

Cashmore, C. with R. Lyall (1991) *Business Information Systems and Strategies*, Prentice Hall, London.

Cowling, A. and P. James (1994) *The Essence of Personnel Management and Industrial Relations*, Prentice Hall, Hemel Hempstead.

Doyle, P. (1994) *Marketing Management and Strategy*, Prentice Hall, London.

Earl, M. (1989) *Management Strategies for Information Technology*, Prentice Hall, London.

Emmanual, C., D. Otley and K. Marchant (1991) *Accounting for Management Control* (2nd edn), Chapman and Hall, London.

Hiromoto, T. (1988) 'Another hidden edge: Japanese management accounting', *Harvard Business Review*, vol. 66, no. 4, pp. 22–7.

Hopper, M. (1990) 'Rattling SABRE: new ways to compete on information', *Harvard Business Review*, vol. 68, no. 3, pp. 118–25.

Jobber, D. (1995) *Principles and Practice of Marketing*, McGraw-Hill, London.

Kochan, T.A. and T.A. Barocci (1985) *Human Resource Management and Industrial Relations: Text, readings and cases*, Little Brown, Boston, MA.

Kotler, P. (1991) *Marketing Management* (7th edn), Prentice Hall, Englewood Cliffs, NJ.

Large, J. (1986) 'Information's market force', *Management Today*, August, pp. 64–80.

Maher, M.W., C.P. Strickney, R.L. Weil and S. Davidson (1991) *Managerial Accounting* (4th edn), Harcourt, Brace and Jovanovich, London.

Miles, R.E. and C.C. Snow (1978) *Organizational Strategy, Structure and Processes*, McGraw-Hill, New York.

Murphy, T. (1989) 'Pay for performance: an instrument of strategy', *Long Range Planning*, vol. 22, no. 4, pp. 40–5.

Simmonds, K. (1981) 'Strategic management accounting', *Management Accounting*, April, pp. 26–9.

Simons, R. (1987) 'Accounting control systems and business strategy: an empirical analysis', *Accounting, Organizations and Society*, vol. 12, no. 4, pp. 357–74.

Simons, R. (1990) 'The role of management control systems in creating competitive advantage', *Accounting, Organizations and Society*, vol. 15, no. 1/2, pp. 127–43.

Snow, C.C. and L.G. Hrebiniak (1980) 'Strategy, distinctive competence and organizational performance', *Administrative Science Quarterly*, vol. 25, June, pp. 317–36.

Storey, J. (1995) 'HRM: still marching on, or marching out', in J. Storey (ed.), *Human Resources Management*, Routledge, London.

Swiercz, P. and Spencer, B. (1992) 'HRM and sustainable competitive advantage: lessons from Delta Airlines', *Human Resource Planning*, vol. 15, no. 2, pp. 35–46.

Ward, J., P. Griffiths and P. Whitmore (1990) *Strategic Planning for Information Systems*, Wiley, Chichester.

Wiseman, C. (1985) *Strategy and Computers*, Dow Jones, Irwin, IL.

Zabriskie, N. and A. Huellmantel (1989) 'Implementing strategies for human resources', *Long Range Planning*, vol. 22, no. 2, pp. 70–7.

Discussion topics/exercises

1. For an organization of your choice, describe the key interfaces between the appropriate functional strategies.

2. Use practical examples to illustrate the generic strategy classification of Miles and Snow.

3. 'In a service organization there is little difference between the marketing strategy and the operations strategy.' Use examples to discuss this statement.

4. Use illustrations to distinguish between the systems and the technology aspects of an information strategy.

Chapter 5

Operations strategy

Chapter outline

☆ Competitive dimensions
☆ Order-winning and order-qualifying criteria
☆ Strategic service vision
☆ Stages of service organization competitiveness
☆ Focused operations
☆ Operations strategy formulation process

Introduction

The operations strategy is one of the key functional strategies in any service organization, and it must be developed in such a way that it supports the corporate strategy of the enterprise as a whole. It is often convenient to think of the strategy development process as starting with the organization's corporate strategy, and after developing this, to proceed systematically to develop the separate functional strategies for operations, marketing, human resources management (HRM) and so on. Indeed, this view has in part been reinforced by the structure in the presentation of corporate strategy in Chapter 3, followed by the functional strategies in Chapter 4.

However, it will have been apparent in reading both these earlier chapters that there was a degree of overlap between issues, ideas and concepts introduced in the different sections. The Miles and Snow (1987) strategy types of defender, prospector, analyzer and reactor were introduced in the context of accounting finance strategies, in Chapter 4. Would these not have been better covered in Chapter 3 on corporate strategy? Marketing channel strategies are linked to the fourth P of marketing place. As such, issues like location, layout and distribution are fundamental. However, an operations manager would regard decisions in these areas a key responsibility. An important area in HRM is strategic personnel planning. A major area of strategic planning associated with this is recruitment, training and development. It is clear that important inputs into this process are the job specifications of the tasks required and knowledge of the necessary skills and competences. Again this is an area where operations management can make a significant contribution.

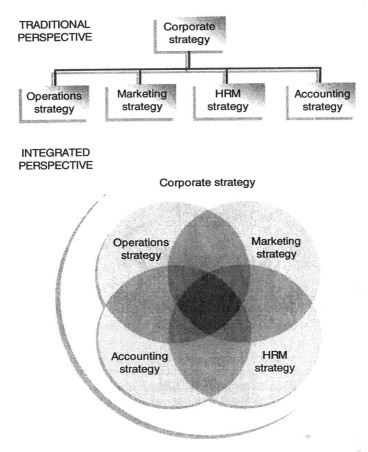

Figure 5.1 Traditional and integrated views of functional strategies

What is becoming apparent is that, while it is necessary to consider the corporate strategy in developing each individual functional strategy, the various aspects of each functional strategy cannot be considered generally in isolation from the other functional strategies. Often it is not sufficient to think of them as being linked via the corporate strategy. It is necessary to recognize this overlap and view the process from an integrated perspective. This is presented diagrammatically in Figure 5.1.

The extent and nature of the overlaps will depend in part on the characteristics of the particular service organization. It is less important whether a particular issue is regarded as being associated with, say, marketing strategy or operations strategy; but key that it be an issue which requires full consideration by all interested parties who can bring relevant information, knowledge and expertise to bear on the situation. Generally there will be a natural tendency for each function 'leader' (operations, marketing, HRM and so on) to assume responsibility for the widest range of activities and issues; and this should not be allowed to generate friction and detract from the effective development of the various strategies. They should be integrated and there should be corporate responsibility for them.

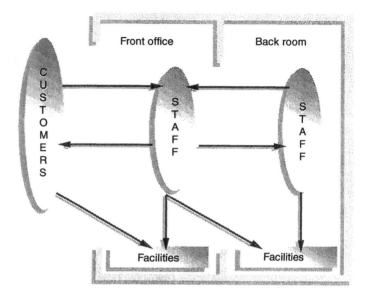

Figure 5.2 The front office/back room of service organizations

A useful concept in examining service situations is the split between what are sometimes referred to as 'front office' and 'back room' activities, which was introduced in Chapter 2. This split can have significance for the characteristics of the service organization, as well as having implications for the development of an operations strategy. It is shown diagrammatically in Figure 5.2.

The front office is the area where customer contact takes place, and where the customer is present. The back room is where the support activities take place: the customer normally does not come into contact with this area or its personnel. The terms 'back room' and 'front office' are actually *used* in some environments, such as banking, whereas in a restaurant, the front office is represented by the actual dining room where the meal is served and eaten, and the back room is the kitchen where it is prepared and cooked. In a solicitor's office, both front office and back room activities may be carried out at different times, depending on the presence of the client.

A service organization can be characterized by the balance between front office and back room activities, and the relative sizes of these two areas. A hairdressing salon might have minimal back office activity, whereas a building society might have a large activity handling mortgage application paperwork in comparison to direct customer contact. Both a fast-food restaurant and the French bistro might have the same space allocated to cooking and to eating meals. However, there is likely to be a higher degree of customer contact in the French bistro. In the front office areas, with the high levels of customer presence and contact, the distinctions between the different functional roles of marketing, operations and HRM become blurred, particularly marketing and operations. Consider the location and the layout of a restaurant, and the timing/schedule for a flight from London to Paris. McLaughlin and Pannesi (1991) state that 'virtually all strategic issues involving customer contact and front office activities must be the result of joint decision making involving marketing, operations, finance and human resources' (p. 63).

In the next section, some of the concepts supporting operations strategy will be developed. This will include revisiting some of the ideas introduced in earlier chapters, and examining them in rather more detail from an operations perspective.

Some concepts supporting operations strategy

Competitive dimensions

It is important to recognize the different dimensions along which organizations compete, and to ensure that the operations function has the capability to support them. Moreover, the decision about which dimensions to compete on should be made formally at the highest levels within the organization, and be consistent with (and part of) the organization's corporate strategy.

A number of authors have presented a variety of different sets of dimensions along which organizations compete (e.g. Platts and Gregory, 1990; Department of Trade and Industry, 1994; Hill, 1993; McLaughlin and Pannesi, 1991). This set includes quality, location, service features, cost, speed of provision, reliability of timing of provision, delivery/design flexibility and volume flexibility. There is much debate around the issue of service quality, and this topic is covered in Chapter 13. However, it is worth listing here one set of subdimensions of service quality proposed by Parasuraman *et al.* (1988):

- Tangibles.
- Reliability.
- Responsiveness.
- Competence.
- Courtesy.
- Credibility.
- Security.
- Access.
- Communication.
- Understanding the customer.

This gives a flavour of the different ways in which a customer might choose to assess the quality of a particular service. The weight attached to each will vary both between different services and between consumers for the same service.

McLaughlin and Pannesi (1991) note that, because services cannot be stored, location and capacity are two further dimensions which could be added to the above list (although there is overlap between capacity and volume flexibility). Moreover, they claim that since contact between the customer and server is an essential feature of many service organizations, and forms a key part of its competitive strategy, operations strategy should be viewed separately for the front office and for the back room.

Table 5.1 illustrates some competitive dimensions for a range of service organizations. The business person wants the aircraft to depart and arrive on time for an important meeting. The hairdresser must have the flexibility to do customers' hair to their exact requirements. The hotel must have the bed capacity for the last-minute booking and arrival. Although only a single dimension is shown against each situation in the table, in practice there could be a range with different levels of importance. The next section presents a framework for tackling this.

Table 5.1 Some illustrative competitive dimensions for service organizations

Organization/service	Illustrative key competitive dimension
Airline	Reliability of timing of provision
Hairdresser	Delivery/design flexibility
Hotel	Capacity
Professional accountant	Quality: competence
Coach service	Cost
Corner shop	Location

Order-qualifying and order-winning criteria

Hill (1993) introduced the concepts of order-qualifying and order-winning criteria (OQC and OWC) as means for understanding how an organization's services compete in the market place. An OQC is one which the service must have to be able to enter the market, while an OWC is one which enables an organization's service to gain advantage over similar services offered by competitors. At a simple level, in fast-food catering, speed of delivery could be considered an OQC, while an organization might target the market which has price as an OWC.

To take a rather more complex example, consider a student at a college starting the process of selecting a university at which to go and study. In general terms, the criteria of importance could be considered under the generic headings of cost, quality, features and flexibility. However, what do these criteria mean in terms of the specific aspects of the degree programme? Some of them are presented in the first column of Table 5.2. This is not intended to be a definitive list, rather to give a flavour of some of the relevant criteria under the generic headings. Thus under 'cost' the student might have both the cost of accommodation and the cost of living (food, transport) as criteria. Features might be a mix of those related to the university (e.g. a good social life) and those related to the particular programme of study (e.g. a placement year spent working). Flexibility could refer to opportunities to tailor or customize the programme to the individual's own specific requirements over time, such as deciding to study abroad for a semester or a year, or selecting options which resulted in either a specialized or a general programme. There are a number of ways in which the quality of a service can be measured, and a more rigorous and formal treatment of this is given in Chapter 13. Indicators of quality are seen by the student as including a high reputation, and small group teaching.

Viewing this from the perspective of the university, it is necessary to establish which criteria from the list are order winning and which are order qualifying. Moreover, Hill (1993) suggests two further refinements. He proposes allocating 100 percentage points across the OWC, and from the OQC identifying the order-losing sensitive qualifiers, i.e. those which, if not provided, lead to a rapid loss of 'custom'. Carrying out this process for the example might give the results presented in the second column of Table 5.2. It is

Table 5.2 OQC, OWC and weightings for a degree programme

Criteria	Category weighting
Cost	
Low fee levels	Q
Cheap accommodation	Q
Low cost of living	Q
Features	
Placement year working	50
Plentiful accommodation	QQ
Good social life	QQ
Flexibility	
Optional semester abroad	10
General or specialized programme	10
Quality	
Good employment prospects	Q
Good degree results	15
High reputation	5
Small group teaching	10

Note: Percentages against OWC sum to 100; Q – order-qualifying criteria; QQ – Order-losing sensitive qualifier.

important to recognize that this is not a static exercise, and that the classification of the criteria and the weightings might change over time. Thus as the employment situation becomes more and more competitive, the placement year feature might become an OQC, and as programmes develop, new OWC like the flexibility to follow a 'fast-track' and complete the course in two years rather than three might occur.

Knowledge of the OQC and the OWC enables the organization to examine those aspects of operations which contribute to the achievement of these criteria. This can form a valuable part of the operations strategy development process, and will be dealt with in more detail later in this chapter.

Strategic service vision

Heskett (1986) describes the development and growth of the French hypermarket chain Carrefour in the 1960s, using this as an illustration of the basic elements of what he calls the strategic service vision. A French retail store owner, Michel Fournier, identified a significant target market segment: young, mobile, two-wage-earning couples who had neither the time nor the inclination to shop at the stores in the local village. From here he went on to develop a service concept which would meet the segment's perceived requirements: the out-of-town (because of space requirements), one-stop shopping centre. He established his competitive strategy of competing on price and quality (freshness), exploiting the generous payment terms offered by wholesalers to the smaller stores and the rapid turnover of stock planned for his hypermarket. This also provided capital for future expansion and growth. Finally, he focused on the service delivery system which

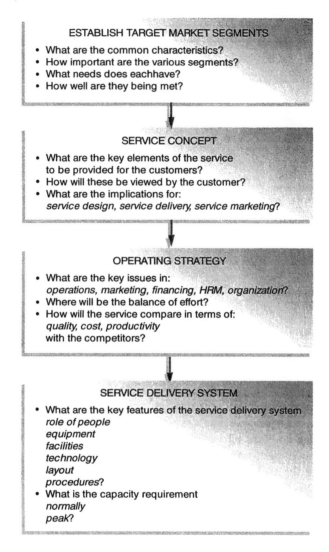

ESTABLISH TARGET MARKET SEGMENTS
- What are the common characteristics?
- How important are the various segments?
- What needs does eachhave?
- How well are they being met?

SERVICE CONCEPT
- What are the key elements of the service to be provided for the customers?
- How will these be viewed by the customer?
- What are the implications for: *service design, service delivery, service marketing?*

OPERATING STRATEGY
- What are the key issues in: *operations, marketing, financing, HRM, organization?*
- Where will be the balance of effort?
- How will the service compare in terms of: *quality, cost, productivity* with the competitors?

SERVICE DELIVERY SYSTEM
- What are the key features of the service delivery system *role of people equipment facilities technology layout procedures?*
- What is the capacity requirement *normally peak?*

Figure 5.3 Basic elements of a strategic service vision (Source: Heskett, 1986, p. 8; adapted and reprinted by permission of Harvard Business School from *Managing in the Service Economy* by J.L. Heskett, Boston, MA, 1986, p. 8. Copyright © 1986 by the President and Fellows of Harvard College, all rights reserved.)

would provide the service for his target market. The key elements in this four-stage process and some of the questions which require answers are presented in Figure 5.3.

In defining and developing the service concept, it is important to distinguish between the core and peripheral services. There are similarities at a detailed level with the order-qualifying and order-winning concepts introduced earlier. The core services are those which are essential to the target market. To a hotel guest this could be a clean room with en suite facilities, while peripheral services might be tea/coffee-making facilities, television (with satellite channels), telephone, minibar and so on.

The stages of service organization competitiveness

The importance of organizations identifying the dimensions on which they compete has been mentioned on several occasions. It is also important that they have a global view of how 'effective' they are in the market place in comparison to the competition. Chase and Hayes (1991) have developed a four-stage model which can be used to categorize a service firm's competitiveness, ranging from 'available for service' to 'world class service delivery'. The definitions of these four stages and some of their key characteristics are given in Table 5.3.

Thus we might use the 'corner shop' because it is convenient and open at 10.00 p.m. on Sunday evening, and we can buy a bottle of fresh milk to go with a pot of tea. We put up with the miserable assistant and the high price. The shop is 'available for service'. Frequently, firms which survive in this category enjoy a monopoly position along some important dimension. However, this survival may not be long lived, when you consider the impact of changes in Sunday trading legislation on small shops. Marks and Spencer might be regarded as being at stage 3 (some might argue stage 4), while it might be suggested that the hotel group Marriot is at stage 4. Some of Marriot's advertising publicity does indeed feature world-class service delivery characteristics. An examination of Table 5.3 will allow the identification of some of the changes of attitude required (see operations function and service quality), and steps to be taken with the customer and workforce, if the organization is to move from one stage to another. It has been suggested that this is a sequential process in which an organization would find it difficult to miss out a stage. An operations strategy might embody the plan of action necessary for operations if a company is to aim to move from, say, stage 2 to stage 4. A more detailed description of the stages can be found in Chase and Hayes (1991).

A key factor in improving competitive positioning is understanding what is important to customers. Chase and Hayes (1991) suggest the use of performance–importance mapping as a tool to present this information. This involves the collection of data from customers concerning both the importance of various measures and how the organization currently performs. This can then be presented on an appropriate graph. As an illustration, consider the service offered by a mid-range restaurant. The various measures of performance might be opening hours (last orders), choice of food (starters, main courses, desserts), range of drinks (soft, beers/ciders, wines, spirits), waiting times (to take orders, between courses), seating arrangements (space, comfort), servers (helpfulness, friendliness), atmosphere (noise, background music, smells). A representative group of customers over an appropriate period of time could be asked to rate these factors (on a 0 (poor) to 10 (excellent) scale) for importance to them and how they perceived the restaurant. The form of these results, averaged out over the group, is presented in Figure 5.4. This clearly indicates some areas which would benefit from further action. The seating and to a lesser extent the service are considered important, yet the perceptions of the restaurant's performance in these areas is not good. Further investigation may be necessary: for example, the tables might be too close together. Clearly, atmosphere and opening hours are not considered important, so investing in a new sound system may not be a sensible proposition.

Table 5.3 Four stages of service firm competitiveness

	Available for service	Journeyman	Distinctive competence achieved	World-class service delivery
Definition	Customers patronize service firms for reasons other than performance	Customers neither seek out nor avoid the firm	Customers seek out the firm based on its sustained reputation for meeting customer expectations	The company's name is synonymous with service excellence, its service doesn't just satisfy customers, it delights them, thereby expanding customer expectations to levels its competitors are unable to fulfill
Operations function	Operations is reactive at best	Operations functions in a mediocre uninspired way	Operations continually excels reinforced by personnel management and systems that support an intense customer focus	Operations is a quick learner and fast innovator, it masters every step of the service delivery process and provides capabilities that are superior to competitors
Service quality	Is subsidiary to cost, highly variable	Meets some customer expectations, consistent on one or two key dimensions	Exceeds customer expectations, consistent on multiple dimensions	Raises customer expectations and seeks challenges, improves continuously
Customer	Unspecified, to be satisfied at minimum cost	A market segment whose basic needs are understood	A collection of individuals whose variation in needs are understood	A source of stimulation, ideas and opportunity
Workforce	Negative constraint	Efficient resource disciplined, follows procedures	Permitted to select among alternative procedures	Innovative, creates procedures
First-line management	Controls workers	Controls the process	Listens to customers, coaches and facilitates workers	Is listened to by top management as a source of new ideas, mentors workers to enhance their career growth

Source: Chase and Hayes (1991), p. 17; reprinted from 'Beefing up operations in service firms' by R.B. Chase and R.H. Hayes, *Sloan Management Review*, Fall, 1991, pp. 15–26, by permission of publisher. Copyright © 1991 by Sloan Management Review Association. All rights reserved.

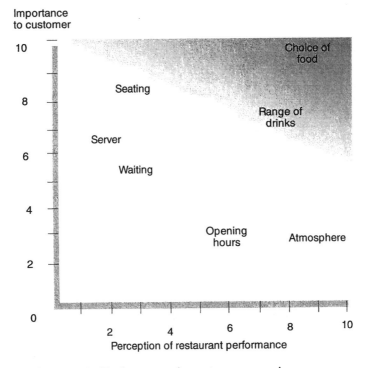

Figure 5.4 Performance importance mapping

Focused operations

The concept of focus was introduced in Chapter 3 in the context of generic corporate strategies. Skinner (1974) developed the idea, emphasizing the producing or operations advantages of concentrating on a narrower range of products or services for a particular market sector. A major benefit was seen to be the higher levels of efficiency and effectiveness possible from the delivery system because of the removal of some of the variety and the elimination of the consequential conflict of objectives. Consider the requirements of different types of airline passenger. The student holiday-maker will want a cheap flight, and will not necessarily mind flying at somewhat 'anti-social' hours if, by getting higher utilization of the aircraft, the costs and therefore fares can be reduced. The business traveller, however, may not be able to plan travel long in advance, and may have a tight schedule which requires transfers and return travel within the day. These two types of traveller have different objectives, and trying to meet the requirements of both equally can cause conflicts for the operations of the airline.

The concept of focus is not new for service organizations, and there are a number of companies which have exploited its benefits: Lunn Poly has focused on the package holiday sector of the holiday market, sixth form colleges in the education system focus on the 16–18-year-olds. Saga Services target the 50+ age group with a range of services from household insurance to holidays. Focus is a key aspect in the ideas developed in the strategic service vision proposed by Heskett (1986).

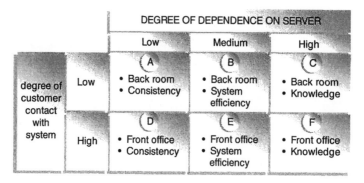

Figure 5.5   A classification of services (Source: van Dierdonck and Brandt, 1988, p. 36)

Van Dierdonck and Brandt (1988) claim that some of the characteristics of service organizations can create special problems in attempting to adopt the idea of focus. The first is the presence of the customer in the delivery system. This can impact on the effectiveness of focusing in a number of ways. Consider a 'haute cuisine' restaurant in an hotel projecting an image and atmosphere contributed to by a dress code that requires males to wear a jacket and tie at dinner. How should the resident in jumper and jeans be handled? In service organizations, there is much less 'control' over some of the 'input materials' (in this case the human element) into the process. The customer also has the direct opportunity to interact with the process and potentially alter or broaden the focus. Consider the wedding meal for which sirloin steak has been chosen as the main course. The kitchen staff are cooking 150 steaks. However, two guests would like theirs underdone! A service consists of a bundle of components and each element should be consistent with the focus. In particular, the facilities and layout often form part of the service rather than simply facilitating delivery of the service. Consider the couple eating an excellently prepared and served meal in a haute cuisine restaurant. There were no complaints whatsoever about the meal. However, the tables were small and it was difficult to accommodate all the dishes and tableware, and they were so close to each other that everyone was talking in whispers. This contributed to a morgue-like atmosphere, certainly not the image the restaurant was attempting to project. A final point made by van Dierdonck and Brandt (1988) is that applying the idea of focus to a service organization can have different implications for the front office, high-contact area and the back room. For example, different skills and competences are required in each area, and general policies resulting from the focus adopted may not be equally applicable in each area.

They make a number of suggestions to improve the situation. The first is a service classification scheme which looks at the degree of customer contact and dependence on the server. The general scheme is illustrated in Figure 5.5. This can be used to identify some of the key characteristics. In a situation where the dependency on the server is low, the customer is likely to be knowledgeable about the service and can therefore be critical. Thus the customer will expect consistency and efficiency in the service, implying clearly specified procedures, tight time control and time-oriented rather than output-oriented planning. An example might be the telecom directory enquiries service, where the degree of customer contact is low. In a situation where the degree of contact is high, the customer will look for visible cues of consistency and efficiency (an uncluttered organized environment, ease of access to information, use of technology) in its front office activity areas. Where the dependency on the server is higher, the customer is likely to be expecting a degree of diagnosis as part of the service, and the presentation of a solution. The focus is on the output, and planning should recognize this. Where there is high dependence on the server, 'diagnosis' is likely to be a dominant feature of the service, and the uncertainty surrounding the resource implications of this make planning a complex issue. In the high-contact situation, customers will look for visible cues for expertise: the white coat of the hospital consultant, the uniform of the airline pilot. The utility of the classification scheme is that it enables the organization to position its focus and then systematically to explore the implications for operations in terms of such issues as customer expectations, staff skills and competences, the planning system, performance measurement and the front office environment.

Van Dierdonck and Brandt (1988) conclude their suggestions for overcoming difficulties associated with focus in services by proposing the possible use of 'a selection process for customers' (e.g. those whose salary has not reached a certain level are not invited to apply for a particular type of credit card), or more indirectly through advertising to project the image of the 'expected customer group'. For example, North West Airlines advertise a chauffeur service between your home and local airport, and while the small print indicates that this is only available in conjunction with business-class tickets, the four homes pictured in the illustrations of the 'convenient departure gates' indicate the type of residence they expect passengers to have. Other examples include the 'family image' for some types of holiday. It is also suggested that training for employees can improve their ability to handle 'difficult customers' who want to broaden or remove the focus in the service being offered (how to say 'no' politely, or without the customer realizing the request has been turned down).

Operations strategy formulation

A variety of approaches have been proposed for the development of an operations strategy, and some of the key and peripheral aspects have been covered earlier in this chapter and in some of the earlier chapters. This section will pull together some of these ideas within a broad framework proposed by the Department of Trade and Industry (1994) and Platts and Gregory (1990), but developed for a service environment. An overview of this process is given in Figure 5.6. As with the development of any of the so-called functional strategies, the starting point is the corporate strategy, with its basic question about the nature of the business which the organization wants to support (indeed, even during the development of this, the operations implications at a macro level should have been considered). There is a clear link, even at this top level, with the customer, and a strong emphasis on meeting customer needs (the so-called customer-focused strategy), although again at this corporate level the focus will be on macro considerations.

The detailed customer requirements can be compared to what the system actually delivers, giving rise to potential gaps. This analysis, with its strategic implications, has to be cast in the longer term, so the impact of the external environment, especially the potential

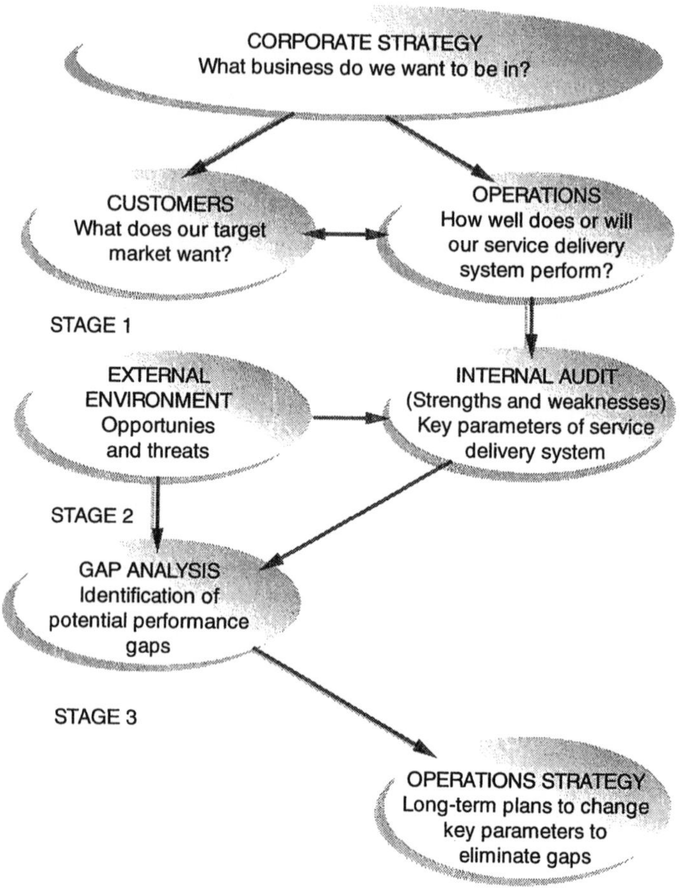

Figure 5.6   Key stages in operations strategy development (Source: Adapted from Department of Trade and Industry, 1994, p. 4)

threats and opportunities, must be analysed. The key parameters of the service delivery system can be specified (paying particular attention to their strengths and weaknesses). These can be viewed alongside the potential gaps to develop the operations strategy, which is the long-term steps which must be taken to eliminate such gaps. Figure 5.6 shows the three stages involved in this, which will now be covered in more detail.

Stage 1

The first stage involves translating elements of the corporate strategy into a 'statement' of the key services which the organization is going to provide for its target markets. This analysis should only include those which the organization feels will have a significant place in the market, so that position in the life-cycle, market growth and potential market are factors to be taken into account when identifying this key group. It is crucial to understand the basis on which these services compete in the market place (see page 81) and the relative importance of these competitive factors to the target group of customers.

Measurement is important for this stage, especially when examining an existing service, since it is crucial to compare market requirements along the key dimensions with how the organization currently performs. At a broad level, an issue like quality can be assessed in terms of customer complaints (reactive) or through customer service questionnaires (proactive) which allow a more sophisticated assessment along a range of dimensions. These questionnaires can be applied passively (posted) or face to face with a sample of customers after the service. Sometimes the service itself offers the opportunity to collect these data (e.g. during the coach transfer back to the airport after a package holiday). Location can be assessed in terms of the average distance a potential customer has to travel for the service, or by looking at the centres of population of potential customers. Speed of provision can be measured by setting targets (linked both to customer expectations and possibly those offered by competitors) and monitoring waiting time in relation to these (e.g. the notice in the bank stating that 'we aim to serve you within two minutes').

The outcome of this stage should be a clear understanding of the factors of importance for the actual or potential customers of the services offered by the organization, supported by some clearly defined targets. For existing services there should also be data which show how the organization currently performs against these, together with systems and procedures in place to ensure these data are collected and analyzed on an ongoing basis.

Stage 2

The next stage involves the identification and assessment of the key parameters of the service delivery system. This assessment should not only view the existing system delivering the existing services, but also take account of new services which are to be added to the portfolio. Figure 5.7 shows some of the major parameters involved. These represent the major areas within operations which will have a significant impact on whether or not the organization is able to deliver the service that meets those factors which the target group consider to be important. At this stage it is also important to consider the existing operations not only internally, but also externally, looking at the opportunities and threats, as well as the political, economic, social and technical factors in the competitive environment. An additional input is through an analysis of the influence of competition (the five forces model: rivalry between existing suppliers, pressure from customers and from suppliers, threat of new entrants and of substitute services). These have all been discussed in more detail in Chapter 3.

Stage 3

This final stage involves initially the identification of the key 'performance gaps' between what the market wants and the service as currently delivered. This has to be linked to a similar assessment for new services where, while no comparison to the existing situation is possible, the key performance parameters have been identified. This should also take account of future developments resulting from the broad analysis of the external environment, outlined at the end of the previous section (e.g. changes in customer expectations over time, use of new technology to provide a superior service delivery system, political

- **Facilities**:
  number, size, location, focus, equipment
- **Capacity**:
  maximum output, how capacity can be
  managed
- **Processes**:
  how delivery is organized, back room–front
  room, multiskilling
- **Span of processes**:
  degree of vertical integration
- **Human resources**:
  payment systems, motivation, training,
  development, recruitment
- **Quality**:
  means of ensuring that the service is
  delivered to the customer's requirements
- **Control policies**:
  systems and procedures to ensure that the
  service is delivered when, where and
  how the customer wants it
- **Suppliers**:
  obtaining materials at the right time, price and
  quality, single and multiple sourcing
- **New services**:
  processes for handling the development and
  introduction of new services

Figure 5.7 Major service delivery system parameters (Source: Adapted from Department of Trade and Industry, 1994, p. 55)

influences, and changing tax structures and consequently costs, such as tax on air travel and increases in value added tax levels).

The key to the development of the operations strategy is the link between, on the one hand, the performance gaps (existing services) and the key performance parameters (new services) and, on the other, the major service delivery system policy parameters listed in Figure 5.7. The strategy developed is the long-term plan for each policy area which will ensure that the gap is closed and/or the performance parameter is met. As a hypothetical example, consider a ferry company providing a car service crossing the English Channel, facing increased competition arising through the 'technology' of the Channel Tunnel. The competitive dimensions could include speed of crossing (including loading and unloading), reliability of timing and features of the service (restaurant, duty-free shopping). Currently the company is not meeting customer requirements in terms of the time taken loading and unloading. This will involve looking at the *process* involved, identifying bottlenecks and so on. Equally there are problems with the reliability of timing: this will involve an examination of the planning and control system. Finally there are potential threats from the government, considering removing the concept of 'duty or tax free' from the on-board shops. The operations strategy will include the long-term plans to develop appropriate processes and planning systems.

Discussion

A key feature in the development of an operations strategy is the adoption of a structured approach which should ensure that no key issues will be overlooked. This chapter has introduced such an approach, together with some concepts which will help you understand the process.

References

Chase, R.B. and R.H. Hayes (1991) 'Beefing up operations in service firms', *Sloan Management Review*, Fall, pp. 15–26.

Department of Trade and Industry (1994) *Competitive Management: A practical approach to the development of a manufacturing strategy*, IFS, Kempston.

Heskett, J.L. (1986) *Managing in the Service Economy*, Harvard Business School, Boston, MA.

Hill, T. (1993) *Manufacturing Strategy* (2nd edn), Macmillan, London.

McLaughlin, C.P. and R.T. Pannesi (1991) 'The different operations strategy planning process for service operations', *International Journal of Operations and Production Management*, vol. 11, no. 3, pp. 63–76.

Miles, R.E. and C.C. Snow (1987) *Organizational Strategy, Structure and Process*, McGraw-Hill, New York.

Parasuraman, A., V. Zeithaml and L. Berry (1988) 'SERVQUAL: A multi-item scale for measuring customer perceptions of service quality', *Journal of Retailing*, vol. 64, no. 1, pp. 12–40.

Platts, K.W. and M.J. Gregory (1990) 'Manufacturing audit in the process of strategy formulation', *International Journal of Operations and Production Management*, vol. 10, no. 9, pp. 5–26.

Skinner, W. (1974) 'The focused factory', *Harvard Business Review*, vol. 35, no. 3, pp. 113–21.

van Dierdonck, R. and G. Brandt (1988) 'The focused factory in service industries', *International Journal of Operations and Production Management*, vol. 8, no. 3, pp. 31–8.

Discussion topics/exercises

1. Select three service organizations and describe what might be regarded as the order-winning, order-qualifying and order-losing sensitive criteria, explaining the reasons. How might the percentage points allocated to the order-winning criteria be established?

2. For three service sectors, give examples of actual organizations which could be said to be at each of the stages of service organization competitiveness ('available for service' to 'world-class service delivery'). Justify your classifications.

3. A multinational company owns a chain of five-star luxury hotels in the major cities throughout the world. The current market is the business traveller and the discerning holidaymaker. The company has a computerized central reservation system, with an international freephone number. Links have been developed with several groups of travel agents specializing in organizing business travel. The company is featured in the brochures of a number of tour operators offering luxury breaks.

The operations director is planning to review the operations strategy. Describe how this might be carried out. Specifically, identify the dimensions or criteria which define the market requirements, and descibe how you would measure how the organization performs across these dimensions. Add a hypothetical assessment of current performance. Examine the mismatches between current performance and market requirements, taking account of any external opportunities and threats. Carry out an audit of current operating policies (e.g. facilities, capacity management, quality, operations planning and so on). Finally, prepare an action plan, identifying the policy areas which contribute to the mismatches, and the steps required to eliminate these.

4. Describe three case situations of organizations which have adopted a focused approach, and the benefits viewed from an operations perspective.

Part III

Service design

Chapter 6

Marketing interface

Chapter outline

Relationship with marketing

In any commercial organization, success will depend upon providing something that the customer wants at a price that gives an acceptable profit margin. If the organization is a non-profit-making organization, success will depend upon providing something that the customer wants in the most efficient, cost-effective way. This is a very simple, but fundamental concept. However, organizations do not always deliver what the customer wants. A widely used illustration of the problem is shown in Figure 6.1.

Little Chef roadside restaurants are recognizing that many travellers do not always want to have a minimum of a half-hour break when they stop for coffee. In the past, it seemed almost impossible to have a short stop at a Little Chef, but now alongside the restaurants are springing up annexes for 'coffee stops' where it is possible to have a quick cup of coffee.

As discussed in Chapter 5, marketing and operations in a manufacturing context are two quite separate functions. This was also illustrated in Figure 2.1. However, in such situations, it is still imperative that there are close links between marketing and operations. Production may have developed particular skills which make them expert makers of 'dodo

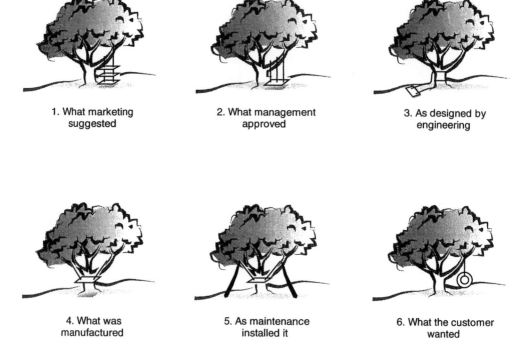

1. What marketing
suggested

2. What management
approved

3. As designed by
engineering

4. What was
manufactured

5. As maintenance
installed it

6. What the customer
wanted

Figure 6.1   Lack of co-operation in designing a swing

traps', but who would buy them? On the other hand, marketing may have identified a potential market for sports cars at a price of £5000, which in terms of production would be quite impossible. There has to be communication between marketing and production.

In services, where the divide between marketing and operations is almost non-existent, responsibilities become unclear. Staff actually providing the service are in contact with the customer, and are thus in a position to identify customer needs. They may also market services other than the one currently being provided. However, from an operations manager's point of view, such tasks as identifying the potential market or deciding on an appropriate method of promotion are beyond their remit.

Whether or not operations staff consciously attempt to market the service, they will always play a major role in the marketing of services. One of the most effective ways of marketing a service is 'word of mouth' advertising: customers tell others of their experiences. As prior testing of a service is usually impossible, recommendations from friends carry much more weight than where a physical product is involved which can be pre-tested. The standard of the service provided, and the friendliness of the staff, can make a lasting favourable impression. A satisfied customer is likely to tell four other people. A dissatisfied customer is likely to tell ten or eleven other people (Horovitz, 1987). Thus, the operations staff actually delivering the product inevitably contribute to the marketing of the service.

Whatever the degree of involvement of the operations manager in the marketing of the service, it is extremely important for an operations manager to have an understanding of what the customer requires. What constitutes a quality service? This is not an easy question to answer, and it has received a great deal of attention over the last decade. No consensus has been reached either on what constitutes a quality service, or how to measure or provide the definitive quality service. This chapter focuses on the work that has been ongoing in this area.

Service quality

The word 'quality' has different meanings and can be used in different ways. Garvin (1984) identified five categories or approaches to the concept of quality:

- The transcendent approach.
- The manufacturing-based approach.
- The user-based approach.
- The product-based approach.
- The value-based approach.

The transcendent approach follows the *Pocket Oxford Dictionary*'s definition: 'degree of excellence, relative nature'. Quality in this sense is *innate excellence*. It reflects the 'best' there is. So, for example, a five-star hotel would be classed as a quality hotel, as opposed to a one-star, family-run hotel. *The Haywain* by Constable would be classed as a quality work of art, as compared to the paintings exhibited at the local craft show.

The manufacturing-based approach relates to conformance with design or specification. A quality service or product would be one which was free of errors, where an error would be defined as non-compliance with specification. The performance of a child playing a simple piece of music with no wrong notes and the correct timing could, with this approach, be classified as a quality performance, while a concert pianist playing a difficult piece of music by Rachmaninov, and hitting the odd wrong note, could be classified as of lower quality.

The user-based approach adopts the attitude that, if a service/product meets the requirements of the user, then it is a quality service/product. Another phrase commonly used with this approach is *fitness for purpose*. A cheap watch which keeps time accurately and meets the requirements of the wearer would be classified as a quality watch. On the other hand, if one of the requirements of the watch was to help create the 'right' image for a successful, well-off, power-wielding young executive, then a gold Rolex would be more appropriate, and the cheap but accurate watch could not be considered a quality watch.

The product-based approach is a quantitatively based approach, and considers measurable characteristics. In most cases, *more* equates with better, and is thus deemed to be of higher quality. For example, 22 carat gold is purer than 9 carat gold and is therefore of higher quality. A car with acceleration of 0–60 mph in 6 seconds would be of higher quality than one which took 8 seconds. A massage which lasted 40 minutes would be considered better than one which lasted only 30 minutes. On the other hand, *less* would sometimes be classified as of higher quality. For example, a dentist who took only 5 minutes, as compared with 10 minutes, to complete a filling would be considered as providing a higher-quality service!

The value-based approach includes cost or price in the equation. How much of something is provided *for the price*. In this case, a one-star hotel which charged only £15 for bed and breakfast may be seen as a better buy than a five-star hotel charging £150 for bed and breakfast.

Which of the above approaches is the most suitable for use by an operations manager? At the end of the day, most firms are in business to make a profit. They also want to be able to continue making profits well into the future. To do that, they need to be able to provide something which they can sell – something that the customer wants and will keep coming back for. It therefore makes sense to employ the *user-based* approach to quality. Quality in operations management books is nearly always taken to mean 'meeting, or exceeding, customer requirements'. In non-profit-making organizations, the main purpose will be to provide a service. Thus, this interpretation of quality makes just as much sense whether the ultimate aim is to make a profit, or to provide a service *per se*. Both profit-making and non-profit-making firms should be concerned with providing the service at a minimum cost to themselves. Exceptions to this latter objective will be where the major aim of the organization is to create jobs. However, even in this case the service provided should still be aimed at meeting customer requirements. In this way, the objective of providing jobs is more likely to be viable in the longer run, as demand for a quality service, i.e. one which meets customer requirements, will be more sustainable than that for a poor service which does not.

One counter-argument to this user-based definition is that two different concepts are being confused. Meeting customer requirements may be considered to be a definition of *satisfaction* and not quality. This is in part reflected in the terminology used by researchers. At times there seem to be at least two different aspects of service being considered. Satisfaction is sometimes seen as what results from one encounter, as opposed to quality which relates to the performance of a service over a period of time. So, for example, if a customer on each visit to a service provider, say a doctor, is satisfied with each outcome, the service may then be described as one of quality. The importance of this debate about what is quality and what is satisfaction is debatable in itself. What is critical is that customers are happy with the service provided, and that they will keep coming back; or perhaps, if it is a one-off service, they will tell others who may become future customers.

The above discussion could apply equally well to either services or physical products. The problem with services, as discussed in Chapter 2, is that they are intangible and, as a consequence, hard to define. As there are often no easily measurable characteristics of a particular service, assessment of performance is very subjective and depends on the perspective of the customer. Additionally, the customers for a service do not often fall into an homogeneous set. Each and every customer may want something different.

Meeting customers' requirements, where they are always different, may seem impossible at first glance. All the answers to these problems have not yet been found. There is no one definitive way of identifying what it is that the customer wants. The rest of this chapter considers the different approaches which have been suggested for identifying just what customers require in a service setting. Most of the time, this task will fall to the marketing department. But it is important for operations managers to understand just what it is that marketing has identified (and the limitations of these findings) if they are to have any hope of success in providing the required service.

Identifying customer requirements

Various different approaches have been taken towards identifying customer requirements, or defining service quality. Parasuraman *et al.* (1985) have played a very prominent role in attempting to pinpoint service quality. They conducted research to try and identify generic underlying dimensions of quality. They suggested that customers would have expectations regarding each of these dimensions of quality. If these expectations were met, then a quality service was deemed to have been delivered. If the customer's perceptions of the service received were higher than expected, then the customers would be delighted. If the customer's perceptions of the service received were lower than expected, then the customer would be dissatisfied.

The consumer behaviour literature takes a slightly different perspective. It is similar in that it looks at the customer's perception of the service delivered, but the premise here is that satisfaction with a service may be, but is not necessarily, the antecedent to service quality. Oliver (1993), for example, states: 'It is possible to be satisfied with a low-quality service encounter if a person expects minimal performance. Similarly, dissatisfaction can result from high-quality performance if expectations exceed the maximum potential of a service provider' (p. 66).

A final approach which will be considered in this chapter is similar to the first two approaches. Customers are seen to have 'scripts', which are just like a script for a play. These scripts outline, in the customer's mind's eye, just what is likely to happen during the provision of a service. If there are then differences between the script and what actually happens, dissatisfaction or delight may result.

All these approaches will now be considered in more detail. The focus in this chapter will be on the identification of what constitutes a quality service. How this may be measured will be covered in Chapter 13.

Parasuraman, Berry and Zeithaml

These three researchers published their first article in a long series in 1985. They had been conducting research which included the use of focus groups, and suggested that service quality occurred when a customer's perception of a delivered service equated with prior expectations. They believed that they had identified ten underlying dimensions of service quality which were applicable to all services. Customers evaluate any service along these dimensions – not necessarily consciously. If expectations regarding the level of performance along each of these dimensions were met, then the customer might be said to have received a quality service. The ten dimensions are presented in Figure 6.2.

The focus groups used in this original research were drawn from customers of four service sectors: securities brokerage, credit card companies, product repair and maintenance, and retail banking.

A model of service quality was developed, which is reproduced in Figure 6.3. This model, sometimes referred to as the gap model, shows how personal needs, word of mouth, past experience and external communications regarding the service influence expectations along the ten dimensions of service quality. If, once service has been delivered, there is a

1. Tangibles

The physical appearance of the facilities, staff, buildings, etc. *e.g. Does the equipment appear modern? How clean is the waitress's apron?*

2. Reliability

The ability to reproduce the same level of service again and again *e.g. Is feedback regarding student progress always given? Are messages always passed on?*

3. Responsiveness

The speed with which queries etc. are dealt with. *e.g. Are letters replied to by return of post, or does it take a month? Is feedback on assignments given within a week, in time for students to assimilate the information, or does the feedback come too late, after the examination has been taken?*

4. Communication

The clarity and understandability of the information given to the client *e.g. Does the doctor take the time to explain, in terms the patient can understand, what is going to happen next? Does the solicitor explain clearly what the legal jargon means?*

5. Credibility

The trustworthiness of the service provider. *e.g. Does the newspaper reporter report all the facts, or only those which support his/her argument? Does the financial adviser present all the options, or only those which earn him/her the most commission?*

6. Security

The physical safety of the customer or privacy of client information. *e.g. Are the medical records of patients kept confidential? Are the stands in the football ground strong enough to support the weight of all the supporters?*

7. Competence

The actual technical expertise of the service provider. *e.g. Is the doctor really qualified to perform heart surgery? Does the financial adviser have sufficient knowledge of all the relevant tax regulations?*

8. Courtesy

The attitude of the service provider and manner adopted by the server. *e.g. Is the receptionist friendly, helpful and polite? Does the doctor treat the patient as an inferior being?*

9. Understanding

How well the provider of the service understands the client's needs. *e.g. Does the bank recognize that most clients cannot get to the bank in working hours? Are there mirrors positioned in the hotel bathrooms which allow guests to see the back of their hair?*

10. Access

How easy is it to reach the service provider, geographically or by phone. *e.g. Are there car parking facilities close to the solicitor's office? Does it always take five attempts to get the solicitor on the phone?*

Figure 6.2 The ten original dimensions of service quality (Source: Adapted from Parasuraman *et al.*, 1985)

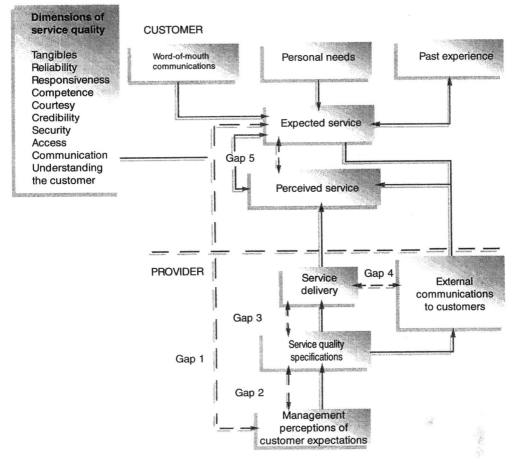

Figure 6.3 Model of service quality (Source: Parasuraman *et al.*, 1985, pp. 44, 48)

difference between expectations and perceptions of the service, then a gap, labelled gap 5, occurs, and a quality service has not been delivered. The rest of the model explains why this is so, by means of four preceding gaps.

The first gap compares customers' expectations with what management *think* customers expect. Clearly, if management are out of tune with their customers, and misunderstand their requirements, then they have little chance of meeting those requirements. The second gap may occur when management fail to translate their understanding of customer requirements into an accurate specification of the service required. If the delivery process is not designed to deliver what the customer wants, then once again there is little chance of providing what the customer wants. Even if the service is correctly specified, there is still room for failure if the front-line employee does not perform according to specification. This is gap 3. A final potential cause of failure to deliver what the customer expects is when an organization, via external communications (e.g. through advertising), raises a customer's expectations beyond what the organization can or does provide. It is all well and good for advertising to attract new customers, but if this is done through false promises, customers are inevitably going to be disappointed. This final gap between what is being provided and what is advertised is gap 4.

This model of service quality may be used to identify *why* a service is not meeting customer expectations. In later chapters, the causes of the gaps and ways to close them will be examined.

What is clearly highlighted by this model is the interdependency of operations and marketing. Communication between the two is pivotal in ensuring, first, that the requirements of the customer are identified and translated into the correct service specification, and second, that marketing know what is being provided by operations, so that the external communications are an accurate reflection of the service provided.

Subsequently, Parasuraman, Berry and Zeithaml developed a questionnaire in an attempt to measure service quality, which they called the SERVQUAL instrument. This is discussed in detail in Chapter 13. An early version of the questionnaire was based on the ten dimensions originally identified by Parasuraman, Berry and Zeithaml in 1985. After factor analysis of the results, the original ten dimensions were reduced to five: tangibles, reliability, responsiveness, assurance and empathy. Communication, credibility, security, competence and courtesy were collapsed into the new dimension labelled assurance, and understanding and access became empathy. These new dimensions are defined as follows:

- Assurance: knowledge and courtesy of employees and their ability to convey trust and confidence.
- Empathy: caring, individualized attention which the firm provides its customers.

In the questionnaire, two sets of 22 questions were asked, first about expectations, and then about perceptions of the service received. The questions related to the five dimensions. The customers were asked to indicate what they expected of an excellent service in each of the 22 cases. For example, customers were asked to state whether they strongly agreed or strongly disagreed with various statements that excellent banking firms *should* perform in some particular kind of way in relation to access, tangibles, etc. The second set of questions matched the first set, but asked how the firms were seen to perform. If the score from the second part of the questionnaire was less than that on the first part for any item, service was seen to be inferior.

This SERVQUAL questionnaire has subsequently been adapted for use in many different contexts, and various questions have been raised regarding the nature of expectations, the generic nature of the underlying dimensions of quality, and whether what is being measured is service quality or satisfaction. Other issues revolve around the measurement technique and these will be considered in Chapter 13.

Expectations, satisfaction and service quality

Concern was originally expressed regarding the use of the word 'should' in respect to the expectations of the customer. When we are talking about expectations of customers, what exactly do we mean? I have expectations regarding my students. I can say that 'I expect students to do the set reading.' I could mean either that 'I think students *ought* to do the reading' or 'I think students *will* do the reading.' The first meaning is perhaps an *ideal* expectation, as opposed to a *predictive* expectation. When defining service quality, which interpretation should be put upon the word 'expectation'?

According to Parasuraman *et al.* (1988, p. 17):

> In the satisfaction literature, expectations are viewed as *predictions* made by consumers about what is likely to happen during the impending transaction or exchange ... In contrast, in the service quality literature, expectations are viewed as desires or wants of consumers, i.e. what they feel a service provider *should* offer rather than *would* offer.

Thus, an out-patient, with an appointment to see the doctor at 9.00 a.m., expects to have to wait for perhaps two hours, and so takes the whole morning off work. In actual fact the patient only has to wait for half an hour. Expectations have been exceeded and the customer is relatively satisfied. However, the patient does not see the service as one of high quality, as he or she may think that they *ought* to see the doctor at the appointed time.

This particular issue has continued to receive attention (Bolton and Drew, 1991a; Parasuraman *et al.*, 1991; Cronin and Taylor, 1992; Boulding *et al.*, 1993; Zeithaml *et al.*, 1993; Teas, 1993; Parasuraman *et al.*, 1994). What has resulted is similar to the fitting of jigsaw pieces together in a puzzle, which still has to be completed. Models linking customer satisfaction, service quality and behavioural intentions have been suggested. Other loose pieces in the jigsaw puzzle relate to the underlying dimensions of service quality and measurement issues.

Zeithaml *et al.* (1993) focus on the expectations element. They conducted sixteen focus group interviews with consumers of insurance, business equipment repair, truck rental and leasing, automobile repair and hotel industries. From the interviews they derived seventeen hypotheses presented here in Figure 6.4.

Boulding *et al.* (1993), working along similar lines, attempted to show the *dynamic* nature of a behavioural process model of perceived service quality. The similarity lies in their view of expectations, which they divide into two categories:

1. Expected service: what *will* happen.
2. Normative expectations: what *should* happen (and which is feasible, as opposed to *ideal*).

Their model is *dynamic* in that they look at the effect over time of expectations on perceived service quality, which in turn affects future behaviour. They conducted two studies: one followed a case study type of approach in the context of a hotel situation, the other was a cross-sectional study at university.

They suggest that *will* expectations are positively related to service quality. They state:

> We believe customers average/integrate past experience with the firm (which is summarized by their prior *will* expectations) and their latest service encounters in making a cumulative assessment of the service quality level of the firm ... We note that the role of *will* expectations is very similar to the role of the 'initial impression' in averaging models of attitude. (p. 11)

They also suggest that *should* expectations are negatively related to service quality. They see the *should* expectation acting as a standard of comparison in relation to competitors.

P1. Customers assess service performance based on two standards: what they desire and what they deem acceptable.
P2. A zone of tolerance separates desired service from adequate service.
P3. The zone of tolerance varies across customers.
P4. The zone of tolerance expands or contracts within the same customer.
P5. The desired service level is less subject to change than the adequate service level.
P6. Enduring service intensifiers elevate the level of desired service.
P7. A positive relationship exists between the level of personal needs and the level of desired service.
P8. In the presence of transitory service intensifiers, the level of adequate service will increase and the zone of tolerance will narrow.
P9. The customer's perception that service alternatives exist raises the level of adequate service.
P10. The higher the level of a customer's self-perceived service role, the higher the level of adequate service.
P11. Situational factors temporarily lower the level of adequate service, widening the zone of tolerance.
P12. Two types of service quality assessment are made by consumers: perceived service superiority which results from a comparison between desired service and perceived service; and perceived service adequacy, which results from a comparison between adequate service and perceived service.
P13. The higher the level of predicted service, the higher the level of adequate service and the narrower the zone of tolerance.
P14. The higher the level of explicit service promises, the higher the levels of desired service and predicted service.
P15. Implicit service promises elevate the levels of desired service and predicted service.
P16. Positive word-of-mouth communication elevates the levels of desired and predicted service.
P17. A positive relationship exists between levels of past experience with a service and the levels of desired service and predicted service.

Figure 6.4 The nature and determinants of customer expectations of service (Source: compiled from Zeithaml *et al.*, 1993, pp. 1–12)

'As the standard set by competitors goes up, all else equal, the firm fares less well in how it is perceived by customers' (p. 11).

The *will* expectations are seen over time to be influenced by previous *will* expectations and present *perceptions of delivered service*. The relative weighting of the two components is seen to change over time. As the level of experience increases, the relative weight given to the prior *will* expectation increases. An example of this might be a passenger travelling by air for the first time. They will have certain *will* expectations concerning the flight. They may well expect that their luggage *will* also arrive in their destination (quite a reasonable expectation). However, their luggage has been temporarily lost. Their *will* expectations on the return flight are likely to have been greatly influenced by the actual service delivered. Contrast this situation with that facing a seasoned air traveller who has never had a problem with lost luggage. On their last flight their luggage went missing. However, the impact of this one-off occurence on their *will* expectations of their next flight is comparatively minimal.

Should expectations, however, are seen to be relatively stable over time, and negative experiences do not change them: what *should* be provided next time remains the same as

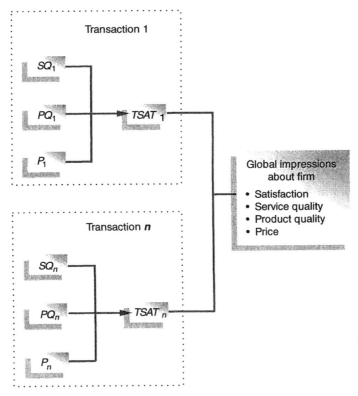

Figure 6.5 Components of global evaluations (Source: Parasuraman *et al.*, 1994, p. 122)

before. *Should* expectations may be positively affected by service provision which has exceeded previous *should* expectations. Having once received superior service, a customer is hardly likely to settle for less in future. External factors are more likely to influence *should* expectations. If competitors are offering more, and if they are able to raise standards, then the *should* expectations of the original firm are likely to rise.

What is recognized in this model is the fact that customers do take feasibility into consideration. The *should* expectations are not an *ideal* standard, and take into consideration such things as price charged and external factors outside the control of service providers, such as weather.

Another direction of causality between satisfaction and service quality has been suggested. Cronin and Taylor (1992) suggest that, if service quality exists, this will lead to a customer being satisfied, which in turn will affect future purchase intentions.

Parasuraman *et al.* (1994) also considered this possibility, and present a new model showing the components of global evaluations, which is reproduced in Figure 6.5. In this model they have introduced two additional elements: product quality and price. They suggest that satisfaction with a transaction (TSAT) will depend upon the perceptions of the quality of the service received, together with perceptions of the quality of the tangible elements involved in the provision of the service, and the price charged for the service.

Over time, satisfaction with many transactions will lead to a global impression about the firm. They do, however, point out that: 'Understanding the roles of service quality, product quality and price evaluations in determining transaction-specific satisfaction is an important area for further research' (p. 122). They also point out:

> This framework, in addition to capturing the notion that the SQ and CS constructs can be examined at both transaction-specific and global levels, is consistent with the 'satisfaction (with specific transactions) leads to overall quality perceptions' school of thought (p. 122)

The relevance of the debate to operations managers revolves around the question of *how* customers' future behaviour in respect of repeat purchasing of the service is influenced by their experience with a service. Are there any critical points in the service delivery process where it is possible to manage customers' perceptions of quality and thus influence future behaviour? Do the underlying dimensions of service quality presented earlier all carry equal weight?

Dimensions of service quality

One of the criticisms levelled at the work of Parasuraman, Zeithaml and Berry relates to their claim that they have identified *the* five generic underlying dimensions of quality. It has been argued that services characterized by high contact with the customer were not included in their studies. For example, although banking does involve some personal contact with the customer, compared to such services as counselling, hospitalization and education, where the customer has to be present throughout the conversion process, contact with the customer is minimal.

Various studies have used the SERVQUAL instrument in different contexts. Upon analysis of the responses, factor analysis has not consistently identified the dimensions suggested by Parasuraman, Zeithaml and Berry. In other studies, additional questions have been added to the questionnaire when researchers have felt that other underlying dimensions exist. Carman (1990) states:

> In sum, our replication of the PZB analysis found most of the dimensions they recommend ... Validity checks suggest, however, that these dimensions are not so generic that users of these scales should not add items on new factors they believe are important in the quality equation. Further, we recommend that items on Courtesy and Access be retained and that the items on some dimensions, such as Responsiveness and Access, be expanded where it is believed that these dimensions are of particular importance. (p. 41)

Table 6.1 presents a summary of some of the studies using SERVQUAL, showing the context and the dimensions identified.

Rosen and Karwan (1994) and Stewart *et al.* (1996) have suggested that, although there may not be generic dimensions across all services, it may be possible to identify common underlying dimensions linked to service characteristics. Rosen and Karwan suggested that the Haywood-Farmer service classification (see Chapter 7) along the three dimensions of contact, customization and labour intensity may be helpful when identifying

Table 6.1 Analysis of SERVQUAL studies by contexts and dimensions

Researchers	Service setting	Dimensions found
1. Walbridge and Delene (1993)	Health care	Reliability, assurance, empathy, responsiveness, tangibles, core medical service, professionalism/skill
2. Brown and Swartz (1989)	Physician/patient	Professionalism, auxiliary communication, professional responsibility
3. Haywood-Farmer and Stuart (1988)	Medical services	Tangibles, reliability, responsiveness, assurance, empathy, customization, knowledge, core services
4. Carman (1990)	Hospitals	Admission service, tangible accommodation, tangible food, tangible privacy, nursing care, explanation of treatment, access, courtesy afforded to visitors, discharge planning, patient accounting
5. Mersha and Adlakha (1992)	Multiservice physician	Good attributes – knowledge of service, thoroughness/accuracy of service, consistency/reliability, willingness to correct errors, follow-up after initial service, timely/prompt service, observance of announced business hours, enthusiasm/helpfulness, courtesy, reasonable cost, pleasant environment, friendliness
6. Bowers *et al.* (1994)	Health care patients	Reliability, responsiveness, competence, access, courtesy, communication, credibility, security, understanding/knowing the customer, tangibles, caring on the part of the physicians and nurses, patient outcomes
7. Rosen and Karwan (1994)	Urgent health care	Assurance, reliability, access, tangibles, knowing the customer, responsiveness
8. Reidenbach and Sandifer-Smallwood (1990)	Hospitals – patient care	Outpatients: patient confidence; emergency room: physical appearance, treatment quality; inpatients: treatment quality, business competence
9. Shewchuk *et al.* (1991)	Hospitals	Tangibles, responsiveness, empathy, reliability/assurance
10. Headley and Miller (1993)	Medical care	Dependability, empathy, reliability, responsiveness, tangibles, presentation
11. Vandamme and Leunis (1992)	Hospital health care	Tangibles, medical responsiveness, assurance, assurance II, nursing staff, personal beliefs and values I
12. Bojanic (1991)	Accountants	Tangibles (location, employee appearance, office appearance), reliability (accuracy of work), responsiveness (promptness, co-operation, responsiveness), assurance (employee knowledge, partner knowledge, professionalism), empathy (accessibility, personal attention)

Table 6.1 *Continued*

Researchers	Service setting	Dimensions found
13. Freeman and Dart (1993)	Accountants – business clients	Tangibles, timeliness, assurance, empathy, fees, professionalism, exceptions, accessibility
14. Dart (1995)	Accountants and lawyers	Tangibles, timeliness, assurance, empathy, fees, professionalism, exceptions, accessibility
15. Witt and Stewart (1994)	Solicitors	Communication with the solicitor, communication with staff, courtesy, reliability/competence, access, tangibles
16. Hedvall and Paltschik (1991)	Swedish pharmacies	General dimensions: willingness to serve, physical and psychological access Pharmacy-specific dimensions: professionalism, commitment, confidentiality, milieu
17. LeBlanc (1992)	Travel agencies	Corporate image, competitiveness, courtesy, responsiveness, accessibility, competence
18. Gagliano and Hathcote (1994)	Apparel speciality stores	Personal attention, reliability, tangibles, convenience
19. Kettinger and Lee (1994)	MIS customers	Level of user knowledge and involvement, quality of information/products, attitudes towards staff and services, reliability/empathy
20. Bouman and van der Weile (1992)	Car service industry	Customer kindness, tangibles, faith
21. Saleh and Ryan (1991)	Hotels	Conviviality, tangibles, reassurance, avoid sarcasm, empathy

Source: Stewart *et al.* (1996).

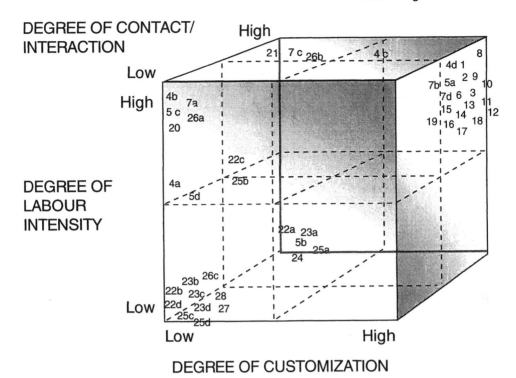

DEGREE OF CONTACT/INTERACTION

DEGREE OF LABOUR INTENSITY

DEGREE OF CUSTOMIZATION

Figure 6.6 Previous SERVQUAL studies plotted on the Haywood-Farmer cube (Source: Stewart *et al.*, 1996)

the order of priority of the dimensions of service quality. Stewart *et al.* categorized previous studies using the SERVQUAL approach, according to the Haywood-Farmer three-dimensional model of service. Consideration of the underlying service quality dimensions identified in these studies supported the suggestion of Rosen and Karwan. The findings of this latter study are presented in Figure 6.6, which plots the studies listed in Table 6.2.

Table 6.2 Studies plotted on Haywood-Farmer (1987) cube

Researchers	Field of research	Where plotted
1. Walbridge and Delene (1993)	Physicians' perceptions of health care	High labour intensity High customization High contact/interaction
2. Brown and Swartz (1989)	Medical services physician/patient	High labour intensity High customization High contact/interaction
3. Haywood-Farmer and Stuart (1987)	Medical services	High labour intensity High customization High contact/interaction
4. Carman (1990)	(a) Tyre store	(a) Medium labour intensity Low customization Low contact/interaction

Table 6.2 (*Continued*)

Researchers	Field of research	Where plotted
	(b) Placement centre	(b) High labour intensity Low customization Low contact/interaction
	(c) Dental clinic	(c) High labour intensity Medium customization High contact/interaction
	(d) Acute hospital care	(d) High labour intensity High customization High contact/interaction
5. Mersha and Adlakha (1992)	(a) Physician services	(a) High labour intensity High customization High contact/interaction
	(b) Retail banking	(b) Low labour intensity Low customization Medium contact/interaction
	(c) Auto maintenance	(c) High labour intensity Low customization Low contact/interaction
	(d) Colleges/universities	(d) Medium labour intensity Low customization Low contact/interaction
6. Bowers *et al.* (1994)	Health care patients	High labour intensity High customization High contact/interaction
7. Rosen and Karwan (1994)	(a) University lecturing	(a) High labour intensity Low customization Low contact/interaction
	(b) Retail bookstore	(b) High labour intensity High customization High contact/interaction
	(c) Medium-price restaurant	(c) High labour intensity Low customization High contact/interaction
	(d) Urgent health care	(d) High labour intensity High customization High contact/interaction
8. Reidenbach and Sandifer-Smallwood (1990)	Hospitals – patient care	High labour intensity High customization High contact/interaction
9. Shewchuk *et al.* (1991)	Hospitals	High labour intensity High customization High contact/interaction
10. Headley and Miller (1993)	Medical care – multispeciality clinic	High labour intensity High customization High contact/interaction
11. Vandamme and Leunis (1992)	Hospital health care	High labour intensity High customization High contact/interaction
12. Bojanic (1991)	Small professional firms	High labour intensity High customization High contact/interaction

Table 6.2 (*Continued*)

Researchers	Field of research	Where plotted
13. Freeman and Dart (1993)	Accountants – business clients	High labour intensity High customization High contact/interaction
14. Dart (1995)	Accontants and lawyers	High labour intensity High customization High contact/interaction
15. Witt and Stewart (1994)	Solicitors	High labour intensity High customization High contact/interaction
16. Hedvall and Paltschik (1991)	Pharmacies	High labour intensity High customization High contact/interaction
17. LeBlanc (1992)	Travel agencies	High labour intensity High customization High contact/interaction
18. Gagliano and Hathcote (1994)	Apparel speciality stores	High labour intensity High customization High contact/interaction
19. Kettinger and Lee (1994)	Management information systems	High labour intensity High customization High contact/interaction
20. Bouman and van der Weile (1992)	Car service industry	High labour intensity Low customization Low contact/interaction
21. Saleh and Ryan (1991)	Hotels	High labour intensity Low customization High contact/interaction
22. Parasuraman *et al.* (1985)	(a) Retail bank	(a) Low labour intensity Low customization Medium contact/interaction
	(b) Credit card company	(b) Low labour intensity Low customization Low contact/interaction
	(c) Securities brokerage	(c) Medium labour intensity Low customization Medium contact/interaction
	(d) Product repair and maintenance	(d) Low labour intensity Low customization Low contact/interaction
23. Parasuraman *et al.* (1988)	(a) Retail bank	(a) Low labour intensity Low customization Medium contact/interaction
	(b) Credit card company	(b) Low labour intensity Low customization Low contact/interaction
	(c) Product repair and maintenance	(c) Low labour intensity Low customization Low contact/interaction
	(d) Long-distance phone co.	(d) Low labour intensity Low customization Low contact/interaction

Table 6.2 (*Continued*)

Researchers	Field of research	Where plotted
24. Taylor *et al.* (1990)	Recreational settings	Low labour intensity Low customization Medium contact/interaction
25. Crompton and Mackay (1989)	Rereational programmes: (a) Physical fitness	(a) Low labour intensity Low customization Medium contact/interaction
	(b) Painting	(b) Medium labour intensity Low customization Medium contact/interaction
	(c) Men's ice hockey	(c) Low labour intensity Low customization Low contact/interaction
	(d) Senior trips	(d) Low labour intensity Low customization Low contact/interaction
26. Chen *et al.* (1993)	(a) Fast food	(a) High labour intensity Low customization Low contact/interaction
	(b) Airlines	(b) Low labour intensity Low customization High contact/interaction
	(c) Long-distance phone co.	(c) Low labour intensity Low customization Low contact/interaction
27. Bressinger and Lambert (1990)	Business to business less than truckload carrier	Low labour intensity Low customization Low contact/interaction
28. Bakabus and Boller (1992)	Electric and gas utility	Low labour intensity Low customization Low contact/interaction

This work, which was preliminary in nature, seems to indicate that the original five or ten dimensions suggested by Parasuraman *et al.* (1985, 1988) have been found appropriate where firms lie in quadrant 1 of the Haywood-Farmer cube, i.e. those exhibiting characteristics of relatively low contact/interaction with the customer, low levels of customization and low labour intensity. In contexts which could be seen to lie in quadrant 8 – for example, professional services – additional underlying service quality dimensions have been identified.

Further research in this area is needed.

Zone of tolerance

In Figure 6.4, Zeithaml *et al.* (1993) use the term 'zone of tolerance'. They suggest that 'a zone of tolerance separates desired service from adequate service' (p. 6). Johnston (1995) examines this zone of tolerance more closely and suggests that there are three sets of zones, for expectations, the process and the outcomes. This is illustrated in Figure 6.7.

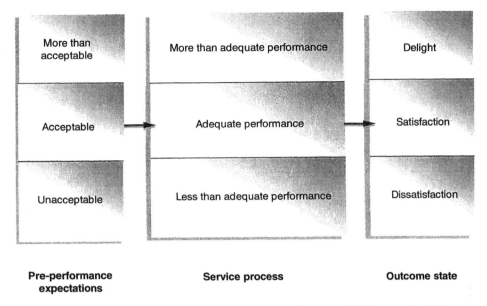

Figure 6.7 Zones of tolerance (Source: Johnston, 1995, pp. 46–61)

Johnston examines factors which influence the relative sizes of the zones and how the three sets of zones are related. In most instances, the widths of the three zones are the same. For example, if the acceptable zone for pre-performance expectations is relatively narrow, then the corresponding adequate/process and satisfaction/outcome zones will also be narrow (see Figure 6.8). As the importance of the service to the customer increases, it is thought that the width of the zone of tolerance reduces.

In many services, such as a haircut, customers are present throughout the transform-ation process. The actual process often comprises different stages. Following on with the hair cutting example, the process will involve reception, waiting, consultation, hair washing, hair cutting, hair drying, etc. At any one stage, performance may be below or above expectations. If the performance is always within the zone of tolerance, then the outcome will be perceived as satisfactory. However, what happens if performance at any one stage falls outside the zone of tolerance? Johnston suggests that, if a sufficient number of the stages are perceived to exceed the upper boundary of the zone of tolerance, then customers will be delighted, and conversely, if a number of stages drop below the adequate boundary, customers will be dissatisfied. If there are a number of less than adequate stages which are compensated by a number of more than adequate stages, the customer is likely to perceive the overall outcome as satisfactory. However, Johnston suggests that the ratio of the two will need to be greater than one, with more positive stages than negative ones.

Johnston also suggests that the size of the zone of tolerance may be dynamic rather than static, and be influenced by excellent or poor service in the early stages of the process. For example, if a customer enters an hotel to find that his or her reservation has been lost, and the receptionist is rude and unhelpful, the reaction of the customer from that point on might be hypercritical throughout the remainder of the stay. Passengers having waited

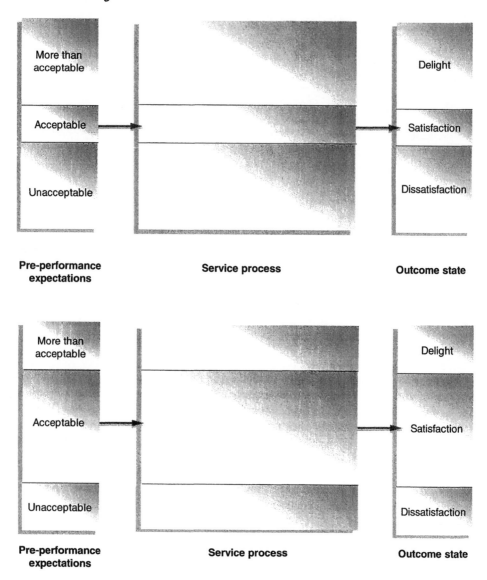

Figure 6.8   Examples of different sizes of zones of tolerance (Source: Adapted from Johnston, 1995)

for a delayed flight are much more likely to be short tempered and willing to find fault with every other aspect of service, which might otherwise have been deemed acceptable. The lower boundary of the zone of tolerance in this case moves upwards for the remainder of the process. This is illustrated in Figure 6.9.

Similarly, a very good start to the service process may result in a lowering of the upper boundary of the zone of tolerance. Perhaps on arrival at an hotel, a guest needs to send an urgent message to her husband; the receptionist goes out of his way to facilitate

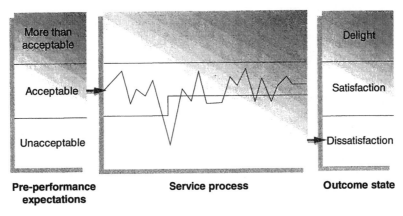

Figure 6.9 The dynamic nature of the zone of tolerance (Source: Adapted from Johnston, 1995)

this. Subsequently, the staff may be viewed sympathetically, with much more patience being exhibited by the guest in the dining room when a large party arrives and causes some delay. This is illustrated in Figure 6.10.

Understanding of this process by the operations manager will help him or her to try and manage the process so that the customer is either satisfied or delighted. However, marketing can influence the zone of tolerance in respect of expectations, and once again the importance of communication between marketing and operations is illustrated. If marketing raise expectations above what would be a feasible upper boundary of the zone of tolerance, then dissatisfied customers are inevitable.

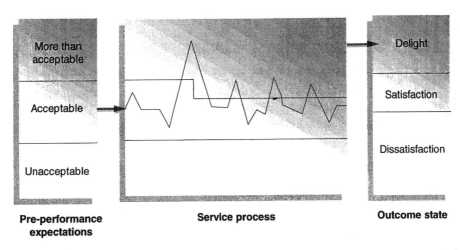

Figure 6.10 The dynamic nature of the zone of tolerance (Source: Adapted from Johnston, 1995)

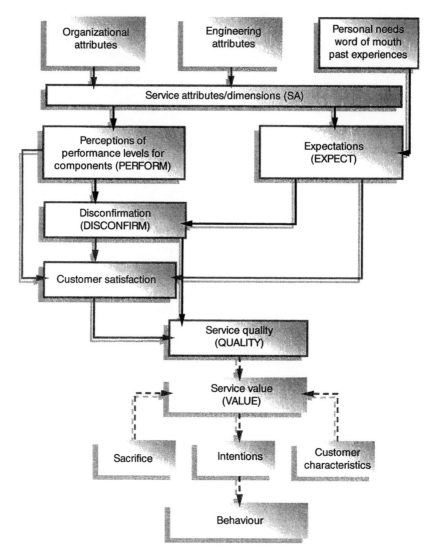

Figure 6.11   A multistage model of customers' assessment of service quality and value (Source: Bolton and Drew, 1991b, p. 376; *Journal of Consumer Research*, published by the University of Chicago. © Journal of Consumer Research Inc., 1991. All rights reserved.)

Value

A final factor in the equation is value, which, as used here, links the user-based definition presented by Garvin to his final *value-based* definition. Zeithaml (1988) and Bolton and Drew (1991b) have considered this additional factor. Zeithaml suggested that: 'Perceived value is the customer's overall assessment of the utility of a product based on perceptions of what is received and what is given' (p. 14). Bolton and Drew suggest that:

After evaluating service quality, the customer assesses service value (VALUE) by trading off the quality of the service versus its costs in a given situation. That is VALUE = v_o (QUALITY, **SACRIFICE, CHAR**), where **SACRIFICE** is a vector of variables describing the monetary and nonmonetary costs associated with customer's utilization of the service, and **CHAR** is a vector of customer characteristics. (p. 377)

They also suggest that performance, expectations and disconfirmation, although already included in the equation through the QUALITY variable, will be weighted by customers differently when considering value, and thus should be included in the equation as separate variables in addition to the quality variable. They found some empirical support for their hypothesis in a study of a local telephone service.

Bolton and Drew (1991b) present a multistage model of customers' assessments of service quality and value, which is reproduced in Figure 6.11.

Scripts

In a recent study by Hubbert *et al.* (1995), a new approach has been suggested for identifying steps in the provision of services. The use of 'scripts' to identify gaps between what the customer expects from a service, and how the provider of the service views the encounter, is seen as a way of overcoming some of the problems (see Chapter 13) which can arise when customers have to recall what their expectations were before receiving a service, in order to answer the first part of SERVQUAL-type questionnaires.

The basic idea is that, based on past experience, people have 'scripts' which describe the component parts of encounters in a given context. For example, regular patients at a doctor's surgery see different stages in the process, such as: make appointment, enter surgery, see receptionist, consultation with doctor, leave surgery. The overall goal would be to see a doctor to get advice leading to a remedy for some illness. Sub-goals would be: enter, register (with receptionist), consult doctor, leave surgery. Associated with each of these sub-goals would be actions. For example, open door and walk to reception area are two actions associated with the first sub-goal. Ring bell, talk to receptionist and fill in form may be expected actions required for the second sub-goal, and so on.

The idea is that customers will have scripts which describe a typical encounter – not a specific one, but a generalized one. Thus the problems encountered when questionnaires are used after the delivery of the service regarding recall of prior expectations for a particular service, and/or the influence that the provision of that specific service delivery had on what the customer thought he or she expected, are eliminated.

The provider of the service will also have a 'script' for the service encounter. It is likely to be more elaborate than the customer's 'script', because that particular type of encounter is being repeated over and over again, every day, with many different customers. The provider's script therefore has to allow for many variants.

Comparison of scripts from customer and provider may be used to identify gaps between what is important to the customer and what the provider perceives as critical components. Hubbert *et al.* (1995) compared scripts of the process of having a haircut. Students and hairdressers were asked to list their sub-goals for the process of having/giving a haircut. These were analyzed and compared. The results are presented in Table 6.3.

Table 6.3 Sub-goals for a haircut

Sub-goals	Percentage of respondents	
	Consumer ($n = 39$)	Service provider ($n = 46$)
Make appointment	51.3	–
Enter	64.1	–
Wait	53.9	–
Greet client	–	100.0
Wash hair	61.5	58.7
Cut hair	92.3	95.7
Pay	79.5	58.7
Talk	–	93.5

Source: Hubbert *et al.* (1995), p. 13.

This showed that the scripts for the providers and recipients of the service were different. Greeting the client and talking to the client did not appear on the customers' list of sub-goals. Similarly, the starting points for the scripts were different. The script for the customer started with the making an appointment. The script of the provider only began with the greeting, and did not even include note of when the client entered the premises. The potential for dissatisfaction with the service is obvious. In this case, one of two things may happen. Either the importance of the process of making an appointment is not given due consideration by the hairdresser, and the customer may be dissatisfied with that part of the service, or, if a receptionist deals with the client at the first contact stage (and has his or her own 'script' for that part of the service encounter), the initial contact may be viewed by the client in a positive light, but the wait before actually being greeted by the hairdresser may fall between the two 'provider scripts' (i.e. that of the receptionist and that of the hairdresser), and once again be potentially a cause for dissatisfaction.

The sampled customer population in the study by Hubbert *et al.* (1995) comprised university students. The generic nature of the findings must therefore be treated with caution as the sample 'customers' could be considered an homogeneous sample. However, such an approach shows promise. Gaps between the scripts of service provider and consumer may be used as a guide for improving service. Also, comparing scripts of successful and less experienced providers may help in the training of new recruits.

Conclusion

In this chapter the interface between marketing and operations has been examined. Considerable time has been spent examining the concept of service quality as perceived by the customer. Emphasis has been placed upon understanding what constitutes service quality: that is, identifying customer requirements. Having identified what the customer requires, the service has to be specified and delivered. It is important that service design involves both marketing and operations. It is then critical that the delivery systems are designed so that the service conforms to specification.

The next two chapters examine issues relating to the specification or design of a service. Part IV of the book considers delivery issues, and thus those factors which will determine quality of conformance.

References

Bolton, R.N. and J.H. Drew (1991a) 'A longitudinal analysis of the impact of service changes on customer attitudes', *Journal of Marketing*, vol. 55, no. 1, pp. 1–9.

Bolton, R.N. and J.H. Drew (1991b) 'A multistage model of customers' assessment of service quality and value', *Journal of Consumer Research*, vol. 17, no. 4, pp. 375–84.

Boulding, W., A. Kalra, R. Staelin and V.A. Zeithaml (1993) 'A dynamic process model of service quality: from expectations to behavioural intentions', *Journal of Marketing Research*, vol. XXX, February, pp. 7–27.

Carman, J.M. (1990) 'Consumer perceptions of service quality: an assessment of the SERVQUAL dimensions', *Journal of Retailing*, vol. 66, no. 1, pp. 33–55.

Cronin, Jr, J.J. and S.A. Taylor (1992) 'Measuring service quality: a re-examination and extension', *Journal of Marketing*, vol. 56, no. 3, pp. 55–68.

Garvin, D. (1984) 'What does "product quality" really mean?', *Sloan Management Review*, Fall, pp. 22–44.

Horovitz, J. (1987) 'How to check the quality of customer service and raise the standard', *International Management*, vol. 42, February, pp. 34–5.

Hubbert, A.R., A.G. Sehorn and S.W. Brown (1995) 'Service expectations: the consumer versus the provider', *International Journal of Service Industry Management*, vol. 6, no. 1, pp. 6–21.

Johnston, R. (1995) 'The zone of tolerance: exploring the relationship between service transactions and satisfaction with the overall service', *International Journal of Service Industry Management*, vol. 6, no. 2, pp. 46–61.

Oliver, R.L. (1993) 'A conceptual model of service quality and service satisfaction: compatible goals, different concepts', *Advances in Services Marketing and Management*, vol. 2, pp. 65–85.

Parasuraman, A., L.L. Berry and V.A. Zeithaml (1991) 'Refinement and reassessment of the SERVQUAL scale', *Journal of Retailing*, vol. 67, no. 4, pp. 420–50.

Parasuraman, A., V.A. Zeithaml and L.L. Berry (1985) 'A conceptual model of service quality and its implications for future research', *Journal of Marketing*, vol. 49, no. 4, pp. 41–50.

Parasuraman, A., V.A. Zeithaml and L.L. Berry (1988) 'SERVQUAL: a multiple item scale for measuring consumer perceptions of service quality', *Journal of Retailing*, vol. 64, no. 1, pp. 14–40.

Parasuraman, A., V.A. Zeithaml and L.L. Berry (1994) 'Reassessment of expectations as a comparison standard in measuring service quality: implications for further research', *Journal of Marketing*, vol. 58, no. 1, pp. 111–24.

Rosen, L.D. and K.R. Karwan (1994) 'Prioritizing the dimensions of service quality', *International Journal of Service Industry Management*, vol. 5, no. 4, pp. 39–52.

Stewart, H.M., C.A. Hope and A.P. Mühlemann (1996) 'Professional service quality: a step beyond other services?' paper presented at the 3rd DIRASS/EIRASS International Conference on Retailing and Services Science, 22–5 June, Telfs/Buchen, Austria.

Teas, R.K. (1993) 'Expectations, performance evaluation and consumers' perceptions of quality', *Journal of Marketing*, vol. 57, no. 4, pp. 18–34.

Zeithaml, V.A. (1988) 'Consumer perceptions of price, quality and value: a means–end model and synthesis of evidence', *Journal of Marketing*, vol. 52, no. 3, pp. 2–22.

Zeithaml, V.A., L.L. Berry and A. Parasuraman (1993) 'The nature and determinants of customer expectations of service', *Journal of the Academy of Marketing Science*, vol. 21, no. 1, pp. 1–12.

Zeithaml, V.A., A. Parasuraman and L.L. Berry (1990) *Delivering Quality Service*, Free Press, New York.

Discussion topics/exercises

1. Service leaders exhibit certain similarities which include customer-conscious and customer-focused delivery systems. Research on companies rated highly on customer service shows that they keep customers up to 50 per cent longer or more, they have lower sales/marketing costs, they have higher returns on sales and as a consequence they have higher net profits, in the region of 7–17 per cent better.

   How do they do this? Explain using examples.

2. How would you define service quality? What do you think the relationship is between satisfaction and quality? What do you think an operations manager should be interested in: satisfaction or quality?

3. How generic do you think the original SERVQUAL dimensions are? Do you agree that they are suitable in all contexts, and if not, why not?

4. What is the role of marketing? What is the role of an operations manager? Who should be responsible for designing the product? Does the operations manager need to understand the customer, or is that the domain of the marketing manager? Who is responsible for what?

Chapter 7

Specifying the service

Chapter outline
☆ Quality of design
☆ The service package
☆ Grönroos – technical/functional quality
☆ The design process
☆ Design considerations
☆ TQM
☆ Measurement difficulties

Quality of design

Because the process itself is often what is being bought, it is not always possible to separate the design of the product from the design of the process. Take a package holiday by air, for example. Part of the product is the process of transporting the holidaymaker from the origin airport to the destination. How well this process is designed will directly affect the experience of the customer.

This chapter considers those operational issues involved in designing and specifying a service to ensure the delivery of a quality product. Various approaches/frameworks to help this process have been proposed, which will be examined in turn.

The service package

As discussed in Chapter 1, services are characterized by intangibility of the product. However, as illustrated in Figure 1.1, very few services do not have some tangible element. What is often used is the concept of the *service package*, which comprises a bundle of goods and services.

Fitzsimmons and Fitzsimmons (1994) break the service package into four components:

- *Supporting facility*: the physical resources that must be in place before a service can be offered. Examples are a golf course, a ski lift, a hospital and an aeroplane.
- *Facilitating goods*: the material purchased or consumed by the buyer or items provided by the customer. Examples are golf clubs, skis, food items, replacement car parts, legal documents and medical supplies.
- *Explicit services*: the benefits that are readily observable by the senses and consist of the essential or intrinsic features of the service. Examples are the absence of pain after a tooth is repaired, a smooth-running car after a tune-up, and the response times of the fire service.
- *Implicit services*: psychological benefits that the customer may sense only vaguely, or extrinsic features of the service. Examples are the status of a degree from an Ivy League school, the privacy of a loan office, and worry-free car repair.

When designing a service, all too often supporting facilities and implicit service do not receive an appropriate level of attention. Administrators of service frequently concentrate on what they see as 'the service provided', which constitutes the *explicit service* only. For example, in education, teachers and lecturers may be chosen with care and a great deal of attention may be paid to curriculum development. In universities, procedures have to be followed to ensure that what is being taught is of the required level. For example, typically, a module will be designed by a lecturer, but has to be approved by a 'Courses Committee' with academic representatives drawn from the whole school, not just from the department. External examiners are employed to ensure that examinations are of an appropriate standard, and examination scripts are scrutinized to ensure that standards have been maintained and students marked fairly.

Compare this approach to the manner in which lecture theatres and teaching rooms are provided and equipped, i.e. the *supporting facilities*. Basic requirements are usually met, but the effect which the environment has on the learning experience of the student is often neglected. The lecture theatre may look smart and new, but how good are the acoustics? Does the air-conditioning blow cool air on just a few students, who need to sit huddled in outdoor clothing to keep warm? Is the overhead projector positioned in a way which makes it difficult for the lecturer to look at his or her notes without blocking the view of students on one side of the lecture theatre? Is there a desk by the overhead projector for the slides being used? How easy is it for the student to rest his or her writing pad on a surface to facilitate note taking?

Facilitating goods usually receive more attention when they are clearly recognized as part of the 'service/product'. For example, in a restaurant, the meal itself will usually be the focus of attention. In this example, it is very clear that the customer is buying the meal. However, when the facilitating goods only *aid* provision of the service – for example, bowling shoes at a ten-pin bowling alley – their overall impact on the perceived level of service is often overlooked. Finding that the pair of shoes provided has broken laces which are difficult to tie does not actually lead to customers leaving the alley, but clearly does nothing to help form an impression of a quality service.

Implicit service is often affected by the supporting facilities, such as the *privacy* afforded by the interview room in a bank or building society. In a small building society branch in South Wales, the interview room is positioned on the left as customers enter the premises.

When there is a queue, some customers actually wait outside the door of the interview room. As the interview room is only formed by partitions which do not reach up to the ceiling, it is possible, while waiting to be served, to be entertained by listening to the conversation going on inside the 'private' facility!

Sometimes the level of supporting facilities and facilitating goods is limited due to shortage of resources/funding. When money is in short supply, it is only natural that the less important elements of the service package are sacrificed. Or, where it is important to serve more people at the lowest cost, high levels of supporting facilities are seen as a luxury. Take, for example, the National Health Service in the UK. Some patients are still treated on wards which contain rows of beds. Anyone who has tried to get a good night's sleep on such a ward knows that it is almost impossible! Patients moan, cough and call out, the phone rings, new patients are wheeled on to the ward, and so on. Recovery is not helped by this environment. A patient's length of stay may be adversely affected. Contrast this with private hospitals with single rooms and en suite facilities. The former situation is managed from an efficiency perspective, the latter from one of effectiveness and the customer. Whatever the context, it is important to recognize the effect on the level of service that *all* elements of the service package have.

Grönroos – technical vs functional

Another analysis of the service package is provided by Grönroos (1984), who suggested that customers consider two aspects of service – the *what* and the *how*. The *what* refers to the core service which is being sought, and is described as the *technical* element. The *how* refers to the process by which the *what* or core service is delivered, and is described as the *functional* element. The functional quality (or element) of a service will be dependent on the supporting and facilitating goods. As discussed above, the design of the lecture theatre will affect how the learning experience takes place.

Another factor which has to be taken into account when designing the service package is the effect that the customer has on *how* the service is provided. Not only will a customer's behaviour affect the success of the transaction for that particular customer, but it may also help or hinder in the provision of the service for other customers. For example, in a restaurant, customers help to create the atmosphere. A group of men out on a stag night, or a group of women out for a hen party, are unlikely to be quiet. If they are at the table next to a couple wanting a peaceful, romantic evening together, then the service package received by the couple will be quite unacceptable.

When designing the service package, therefore, ways of 'selecting' and 'training' the customer must be considered, so that the right type of customer who plays the correct role is attracted. The selection of the customer will in part be the responsibility of marketing. If the correct image of the restaurant has been portrayed, customers will be self-selecting. Other measures designed into the process may be dress codes: for example, pubs often display signs on the entrance drawing customers' attention to the fact that customers wearing jeans will not be served (or only smartly dressed customers will be served). What then needs to be considered is how to enforce such a rule. Who will be responsible for rejecting clients who do not take notice of the sign? Price may act as a signal – restaurants with high prices are less likely to attract a young (and often noisy) crowd, out for a good time.

| No
smoking | Telephone | Gents and
ladies
toilets |

Figure 7.1   Illustrations of signposting

Training often takes the form of signposting. For example, how do patients or visitors to a hospital know where to go, or what to do? In this case, signposts need to be prominently displayed at every entry point directing patients to out-patients, emergency department or wards. On entrance to a department, signs then need to indicate procedures: for example, 'Patients should please report to recepton'. This may seem obvious, but signposting frequently fails. Should a patient take a wrong turn, signposts often disappear. Some patients may be blind – what provision is made for them? Other patients may be illiterate. The important point here is to understand the capabilities of the customer. Who are the customers? Are they all the same? Do they all have the same requirements? Patients going into hospital for a pre-planned operation can be told beforehand where to go and what to bring with them. Visitors and emergency patients may be strangers to the district and have had no previous contact whatsoever with the hospital. The needs of all the different patients have to be taken into account. Only then can appropriate systems be designed which cater for those needs.

Language is sometimes a problem, particularly in international airports. Easily recognizable picture signs may be used. Some of these are truly international in nature: for example, the signposts for ladies' and gentlemen's toilets (Figure 7.1). However, in some countries even these signs are not used: triangles (for men) and circles (for women) are used in Poland – now, did I remember those correctly?!

Some hospitals have different-coloured lines painted on the floor. Patients going from casualty to X-ray are told to follow the yellow line, or patients trying to find their way out have to follow the red line. Whatever the actual method used, it has to be easy to follow, or assistance needs to be readily available to help explain the system.

Failure to inform or train the customer can lead to disruption to the system and/or dissatisfaction for the customer. Travelling by air may be an ordeal for some travellers. Anxious customers, scared of flying, may arrive at an airport for the first time. Even if they have bought a package holiday, have they had clear instructions about what to expect at the airport? Consider a couple who have never flown before. They arrive at a small regional airport and go in the entrance on the right. Then what do they do? There are no directions. They wander to the right, but that only leads to an area which appears to be for arrivals. They then retrace their steps. Going left from their original point of entry, they see other people queuing at desks. As it is only a small airport, they can see the name of the destination above each of the check-in desks. However, they are early (anxious not to miss the flight), and none of the desks has its destination airport showing. They did notice a monitor showing flight arrivals, but they did not see the one with departure informaton.

What do they do? They then notice what seems to be an information desk, so they go and ask. The helpful assistant explains that they have to check in at one of the desks – she does not know which one yet, but she thinks one will be open for their flight in about ten minutes. She points out the way to the snack bar and suggests they might like to wait there. (There isn't much room to sit and wait by the desks.) Eventually, the couple check in and are told to go through the doors behind them by a certain time, but as the boarding gate has not yet been allocated, this information will be announced later. What they have not been told yet, is that, if they look at the television monitors, they will be able to see details of departures, when to go to the gate and so on. They go through passport control immediately and wait, and wait, and wait. The time comes for their scheduled departure, but nothing happens. Eventually, over the information system, the couple are asked to proceed immediately to gate 4.

The couple by this stage are in a state of panic – they do not know their way to the gate, and in the panic they leave a bag behind them, which they have to go back for. Eventually they get to the gate – just as the flight crew are beginning to wonder if they are going to have to unload the plane and find the luggage which has been loaded for the 'missing couple'. The departure slot by this time has been missed, and this flight has to wait for another take-off slot which is an hour later!

Who is to blame? In this case, the tour operator has sold the package to the holidaymaker. Should it have provided very clear instructions to the customer with the tickets? The airport is not under the control of the tour operator, but surely it should consider the inexperienced traveller, who has the potential to cause havoc to schedules. The airline also has to take responsibility for making that part of the holiday as enjoyable as possible. One of the problems in this example is that more than one organization has an input into the service package, even though the customer has only purchased the product from one of them. This also has to be taken into consideration when designing a service.

The design process

Many new services are really adaptations of existing services. Whether this is the case or whether the new service is a revolutionary development, the following stages in the design process need to be followed in order to try and minimize the associated risk (see Figure 7.2).

Idea generation

At the start of the process, the initial idea, which may or may not be followed through to a finished product/service, has to come from somewhere. Essentially, ideas may be internally or externally generated. Customers may approach an organization and ask for a service which at present does not exist. This may be a totally new concept or a variation on an existing service. An example of the latter has occurred in education in the Master of Business Administration (MBA) market. Standard MBAs typically take two formats: full-time study for one or two years, or part-time study with attendance once or twice a week for three years. In both cases, students enrol in the course independently. By contrast, company-specific MBAs, where organizations would fund a whole cohort of students, became popular in the late 1980s. The standard mode of learning was via personal attendance on the courses

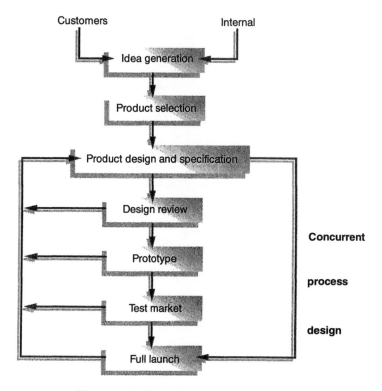

Figure 7.2 Steps in the design process

either at the university or at facilities provided by the company. In the early 1990s, the British Broadcasting Corporation asked for tenders for a new form of MBA, which would entail a distance learning element. The idea of an MBA was not new, nor was the idea of an MBA delivered and tailored for a specific organization. However, the service required was significantly different, and the initial move was instigated by the customer.

In other cases, the initial idea, although coming from the customer, does so indirectly through the efforts of the marketing team as a result of market research exercises. SAS Airlines identified various needs of the business traveller. One of the factors was the availability of direct flights. An implication of this included higher operating costs resulting from smaller aircraft and potentially more empty seats per journey. However, the business traveller was also found to be generally less price sensitive, and quite prepared to pay a premium price for the preferred service.

Internally generated ideas often stem from technological advances. An example of this is automated teller machines. These allow a 24-hour service – in effect a new product. Organizations may look to advances in technology for opportunities to enhance the manner of delivery of the present service, or extend what is being delivered. British Telecom is continually extending the service it provides to customers. Facilities such as video conferencing, telephone pagers and itemized telephone bills have all been made possible because of advances in technology.

Product selection

Not all ideas which are generated by either the customer or internally will be considered for development. Screening should take place to decide which new ideas should be developed. Inputs are needed from the following functions:

- Marketing – who should understand the potential demand.
- Operations – who should have knowledge of such issues as capacity and resource availability.
- Finance – for input regarding availability of cash/capital.
- HRM – for input regarding staffing.

It is important to consider several factors:

- The probability of success.
- The feasibility of developing the service.
- The compatibility with existing operations.

Probability

Some ideas, particularly if they have not come via the market research route, may be considered unlikely to succeed because a large enough target market cannot be envisaged. This may be a function of location. For example, setting up a home catering service may be a very good idea in a fairly wealthy and densely populated region. However, the same idea in a depressed area, where little formal entertaining is likely to take place, and with a scattered population, is unlikely to succeed.

Feasibility

Feasibility may be related to the following:

- Cost.
- Technology.
- Logistics.
- Physical constraints.

The *cost* of producing a service may be prohibitive, if the costs cannot be passed on to the customer. In the earlier example of SAS, business travellers were prepared to pay for the enhanced service. In other cases it is not possible to provide an improved service. For example, in the National Health Service, enhancements to the service in terms of the provision of auxiliary services, such as en suite bathrooms or individual telephones for each patient, may improve the experience for the patient, and in fact provide an environment which is conducive to an early recovery. However, under the Health Service, the resulting increased costs would not be met by increased funding.

In terms of *technology*, developments may not be at a sufficiently advanced stage to allow commercialization of a new concept. Education is taking advantage of the use of CD-Roms to allow access to a wide range of information. However, at present there are still limits to the widespread development and use of this technology. The speed and memory capabilities of personal computers still limit the extent of this new form of education. In particular, at present, the amount of information which can be contained on a CD-Rom limits their usefulness. It can be much slower to access a particular piece of information on CD than it would be to look up that information in a textbook. Present ideas regarding the use of such technology may, in the future, be very successful, but for now they cannot be delivered. To a certain extent this is linked to cost. The technology which would allow a new idea to be developed may be available, but the cost of the advanced technology may be prohibitive.

Another example of this applies to travel agents. What clients often want is to be able to stipulate characteristics of a holiday: for example, destination: Paris; departure airport: Leeds; departure time: between 0700 and 1200 hours; departure date: 10 October; duration: 1 week; accommodation type: three-star hotel, etc. What they would like is a list of the available alternatives offered by a range of tour operators. What will happen is a slow, repetitive process as the travel agent logs on to the various reservation systems of the different tour operators in turn. In many cases it will not be possible to select by criteria other than destination and dates. Unfortunately, at present, the technology in terms of computer hardware and software has not been sufficiently developed to provide this service.

The *logistics* in terms of scheduling and location may preclude the development of an enhanced service. Students at a university during examination periods would prefer a situation in which their suite of examinations are scheduled evenly throughout the examination period. This would facilitate their revision. They may also have a preference regarding the order of their examinations, so that a subject that they perceive to be particularly difficult may be taken first to get it out of the way! However, if courses have been modularized to allow flexibility of choice, the number of potential combinations of examinations is almost certain to preclude such customization of timetables.

In terms of location, service engineers on call-out are likely to order customer visits according to an optimal route which will maximize the number of visits it is possible to complete in a day. It may be deemed infeasible to meet requests from customers to arrive at a specified time, as this would seriously affect the productive time of the engineer. Much more time would be spent travelling between customers, and safety margins would have to be built in between appointments to allow for jobs taking longer than expected.

In both the above situations, solutions which would allow an enhanced service to be provided are possible, but at a cost in terms of increased resources. The feasibility may once again be seen to be limited by resource availability.

The final factor listed above is one of *physical constraints*. This is often a matter of availability of land or building space – there may not be enough available for the extra room needed to house the new service. For example, a health club has identified a need for a child care facility/crèche which would allow parents to visit the club more easily. This is seen as potentially creating a competitive advantage over other health clubs locally. However, unless the club relocates to larger premises, the possibility of providing this new service is precluded.

Physical constraints are not necessarily related to size. Load-bearing factors of floors, or the number of fire escape routes may prevent the provision of a new service.

Compatibility

Some ideas identified by market research may, without doubt, warrant further development. However, should *we* develop the idea? This is an issue of strategy. Does the proposed new service fit in with the image of the organization? Is it outside our area of expertise? If it is not in line with present operations, what is it about the new service that justifies diversification? Marks and Spencer in the past built a reputation for quality clothes at a reasonable price. How much sense would it make for it to start selling designer clothes? Extending the range of goods sold from clothes to household goods (e.g. towels and bedding) did make sense because it was still maintaining its image of reasonably priced, quality goods. Designer clothes are not what Marks and Spencer is associated with, and would start to blur its brand image.

It may well be that the new product does fit in well with the perceived direction that the organization wishes to follow, and is one that requires expertise which already exists within the organization. However, one danger which is often overlooked is capacity. Is there spare capacity *when it is needed*? Whenever there are fluctuations in demand, be they seasonal, as is the case in the tourism industry, or monthly, for example in a department issuing invoices at the month end, overall figures of capacity utilization may present a misleading picture. If the new service is complementary in timing terms, i.e. it requires resources when existing activities are quiet, then this is an ideal opportunity which should be followed up. However, all too often, consideration at a superficial level results in misleading conclusions.

Screening framework

A useful framework for 'scoring' ideas considers ideas along relevant dimensions, as illustrated in Table 7.1. The overall score in the example is obtained by allocating weights to each factor and then summing the product of the weight and the score across all the factors. In this example the score was 3.6. The maximum score would be 5 and the minimum 1. The score might be compared to a minimum cut-off value: for example, if this were set at 3.0 and product scored less than this, it would not be considered further. Or the score might be compared with those of other new ideas, and the lowest 50 per cent could be dropped.

Table 7.1 Screening framework

Factor	Weight	Weak Score: 1	Poor 2	Reasonable 3	Good 4	Excellent 5
Potential market	0.25				x	
Cost	0.20			x		
Logistics	0.10			x		
Technology	0.10			x		
Physical constraints	0.10				x	
Compatibility	0.25				x	

Overall weighted score:
$(0.25 \times 4) + (0.2 \times 3) + (0.1 \times 3) + (0.1 \times 3) + (0.1 \times 4) + (0.25 \times 4) = 3.6$

Just how this framework is used will vary between different situations. The factors used and factor weighting are subjective. Past products may be scored on a proposed framework to see whether the scores obtained show any correlation with success and failure. Adaptation of the framework should take place until it appears to possess reasonable predictive power. However, care should still be exercised if it is believed that changes to the economic environment will have affected the relationship between the factors.

In some situations one factor may be essential: for example, if there is no existing technology which is capable of producing the service, then the rest of the exercise ceases to have any meaning.

Product design and specification

At this point, ideas which have survived the screening process described above are considered at a more detailed level. *What* the service is and *how* it will be delivered should be defined in great detail. This is particularly difficult in services because of the fact that the service often has to be tailored to meet the needs of the individual customer. For example, a counselling service for students cannot be specified exactly; much will depend upon the needs and personality of the student seeking help. Some facets of the service can, however, be defined precisely:

- Location (e.g. the communal centre of the university to maximize accessibility).
- Room requirements (e.g. specified minimum and maximum size, lighting).
- Facilities in the room (e.g. type of seating, size of desk, coffee machine etc.).
- Records (e.g. a format for the type of records which should be kept).
- Security (e.g. who has access to records, where should they be kept).
- Access (e.g. when is the service on offer – will there be a 24-hour help line?).
- Staff (e.g. details of qualifications and experience needed).
- Process (e.g. length of sessions, provision for back-up in an emergency).
- Customer (e.g. all students or specialized problems only).

Exactly *how* the counselling sessions should go cannot be specified in exact terms. There will be professional guidelines which should be followed, and these should be included in the specification. It may be considered appropriate that all sessions be tape recorded, or not, in which case this should also be included in the specification. Should interruptions be possible or prevented: for example, is the phone switched off during counselling sessions? Review procedures should be included in the specification to allow some safeguard for both the student and the counsellor. At all times, the objectives of the service should be considered and each element in the service package assessed in terms of their contribution towards achieving the aims of the service. The PZB dimensions of service quality provide a helpful *aide-mémoire*. Consideration of each dimension in turn, with questions asked such as 'What measures can be built into the specification to ensure responsiveness?' will help the service provider view the product from all perspectives.

Value analysis is a technique which has been used extensively in the manufacturing sector. It is simply a systematic approach which can be used to consider all aspects of a product in terms of the value added by each part of the product. What is the function of the part? How else could the function be achieved? Is there a better, more efficient and effective way of achieving the same function? A similar approach can be taken in services. In this case it will be important to remember the concept of the 'service package' and include the supporting facilities, the facilitating goods and the implicit service as well as

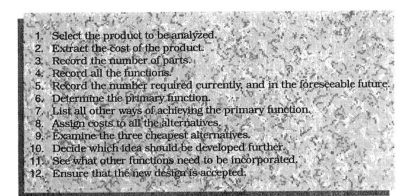

1. Select the product to be analyzed.
2. Extract the cost of the product.
3. Record the number of parts.
4. Record all the functions.
5. Record the number required currently, and in the foreseeable future.
6. Determine the primary function.
7. List all other ways of achieving the primary function.
8. Assign costs to all the alternatives.
9. Examine the three cheapest alternatives.
10. Decide which idea should be developed further.
11. See what other functions need to be incorporated.
12. Ensure that the new design is accepted.

Figure 7.3 Gage's twelve steps (Source: Adapted from Mühlemann *et al.*, 1992, pp. 92–4)

the explicit service. Twelve steps are suggested by Gage, and these are presented in Figure 7.3.

Part IV of this book looks more closely at delivery issues such as location and process design, so these aspects of service design will not be considered further here. However, it is extremely important to recognize that *how* delivery takes place is specified alongside the specification of *what* is being delivered. As pointed out earlier, the *what* often cannot be divorced from the *how* in services because of simultaneity of production and consumption. However, even in situations where 'back room' type operations are possible, consideration of *what* without the *how* may prove problematic. For example, in a hospital, patients have expressed a need for lighter, more appetizing dishes at meal times. Consideration of this request resulted in the suggestion that soufflés could be included on the menu. A recipe was identified and was unanimously proclaimed delicious by all who tasted the dish in the kitchen. However, no thought had been given to the problem of their distribution to the patients before the soufflés collapsed!

Design review

At this stage, the idea has been developed to a full specification. It is no longer vaguely described in broad terms. The next step, therefore, is a review by a broader representation of the organization than the development team. This is an ideal opportunity for feedback. It is quite possible that a wider perspective is needed to confirm that the new idea is still considered compatible with the other operations of the organization. In broad terms, the idea might have sounded suitable, but once the detail has been completed, the idea may not seem quite as appropriate for further development. In addition, it should be possible at this stage to estimate what resources will be required, in what mix and when.

In the counselling example, it may have become clear that, to meet student requirements, the service should be provided in the evenings and at weekends. At the original screening stage, it may have been assumed that only spare capacity during the day would be employed. As a result of this review, the idea may be passed back to the planning team to look at the alternatives, when, for example, questions such as 'What impact would providing the service during the day have on demand?' and 'What would the effect on costs be if additional staff were recruited for evening sessions?' could be considered.

Prototype

Prototypes conjure up visions of concept cars. In services, ideas can be tested by setting up a trial run, very much like a rehearsal for a television programme. On one occasion, A-level economics students took multiple choice examination papers alongside the standard papers which had been in use previously. Both sets of examination were marked, and the results were compared. The results from the multiple choice did not actually count towards the qualification. At this point, the 'prototype' of this new approach had been designed and developed to a testing stage. The examiners, by comparing the results, could check to see whether the new mode of examination discriminated between students in the same way as the standard approach. They also had feedback from tutors who gave their opinion of the new format. Other examples would be a building society or bank offering a new service in one branch. This might involve redesign of the layout of the branch. The new idea could then be tested to see whether the new service was successful; or, on the other hand, problems could be identified and the idea referred back to the design team.

Test market

The example of the building society or bank described above may be thought of as a test market for a new product. However, a test market would usually involve trying out the new service in more than just one branch where numerous branches exist. Typically, a new idea may be tried out in a particular region, or be available for a limited period of time. After what could be considered a representative period, a review of the new service should be undertaken to assess how successful the test has been. As was the case at the end of the previous stage, feedback to the design team should be given to allow adjustments to the specification to be made.

Full launch

The process described above, from service design and specification to test market, is an iterative one. Only when the service has been refined to meet customer requirements should it be fully launched.

The above process is a generic framework. Some of the stages may in effect merge. If the service provider in question is a small single unit, the opportunity to develop a prototype may be somewhat limited, and the same applies to the test marketing stage. However, even here it may be possible to obtain feedback from customers regarding their interest in a proposed new service, or to offer a new service for a limited period.

Review

Once a service has been designed and successfully launched, it is important to realize that the design should periodically be reviewed. Many changes will occur during the life of a product, either in respect of technological developments which permit a radical change in modes of delivery, or of the external environment. The latter could involve changes in the behaviour of competitors or, more generally, changes in the economic climate. For whatever reason, customers' requirements are going to change over time. Periodic reviews of existing services which examine whether a gap has opened between what is being provided and what the customer now wants are essential for long-term survival. To remain successful, the service should go through an evolutionary process, sometimes changing in small incremental steps; at other stages the change may be quite radical.

The frequency of design review will depend upon the nature of the industry. In a fast-moving environment, the review period should be short. For example, in information technology advances have been rapid, allowing enhanced service in all types of reservation system. Firms using inferior technology capable of providing a more limited service will soon find customers complaining and quite possibly defecting. In a slower-moving environment, service reviews may be less frequent. However, even in these environments it is dangerous to become complacent. Value analysis and Gage's twelve steps are equally effective when conducting a review as when designing a product from scratch.

What must also be considered concurrently in the review process is the delivery system. If the system *is* the product, then of course this occurs simultaneously.

Design considerations

Various frameworks have been developed which may be used to aid the design process, highlighting which factors should receive particular attention in which circumstances. Services differ tremendously across the various dimensions of *simultaneity, heterogeneity, intangibility* and *perishability*. Two frameworks will be examined here, which have been presented by Chase and Aquilano (1995) and Haywood-Farmer (1988).

The framework provided in Table 7.2 is particularly useful as a prompting device. Have implications regarding each of the decision areas been fully considered? For example, in a restaurant, a chef may have been hired based on his or her abilities as a culinary expert. Management have decided to launch a new product – a series of lunch-time demonstrations by their 'expert', with the opportunity for the customers to ask questions. The idea is seen as novel, and market research has identified keen interest from existing customers. Lunch times have been slow in terms of business, and this is seen as an ideal product to create a complementary new service using spare capacity. The problem is that the chef does not possess the interpersonal skills necessary to interact successfully with the customers. In this example, 'worker skills' in Table 7.2 had not been considered.

In Figure 7.4, success in delivering the service as required by the customers is seen to depend upon the correct mix of professional judgement, physical processes and the behaviour of people. Too much emphasis on any one area may result in the wrong message being transmitted to the customer, as illustrated by the examples given. The correct mix of the three elements will depend upon the nature of the service being provided.

In Figure 7.5, Haywood-Farmer presents a model to help in the analysis of the nature of the service. The three dimensions are degree of contact and interaction (e.g. does the customer have to be present, as is the case with a haircut); degree of labour intensity (e.g. is it possible to automate the service, as with automatic teller machines); and degree of

Table 7.2 Major design considerations in high- and low-contact systems

Decision	High-contact system	Low-contact system
Facility location	Operations must be near the customer	Operations may be placed near supply, transport or labour
Facility layout	Facility should accommodate the customer's physical and psychological needs and expectations	Facility should enhance production
Product design	Environment as well as the physical product define the nature of the service	Customer is not in the service environment so the product can be defined by fewer attributes
Process design	Stages of production process have a direct, immediate effect on the customer	Customer is not involved in majority of processing steps
Scheduling	Customer is in the production schedule and must be accommodated	Customer is concerned mainly with completion dates
Production planning	Orders cannot be stored, so smooth production flow will result in loss of business.	Both backlogging and production smoothing are possible
Worker skills	Direct workforce comprises a major part of the service production and so must be able to interact well with the public	Direct workforce need only have technical skills
Quality control	Quality standards are often in the eye of the beholder and hence variable	Quality standards are generally measurable and hence fixed
Time standards	Service time depends on customer needs, and therefore time standards are inherently loose	Work is performed on customer surrogates (e.g. forms), thus time standards can be tight
Wage payment	Variable output requires time-based wage systems.	'Fixable' output permits output-based wage systems
Capacity planning	To avoid lost sales, capacity must be be set to match peak demand	Storable output permits capacity at some average demand level
Forecasting	Forecasts are short-term, time-oriented	Forecasts are long-term, output-oriented

Source: Chase and Aquilano (1985), p. 89.

service customization (e.g. how much standardization is possible – in a fitness gym can a standard routine be devised for all customers?).

Figures 7.4 and 7.5 are used together to help focus attention on the important factors associated with the characteristics of the particular service. The first step is to identify where the proposed service lies in the cube in Figure 7.5. Take water supply. This is characterized by low degrees of contact and interaction, low labour intensity and low service customization, and would be located in quadrant 1. Linking this to Figure 7.4, the focus of attention in the design process should be on the physical processes needed to deliver the service. As there is little interaction and customization, little professional

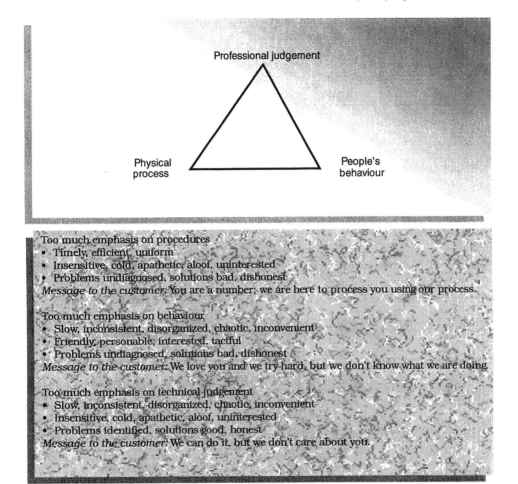

Figure 7.4 shown: triangle with vertices labelled "Professional judgement" (top), "Physical process" (bottom left), and "People's behaviour" (bottom right).

Too much emphasis on procedures
• Timely, efficient, uniform
• Insensitive, cold, apathetic, aloof, uninterested
• Problems undiagnosed, solutions bad, dishonest
Message to the customer: You are a number; we are here to process you using our process.

Too much emphasis on behaviour
• Slow, inconsistent, disorganized, chaotic, inconvenient
• Friendly, personable, interested, tactful
• Problems undiagnosed, solutions bad, dishonest
Message to the customer: We love you and we try hard, but we don't know what we are doing.

Too much emphasis on technical judgement
• Slow, inconsistent, disorganized, chaotic, inconvenient
• Insensitive, cold, apathetic, aloof, uninterested
• Problems identified, solutions good, honest
Message to the customer: We can do it, but we don't care about you.

Figure 7.4 Haywood-Farmer's model of service quality (Source: Haywood-Farmer, 1988, p. 23)

judgement is required, and there is less need to concentrate on such factors as the ability of staff to interact with customers.

Solicitors typically provide a service which involves a relatively high level of service customization, a high level of labour intensity and a medium level of contact and interaction, and would thus lie somewhere between quadrants 4 and 8. Linking this example to the triangle, professional judgement will be required to decide what is best for the client, and personal behaviour is important as the service is labour intensive. Processes will still be important because clients are in a position where they do not have the expert knowledge to tell whether the service is being provided competently, and *how* the process is handled (e.g. letters answered promptly) will indicate efficiency.

Generally, service customization requires professional judgement; low contact and interaction requires more attention to the physical process; and high labour intensity requires close attention to people's behaviour.

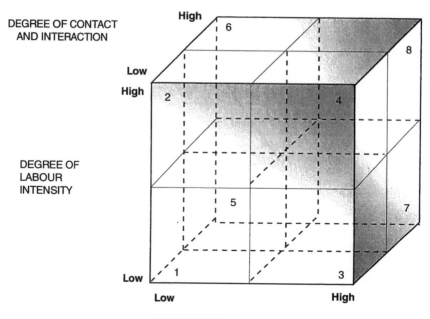

DEGREE OF CONTACT
AND INTERACTION

DEGREE OF
LABOUR
INTENSITY

DEGREE OF SERVICE CUSTOMIZATION

Some examples of services in each octant:

1. Utilities, transportation of goods
2. Lecture teaching, postal services
3. Stockbroking, courier services
4. Repair servies, wholesaling, retailing
5. Computerized teaching, public transit
6. Fast food, live entertainment
7. Charter services, hospitals
8. Design services, advisory services, healing services

Figure 7.5 Haywood-Farmer's three-dimensional classification scheme (Source: Haywood-Farmer, 1988, p. 25)

Total quality management

Total quality management (TQM) is an approach to improving the effectiveness and flexibility of businesses as a whole. It is essentially a way of organizing and involving the whole organization; every department, every activity, every single person at every level. (Oakland, 1989, p. 14)

Figure 7.6 is a model of total quality management (TQM) presented by Oakland (1993). Many of the component parts of the model stem from good operations management practice techniques, which were tried and tested for many years before the philosophy of total quality management became popular. For example, 'tools' include techniques such as statistical process control. These different elements will be covered in the appropriate sections of this book.

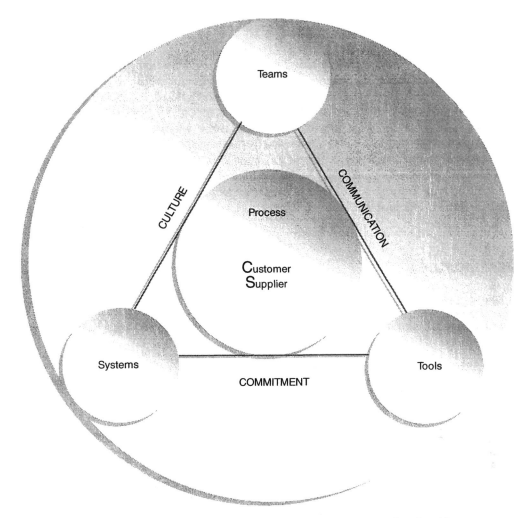

Figure 7.6 The TQM model (Source: Oakland, J.S., *Total Quality Management*, Heinemann, 1993, p. 40)

In terms of specifying the service, TQM has implications for the design of systems to ensure that the service is produced right first time, every time. The overriding philosophy for any organization professing to follow TQM principles is a commitment to meeting customer requirements. Thus, as discussed in Chapter 6, quality of design (i.e. specifying exactly what the customer wants) and quality of conformance (i.e. the ability to meet the specification) form two key features of a TQM approach. The design process and other frameworks and approaches presented in this chapter help an organization achieve these goals. More attention is paid to the design of systems to deliver services in Part IV of the book.

Measurement difficulties

One of the major problems when specifying a service is definition. It is easy to write a specification for a table: the wood – pine; height – 77.5 cm; width – 43 cm; depth – 41 cm; finish – clear lacquer, etc. Drawings to 'scale, showing fine detail, will be prepared. It is possible to define all the parameters to ensure that no uncertainty exists, and the table which is produced can be measured/inspected to check whether or not it conforms to specification. It is not possible to define an experience in the same way. For example, the service provided by a job centre cannot be specified in terms of physical measurements; nor can an accompanying drawing be provided for staff delivering the service. Ambiguity and subjectivity are major problems when trying to compile a specification. Chapters 9 and 13 address this problem.

References

Chase, R.B. and N.J. Aquilano (1995) *Production and Operations Management: A life cycle approach* (4th edn), Irwin, Homewood, IL.

Fitzsimmons, J.A. and M.J. Fitzsimmons (1994) *Service Management for Competitive Advantage*, McGraw-Hill, Inc., New York.

Grönroos, C. (1984) 'A service quality model and its marketing implications', *European Journal of Marketing*, vol. 18, no. 4, pp. 36–44.

Haywood-Farmer, J. (1988) 'A conceptual model of service quality', *International Journal of Operations and Production Management*, vol. 8, no. 6, pp. 19–29.

Oakland, J.S. (1989) *Total Quality Management* (1st edn), Heinemann, Oxford.

Oakland, J.S. (1993) *Total Quality Management* (2nd edn), Heinemann, Oxford.

Mühlemann, A., J. Oakland and K. Lockyer (1992) *Production and Operations Management* (6th edn), Pitman, London.

Discussion topics/exercises

1. Why is there a need continually to design new services? What stages are involved in the design process? Think how the stages would relate to the design of a new degree programme. What would have to be considered?

2. The context is a doctor's surgery. Discuss those elements which will affect the technical quality of the service, and those which will affect the functional quality.

3. Using the Haywood-Farmer model of service quality, consider where the following should be positioned:
    (a) a firm of solicitors
    (b) a sixth form college
    (c) a hairdressing salon
    (d) a small local branch of a bank
    (e) the post office.

4. Consider how the level of contact with the customer will affect the design of a service. What constraints will high contact with the customer place on service design?

Chapter 8

Specification parameters

Chapter outline

Introduction

Specifying the actual parameters for a service is probably the most difficult task facing an operations manager. The explicit service being provided may differ each time it is provided, as each customer is different and has individual needs. The interaction between two individuals can never be exactly the same on every occasion. This is a consequence of the heterogeneous nature of services. The product itself is intangible – and is often an experience. Comedians are supposed to make an audience laugh. People, however, have different senses of humour. Assessment of the performance is subjective. How can 'funny' be specified? With jokes, the timing and delivery can make a difference – *how* the punchline is delivered is important. So, even if the service being provided has been 'scripted', i.e. the service provider has learnt a set of lines to use when delivering a service, the actual service may not meet customer requirements. In this chapter, some of the steps that can be taken to try and ensure that the service is specified so that it is delivered as conceived are considered. The emphasis will be on those factors which affect what Grönroos (1984) called the *functional quality*, i.e. *how* the service is delivered, as these factors will tend to be generic. *Technical quality* will be more context specific and will tend to be reliant upon training in the specific area concerned. For example, *what* is provided by an accountant when doing an audit for a company will be governed by standards and procedures laid down by the professional body, i.e. the Institute of Chartered Accountants.

Supporting facilities and facilitating goods

Often, it is the management of the supporting facilities and the facilitating goods which determines the quality of the customer experience. For example, in the building society example discussed in Chapter 7, privacy for the customer could have been ensured by redesigning the supporting facility – the interview room should have been designed to be sound proof. Sometimes the supporting facilities and facilitating goods are designed with the service provider in mind rather than the customer. For example, the design of hospital wards has often focused more on the efficiency of the layout from the perspective of the medical staff than from the viewpoint of the patient. What should happen is that 'The organization's environment should support the needs and preferences of both service employees and customers simultaneously' (Bitner, 1992, p. 58).

A great deal of research has been conducted which considers the effect of the physical setting on organizational behaviour. However, one of the lessons from the famous Hawthorne experiments (Roethlisberger and Dickson, 1939) was that caution is needed when attributing behaviour changes to alterations to the environment: the effect of changes in the environment on behaviour is complex, and it can be difficult to differentiate between the effects of the changes in the environment and the reactions arising due to sociological factors.

In comparison to the mass of literature related to the effect of the environment on performance at work, little research has been conducted on the effect of the environment on the customer in a service environment. However, when the process itself is the product or part of the product, the environment in which the service takes place will clearly impinge upon the perceptions of the customer and thus needs to be considered when specifying the service. In addition, the customer often performs the role of an employee, particularly when aspects of service are *self*-service. It is thought likely that many of the findings from the work on organizational behaviour and ergonomics will apply equally to both the customer and the paid employee.

Bitner (1992) developed the framework for understanding environment–user relationships in service organizations presented in Figure 8.1. The individual environmental dimensions combine to create a setting which is perceived by the customer or employee. The way the environment is perceived will be influenced by factors pertaining to the individual, i.e. personality, mood, etc. Internal responses will be triggered by the environment, cognitively, emotionally and physiologically, which will lead to certain behaviour. The aim of the organization must be to create the environment which elicits the desired behaviour. For example, in a fast-food restaurant, the organization will want to maximize the number of customers served. To achieve this it will not want the customers to linger,

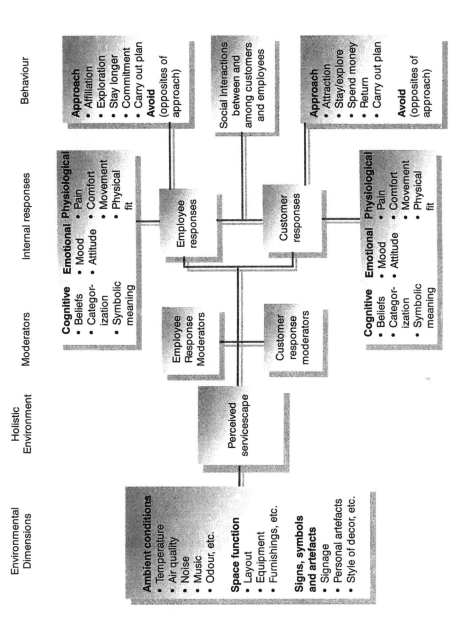

Figure 8.1 Framework for understanding environment–user relationships in service organizations (Source: Bitner, 1992, p. 60)

P1. Positive (negative) internal responses to the servicescape lead to approach (avoidance) behaviours.
     (a) For employees, approach includes such behaviours as affiliation, exploration, staying longer,
     expressions of commitment, and carrying out the purpose for being in the organization. Avoidance is
     represented by the opposite behaviours.
     (b) For customers, approach includes such behaviours as coming in, staying, spending money, loyalty,
     and carrying out the purpose of being in the organization. Avoidance is represented by the opposite
     behaviours.

P2. For interpersonal services, positive (negative) internal responses to the servicescape enhance (detract
     from) the nature and quality of social interactions between and among customers and employees.

P3. Optimal design for encouraging employee (customer) approach behaviour may be incompatible with
     the design required to meet customer (employee) needs and/or facilitate positive employee–customer
     interactions.

P4. Perceptions of the servicescape and associated positive (negative) cognitions can lead to positive
     (negative) beliefs and attributions associated with the organization, its people and its products.

P5. Perceptions of the servicescape influence how people categorize the organization; thus, the
     environment serves as a mnemonic in differentiating among firms.

P6. The servicescape's influence on beliefs, attributions and categorization of the organization is stronger
     for inexperienced customers or new employees, and when few intrinsic cues are available on which to
     categorize or base beliefs.

P7. Customer and employee emotional responses to the servicescape can be captured by two dimensions,
     pleasure and arousal.
     (a) Pleasure increases approach behaviours.
     (b) Arousal, except when combined with unpleasantness, increases approach behaviours.

P8. Perceptions of greater personal control in the servicescape increase pleasure.

P9. Complexity in the servicescape increases emotional arousal.

P10. Compatibility, the presence of natural elements and the absence of environmental 'nuisances' in the
     servicescape enhance pleasure.

P11. Perceptions of the servicescape and associated positive (negative) emotions can lead to positive
     (negative) feelings associated with the organization, its people and its products.

P12. Positive (negative) physiological responses to the servicescape can result in positive (negative) beliefs
     and feelings associated with the organization, its people and its products.

P13. Personality traits (such as arousal-seeking tendencies and ability to screen environmental stimuli)
     moderate the relationship between the perceived servicescape and internal responses.

P14. Situational factors (such as expectations, momentary mood, plans and purposes for being in the
     servicescape) moderate the relationship between the perceived servicescape and internal responses.

P15. Customers and employees perceive the environment holistically as a composite of three dimensions:
     ambient conditions; spatial layout and functionality; signs, symbols and artefacts. Each dimension
     may affect the overall perception independently and/or through its interactions with the other
     dimensions.

P16. The effects of ambient conditions on the overall, holistic perception of the servicescape are especially
     noticeable when they are extreme (e.g. loud music, high temperature), when the customer or employee
     spends considerable time in the servicescape (e.g. hospital stay vs visit to dry cleaner), and when they
     conflict with expectations (e.g. loud music in a law office).

P17. The effects of spatial layout and functionality are particularly salient in self-service settings, when the
     tasks to be performed are complex, and when either the employee or customer is under time
     pressure.

P18. Signs, symbols and artefacts are particularly important in forming first impressions, for
     communicating new service concepts, for repositioning a service, and in highly competitive industries
     where customers are looking for cues to differentiate the organization.

Figure 8.2 Bitner's eighteen propositions (Source: Bitner, 1992)

and the seating arrangements in fast-food restaurants are usually slightly uncomfortable:
hard, fixed in position, just too close together, etc. The colour red has also been found to
encourage diners to eat more quickly (Cumming and Porter, 1990).

Bitner made a series of propositions related to her framework. These are presented
in Figure 8.2. These propositions attempt to summarize the underlying factors which cause

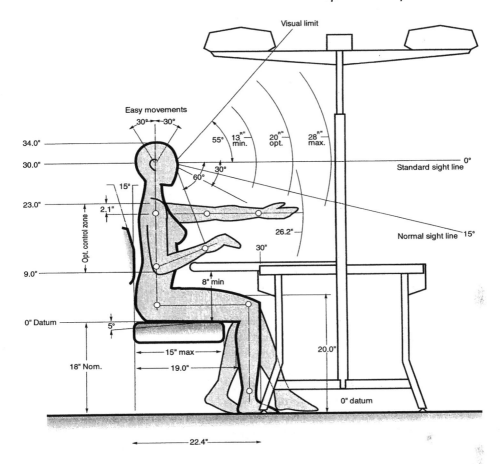

Work station for the 50-percentile American female. When using anthropometric data it is important for the designer to realize that it is rare to find a 50-percentile female in real life. The dimensions shown are merely averages, and anything designed to those specs must be adjustable for maximum and minimum tolerances. Usually a dimensional tolerance of plus or minus 4 inches from those shown on the chart will suffice, but not in all cases. There are a few standards, such as 30-inch table height, 18-inch chair height, etc. that will hold true for up to the 95-percentile female. Visual limits and reacting distances also vary with the individual, and in some cases the variation is considerable.

Figure 8.3 Anthropometric data for a 50-percentile American female (Source: Heizer and Render, 1988, p. 424)

customers and employees to react to the service setting (which Bitner refers to as the 'servicescape') in the way that they do.

The environment or 'servicescape' may be considered from various perspectives:

- Anthropometric factors.
- Neurological factors.
- Illumination.

- Colour.
- Temperature and humidity.
- Noise.
- Smell.
- Signs, symbols and artefacts.
- Spatial layout.
- Personal space.

All of the factors listed above will have some impact on a customer's perception of the service being provided. The actual influence on perceptions will depend upon the context. In situations where contact is prolonged, the environment will have a greater impact than when the contact is fleeting. However, whenever a customer is present during the delivery of a service, parameters should be specified for all the relevant environmental factors, i.e. precise specifications are needed for the supporting facilities and facilitating goods. Each of these factors will now be examined.

Anthropometric factors

These factors are related to the physical attributes of people, such as their size. For example, how high should a ledge be in a bank to enable customers to fill in forms comfortably when standing? Figure 8.3 illustrates anthropometric data taken in relation to an American female. The problem with such data is that the measurements given are averages and additional data will be required relating to variations from the mean.

Human diversity is really quite extensive. Figure 8.4 illustrates the variation of average heights of adults in the human race. This shows that British adults are above the overall average height. Efe and Basua are 'pygmies' of central Africa, who, according to Roberts (1975), are the shortest people in the world. By contrast, the Dinka Nilotes of the southern Sudan are the tallest.

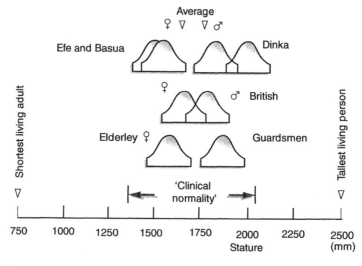

Figure 8.4   Variation in adult stature in the human race as a whole (Source: Pheasant, S., *Bodyspace*, Taylor and Francis 1986, p. 43)

Tables exist which present anthropometric estimates for different races and ages of people. Table 8.1 presents such data for British adults aged 19–65 years. Note that three estimates are given for each feature measured: for example, for the stature (height) of men, the dimensions 1625 mm, 1740 mm and 1855 mm are given under the headings 5th, 50th and 95th %iles. The variation in the size of people follows a normal distribution, so these statistics may be interpreted as follows: 5 per cent of men are shorter than 1625 mm, the mean height is 1740 mm (i.e. 50 per cent of men are shorter, and 50 per cent taller than this height), and 5 per cent of men are taller than 1855 mm.

Table 8.1 Anthropometric estimates for British adults aged 19–65 years

Dimension	Men				Women			
	5th %ile	50th %ile	95th %ile	SD	5th %ile	50th %ile	95th %ile	SD
1. Stature	1625	1740	1855	70	1505	1610	1710	62
2. Eye height	1515	1630	1745	69	1405	1505	1610	61
3. Shoulder height	1315	1425	1535	66	1215	1310	1405	58
4. Elbow height	1005	1090	1180	52	930	1005	1085	46
5. Hip height	840	920	1000	50	740	810	885	43
6. Knuckle height	690	755	825	41	660	720	780	36
7. Fingertip height	590	655	720	38	560	625	685	38
8. Sitting height	850	910	965	36	795	850	910	35
9. Sitting eye height	735	790	845	35	685	740	795	33
10. Sitting shoulder height	540	595	645	32	505	555	610	31
11. Sitting elbow height	195	245	295	31	185	235	280	29
12. Thigh thickness	135	160	185	15	125	155	180	17
13. Buttock–knee length	540	595	645	31	520	570	620	30
14. Buttock–popliteal length	440	495	550	32	435	480	530	30
15. Knee height	490	545	595	32	455	500	540	27
16. Popliteal height	395	440	490	29	355	400	445	27
17. Shoulder breadth (bideltoid)	420	465	510	28	355	395	435	24
18. Shoulder breadth (biacromial)	365	400	430	20	325	355	385	18
19. Hip breadth	310	360	405	29	310	370	435	38
20. Chest (bust) depth	215	250	285	22	210	250	295	27
21. Abdominal depth	220	270	325	32	205	255	305	30
22. Shoulder–elbow length	330	365	395	20	300	330	360	17
23. Elbow–fingertip length	440	475	510	21	400	430	460	19
24. Upper limb length	720	780	840	36	655	705	760	32
25. Shoulder–grip length	610	665	715	32	555	600	650	29
26. Head length	180	195	205	8	165	180	190	7
27. Head breadth	145	155	165	6	135	145	150	6
28. Hand length	175	190	205	10	160	175	190	9
29. Hand breadth	80	85	95	5	70	75	85	4
30. Foot length	240	265	285	14	215	235	255	12
31. Foot breadth	85	95	110	6	80	90	100	6
32. Span	1655	1790	1925	83	1490	1605	1725	71
33. Elbow span	865	945	1020	47	780	850	920	43
34. Vertical grip reach (standing)	1925	2060	2190	80	1790	1905	2020	71
35. Vertical grip reach (sitting)	1145	1245	1340	60	1060	1150	1235	53
36. Forward grip reach	720	780	835	34	650	705	755	31

Source: S. Pheasant, *Bodyspace*, Taylor and Francis (1986), p. 85.

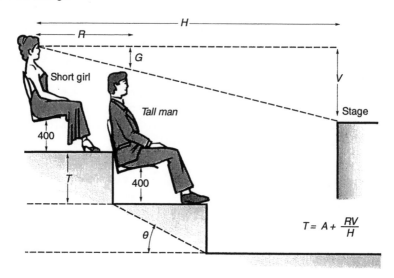

Figure 8.5   Sight lines in auditorium seating (Source: Pheasant, S., *Bodyspace*, Taylor and Francis, 1986, p. 190)

These statistics may be used in the design of facilities. For example, in a theatre it is possible to estimate the incline needed so that the vision of the audience is not impeded by those seated in front of them. Figure 8.5 and Table 8.2 illustrate this. The actual incline (θ) needed to ensure that a short girl seated behind a tall man can see the stage has been calculated based on the spacing between rows (R) and the position of the stage relative to the seating (V/H). Table 8.2 presents alternatives indicating whether the incline is suitable for a ramp or whether stairs would be needed.

One solution to the problem of diversity is to have adjustable facilities. For example, in the new United Airlines Boeing 777, the back of the seats in economy class has been made higher in response to customer feedback, and there is a head-rest which may be adjusted by the customer.

Neurological factors

These factors relate to how people respond automatically or intuitively in situations. If steering a car to the right, the natural direction to turn the steering wheel is clockwise. Other examples include turning a handle clockwise to open a door. Some of these actions are learned behaviour. In the UK light switches are pressed down to turn the light on. Generally in the USA the reverse is true.

However, what appears 'natural' is not always the most effective in terms of desired behaviour. Designing knobs and dials is an example of this. Consider Figure 8.6. The natural way to position a bank of dials is with the pointers pointing upwards when off. When the equipment is turned on, however, the 'normal' range for each dial may be at any position on the dial. To identify any dial indicating performance outside the 'normal' range, the observer needs to look at each dial in turn. If, however, the dials are positioned

Table 8.2 Gradient (θ) required for unimpeded vision in an auditorium as a function of row spacing (*R*) and location (*V/H*)

V/H	R (mm)				
	800	1000	1200	1400	
0	17	14	11	10	Use ramps
0.1	22	16	17	16	
0.2	27	23	22	21	Acceptable for stairs
0.3	31	28	27	26	
0.4	35	32	31	30	Preferred gradient for stairs
0.5	39	36	35	34	
0.6	42	40	39	38	Acceptable for stairs in MIL-STD-1472[a] but not in certain fire regulations
0.7	45	43	42	41	
0.8	48	46	45	44	
0.9	50	49	48	47	
1.0	53	51	50	50	
1.1	55	53	53	52	Definitely unacceptable

Note: [a]MIL-STD-1472C considers gradients 20–50° to be acceptable for staircases, but 30–5° is preferred.
Source: S. Pheasant, *Bodyspace*, Taylor and Francis (1986), p. 191.

so that the pointer points upwards when operating within the 'normal' range, any problems can be spotted at a glance.

These kinds of factor are particularly important in service settings where the customer uses equipment, such as motorized buggies on a golf course, automatic teller machines and self-service petrol stations.

Ilumination

Natural light is usually the most comfortable source of light. Strip lighting, particularly when it flickers, can cause actual discomfort for some people, whether customers or employees. In some cases it can even cause migraines. Unfortunately, the amount of natural light varies with the time of day and weather conditions. Glare from sunlight on screens can also cause problems. For example, at certain times of day the sun's glare on automatic teller machine monitors can actually make them impossible to use. It is similar with arrival and departure information monitors at railway stations. In such cases excess light is a problem and appropriate shades are needed. Sometimes it is not feasible to use natural daylight: for example, in a lift. Therefore artificial light sources are needed, but the characteristics of different types of lighting need careful consideration.

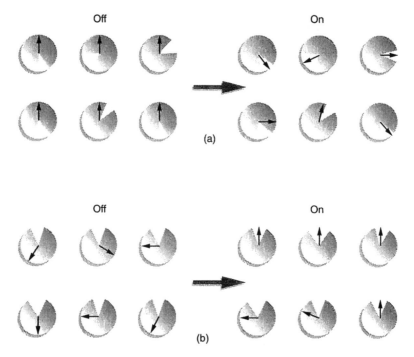

Figure 8.6 Alignment of dials (Source: Meredith, 1987, p. 343; *The Management of Operations*, J.R. Meredith, Copyright © Wiley 1987. Reprinted by permission of John Wiley & Sons, Inc.) (a) Zero values aligned (b) Shaded ('normal') ranges aligned

On a functional level, different illumination levels are needed to perform tasks, depending on the level of detailed attention required. An example of inappropriate lighting is the lighting in the en suite facilities of many hotels. Good light is needed for putting make-up on or shaving, and yet frequently the lighting provided is very poor. The actual measure of light now in use is the *lux* (lx) which is equal to 1 lumen (lm) per square metre, the lumen being a unit of luminous flux. Light used to be measured in *footcandles*, where 1 footcandle is approximately equal to 10 lux. Table 8.3 gives an indication of the different levels of illumination needed to perform various tasks.

Lighting can also contribute to the creation of atmosphere. Low levels of lighting are associated with romantic settings. Strobe lighting is often used in nightclubs to excite and arouse. Well-lit passages will feel safer than those which are poorly lit. Light bulbs which have failed and not been replaced create an ill-kept, inefficient image.

Colour

Colour and illumination are often used in conjunction. A colour at different levels of illumination may look quite different. The effect of neighbouring colours also changes the impact of a colour: some clash and have a disturbing or arousing effect; others complement

Table 8.3 Examples of suitable lighting levels in workrooms

Type of work	Examples	Recommended lighting (lx)
General	Storeroom	80–170
Moderately precise	Packing: despatch; works laboratory; simple assembly; winding thick wire on to spools; work on carpenter's bench; turning; boring; milling; locksmith's work	200–250 250–300
Fine work	Reading; writing; book-keeping; laboratory technician; assembly of fine equipment; winding fine wire; woodworking by machine; fine work on tool-making jig	500–700
Very fine to precision work	Technical drawing; colour proofing; adjusting and testing electrical equipment; assembling delicate electronics; watchmaking; invisible mending	1000–2000

Source: E. Grandjean, *Fitting the Task to the Man*, Taylor and Francis (1988), p. 256.

and have a more soothing or calming effect. Greens and blues are 'cool' colours, often used for quiet or rest areas. 'Warm' colours are reds, oranges and yellows. Mudie and Cottam (1993) provide some examples of the use of colours, based on work by Cumming and Porter (1990). These are presented in Figure 8.7.

Temperature and humidity

Temperature and humidity affect the comfort of customers. This can be difficult to control in situations where the number of customers in the system fluctuates. For example, a crowded train or theatre may become unbearably hot because there are so many customers in the system. The converse of this is the lecture theatre where the air-conditioning is fine when the theatre is full of students, but when half-empty leaves students huddling in their coats. The negative impact on perceptions of the service can be quite severe.

The level of activity undertaken during the service will also be relevant: the higher the level of exercise, the lower will be the requirement for heat. Table 8.4 gives recommended room temperatures for various activities in a work context and Table 8.5 examines the effects on work of deviations from a comfortable working temperature.

Table 8.4 Recommended room temperatures for various activities

Type of work	Room temperature (°C)
Sedentary mental	21
Sedentary light manual	19
Standing light manual	18
Standing heavy manual	17
Severe work	15–16

Source: E. Grandjean, *Fitting the Task to the Man*, Taylor and Francis (1988), p. 317.

> **Red.** The colour of fire and passion, suggesting activity, energy, joy. It is used by interior designers to increase comfort levels in unheated spaces and is also regarded (along with pink) as good for restaurants, especially the fast-food variety. One study showed that red-stimulated diners tend to eat more quickly and move on for the next person.
>
> **Orange.** Although researchers have claimed that an orange environment improves social behaviour, cheers the spirit and lessens hostility and irritability, it is seldom used by professional designers.
>
> **Yellow.** Conflicting evidence here which on the one hand suggests its ideal stimulative effect where concentration is required. However, if it is used too strongly, those in its environment are likely to get 'stressed up'.
>
> **Green.** Symbolizes the natural world and is widely believed to be a calming hue. Ideal for areas where relaxation is required and along with blue is found to enhance our appetite; thus good for dining areas.
>
> **Blue.** Symbolizes authority and implies truth, prudence and wisdom - ideal for banks and building societies. It is considered as having a calming effect which makes it ideally suited for hospital cardiac units.
>
> **Purple.** Regarded as disturbing and psychologically 'difficult'. In a Swedish study it was the most disliked colour in terms of environmental settings.

Figure 8.7   Insights into colour psychology (Source: Mudie and Cottam, *The Management and Marketing of Services*, Butterworth Heinemann, 1993, p. 68)

Once again conflicts between what the customer wants and what the service provider would prefer can occur. For example, in winter when shoppers enter stores dressed in outside clothing, the heat inside often prompts them to remove their coats and carry them around. This can be a nuisance, particularly when trying to examine goods with shopping bags in one hand and a coat in the other! However, the shop assistant who is on check-out duties clearly requires a warm environment in which to work.

According to Grandjean (1988, p. 312) relative humidity (RH) has little influence on effective temperature. He suggests that, for temperatures of 18–24 degrees centigrade the relative humidity can fluctuate between 30 and 70 per cent without causing thermal discomfort. He suggests that the threshold at which a room will begin to feel stuffy lies between the following pairs of values:

- 80% RH and 18°C
- 60% RH and 24°C

and that relative humidity below 30 per cent will result in an atmosphere which is too dry.

Table 8.5 Effects of deviations from a comfortable working temperature

20 °C	Comfortable temperature	Maximum efficiency
	Discomfort: increased irritability; loss of concentration; loss of efficiency in mental tasks	Mental problems
	Increase of errors: loss of efficiency in skilled tasks; more accidents	Psycho-physiological problems
	Loss of performance of heavy work; disturbed water and salt balances; heavy stresses on heart and circulation; intense fatigue and threat of exhaustion	Physiological problems
35–40 °C	Limit of tolerance of high temperature	

Source: E. Grandjean, *Fitting the Task to the Man*, Taylor and Francis (1988), p. 318.

Noise

Once again, in the work environment, the effects of noise have been studied. In particular, the loss of performance and long-term damage to hearing are areas which have received a great deal of attention. Background noise often interferes with concentration and can make learning difficult. The unit of measurement of sound is the decibel and this is related to the physical unit of sound pressure called the micropascal. The minimum sound that a human ear can hear is 20 micropascals, and this is equivalent to 1 decibel. The relationship between micropascals and decibels is logarithmic, so that each time sound pressure in micropascals is multiplied by 10, 20 decibels are added to the decibel level. Bearing in mind the fact that a logarithmic scale applies to decibels, Table 8.6 gives an indication of noise levels in decibels for various activities. The generally recommended maximum level to which workers should be exposed over a working day is 90 decibels.

Table 8.6 Noise levels for various activities

Noise	Decibels (dB)
Quiet speech	40
Light traffic at 25 metres	50
Large busy office	60
Busy street, heavy traffic	70
Pneumatic drill at 20 metres	80
Textile factory	90
Circular saw – close work	100
Riveting machine – close work	110
Jet aircraft taking off at 100 metres	120

Source: Slack *et al.* (1995), p. 366

Research in the context of service provision is more limited. But noise clearly does affect the experience of the customer. In some cases, noise is a central part of the service, as in a nightclub. Concern has been expressed over the effect of the level of noise on the hearing of young people attending such functions. Temporary deafness can result from exposure to noise over 80–90 decibels: the longer the exposure to the noise, the greater the effect and the longer it takes for the temporary deafness to disappear. Research has also shown that temporary and permanent deafness are closely related.

Background noise, on the other hand, can help to create a romantic or relaxing atmosphere. In both of these cases the volume should be such that the music is not intrusive.

The perception of noise varies between individuals. Some people are just better than others at 'screening out' noise, and may be oblivious to the loud music from next door. The maker of the noise is often either oblivious to the noise (e.g. a typist) or enjoys the noise (e.g. a pianist). In a hospital ward, the potential problem of noise is recognized and all patients have earphones to listen to whatever they wish to hear on the radio without disturbing fellow patients. Passengers on trains can often be seen listening to music on walkmans (portable tape recorders fitted with personal earphones). The problem with the latter is that, although some consideration has been shown, the background rhythm is frequently still audible to the other passengers, which is often highly infuriating. Lack of control over the source of the noise is in itself stressful. Circumstances may also affect sensitivity to noise. Students sitting examinations may find the rustling of sweet papers highly distracting, when normally they would not even notice the noise. Some factors affecting the level of annoyance caused by noise are summarized in Figure 8.8.

Noise can have a surprisingly large, but subconscious impact on a customer's perceptions of the quality of the service provided. It can have either a positive or negative impact and should thus be actively managed. Where possible (e.g. in a greenfield site situation), building specifications need to address the transmission of noise specifically. What levels of sound proofing have been incorporated in the design? What are the acoustics

1. The louder the noise, and the higher the pitch, the greater the annoyance.
2. Intermittent and unfamiliar noises intrude on the consciousness more than continuous or familiar sounds
3. Previous experience or exposure to noise can influence perceptions of sounds: for example, the sound of a dentist's drill, or a similar sound, can arouse anxiety.
4. Non-participation in the creation of the noise increases the likelihood of annoyance. This effect will be influenced by the degree of dislike of the sound (e.g. the type of music), by the attitude towards the person creating the sound, and by the inability to control the source of the noise.
5. The situation in which the noise is experienced. If a person is trying to get to sleep, or concentrate on a difficult task, a noise which would otherwise be acceptable, or not even noticed, may become extremely annoying.

Figure 8.8 Factors affecting the level of annoyance from noise

like in a lecture theatre? Location decisions may be relevant – is the resort hotel under the approach flight path to the local airport? Noise should also be taken into consideration when deciding on an appropriate layout of a building. For example, the hotel disco should be located as far away from the bedrooms as possible.

Control of noise emitted by customers and which affects other customers is more difficult to control. Pre-selection and 'training' of customers are two ways which can help to minimize possible undesirable noisy behaviour.

Smell

The smell of freshly baked bread or freshly ground coffee has a very positive appeal to many people. In contrast, many people find the smell of cigarette smoking obnoxious. Once again, however, the service provider must recognize that all customers will perceive odours in different ways. Smoking, in particular, causes problems. In some countries, smoking in public places is prohibited. This is fine for the non-smoker, but for the 50-cigarettes-a-day smoker, having to refrain from smoking on a flight lasting two hours or more can be very uncomfortable, particularly if he or she is anxious about flying. Grandjean (1988) states that:

> Calculation showed that *a fresh air supply of 33 m³/h and per smoked cigarette is necessary to keep the ΔCO concentration below the proposed upper limit of 2.0 ppm; for the lower limit, 50 m³/h of fresh air per smoked cigarette are required.* Depending on the number of people present in a room, a fresh air supply of 25–45 m³/h/person is necessary in order not to exceed the upper limit. In other words: the ventilation has to be 2–4 times higher than in a room where nobody smokes (in which only 12–15 m³/h/person are required). (p. 328)

The implication of this is that more has to be spent on ventilation to minimize the effect on non-smokers if some customers are to be allowed to smoke. Segregation is one way of trying to minimize the impact. The problem with this is that smoke drifts, and many non-smokers will notice when a cigarette has been lit even if at the opposite side of the room. The smell of smoke also lingers well after the smoker has gone. Hotel bedrooms which have been occupied by smokers previously can be unacceptable to non-smokers. Probably the best answer to this problem is to have totally separate rooms for smokers. However, the actual solution will depend upon the mix of customers and the country in which the service is being provided.

In contrast to this, scents can be used in a very positive way. Movenpick hotels provide essential oils together with an oil burner in some of their hotel rooms. Essential oils are thought to have a variety of effects and have been used for therapy for thousands of years. The aroma from the oils is thought to be able to help create a warming, stimulating, relaxing or uplifting environment. For example, camomile has a refreshing and relaxing effect, while lemon has a refreshing and stimulating effect. The conscious use of aroma in service settings has been very limited in recent years. However, as there has been a growing awareness and popularity of essential oils generally, this state of affairs is likely to change.

Signs, symbols and artefacts

There are two aspects to signs, symbols and artefacts. First, they may help customers to orientate themselves within the service environment, and second, they provide cues about the service being provided.

In terms of orientation, signs indicate where customers should go: for example, in hospitals, signs usually indicate where out-patients should report. They may also be used to instruct customers: for example, in a launderette signs may be used to instruct the customer how to use the washing machine. The effect on the customer's perception of the service can often be negatively affected by the lack of signs, or by ambiguous signs. Getting lost in the railway station and missing a train can be extremely annoying, and of course it is always when the passenger is short of time that clear, prominent signs which are essential in such circumstances are non-existent!

Signs often represent the first encounter that a new customer has with the organization, and influence those 'first impressions' which are so very important. Being able to find the way quickly and without trouble encourages a positive frame of mind. On the other hand, getting lost before the service being sought has even begun is likely to put the customer in a negative frame of mind at the outset, just ready to pounce on the first shortcoming in the service: that is, raising the lower boundary of the zone of tolerance (as discussed in Chapter 6). An example of poor use of signs is the Fort Worth-Dallas Airport, where extra staff had to be employed to help passengers find their way to the bagage reclaim area, as 20 per cent of incoming passengers got lost (Wener, 1985).

Various design aspects of signs are important, and they will affect the visibility, legibility and intelligibility of the message. The orientation of the signs will also have an impact on their ease of use.

Visibility of signs refers to their positioning in such a way that they can easily be seen.

Legibility refers to the clarity of the message on the sign. The distance of the viewer from the sign, the contrast between the sign and the background, illumination, the style of printing used, the length of time that the sign is visible and the familiarity with the message will all affect the legibility of the sign. Data on the size of lettering needed, and the legibility of different letter styles and fonts, are available. Details of spacing between letters and lines for ease of reading are also obtainable. Generally the use of a mix of capitals and lower case has been found to be more legible than all capitals alone.

Intelligibility refers to the sense of the message. The sign itself may be perfectly visible and the shapes distinct, but can the customer understand the message? Signs in foreign languages, although visible and legible, will not help tourists if they do not understand the language. In Bradford, many of the signs in the hospitals and other public service offices are translated into various languages, such as Urdu, Hindi, Gujurati, Punjabi and Bengali.

In services, some customers may be illiterate. Symbols can overcome the language and literacy problems, but are sometimes themselves unclear.

The *orientation* of signs on a wall which take the form of a plan or map, with a little arrow pointing to a 'You are here' message, can be difficult to follow if they are not aligned so that up relates to straight forward. The problem is that most maps or plans are drawn once and then copied. The only difference, once they are in place, is the position of the arrow. The implication of correct orientation is that the writing on the map needs to be typeset according to the final siting of the map, and thus, as multiple versions will be

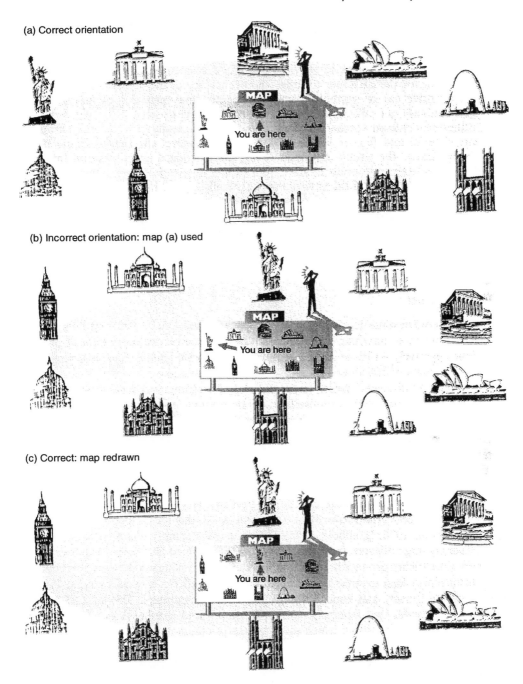

(a) Correct orientation

(b) Incorrect orientation: map (a) used

(c) Correct: map redrawn

Figure 8.9 Orientation of 'you are here' maps

needed, costs of preparation increase. Figure 8.9 illustrates both the correct and incorrect ways of using this type of sign.

Symbols and artefacts may act as cues. As service is intangible, and often there is an expertise gap between the service provider and the customer (e.g. doctor and patient), it is often difficult for the customer to judge the proficiency of the 'expert'. Certificates on walls are a visible cue or symbol of achievement and may provide reassurance to the customer. Similarly, an office lined with bookshelves suggests knowledge, while original oil paintings may indicate success. The style of the décor generally can create an impression of cheap, cheerful and fun, or sedate, serious and expensive, etc. Inappropriate use of artefacts can create the wrong impression completely: leopard skins hung on the office wall would hardly be appropriate in an organization trying to project an image of concern for wildlife and the future of the environment generally.

Artefacts such as paintings, plants and sculptures can also be used in conjunction with the spatial layout to create a type of landmark along a corridor, helping navigation around a building with a symmetrical layout. In such buildings, it is sometimes difficult to tell the difference between floors or corridors. A distinctive plant in the north-west corner of the fifth floor, for example, provides a point of reference when trying to get one's bearings.

Spatial layout

Layout is covered in some depth in Chapter 11 and will therefore be mentioned only briefly here. For a customer, anything which makes receiving the service more difficult is likely to impinge negatively on his or her perception of the service quality. Ease of access, good visibility, proximity of linked services and so on will help to make a customer feel in control of the process. As discussed earlier in the chapter, if a customer is lost, stress levels rise. Unless the whole point of the exercise is to create a sense of mystery and excitement, as in a maze in a theme park perhaps, then one of the main objectives for the design of the layout of the facilities should be to facilitate ease of use for the customer.

Personal space

Linked with spatial layout is the concept of personal space. Every person needs space around them to feel comfortable. If other people enter this space, stress levels will rise (Middlemist *et al.*, 1976; Lundberg, 1976). Personal space comprises four zones, each with an increasingly large distance from the individual. Figure 8.10 illustrates these four zones. Only very close friends can be admitted to zone A without causing psychological discomfort, which in turn may lead to stress and associated physical effects, such as sweating. Zone B is reserved for friends, and zone C for business-type encounters. The limit of zone C represents the closest that strangers can approach without causing discomfort. Zone D extends to that distance within which the presence of others is noted.

The size of the zones varies among people, and in particular among people of different cultures. Touching is much more acceptable in some cultures than in others, which clearly necessitates close proximity. Other variables which affect the size of the different zones are age, personality, sex and status of the individuals involved. When personal space is breached, as is the case in a crowded underground tube in London, or in a lift, coping mechanisms are used: for example, no eye contact is made with the people within the personal space. Commuters will look anywhere but at the person next to them.

A Intimate distance
B Personal distance

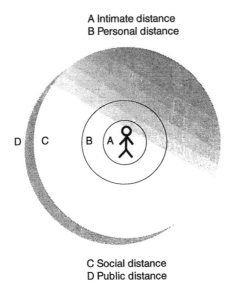

C Social distance
D Public distance

Figure 8.10 Personal space zones (Source: *Ergonomics at Work*, Oborne, D.J. Copyright 1987 John Wiley and Sons Ltd. Reprinted by permission of John Wiley and Sons Ltd)

The implications of this for the design of the service are to recognize that expecting customers to share their 'space' with others will lead to increased stress levels and is likely to have a negative impact on their perception of the service received, or at least make them feel uncomfortable. This can be used to some advantage if the aim is to encourage customers to vacate tables quickly, as in a fast-food restaurant, or when the aim is to arouse, as in exciting/scary experiences. However, if the aim is to create a relaxing atmosphere, crowding must be avoided.

Psychology of queuing

Queuing is inevitable whenever spare capacity is not available to meet demand when it occurs. Over a period, capacity is likely to exceed demand, but unless demand is constant and only occurs when an organization is open, queues will form. For example, in the National Health Service in the summer months, there is excess capacity of intensive care beds for children. However, in the winter months, demand often exceeds supply and a search has to be made of other hospitals to find an empty bed. The cost of equipping and staffing such a bed is in the region of £250,000 per year, and therefore maintaining excess capacity for a large part of the year cannot be undertaken lightly. However, the cost of having insufficient intensive care beds, necessitating critically ill children to wait/queue for a bed is likely to be loss of life.

All organizations face this trade-off. Providing sufficient capacity to prevent queues involves the cost of paying for resources which will be idle for considerable periods. The cost of not having sufficient capacity is, in the case of services, dissatisifed customers. The longer a customer waits, the greater the dissatisfaction, and ultimately custom will be lost to competitors, because the customer (1) leaves the queue before being served, (2) stays in the queue this time, but decides never to return and/or (3) tells others and influences their choice of organization.

Decisions which will affect capacity are dealt with in Chapter 12. However, the psychology of queuing, which will be covered here, concerns factors which will affect customers' perceptions of the queuing experience. Often the perceived time of waiting is inaccurate, but it is the perceptions which will affect customer satisfaction, so that customer *perceptions* of the queuing time are more important than *actual* time. In a study by Katz *et al.* (1991), customers at a bank were videoed and the length spent in the queue was timed. On leaving the bank, these customers were asked how long they had queued. On average, the time spent in the queue was 4.2 minutes, but the average perceived time was 5.1 minutes.

Further work by Katz *et al.* found that informing customers of the expected length of wait could prove negative if the estimated time was an underestimate, in which case customers became more infuriated because 'You said it would be 20 minutes, and I've been here 30 minutes!' In some cases, if the queuing experience is managed very well, and the time of the queuing customers is enjoyably occupied with some diversion or entertainment, advertising the expected waiting time can also be negative, as it draws attention to the time wasted queuing. On the other hand, advising customers of the expected length of delay provides a measure of control for the customer: for example, at an airport, a customer who knows that there will be a 20 minute delay may decide that she has time to go to the snack bar and have another coffee. Had she not been informed, uncertainty would have occurred and she would not have had that extra coffee, in case she was called to the departure gate. This would have made the queuing time *seem* much longer. Care therefore has to be taken when advising customers of the expected waiting time.

Yalch and Spangenberg (1988) found that, when background music was played, unfamiliarity with the music increased the perception of time spent shopping. It is posited that the same effect will also apply to perceived time spent in a queue.

Maister (1985) also examined the factors which influence perceived waiting time. Figure 8.11 presents a summary of the factors which have materialized from the research of Maister and Katz *et al.* which affect customers' perceptions of queuing, and the posited link to the work of Yalch and Spangenberg.

Body language and communication

One of the ways to try and standardize the service provided is to prepare 'scripts' for employees to follow. These may be quite detailed or simply provide an outline. For example, telephone sales operators are often trained to follow a script, with the exact opening lines and follow-up questions being predefined. In fast-food restaurants, the opening and closing lines that the server has to use may be prescribed. However, 'Have a nice day' can become an irritant to customers who perceive the lines as stilted and false. The reason why customers often feel that the words spoken are not meant is because the accompanying body language is conveying another message.

1. Unoccupied time feels longer than occupied time and increased distractions make the waiting experience more interesting and tend to increase customer satisfaction.
2. Pre-process waits feel longer than in-process waits.
3. Anxiety makes waits seem longer.
4. Uncertain waits are longer than known, finite waits.
5. Unexplained waits are longer than explained waits.
6. Unfair waits are longer than equitable waits: can newcomers push in front of customers who arrived before them?
7. The more valuable the service, the longer people will wait. Can the service be obtained elsewhere?
8. Solo waiting feels longer than group waiting.
9. Customer attitudes: what time pressures do customers face?
10. Environment: is waiting comfortable? Does the customer have to freeze in the cold or bake in the sun?
11. Unused facilities and idle staff who are not attending to waiting customers increase annoyance of those customers.
12. Unfamiliar music makes the perceived time spent in activities seem longer than when familiar music is played in the background.

Figure 8.11 Factors affecting perceptions of queuing time (Sources: Adapted from Maister, 1985; Katz *et al.*, 1991; Yalch and Spangenburg, 1988)

Body language, which includes facial expression and bodily positioning, conveys emotion or attitude. Spoken language conveys information, although the way something is said can also convey emotion. Greeting a customer or thanking a customer without making eye contact or smiling will not have the effect that management would like the lines to have. It is relatively easy to tell employees to learn a script, but it is far more difficult to foster the desired body language.

Training is needed here, but as such interpersonal behaviour is a skill, it cannot be learnt without practice and feedback. This form of training is time consuming and costly. More often than not, it is not provided, as front-line serving staff are frequently part time or temporary, and such an investment is not perceived to be justified. A well-known exception to this is Disneyland, where even the street cleaners undergo a week's training before being allowed exposure to the public (Miller, 1992).

Conclusion

Most of this chapter has focused on factors relating to the supporting facilities of a service. The issues discussed here are often neglected and go unmanaged. What is frequently not recognized is the direct role that the supporting facility has in the intangible service provided, and the influence that the supporting facilities play in creating the experience of the customer. This is evidence of a lack of understanding of the service package and of the importance of *all* the elements.

Other aspects of the service which must be specified include the technical aspects. However, these will tend to be context specific. For example, in a teaching context, the breadth and depth of material covered should be clearly specified, together with mode of delivery, etc. The role of the students should also be clearly specified. What, how, by whom and when all need to be defined.

It is difficult to separate the *product* from the *process* in services. Writing a specification for a service often cannot be divorced from the specification of the process. Additional parameters which will need formal specification may therefore relate to location, transportation, process design and so on. These additional features are examined in Part IV of the book.

References

Bitner, M.J. (1992) 'Servicescapes: the impact of physical surroundings on customers and employees', *Journal of Marketing*, vol. 56, no. 2, pp. 57–71.

Cumming, R. and T. Porter (1990) *The Colour Eye*, BBC Books, London.

Grandjean, E. (1988) *Fitting the Task to the Man*, Taylor and Francis, London.

Grönroos, C. (1984) 'A service quality model and its marketing implications', *European Journal of Marketing*, vol. 18, no. 4, pp. 36–44.

Heizer, J. and B. Render (1988) *Production and Operations Management* (international student edition), Allyn and Bacon, Boston, MA.

Katz, K.L., B.M. Larson and R.C. Larson (1991) 'Prescription for the waiting-in-line blues: entertain, enlighten and engage', *Sloan Management Review*, Winter, pp. 44–53.

Lundberg, U. (1976) 'Urban commuting: crowdedness and catecholamine excretion', *Journal of Human Stress*, vol. 2, pp. 36–42.

Maister, D.H. (1985) 'The psychology of waiting lines', in J.A. Czepiel, M.R. Soloman and C.F. Surprenant (eds.), *The Service Encounter: Managing employee/customer interactions in service businesses*, Lexington Books, Lexington, MA.

Meredith, J.R. (1987) *The Management of Operations* (3rd edn), Wiley, New York.

Middlemist, R.D., E.S. Knowles and C.F. Mutter (1976) 'Personal space invasions in the lavatory: suggestive evidence for arousal', *Journal of Personality and Social Psychology*, vol. 33, pp. 541–6.

Miller, B.W. (1992) 'It's a kind of magic', *Managing Service Quality*, vol. 2, no. 4, pp. 191–3.

Mudie, P. and A. Cottam (1993) *The Management and Marketing of Services*, Butterworth-Heinemann, Oxford.

Oborne, D.J. (1987) *Ergonomics at Work* (2nd edn), Wiley, Chichester.

Pheasant, S. (1986) *Bodyspace*, Taylor and Francis, London.

Roberts, D.F. (1975) 'Population differences in dimensions, their genetic basis and their relevance to practical problems of design', in A. Chapanis (ed.), *Ethnic Variables in Human Factors Engineering*, John Hopkins University Press, Baltimore, MD.

Roethlisberger, F.J. and W.J. Dickson (1939) *Management and the Worker*, Harvard University Press, Cambridge, MA.

Slack, N., S. Chambers, C. Harland, A. Harrison and R. Johnston (1995) *Operations Management*, Pitman, London.

Wener, R.E. (1985) 'The environmental psychology of service encounters', in J.A. Czepiel, M.R. Soloman and C.F. Surprenant (eds.), *The Service Encounter: Managing employee/customer interactions in service businesses*, Lexington Books, Lexington, MA.

Yalch, R.F. and E. Spangenberg (1988) 'An environmental psychological study of foreground and background music as retail atmospheric factors', in G. Frazier, C. Ingene, D. Aaker, A. Ghosh, T. Kinnear, S. Levy, R. Staelin and J. Summers (eds.), *Efficiency and Effectiveness in Marketing: 1988 AMA Educators' Proceedings*, American Marketing Association, Chicago, IL.

Discussion topics/exercises

1. Critically assess a lecture theatre in terms of the supporting facilities. What aspects of the design enhance the service provided, and which need improvement?

2. What factors would you consider in the design of an 'up-market' restaurant? How would these differ from a 'fast-food' restaurant?

3. Should customers ever have to queue, or should there always be adequate capacity to meet demand at all times? How can queues be managed to minimize any negative consequences of queuing?

4. Think of ways that body language can be used to convey a message to a customer. Consider situations where you have not believed what the server was saying. Why did you disbelieve them?

Part IV

Delivery issues

Chapter 9

Location decision making

Chapter outline

☆ Context of the location decision
☆ Two-stage approach
☆ Conceptual model of retail location drivers
☆ Rule of retail compatibility
☆ Reilly's law of retail gravity
☆ Spatial interaction models
☆ Regression analysis models
☆ Checklists and analogs

The context of the location decision

The location decision can be one of the key strategic decisions facing an organization. Indeed, in Chapter 4 it was identified as one of the four Ps of the marketing mix: place. It is an area where marketing and operations specialists must work closely together to ensure that all relevant factors are considered, and that the final decision is in the long-term interests of the organization. It is the long-term implications of such decisions and the significant financial aspects which in part indicate the fact that location decisions are generally strategic in nature. They thus involve not only operations and marketing (as mentioned earlier), but also the other functions within the organization: accounting/finance, human resources and information (communications). It is important that such decisions are consistent with and support the corporate strategy of the enterprise.

Location decisions can arise for a whole range of reasons. Probably that which most readily comes to mind is the new business start. Someone working for a hairdresser decides to 'go it alone'. He looks for premises which he can afford, close to a (hopefully) large group of potential customers. A local entrepreneur decides to start a 'local bus service' – where should this be based and what routes should be covered? (Which of these is in fact the location decision?). The routes will be determined, in part, by existing provision of transportation services, local demand and costs. The base will depend on which routes are offered and the availability and costs of space, buildings and equipment to garage and maintain the buses.

A second type of location decision is to relocate an existing business. The existing location may have become unsuitable because of size. Thus the school, admitting increasing numbers of students, perhaps being unable to expand because land is not available adjacent to existing buildings, may choose to relocate to a new site which has provision for playing fields as well as the extra buildings required. Factors of importance here could be land availability and costs, building costs, and existing and future population figures by area to predict student numbers. A multiple store might have occupied a prime high street site. However, a city centre redevelopment could have taken place involving a central pedestrian area, resulting in the store being left on a busy road used by through traffic. Clearly, to remain viable the store will need to relocate. A factor of importance in selecting a site in this case will be the location of competitors.

A third cause of the location decision is an expansion of existing operations, linked to the identification of a 'business opportunity'. The owner of a successful French restaurant in an up-market area of Bradford may decide to open a second restaurant in a similar type of area in Leeds. A factor of importance will be the ability to find a second chef able to create the attractive cuisine which contributed to the success of the first restaurant. An organization which has a chain of 'travel lodges' is looking to expand the network. Clearly a location is required which is on or very near to a major road network (perhaps even on a motorway service area). A food supermarket chain is seeking to expand its set of outlets. It has chosen to move outside its existing geographic area. It might be looking for a location on a retail park with other complementary (rather than competing) outlets, such as electrical household appliances, discount footwear and clothing.

Location decisions arise in all environments. However, one of the core characteristics of services, the high customer contact, means that the location decision is even more important in this type of environment. This is, in part, because the high levels of customer focus necessary for a successful service, linked to the frequent perishability of services (discussed in Chapter 2 as part of SHIP), mean that location is of strategic importance to the typical service firm.

In a service encounter, the service provider can be regarded as being in the 'middle', linked forwards to the customers, and backwards to suppliers of 'materials' to support the delivery of the service.

In a retailing situation, the service provider is normally a shop or store of some type, and there might be several direct links back up the supply chain, involving warehouses and manufacturers of the products/services which are being sold or provided. This can raise a second set of decisions associated with the location: the 'best' way to handle this distribution. This can become a significant issue when the service provider is part of a chain of branches and there are multiple suppliers. Consider the decisions which must be made in organizing the supply and delivery of perishable food stuffs to a supermarket chain (for example, Sainsbury, ASDA or Marks and Spencer).

Some of these distribution problems are considered in Chapter 10. In non-retail service situations, provision of the 'support materials' can become of less importance and can be regarded as part of the purchasing function of the organization, the restaurant purchasing its ingredients for meals to be served, the hotel purchasing the 'toiletries' (soap, shampoo and so on) to be put in the bathrooms. There are many texts which give a comprehensive coverage of this topic (e.g. Bailey *et al.*, 1994).

The involvement of the customer in the process and the perishable nature of the service mean that the links between service provider and customer can be crucial. These links may involve physical movement in either direction (patients go to hospital, students to college and travellers to the airport, but a general practitioner may visit a patient at home, a service engineer will repair the boiler in the house, and a fire engine will attend a factory fire). The relative locations of the service provider and customer in all these cases can have a significant impact on the level or 'quality' of the service which is experienced by the customer.

It is important, however, not to overlook the impact of communications technology on these aspects. Voice links via telephone lines can be used effectively to provide information services and general fault diagnosis. These can be and are being extended to video phone and through computers to electronic mail (e-mail). The effect of the location of the service provider in these cases can be reduced, and it can be diminished still further by the use of the Telecom facility to dial a number and be charged the lowest (local) call rate, irrespective of the location of the recipient of the call. A computer manufacturer could provide a telephone helpline service based in the north of England, yet all users, irrespective of location, could be charged at the lowest call rate, even if phoning from the south. Thus the actual location of the base becomes less important.

It is clear that there is a whole range of inputs into the location decision. These are sourced within the organization, from the external environment and from professional agencies. Some of them are illustrated in Figure 9.1, which shows not only the source of these inputs to the decision, but also some of the relationships among the different sources. Thus the marketing department of the supermarket chain might approach a 'local' independent market research consultancy in an area being considered, for information concerning the locations and purchasing patterns of inhabitants (potential customers). The accounting/finance group within the organization will get information concerning land availabilities and costs from local estate agencies, and will approach central and local government departments for information about local financial incentives to develop in the particular area. The relative importance of the information and its impact on the decision will clearly vary from situation to situation. For the location of a theme park, weather will be a factor; for a hospital it might be proximity of patients, for a hotel, convenience for the city centre; for a mail order distribution centre, a good road network. As will be seen later, a comprehensive list of possible factors can be a starting point to the decision process.

Of the examples described earlier, a large number (although not all) are in the retail sector. As a consequence, most texts on retail management include at least one chapter on this important decision-making area (see, for example, McGoldrick, 1990; Mason and Mayer, 1990). Clearly, the factors of importance and approaches taken will depend on the nature of the retail outlets, which can include superstores (food, clothes, furniture, electrical, mixed), discount stores, specialist shops, franchise operations and so on. Sometimes benefit can be gained by classifying the different types of outlet by their key features (e.g. size, target market). However, there is no really unique, universal scheme which assists significantly the location decision-making process.

In the next section, some basic concepts will be introduced which help clarify the location decision-making process. They will be followed by some examples of the key models which can be used by planners.

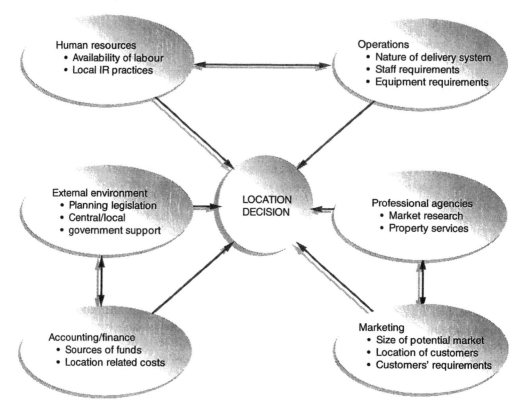

Figure 9.1 Some of the involvements of the different functions and agencies in the location decision

Concepts supporting location decision making

A two-stage approach

Schmenner (1994) suggested a two-stage approach to the service location decision. The first-level decision concerns the general geographic area in which the 'service provider' is to be based, while the second-level decision involves the selection of the particular site, in a sense dividing the decision into macro- and micro-level considerations. Thus the supermarket chain seeking to expand its network of outlets might identify geographic areas in which it does not currently trade. These might then be examined from a variety of perspectives, including the size and profile of the potential market. In the evaluation and selection of the area, first the essential features and then the desirable features are considered. For those areas 'selected' for further development, the next decision will involve the selection of an appropriate site. This site selection decision might be made from a finite range of identified potential sites or based on a 'blank map' of the area. Again the site evaluation might be carried out against both essential and desirable features.

Thus an essential feature of the geographical area for the supermarket might be the availability of development grants from central government, while a desirable feature might be a favourable attitude towards development from the local authorities. At the site level, an essential feature might be the proximity of complementary retail outlets, and a desirable feature could be easy access to a good road transport system.

The scheme described presupposes that the decisions at the two levels can be 'decoupled' and considered separately. While this simplifies the decision-making process, it need not always be the case. There may well be trade-offs between the factors at the two different levels. For example, the lack of availability of attractive business property tax rates within a particular area might be compensated for by cheap land or rental rates for a particular site.

Clearly, with this approach it is helpful to identify an appropriate and comprehensive list of factors from which to select, together with a suitable method for evaluation and selection. Some of the ways of tackling these issues will be outlined later in this chapter. A key issue in this process is measurement. While some issues, like tax incentive schemes, are readily quantifiable, others are far more subjective and involve softer issues: for example, the view of the local population about a particular development. However, if they are important, it is possible to collect relevant data about a number of these less easily quantified aspects, for instance by attitude surveys.

A conceptual model of retail location drivers

Davies and Clarke (1994) present a model of some of the key factors which can be thought of as driving the retail location decision. This is shown in Figure 9.2. They divide the decision along a number of dimensions. One such dimension has *convenience* at one end, identifying with products which in some sense need replenishing ('consumable' goods, like petrol and perishable foods), and *comparison* at the other, where the consumer is likely to want to examine a range of products possibly sold at more than one outlet (e.g. durables like clothes and electrical equipment). They suggest that at the 'comparison' end of the spectrum behaviour is in some way *leisure* driven, while at the 'convenience' end *time* is an important factor. The second dimension relates to the size of the product, which can range from bulky to portable. This gives rise to four types of location: solus or free-standing outlets, retail parks, high street/town centre outlets, and parades of outlets in peripheral centres.

Figure 9.2 also summarizes the key factors, split into primary and secondary, for each of these types of outlet. Thus for free-standing (solus) outlets (e.g. a store specializing in pine furniture for the whole house), ease of access is important, while the extent of the competition is less crucial. For shopping parades (e.g. a fish and chip shop), the geodemographic profile of the local population is likely to be an important consideration in evaluating the performance of such an outlet. For an outlet in a retail park (e.g. a store selling domestic electrical equipment), the number of competitors, indicating the range of choice, is likely to be more important than the geodemographic profile of the local population. For the high street outlet (e.g. a chemist), the variety in other outlets is likely to be an important influence. This model is described and illustrated in more detail in Davies and Clarke (1994).

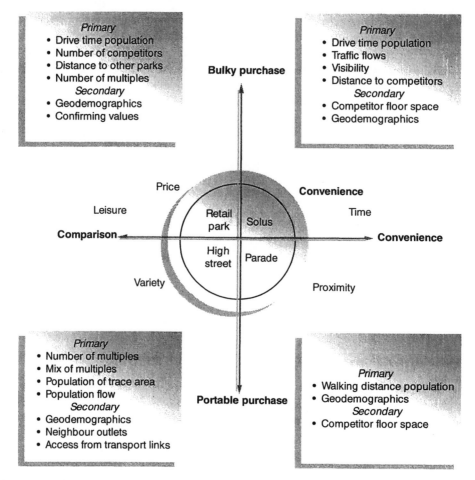

Figure 9.2 A conceptual model of retail location drivers (Source: Davies and Clarke, 1994, p. 7)

It is interesting to note how a number of retail chains have adapted to operate in more than one type of location. Davies and Clarke (1994) quote the example of Marks and Spencer, which operates very effectively both in the high street and on retail parks, although altering its offering (for example, the balance between food, clothes and soft furnishing) according to the location. The important aspect is that the location decision should be seen as part of the retailing strategy of the organization. The model helps organizations formally consider the four broad options and identify and understand the factors influencing the choice.

The rule of retail compatibility

Mason and Mayer (1990) describe some work completed by Nelson (1958), examining the influences that two compatible outlets have on each other's overall business. This work was based on an analysis of 10,000 consumer shopping trips. These influences can have a significant impact on the location decision. The concepts of generative, shared and suscipient business were introduced to help explain the various relationships.

Generative business is that which an outlet generates through significant advertising or other related means. It is suggested that an organization that generates all of its own business needs an exceptional location.

Shared business is obtained by an outlet as a result of the 'traffic-generating' power of its neighbours. The tobacco shop in the busy shopping centre relies on this type of business. Indeed, the traffic-generating power of outlets is key to the concept of the 'anchor tenant': big name retailers which will draw potential customers to a shopping area (examples are Marks and Spencer and British Home Stores). The existence and location of these anchor tenants can be key to the development of retail parks and high street areas.

Suscipient business is when customers use an outlet even when their reasons for being in the area are other than for purchasing. An example is the 'boutiques' found on board ferry-boats and at airports.

The rule of retail compatibility, as developed by Mason and Mayer (1990), states that when two compatible businesses are located close to each other, there will be an increase in business volume which is proportional to:

- the extent of total customer interchange between them;
- the sum of the ratios of purposeful purchasing; and
- the ratio of the business volume of the smaller and larger store.

Thus:

$$IV = DI\,(TV_L + TV_s)\,\frac{TV_s}{TV_L}\left\{\frac{PP_L}{TV_L} + \frac{PP_s}{TV_s}\right\}$$

where:

IV = increase in volume of purchases
DI = degree of interchange of customers between the outlets
TV_L = total volume of retail sales for the larger outlet
TV_s = total volume of retail sales for the smaller outlet
PP_L = volume of purposeful purchasing at the larger outlet
PP_s = volume of purposeful purchasing at the smaller outlet.

Consider a large department store with annual retail sales of £12.5 million, and a small specialist clothes retailer 'next door' with sales of £850 000. From surveys and other sources, it is estimated that the degree of interchange is one customer in ten, while the purposeful purchasing in the department store is 60 per cent, and in the clothes shop is 90 per cent. The application of the rule shows an estimated increase in volume of the order of:

$$0.1\,(12.5 + 0.85)\,\frac{0.85}{12.5}\,(0.6 + 0.9)$$

$$= 0.13617, \text{ or just under } £140,000$$

Reilly's law of retail gravity

While the previous rule examined the added benefit to be gained by the close proximity of two compatible outlets, Reilly's law proposes the limits of the attraction of one shopping centre in relation to its distance (in miles) from a second. As the analogy with gravitational forces suggests, as a consumer gets further from one shopping centre and closer to a second, the attraction of the first centre gets less. It is assumed that the populations of the communities in which the centres are based and the distance between the two centres are key factors in this relationship. (This result was based on an empirical study, and it was claimed that this could be interpreted as a form of regression: the break-even point as dependent variable determined as a function of the population and distance – the independent variables.)

The law provides a formula for calculating that point at which a consumer is indifferent to the choice of shopping centre A or centre B (Figure 9.3). This point is found as follows:

$$\text{Distance of point of indifference from A} = \frac{\text{Distance from A to B}}{1 + \sqrt{\dfrac{\text{Population of B}}{\text{Population of A}}}}$$

For illustration, suppose A has a population of 200,000 and B a population of 320,000, and that they are 15 miles apart. Reilly's law states that the point/line of indifference is at:

$$\frac{15}{1 + \sqrt{\dfrac{320,000}{200,000}}} \text{ miles from A}$$

i.e. 6.62 miles from A, or:

$$\frac{15}{1 + \sqrt{\dfrac{200,000}{320,000}}} \text{ miles from B}$$

i.e. 8.38 miles from B.

Jones (1989) suggests how this approach can be extended to more than two centres by looking at all the neighbouring centres around the one of interest, and establishing its catchment area. This is obtained by linking the points of indifference obtained by considering the centre of interest with each neighbouring centre in turn.

One of the criticisms of the approach is the use of population to measure the 'attractiveness' of the centres. Alternatives to this suggested by Jones (1989) involve identifying other factors which measure attractiveness (e.g. range of shops, parking facilities), weighting these for importance, scoring the two centres for the measures and using the weighted scores instead of the population figures. The use of scoring methods generally will be considered again later in the chapter.

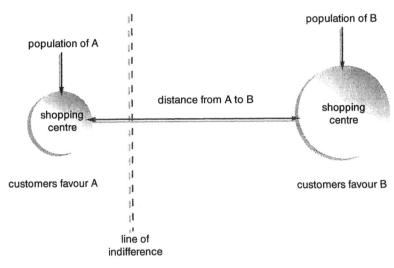

Figure 9.3 Reilly's law of retail gravity

Basic location models

A variety of approaches have been adopted to the location decision-making process. This section will present and review some of these. The interested reader can find examples of the more recent, but possibly untested models in such journals as the *Journal of Retailing* and the *International Journal of Retail and Distribution Management*.

The approaches can be broadly grouped into a number of sets:

- Gravity models, sometimes also referred to as spatial interaction models.
- Regression analysis models.
- Checklists and analogues.

The first two sets of approaches are frequently grouped together and classified as mathematical modelling of the situation, and it is in this broad area that much of the current research is taking place.

It is interesting to note the approaches which have been adopted by retailers. Simkin (1989) reports on a comprehensive study involving a mail questionnaire of 200 retailers with large (30 +) branch networks, complemented by 40 in-depth interviews. His results in terms of the techniques adopted by UK multiple retailers are presented in Table 9.1. There is still a high reliance on checklists and intuition, although there is some evidence that some of the larger retailers are adopting more sophisticated approaches.

Gravity or spatial interaction models

These are based on the law of retail gravity developed by Reilly and described earlier. The basic principle behind these models is that movement of customers attracted to a particular

Table 9.1 Results of a survey of assessment techniques used by retailers

Type	Assessment technique
Department stores	Checklists and financial appraisal
Variety stores	Checklists and analogs
Out-of-town warehouses	Analogs based on checklists
Grocery superstores	Analogs based on regression
Larger company multiples (high street)	Intuition/gut feeling and analogs
Small company multiples	Intuition/gut feeling
Convenience stores	Intuition and analogs
Financial outlets	Intuition/gut feeling

Source: Reprinted from *Omega*, vol. 17, Simkin, L.P., 'SLAM: Store Location Assessment Model – theory and practice', pp. 55–8, 1989, with kind permission from Elsevier Science Ltd, The Boulevard, Langford Lane, Kidlington, OX5 1GB, UK.

retail outlet is inversely proportional to distance and directly proportional to the attraction of the outlet (frequently measured by its size). It is claimed that the general principles of spatial interaction are widely accepted (McGoldrick, 1990). While these models can be used as part of the process of evaluating a location, they can also be used more broadly as part of a simulation to predict the impact of expanding the size of an outlet, or the possible consequences of a new outlet on an existing outlet.

Probably the most widely quoted model is that developed by Huff. Ghosh and Craig (1983) describe this model as stating that 'the probability of any individual choosing a particular retail store is equal to the ratio of the utility of that store to the sum of the utilities of all the other stores that the individual considers' (p. 57). In this context the utility is considered to be dependent on the size of the store and the distance between the individual customers and the stores. Expressing this relationship in mathematical terms:

$$P_{ij} = \frac{\dfrac{S_j}{D_{ij}^{\beta}}}{\displaystyle\sum_{k=1}^{n} \dfrac{S_k}{D_{ik}^{\beta}}}$$

where:

P_{ij} is the probability that an individual in zone i ($i = 1, \ldots, m$) will travel and shop in facility j ($j = 1, \ldots, n$).
S_j is the size of shopping facility j
D_{ik} is the distance or travel time between zone i and shopping facility k
m is the number of zones
n is the number of shopping facilities
β is a parameter which has to be estimated empirically.

The parameter β reflects the influence of travelling time on various types of product purchase, and it is suggested that it might lie between 0.5 and 3.0, taking larger values for convenience goods and where distance has a major impact: for example, shopping for food (Jones and Simmons, 1990).

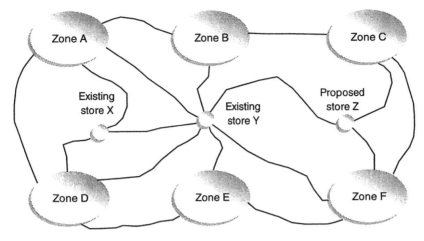

Figure 9.4 Site selection problem

This model can be used to support a variety of decisions, including that involving the selection of an appropriate site for a new store. The following example will illustrate the process.

Currently two major supermarkets located at X and Y provide a service for six small towns/zones (A, B, C, D, E and F). A national supermarket chain is considering opening a new store at location Z. These locations, together with some of the major roads, are shown in Figure 9.4.

Some data concerning the stores are presented in Table 9.2. This shows their travelling distances from the six towns, the floor area of the existing stores and that proposed for the new store, and the populations of the towns. Since distance has a significant, but not dominant impact and the stores are dealing largely in convenience foods, a value for β of 2 will be taken (a detailed discussion of more comprehensive methods for estimating β is given in Jones and Simmons (1990)).

Table 9.2 Data for the site selection problem

Zone	Population	Distance in km to shopping facility		
		X	Y	Z
A	20 000	10	15	20
B	30 000	20	10	15
C	25 000	20	10	5
D	40 000	15	15	20
E	15 000	20	10	15
F	20 000	15	5	5
Floor area (sq. metres)		1500	2500	3000

The first step in the analysis is the calculation of the probabilities. The probability that an individual from town A will shop in facility X is given by:

$$\frac{\dfrac{1500}{10^2}}{\dfrac{1500}{10^2} + \dfrac{2500}{15^2} + \dfrac{3000}{20^2}} = 0.446$$

The remaining probabilities are shown in Table 9.3. It is then possible to explore in more detail the potential sales revenue. The starting point is the population (or households) in each town and the average expenditure per household (Jones and Simmons (1990) discuss how this can be estimated). Simply multiplying the probability figures in Table 9.3 by the population gives estimates of the potential customers visiting each shopping facility. Thus, for example, the potential customers from zone A to facilities X, Y and Z are 8.92, 6.62 and 4.46 respectively (in 000s). This gives the organization the opportunity to evaluate the proposed site in terms of its sales potential (particularly if there are estimates of the sales per potential customer). Mason and Mayer (1990) discuss some of the other analysis which can be carried out to explore the potential of different sites.

Table 9.3 Probability values

From town	To shopping facility		
	Existing X	Existing Y	Proposed Z
A	0.446	0.331	0.223
B	0.089	0.594	0.317
C	0.025	0.168	0.807
D	0.264	0.440	0.297
E	0.089	0.594	0.317
F	0.029	0.441	0.529

The model is perhaps best set up using a spreadsheet. It is then possible to investigate the alternative scenarios very quickly. A second proposed site can be considered simply by altering the appropriate distances from the six towns. Trade-offs between the extra sales generated at the shopping facility by increasing the sales area and the cost of this extra sales area can be evaluated. This is illustrated in Figure 9.5, where a range of possible sizes for the proposed store at Z are presented.

It is worth noting that it also shows the impact on the potential customers visiting the two other facilities. It is also possible to test the sensitivity of the model to the other input parameters: for example, the travelling time parameter, β. Again, having set up the model on a spreadsheet makes these analyses rapid and very easy to complete.

A number of developments have been made to this basic model to enhance its potential and to attempt to make it a better fit to reality. Descriptions of some of these can be found in the references at the end of the chapter (see, for example, McGoldrick, 1990). However, generally these require more data, which are not necessarily easy to collect, and a level of

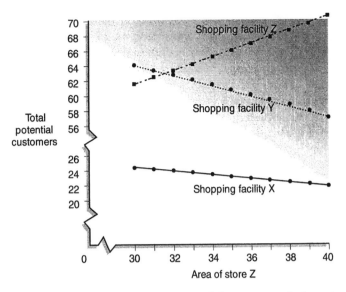

Figure 9.5 Impact of increasing the area of the proposed shopping facility

sophistication which the practitioner may find difficult to understand. This often presents a barrier to the application in practice.

Regression analysis models

These are not dissimilar to the spatial interaction models, in that they attempt to predict store performance. Thus they can be used as part of the process by which a store location is assessed.

Normally, regression models are used to predict store turnover, which is the dependent variable, considered to be a linear function of a number of independent variables which will be used as part of the forecasting process. Thus store turnover might be considered dependent on the sales area of the store, the number of competitors, the cost of parking, the population size in the catchment area, and so on. The general form of this model is as follows:

$$Y = a_0 + a_1 x_1 + a_2 x_2 + a_3 x_3 + \ldots + a_n x_n + \varepsilon$$

where:

y = the estimated turnover
x_i = the ith independent variable
a_i = a constant, the coefficient of the ith independent variable
a_0 = a constant
ε = an error term.

It is likely that the set of independent variables and their relative importance will vary with store type. Simkin (1989) reports on the criteria used in a survey of retailers' practices. These are shown in Table 9.4. Thus for a department store 'competition' might be one of the main factors, while for a grocery superstore 'accessibility' might be a key issue. Simkin (1989) groups these factors into five categories: competition, trading area composition, store accessibility, store characteristics and catchment demographics. Some of the information from which to select likely independent variables which could be derived from this set is presented in Figure 9.6.

Table 9.4 Factors in assessing store location

Type of store	Location factors
Department stores	Competition Demographics Local economy Site size and characteristics
Variety stores	Population size Presence of variety stores Site size Turnover threshold
Out-of-town warehouses	Accessibility Road layout Competition Population size Planning permission Site size
Grocery superstores	Accessibility Road layout Competition Population size by drive time Planning permission
Large and small high-street multiples	Location of key traders Prime pitch Pedestrian flow Population size Turnover
Convenience stores	Site prominence Pedestrian and traffic flow Competition
Financial outlets	Business structure of area Planning permission Success of agencies

Source: Reprinted from *Omega*, vol. 17, Simkin, L.,P., 'SLAM: Store Location Assessment Model – theory and practice', pp. 55–8, 1989, with kind permission from Elsevier Science Ltd, The Boulevard, Langford Lane, Kidlington, Oxford, OX5 1GB, UK.

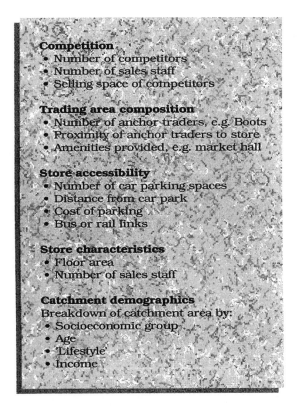

Figure 9.6 Store turnover indicator factors (Source: Reprinted from *Omega*, vol. 17, Simkin, L.P., 'SLAM: Store Location Assessment Model – theory and practice', pp. 55–8, 1989, with kind permission from Elsevier Science Ltd, The Boulevard, Langford Land, Kidlington, OX5 1GB, UK)

The first step in using multiple regression is to establish the likely set of dependent variables. Simkin (1989) describes a process whereby discussions with retail managers can be used for this step, and might give rise to as many as 60–70 potential independent variables. These must be refined down into those which are likely to be relevant for the particular store type under consideration. Data on these parameters must then be collected from existing stores of this type. Suppose interest were focused on a city centre department store, and the independent variables were identified as follows:

- Selling space of competitors in city centre.
- Number of anchor traders.
- Distance from car park.
- Floor area of actual store.
- Average income in catchment area of city centre/store.

For illustrative purposes, one variable only has been selected from each of the headings in Figure 9.6. The format of the data is shown in Table 9.5. This includes not only the five independent variables, but also the dependent variable: store turnover.

Table 9.5 Data from existing stores

Store	Competitors' selling space (m²)	No. of anchor traders (units)	Distance from car park (m)	Floor area of store (m²)	Average income (£)	Store turnover (£)
A	4200	4	100	1100	15 500	101 000
B	2480	5	50	1320	20 000	192 000
C	1350	2	20	1520	11 300	184 000
D	1580	4	90	1240	13 000	164 000
E	4500	2	50	990	16 000	91 000
F	3200	4	20	1520	14 300	166 000
G	2310	5	10	1140	15 000	152 000
H	1980	2	20	1450	12 700	171 000
I	1530	5	60	1230	13 800	162 000
J	1420	3	40	1890	14 700	800 000
K	3200	5	20	1420	15 600	161 000
L	2300	4	40	1500	13 400	176 000
M	1200	2	70	1270	12 900	171 000
N	1580	1	10	1420	11 200	171 000
O	1990	3	30	1390	12 000	162 000

Normally, these data would be split into two sets: one set to estimate the parameters (the values for $a_0, a_1, a_2, a_3, a_4, a_5$ in the earlier equation) and the second set to validate the model (to test how well it forecasts the store turnover figures with these values of a_i and this second set of stores). It has been suggested (McGoldrick, 1990) that six stores (sets of observations) are required for each variable in the model.

A stepwise approach is often adopted, whereby the independent variables are added into the model one at a time, with those contributing the largest amount toward the dependent variable joining first. The process stops when the remaining variables contribute negligibly. Most statistical texts describe in detail the process by which multiple regression can be applied to the above type of situation, and there are many computer programs which will perform the analysis given data in the format specified in Table 9.5. The key output, the regression equation, might resemble the following:

Store turnover = 12 407
$-$ 21.6 × Floor space of competitors
$+$ 4.56 × Number of anchor stores
$-$ 12.6 × Distance from car park
$+$ 96.2 × Floor space of store itself
$+$ 5.1 × Average income of potential customer

Thus the organization may evaluate future potential sites in terms of their profitability.

It is worth noting the significance of the signs in the equation: each extra square metre of floor space taken by competitors reduces turnover by 21.6, whereas each extra square metre of floor space of the store itself increases turnover by 96.2.

Table 9.6 shows the predicted store turnover for three locations: X – a new centre being developed (without many anchor tenants); Y – an established popular centre; and

Z – a less popular centre, but with a more affluent catchment area than Y. For each of

Table 9.6 The evaluation of three locations

Store	Competitors' selling space (m²)	No. of anchor traders (units)	Distance from car park (m)	Floor area of store (m²)	Average income (£)	Store turnover (£)
X	1000	1	10	1200	15000	182666
Y	5000	6	90	1200	12500	82736
Z	3000	3	50	1200	13500	131403

the three locations, the independent variables (competitors' selling space and so on) are known and the regression equation can be used to estimate/calculate the final column, the store turnover. It appears that location X is preferable, since it has the highest predicted turnover. However, the model also facilitates the evaluation of how the centres might develop over time. Suppose location X is likely to acquire more competitor stores (a negative factor), but also more anchor stores (positive). These can be reflected in the 2 year hence (with more competitors selling space) and 3 year hence (with still more competitors selling space and more anchor sites) scenarios presented in Table 9.7. Clearly, unless some steps are taken, a store at location X will see a drop in turnover, to a level which is less than that predicted for location Z, where the situation is more static. Management have a much better basis on which to evaluate the alternative sites, and as with the model described in the previous section, all of the calculations which underpin these evaluations can be readily and rapidly carried out using a spreadsheet.

Table 9.7 Future developments for the locations

Store	Competitors' selling space (m²)	No. of anchor traders (units)	Distance from car park (m)	Floor area of store (m²)	Average income (£)	Store turnover (£)
After two years						
X	3000	1	10	1200	16000	144567
Y	5000	6	90	1200	13500	87837
Z	3000	3	50	1200	14500	136504
After three years						
X	4000	3	10	1200	16500	125608
Y	5000	6	90	1200	14000	90387
Z	3000	3	50	1200	15000	139054

A number of authors have mentioned some of the difficulties with this approach. One is the amount of data required from 'compatible' stores, as mentioned above. A second results from incorporating independent variables into the model that are themselves related: for example, number of competitors and total floor space of competitors. McGoldrick (1990) discusses the use of factor analysis to overcome this influence.

Checklists and analogs

As can be seen from Table 9.1, many existing organizations rely on checklists, analogs and intuition to support the solution to their location decision problems. In fact, intuition frequently has as its foundation the unstructured checklist. A variety of authors have suggested a range of these checklists for the location situation. Their advantage is that they systematically take the analyst through what can be regarded as all of the key factors of potential importance. McGoldrick (1990) presents a checklist based around four sets of factors related to population, accessibility, competition and costs. The complete checklist is presented below in Table 9.8. The original text includes detailed discussion under each of these headings.

Table 9.8 Location checklist

Population	Accessibility	Competition	Costs
Population size	Pedestrian flow	Existing retail activity	Purchase price
Age profile	Pedestrian entry routes	Direct competitors	Leasing terms
Household size	Public transport	Indirect competitors	Site preparation
Income levels	Types	Anchor stores	Building restrictions
Disposable income per capita	Cost	Cumulative attraction	Building costs
Occupation classifications	Ease of use	Compatibility	Development
Main employers	Potential	Existing retail specs	concessions
Economic stability	Car ownership levels	Selling areas	Rates payable
Unemployment levels	Road network	Turnover estimates	Refurbishment needs
Seasonal fluctuations	Conditions	Department/product	Maintenance costs
Housing density	Driving speeds	analysis	Security needs
Housing age/type	Congestion	Trade areas	Staff availability/
Neighbourhood classification	Restrictions	Age of outlets	rates
House ownership levels	Plans	Standard of design	Delivery costs
Building/demolition plans	Parking	Car parking	Promotional media/
Lifestyle measures	Capacity	Saturation index	costs
Cultural/ethnic groupings	Convenience	Competitive potential	Turnover loss –
Current shopping patterns	Cost	Outlet expansion	other branches
	Potential	Refurbishment	
	Visibility	Vacant sites	
	Access for staff	Interception	
	Access for transport and	Repositioning	
	deliveries	Competitor policy	

Source: McGoldrick (1990), p. 161.

This approach can be extended into a subjective scoring and weighting model (see, for example, Murdick *et al.*, 1990). Within this framework the factors of importance in locating a 'service outlet' are identified. Clearly, the group of individuals involved in this process will have a key impact, so it is important that it has representatives from all parties with a contribution to make to the decision. For each potential location, its 'performance' in relation to the factors is assessed. Weightings reflecting relative importance are assigned by the group, and a composite weighted performance is calculated for each location.

Consider a local authority looking for a location for a new school. The planning department identifies three possible sites. The group responsible for the recommendation identifies six factors of importance. These are shown in Table 9.9. After much debate they also come up with weightings (on a percentage scale) which can be allocated to these factors. Finally, they rate each location according to each factor on a scale from 0 (poor) to 5 (excellent). These results are shown in Table 9.9. Some of these ratings can be based on hard data (e.g. building costs), while others (e.g. attitude of local community) are more subjective. However, this should not detract from the use of these factors, or collection of data on them where possible (e.g. using attitude questionnaires).

Table 9.9 Data for school location decision

Factor	Weighting (%)	Scores of locations		
		A	B	C
Building cost	30	4	3	3
Land availability	25	3	4	3
Transportation	15	4	3	3
Proximity to catchment area	20	3	4	4
Availability of ancillary staff	5	2	4	4
Attitude of local community	5	3	4	3
Overall rating		(3.4)	(3.55)	(3.25)

Notes: Weights sum to 100%.
Scores: 0 poor, 1 fair, 2 average, 3 good, 4 very good, 5 excellent.

The overall ratings can be calculated, and are shown in brackets. Based on the data provided, B would appear to be the best location with an overall rating of between good and very good. If these overall figures are close, then sensitivity analysis can be carried out on the weightings or the factor scores (whichever have the most uncertainty associated with them) to see by how much they will need to change before the decision changes. This might result in attempts to collect more 'accurate' data (e.g. a more comprehensive attitude survey with a larger sample size).

Analog methods can be thought of as a less statistically based approach, similar to but without the rigour of multiple regression. McGoldrick (1990) summarizes the key steps as follows:

1. Identify other stores which have the same key characteristics as the proposed store/location.
2. Quantify the key features of these stores and their trading areas.
3. Extrapolate from these 'analog' stores to estimate key parameters (turnover) of the proposed store/location.

Analog methods are most successfully used by large organizations with a branch network structure. In this type of situation, there is ready access to a set of 'analog' stores and the appropriate data which are necessary for the use of these methods. It is suggested (Mason and Mayer, 1990) that some of these necessary data can be collected by customer questionnaires at the existing stores. It is assumed that the attraction of a store can be estimated by determining the percentages of total customers coming from each of a series of bands at different distances from the store. The total sales can be used, together with these percentages, to calculate the sales in each band, while the population figures for each band allow the per capita sales per band to be calculated. This set of calculations for a specimen analog store is shown in Table 9.10.

Table 9.10 Analog store data

Distance from store (km)	Percentage of sample	Total sales	Population	Per capita sales
0–2	42	79 800	31 000	2.57
2–5	28	53 200	16 000	3.33
5–10	16	30 400	10 000	3.04
Over 10	14	26 600	22 000	1.21

Note: Based on total sales of 190 000.

A sample of customers could be used to estimate the percentages which come from each of the bands (which therefore sum to 100). Given the total sales figure of £190 000, multiplying by these percentages gives estimates of the total sales in each band. Finally, the (known) population figures for each band could be divided into the total sales figures to arrive at the per capita sales. The analyst would have similar sets of data for a whole range of analog stores in the branch network. The characteristics of the store would determine an appropriate set of distances at which to break down the samples. These could equally be set at travelling times. Based on the figures for the analog (i.e. a number of sets of data as in Table 9.10), and with use of the analyst's 'local knowledge' of the potential location of a new store, it is possible to estimate the proportion of customers in each 'zone' and the associated per capita sales. Knowledge of the total population in each of these zones permits the calculation of the total sales values in each zone, which can be summed to estimate the overall store revenue at the new location.

Many of the models described have as a key objective the estimation of store turnover. While this can be useful in the comparison of alternative locations, it can also form a useful input into a more formal financial appraisal. Indeed, the financial appraisal was one of the assessment techniques identified as being used by department stores in the survey by Simkin (1989). In general terms, this involves the identification of all of the costs and revenues associated with the location of a store in a particular position, over the 'lifetime' of the store, and the 'discounting' of these to present value. This process takes account of the time value of money, and allows for the fact that £1 to be received in ten years' time has less value than £1 received today. More details of this accounting process – discounted cash flow and the calculation of the net present value – can be found in most accounting texts.

Discussion

In retail location decision making, a major input is the profile of the catchment area of the various shopping areas. In the past, much of the relevant data on such aspects as expenditure profiles between different socioeconomic groups was available from national census data. However, provision of this and related data is now coming from the private sector consultancy organizations. Examples are CACI and Pinpoint Analysis Ltd, whose 'products' include retail potential reports, and national typologies which classify areas by their dominant socioeconomic characteristics, allowing the determination of the different purchasing characteristics for various ranges of goods and services. The well-known typologies are ACORN, PiN and Super Profiles (see Wrigley, 1988).

It is important that organizations approach the location decision in a structured and systematic manner. This decision is of key strategic significance to service organizations. There are a variety of approaches which may be adopted, the major examples of which have been included in this chapter. A number of organizations have reported using some of these approaches in practice. Penny and Broom (1988) describe the approach to store location adopted by Tesco. A key input into this was a spatial interaction model. Tesco was operating a specific store development strategy orientated towards opening approximately twelve new stores per year. Strategic guidelines were provided for the board by the research team. The model provided important data for this process.

References

Bailey, P., D. Farmer, D. Jessop and D. Jones (1994) *Purchasing Principles and Management*, Pitman, London.

Davies, M. and I. Clarke (1994) 'A framework for network planning', *International Journal of Retail and Distribution Management*, vol. 22, no. 6, pp. 6–10.

Ghosh, A. and S.C. Craig (1983) 'Formulating retail location strategy in a changing environment', *Journal of Marketing*, vol. 47, no. 3, pp. 56–68.

Jones, G. (1989) *Retailing* (Natwest Small Business Bookshelf), Pitman, London.

Jones, K. and K. Simmons (1990) *The Retail Environment*, Routledge, London.

Mason, J.B. and J.B. Mayer (1990) *Modern Retailing: Theory and practice* (5th edn), Irwin, Homewood, IL.

McGoldrick, P.J. (1990) *Retail Marketing*, McGraw-Hill, London.

Murdick, R.G., B. Render and R.S. Russell (1990) *Service Operations Management*, Allyn and Bacon, London.

Nelson, R.L. (1958) *Selection of Retail Locations*, Dodge, New York.

Penny, N.J. and D. Broom (1988) 'The Tesco approach to store location', in N. Wrigley (ed.), *Store Choice, Store Location and Market Analysis*, Routledge, London.

Schmenner, R. (1994) 'Service firm location decisions: some midwestern evidence', *International Journal of Service Industry Management*, vol. 5, no. 3, pp. 35–56.

Simkin, L.P. (1989) 'SLAM: Store Location Assessment Model – theory and practice', *Omega*, vol. 17, no. 1, pp. 53–8.

Wrigley, N. (1988) *Store Choice, Store Location and Market Analysis*, Routledge, London.

Discussion topics/exercises

1. Describe four different, actual situations where service organizations have sought a new location, highlighting the reasons for this, the objectives and information requirements.

2. Use actual examples to describe how the characteristics of service organizations add complexity to the location decision-making process.

3.   A company has a chain of do-it-yourself stores in the south of England. The board has an ambitious two-stage expansion programme. Initially (over the next two years) it intends to move into the rest of the UK. Over the next five years, it proposes to expand into the rest of mainland Europe (initially France, Spain and Germany).

Prepare action plans showing time scales and major activities which will be involved in the selection and evaluation of the geographical areas and sites for the expansion. Identify key data sources.

4.   An international leisure company is planning to expand its network of theme parks, and is considering three possible locations: Cornwall, Avon and Teesside. It plans to establish a project team to investigate the situation further. Discuss the composition of the project team, and any outside representation/inputs necessary. Identify an appropriate approach to the decision-making process, outlining the data requirements and sources. Using your own experience, estimate the appropriate values for parameters, scores and so on to illustrate the application of your chosen framework.

Chapter 10

Transportation and distribution systems

Chapter outline

- ☆ Context of logistics problems
- ☆ Transportation problem
- ☆ Transhipment problem
- ☆ Warehouse location model
- ☆ Travelling salesman problem
- ☆ Vehicle scheduling and routing
- ☆ Distribution resource planning
- ☆ Contracting the distribution process
- ☆ Contribution of IT to distribution

The context of transportation and distribution systems

Transportation and distribution systems are frequently seen in larger organizations within the activity referred to as 'logistics'. In simple terms, Sussams (1991) defines logistics as 'the science which integrates all the activities required to move goods from the original sources of raw materials to the location of the ultimate consumer of the finished product' (p. 5). The major focus within this chapter will be on those aspects of logistics which impact on the ultimate consumer, especially from a service perspective. As with Chapter 9, retailing has a major, although not sole, presence in this area. While in this context a tangible product is frequently the focus of the consumer's attention, logistics can have a significant impact on the service surrounding the acquisition of this product, including such key parameters as choice and availability. Equally, there are a range of additional decisions in different types of service environment which have elements of transportation and distribution within their structure. These include the following issues:

- The development of appropriate timetables/schedules for human transportation systems (e.g. buses, trains, ferries, aircraft).

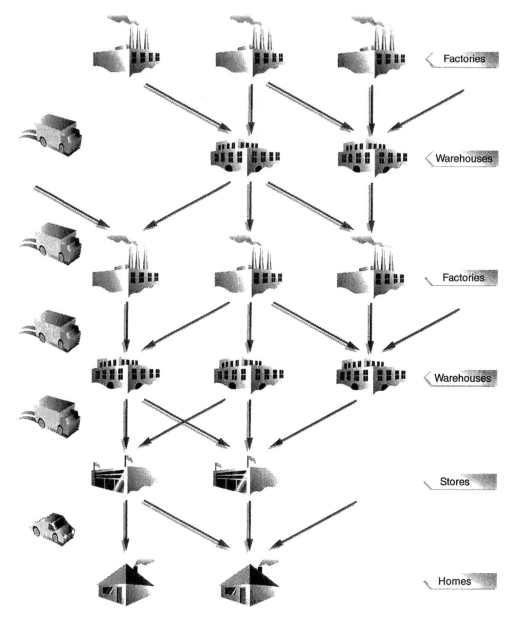

Figure 10.1   Typical logistics situation

- The scheduling of routes for field-based service staff (e.g. utility meter readers, repair people, post).

It is sometimes possible to decompose the problem into two parts: an allocation part, where the resources are assigned to some of the 'customers' (e.g. trains to certain routes, repair staff to certain geographic areas); and a scheduling part, where the best (or at least a good) timetable is developed (e.g. the timing of the trains on the routes selected, the routes to be followed by the repair staff in visiting customers requiring service in the towns they cover).

A typical logistics situation is shown in Figure 10.1. This identifies the major links between the raw materials and the ultimate consumer of the finished product. Emphasis will be on issues concerning logistics towards the bottom part of the figure, where the links are nearer to the customer, rather than the top, where concerns are closer to manufacturing. Figure 10.1 also demonstrates one of the reasons for the complexity of logistics decision making: the number of possible links in the distribution system – the possibilities that should be considered, sometimes referred to as the combinatorial aspect of the problem.

Bessen (1993) claims that the average grocery store stocks around 20 000 items, larger stores stocking two or three times this number; and that annually approximately 10 000 new items are added. When account is taken of pack sizes, colours and other basic variations, this can amount to several hundred thousand stock-keeping units (a stock-keeping unit (SKU) is an individually identified shelf product, e.g. a 200 g jar of 'own-label', decaffeinated, freeze-dried instant coffee). IKEA (the Swedish retailer of home furnishings) has 1800 suppliers located in more than 50 countries around the world, operating with a network of warehouses, the largest of which occupies 135 000 square metres, supplying over 100 stores. Brown (1994) quotes the Sainsbury supply chain handling 17 000 commodities from over 1000 suppliers through 21 warehouse depots. Some 340 stores are served with 11 million cases of goods each week by a fleet of nearly 1000 lorries. DHL annually delivers 80 million business documents and parcels to 70 000 destinations in more than 200 countries.

Another perspective can be put on the size/scale problem by thinking about the repair engineer planning a route to visit ten homes to service/repair gas equipment. Any of the ten customers can be visited first, followed by any of the remaining nine next, followed by any of the remaining eight next and so on. In all there are $10 \times 9 \times 8 \times 7 \ldots = 10! = 3\,628\,800$ different routes which the repair engineer could take.

A second reason for the complexity of the logistics problem concerns the identification of the criteria by which the performance of the solution is to be judged. The supplier to the supermarket might want to make large regular deliveries to fill its vans and reduce transport costs. The supermarket itself, however, wants small deliveries more frequently in order to keep stock levels (and the space required) at a low level, and product 'freshness' as high as possible. The service engineer might consider planning the route to minimize the distance travelled (as this adds costs but not value), whereas there may be priorities in terms of customer needs. The consumer whose central heating boiler has broken and who has no other means of heating will need to be visited before the home where the cooker is due for a routine service. Hence there can be conflict between different objectives and a balance has to be achieved.

A final complexity is the uncertainty surrounding the decision process, particularly in terms of the inputs. What happens when demand for a product is higher than expected, and a stockout is likely to occur before the next delivery is due? What happens when a repair takes longer than planned, or a trip back to the depot is needed to pick up spare parts? What happens when an aircraft is delayed by fog and a connecting flight is missed? The planner must be aware of some of the areas where uncertainty is likely to occur, and recognize the potential impact of this on the decision.

Logistics is increasingly being seen as a significant activity within a range of organizations, especially those in the retailing sector. The distribution director of Sainsbury is quoted as saying that efficient logistics and distribution contributed around 1 per cent towards the company's net margin of 6.2 per cent (Fernie and McKinnon, 1991). The group distribution director of Safeway stated that expenditure of £2 million on hitting the right store delivery time slots saved £12 million in in-store labour costs (Bristow, 1990). It is claimed that the contents of the average shopping basket are reckoned to have travelled over 4000 kilometres before reaching the supermarket shelves (Wilsher, 1994).

It is important to recognize the role that the customer plays in the logistics function. Indeed, in many environments the customer provides the final link. Few grocery stores these days provide a delivery service. This in itself can cause problems and difficulties as any chain is only as strong as its weakest link. Few consumers use cool boxes to maintain the temperature of frozen or fresh food in transit back from the supermarket. According to a survey, only one in five people knew at what temperature their refrigerator should operate, linked to the fact that 80 per cent of domestic refrigerators were over 5 °C at the warmest spot (Bristow, 1990). It is not known how this has contributed to the consumer's assessment of the quality of the product when finally consumed, and ultimately to the assessment of the service offered. In other cases, the consumer has been encouraged to take on new roles in the logistics chain. IKEA, for example, will lend roof racks to customers to enable them to transport to their homes self-assemble furniture, which otherwise would have had to be preassembled and transported by the organization itself.

In the next section some of the models which can be used to support various distribution and transportation problems will be presented and described. This will be followed by a discussion of some recent trends, including subcontracting the logistics function and the influence and impact of information technology developments.

Models for transportation and distribution systems

The transportation problem

At its simplest, this problem is normally associated with situations like a series of warehouses supplying a set of retail outlets. The following example will be used to demonstrate the general structure of the problem and its main parameters, and to illustrate an appropriate solution procedure.

An illustrative example

An organization has a chain of five superstores located in Oxford, Birmingham, London, Manchester and Newcastle. These are serviced with perishable goods from three regional distribution centres (RDCs) in York, Norwich, and Southampton. Both the stores and the RDCs have been added to the network as the organization has grown from its origins as a single store in London. The decisions over the actual locations of the stores and the RDCs were made over an extended period of time, in the light of the information available at the time the decision was made. Relevant factors included the geographic distribution of customers in the appropriate socioeconomic groups in determining store location, and the sources of the perishable goods in locating the RDCs. Chapter 9 includes discussion

		SUPERSTORE					
		Oxford	Birmingham	London	Manchester	Newcastle	Containers available
REGIONAL DISTRIBUTION CENTRE	York	18	13	17	7	9	70
	Norwich	14	16	12	19	23	35
	Southampton	7	13	8	23	32	85
Containers required		25	30	55	45	35	

Figure 10.2 Data for the transportation problem

of the other factors the organization should have taken account of, and a choice of more structured approaches which it could (or should?) have adopted. The result, however, is that the current situation is not necessarily the best, and that the RDCs are limited in terms of their capacities. However, the financial position for the organization at present is such that no further growth, expansion or capital expenditure is possible.

For convenience, the products are packed in standard-sized containers, and stores are supplied daily with prescribed numbers of these. The capacities of the RDCs mean that only a certain number are available from each of these RDCs to meet the requirements of the stores. The relative locations of the stores and RDCs mean that there are different unit costs for each RDC supplying each store with one container of products (in part this results from the different distances, travel times and so on). These data are given in Figure 10.2.

It is worth noting that the problem can be formulated in mathematical terms. If the RDCs are numbered 1, 2 and 3 and the stores 1, 2, 3, 4 and 5, then the variable x_{ij} can represent the number of containers shipped from RDC i to j, and the objective is to minimize the total cost, which can be expressed as:

$$18x_{11} + 13x_{12} + 17x_{13} + 7x_{14} + 9x_{15} +$$
$$14x_{21} + 16x_{22} + 12x_{23} + 19x_{24} + 23x_{25} +$$
$$7x_{31} + 13x_{32} + 8x_{33} + 23x_{34} + 32x_{35}$$

However, each RDC only has a certain number of containers available, so these three limitations (or constraints), one for each RDC, can be written as follows:

	Oxford	Birmingham	London	Manchester	Newcastle	Containers available
SUPERSTORE						
York	(1) 25	(2) 30	(3) 15			70
Norwich			(4) 35			35
Southampton			(5) 5	(6) 45	(7) 35	85
Containers required	25	30	55	45	35	

REGIONAL DISTRIBUTION CENTRE

Cost = (25 x 18) + (30 x 13) + (15 x 17) + (35 x 12) + (5 x 8) + (45 x 23) + (35 x 32) = 3710

Note: Figures in brackets show the sequence in which the solution was developed.

Figure 10.3 Initial solution found using the north-west corner rule

$$x_{11} + x_{12} + x_{13} + x_{14} + x_{15} = 70 \text{ (York)}$$

$$x_{21} + x_{22} + x_{23} + x_{24} + x_{25} = 35 \text{ (Norwich)}$$

$$x_{31} + x_{32} + x_{33} + x_{34} + x_{35} = 85 \text{ (Southampton)}$$

Finally, each store should only receive in total the number of containers it requires:

$$x_{11} + x_{21} + x_{31} = 25 \text{ (Oxford)}$$

$$x_{12} + x_{22} + x_{32} = 30 \text{ (Birmingham)}$$

$$x_{13} + x_{23} + x_{33} = 55 \text{ (London)}$$

$$x_{14} + x_{24} + x_{34} = 45 \text{ (Manchester)}$$

$$x_{15} + x_{25} + x_{35} = 35 \text{ (Newcastle)}$$

(In this case the total availability from the RDCs equals the total requirement of the stores. This need not always be the case, as will be discussed later in this section.)

The problem expressed above is an example of what is called a *linear program*: all of the equations involve constants multiplied by the variables (there are no terms which include the variables raised to higher powers or multiplied by each other).

	SUPERSTORE					
REGIONAL DISTRIBUTION CENTRE		Oxford	Birmingham	London	Manchester	Newcastle	Shadow cost of dispatch

REGIONAL DISTRIBUTION CENTRE		Oxford	Birmingham	London	Manchester	Newcastle	Shadow cost of dispatch
	York	18	13	17			u_1
	Norwich			12			u_2
	Southampton			8	23	32	u_3
Shadow cost of receipt		v_1	v_2	v_3	v_4	v_5	

Figure 10.4 Shadow costs for initial solution

The objective is to minimize a linear cost equation subject to a set of linear constraints. There are standard procedures for solving such problems (widely available as a software package on all sizes of computer). The transportation problem is a special type of linear programme and there is a specialized procedure for its solution. This will be illustrated here.

The first step in this process is to develop an initial feasible solution (not the best one, but one which does satisfy the constraints on availability and requirements). A simple approach to this is by using the north-west corner rule, as follows.

The process starts at the top left of the matrix with the link York to Oxford, allocating as much as possible, 25 containers, and meeting Oxford's requirements. It then moves to the link York to Birmingham, allocating as much of what remains (70–25 = 45) as possible, 30 containers, satisfying Birmingham's needs and leaving 15. These are allocated to York to London, exhausting York's availability and leaving London still requiring (55–15 = 40). It is then necessary to move down and consider Norwich to London, allocating the entire availability of 35 and leaving London still requiring 5. These are satisfied by Southampton, which also satisfies the demand for 45 from Manchester and 35 from Newcastle. This initial solution is summarized in Figure 10.3. The cost can be simply calculated by multiplying the number of containers handled by each link and the appropriate unit cost.

The mathematics behind the linear programme formulation indicates that any 'regular' solution should have $n + m - 1$ links, where n is the number of destinations (stores) and m is the number of sources (RDCs). In this case $n + m - 1 = 3 + 5 - 1 = 7$.

While the north-west corner rule does not guarantee to produce a good solution, it is systematic and produces a solution rapidly which is feasible (that is, it meets the constraints).

		Oxford	Birmingham	London	Manchester	Newcastle	Shadow cost of dispatch
				SUPERSTORE			
REGIONAL DISTRIBUTION CENTRE	York	18	13	17			0
	Norwich			12			−5
	Southampton			8	23	32	−9
Shadow cost of receipt		18	13	17	32	41	

Figure 10.5   Summary calculation of initial shadow costs

The next step is to develop a procedure which will indicate how to improve the solution if this is possible.

'Shadow costs' are associated with each RDC (the cost of dispatch) and each store (the cost of receipt), such that for the links in the solution the actual cost is the sum of the two appropriate shadow costs. These are shown in Figure 10.4, with the shadow costs of receipt shown as v_1, v_2, v_3, v_4 and v_5, and the shadow costs of dispatch being u_1, u_2 and u_3. This gives the following equations:

$$u_1 + v_1 = 18, \qquad u_1 + v_2 + 13, \qquad u_1 + v_3 = 17$$
$$u_2 + v_3 = 12$$
$$u_3 + v_3 = 8, \qquad u_3 + v_4 = 23, \qquad u_3 + v_5 = 32$$

Now it is clear that there are eight unknowns but only seven equations. In fact, there will normally be one fewer equation than unknowns, so we set $u_1 = $ zero.

$$\text{Thus} \quad v_1 = 18, \qquad v_2 = 13, \qquad v_3 = 17$$
$$\text{and} \quad u_2 + 17 = 12 \quad \text{so} \quad u_2 = -5$$
$$\text{and} \quad u_3 + 17 = 8 \quad \text{so} \quad u_3 = -9$$
$$\text{and} \quad -9 + v_4 = 23 \quad \text{so} \quad v_4 = 32$$
$$\text{and} \quad -9 + v_5 = 32 \quad \text{so} \quad v_5 = 41$$

Figure 10.6 Selection of the link to be included in the improved solution

Normally these calculations are carried out directly on the table of results, as shown in Figure 10.5.

It is now possible to consider how the solution might be improved. This is achieved simply by examining the links which are not currently in the solution. Those which are attractive are those where the sum of the shadow costs exceeds the actual costs. Figure 10.6 shows these differences (sum of shadow costs − actual cost) for the links not in the solution.

These differences represent the reduction in overall cost obtained for each container which can be 'transferred' to that link. The most attractive link is York to Newcastle, with unit cost reduction of 32. If Y containers (the value for Y is not yet known, but to be determined) are allocated to that link, then in order to balance the requirement into Newcastle, Y must be taken off the supply *from* Southampton, so Y must be added *on to* the supply to Manchester *or* London. If it is added on to Manchester, it cannot be taken off the supply from some other RDC to Manchester, so it must be added on to London. It must then be taken off some other supply to London to balance this. Norwich and York are possibilities, but York allows the balancing to be complete. The process is summarized in Figure 10.7.

Clearly, it is advantageous to make Y as large as possible. There are two links which limit this, $15 - Y$ and $35 - Y$, and this indicates that Y should be set at 15. The new improved solution is shown in Figure 10.8. Note that a new link has been introduced and one has disappeared, and that the cost has been reduced by 15×32 (the value of Y multiplied by cost reduction).

		\multicolumn{5}{c	}{SUPERSTORE}
		Oxford	Birmingham	London	Manchester	Newcastle
REGIONAL DISTRIBUTION CENTRE	York	25	30	$15-Y$		Y
	Norwich			35		
	Southampton			$5+Y$	45	$35-Y$

Figure 10.7 Adjustments for the allocation to new link

The whole process can now be repeated, starting again with the shadow costs associated with the new solution (Figure 10.8). The process is summarized below.

The procedure

- *Step 1.* Develop initial solution using the north-west corner rule.
- *Step 2.* Calculate the shadow costs of dispatch (u_i) and receipt (v_j) corresponding to the links in the solution. There should be $n + m - 1$ links and normally $u_1 = 0$.
- *Step 3.* For those links *not* in the solution (k to l), compare the actual cost (a_{kl}) with the sum of the shadow costs $(u_k + v_l)$, (calculate the difference $(u_k + v_l - a_{kl})$).
- *Step 4.* If a_{kl} is greater than or equal to $u_k + v_l$ for all links not in the solution (all of the differences are negative or zero), then the current solution is the best solution and the procedure terminates.
- *Step 5.* Otherwise select the link not in the solution which has the largest difference $u_k + v_l - a_{kl}$. This represents the potential saving for each container transferred to this link.
- *Step 6.* Allocate an unknown quantity Y to this link and make balancing adjustments to the other links in the solution, so that the requirements and availabilities are not violated.
- *Step 7.* Determine the largest value of Y at which point one of the links currently in the solution becomes zero, thus retaining $n + m - 1$ links in the solution.
- *Step 8.* This is the new solution with this value of Y. The cost has been reduced by Y multiplied by the saving calculated at step 3. Go to step 2 and repeat the process.

			SUPERSTORE			
		Oxford	Birmingham	London	Manchester	Newcastle
REGIONAL DISTRIBUTION CENTRE	York	25	30			15
	Norwich			35		
	Southampton			20	45	20

New cost = 3710 −(32 x 15) = 3230

Figure 10.8 New solution after first iteration

It can be seen that when the stage is reached that, for links not in the solution, the actual cost exceeds the sum of the appropriate shadow costs, then this solution is the best. If for some of these links the actual cost *equals* the sum of the shadow costs, then there are a number of alternative solutions each with minimum cost.

In the next (second) iteration, the link Southampton to Oxford is introduced with 20 containers; in the third iteration, the link York to Manchester is selected with 5 containers; in the fourth iteration, the link Norwich to Birmingham is selected with 30 containers; in the fifth iteration, the link Norwich to Manchester is selected with 5 containers. The result of the sixth iteration is shown in Figure 10.9. Confirmation that the best solution has been found is given in Figure 10.10.

The solution for this example is then as follows:

- York supplies 35 containers to Manchester, 35 containers to Newcastle.
- Norwich supplies 25 containers to Birmingham, 10 containers to Manchester.
- Southampton supplies 25 containers to Oxford, 5 containers to Birmingham and 55 containers to London.

The total cost is £1830.

It is worth noting the additional information given in the final table of shadow costs (Figure 10.10). The figures represent the additional costs incurred if the organization is forced to use a particular link: for example, if York has to supply Oxford, each container will increase the cost by 20. Viewed from another perspective, if a new road network were

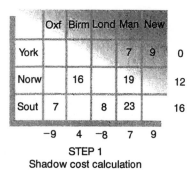

	Oxf	Birm	Lond	Man	New	
York				7	9	0
Norw		16		19		12
Sout	7		8	23		16

$$-9 \quad 4 \quad -8 \quad 7 \quad 9$$

STEP 1
Shadow cost calculation

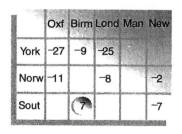

	Oxf	Birm	Lond	Man	New
York	-27	-9	-25		
Norw	-11			-8	-2
Sout	⑦				-7

STEPS 3, 4 and 5
Calculation of the differences between
sums of shadow costs and actual cost

	Oxf	Birm	Lond	Man	New
York				35	35
Norw		30-Y		5+ Y	
Sout	25	Y	55	5-Y	

$Y = 5$

STEP 6
Allocate Y to the largest
difference and adjust

	Oxf	Birm	Lond	Man	New
York				35	35
Norw		25		10	
Sout	25	5	55		

$\text{Cost} = 1865 - (5 \times 7) = 1830$

STEPS 7 and 8
Determine value of Y
giving new solution

Figure 10.9   Results of iteration 6

opened on the route between Norwich and Birmingham which reduced the unit transportation cost by 2, then since the difference is currently -1, it would mean that this link was worth considering.

Some extensions
A situation which occurs quite frequently is that the availabilities from the warehouse exceed the requirements. The approach can be extended quite easily to handle this situation. Suppose the number of containers which can be kept at Norwich increases from 35 to 45, resulting in a 'surplus' of 10 containers. The problem is dealt with by introducing a 'dummy' superstore, for which the unit costs are zero and which has a requirement of 10 containers. In the final minimum cost solution, any shipments from the RDCs to this dummy represent the amount left at the RDC.

A second more complex version of the transportation problem is when the analysis extends one level further back into the supply chain, and the examination includes the suppliers to the warehouses. This is sometimes referred to as a transhipment problem. It is possible to build a composite table of data combining the two decision-making processes. This is shown in Figure 10.11, where the two separate factory–warehouse and warehouse–

	Oxf	Birm	Lond	Man	New	
York			7	9		0
Norw		16		19		12
Sout	7	13	8			9
	-2	4	-1	7	9	

STEP 1
Shadow cost calculation

	Oxf	Birm	Lond	Man	New
York	-20	-9	-18		
Norw	-4		-1		-2
Sout				-7	-14

STEPS 3, 4 and 5
Calculation of the differences between
sums of shadow costs and actual cost

As all differences are negative, the best solution has been obtained.

Figure 10.10 Confirmation that the solution has been found

store problems are shown composed into a combined problem, only using the cost values associated with legitimate links. The procedure described earlier can be applied directly to this problem. Software programs are widely available to solve both transportation and transhipment problems, and these will run on all sizes of computer. However, it is important that the user understands the process being followed in order to present the input data in the correct form, to understand the assumptions made in arriving at the solution and to interpret the results correctly. Use of such models/programs should be seen as a support for the decision-maker, rather than as a replacement, since there are soft issues that cannot directly be incorporated into the model, but which needed to be allowed for. Moreover, sensitivity analysis (rerunning the model with different values of the uncertain parameters) can frequently help the decision-maker handle risk and uncertainty. Thus it is possible to look at the effects on the solution of uncertainty in requirements or availabilities, a new road reducing distribution costs or a major road development increasing distribution costs in the short/medium term.

A warehouse location model

At first sight, it might appear that this problem should have been covered in an earlier chapter, since it concerns location. However, it is placed here because it has a major impact on logistics and distribution. The problem is best illustrated with an example (based broadly on an illustration in Evans (1993)).

An organization has five stores located throughout England, which are serviced by a single warehouse. This has now reached its maximum capacity and its location was selected before the organization had grown to its current size, when it had only two stores. A new site is being sought for a replacement. The current stores are in Exeter (100), London (800), Liverpool (600), Hull (200) and Newcastle (400). The figures in brackets are the forecast numbers of containers of produce required from the warehouse on a daily basis. The organization is keen to determine a location for the new warehouse which minimizes the distance travelled to distribute the goods, weighted by the numbers of containers carried.

		Warehouse X	Warehouse Y	Warehouse Z	Available
	A	12	13	16	12
Factory	B	10	12	9	34
	C	14	19	21	9
Required		20	15	20	

FACTORY–WAREHOUSE PROBLEM

		Store 1	Store 2	Store 3	Store 4	Available
	X	19	24	16	7	20
Warehouse	Y	12	13	19	16	15
	Z	14	12	17	8	20
Required		11	19	8	17	

WAREHOUSE–STORE PROBLEM

		Warehouse X	Warehouse Y	Warehouse Z	Store 1	Store 2	Store 3	Store 4	Available
	A	12	13	16					12
Factory	B	10	12	9					34
	C	14	19	21					9
	X				19	24	16	7	20
Warehouse	Y				12	13	19	16	15
	Z				14	12	17	8	20
Required		20	15	20	11	19	8	17	

COMPOSITE TRANSHIPMENT PROBLEM

Figure 10.11 Illustrative transhipment problem

The approach to the solution is based on the calculation of the *centre of gravity*. The first step is to place the locations of the stores to scale on a plan, and to introduce an arbitrary origin and horizontal (x) and vertical (y) scale. This has been done in Figure 10.12. The figure in square brackets by each store is the number of containers required; the other figures are the x coordinate and y coordinate respectively, relative to the arbitrary origin.

The process involves finding the 'centre of gravity', the coordinates of which are given in general terms by:

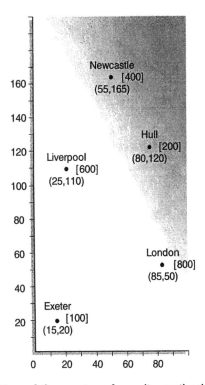

Figure 10.12 Application of the centre of gravity method to warehouse location

$$c(x) = \frac{d(1,\ x)w(1) + d(2,\ x)w(2) + d(3,\ x)w(3) + \ldots}{w(1) + w(2) + w(3) + \ldots}$$

$$c(y) = \frac{d(1,\ y)w(1) + d(2,\ y)w(2) + d(3,\ y)w(3) + \ldots}{w(1) + w(2) + w(3) + \ldots}$$

where:

   $c(x)$ is the x coordinate of the centre of gravity
   $c(y)$ is the y coordinate of the centre of gravity
   $d(i, y)$ is the x coordinate of location i
   $d(i, y)$ is the y coordinate of location i
   $w(i)$ is the number of containers moved to location i.

For the data provided above, this gives an x coordinate of 58.3 and a y coordinate of 94.2. Examining this in the context of a detailed map of the area indicates that, from the perspective of distance weighted by the number of containers, a site somewhere between Stafford and Nottingham should be selected. It is now possible to incorporate other issues into the analysis.

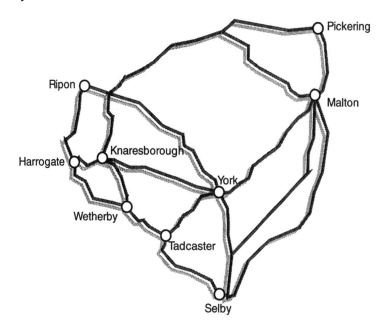

Figure 10.13 Locations of service engineer's calls

The travelling salesman problem

The nature of this problem derives from its title, and finding an efficient solution to it has challenged researchers for decades. Essentially, a salesperson has to plan a visit route which takes him or her to all the cities in the salesperson's itinerary, and back to base again in minimum time (or minimum distance), without visiting any city more than once. A number of approaches have been proposed (see, for example, Ackoff and Sasieni, 1968): those which claim to provide the best solution are somewhat complex and time consuming, and often involve unrealistic assumptions. The following example illustrates a more practically based approach to a problem which has a stronger service slant to it.

An illustrative example

A service centre is based in Harrogate covering the major parts of Yorkshire. This covers major domestic gas appliances, including cookers, fridges, gas fires, boilers and complete central heating systems. The work covers both regular servicing and emergency breakdowns. A significant number of customers have regular service agreements which provide for an annual service and guaranteed response in case of an emergency. Other (casual) customers call as a result of the organization's advertising and entries in the *Yellow Pages*.

On Friday, a particular service engineer is given a list of nine calls which have been allocated for that day. Each call is expected to take an average of 30 minutes, with travelling time added on top. Normally between five and ten calls are allocated per person depending on the locations and nature of work. The locations of these calls are shown in Figure 10.13. Details of the calls are given in Table 10.1. It has also been possible to collect the approximate

from \ to	1 H	2 K	3 M	4 P	5 R	6 S	7 T	8 W	9 Y
1 Harrogate	–	6	54	62	16	43	25	13	34
2 Knaresborough		–	51	55	16	38	24	12	25
3 Malton			–	14	55	48	47	53	30
4 Pickering				–	62	61	55	58	48
5 Ripon					–	51	42	31	38
6 Selby						–	22	33	23
7 Tadcaster							–	11	17
8 Wetherby								–	21
9 York									–

Figure 10.14 Distances between all pairs of locations for calls (in kilometres)

travelling distances between the locations of the different calls. These are shown in Figure 10.14.

Table 10.1 Details of the service calls

Call	Location	Details
1	Harrogate	Routine gas fire service (agreement)
2	Knaresborough	Routine gas boiler service (casual)
3	Malton	Boiler breakdown (agreement)
4	Pickering	Routine central heating service (agreement)
5	Ripon	Routine cooker service (agreement)
6	Selby	Routine boiler service (casual)
7	Tadcaster	Routine fridge service (agreement)
8	Wetherby	Gas fire breakdown (casual)
9	York	Routine central heating service (agreement)

The majority of the formal approaches to the 'travelling salesman problem', as applied to this case, would take the travelling distances and derive the route, starting from Harrogate, visiting all of the other locations and returning to Harrogate, which minimized the total distance travelled by the service engineer. With the narrow focus of cost minimization, they would not have taken into account any other factors associated with the problem, like relative priorities of the different types of customer and their circumstances.

The approach developed here is based on a well-known 'heuristic' for this type of problem. This is a commonsense-based 'rule of thumb' designed to give a good (rather than the best) solution, in a fast, easy-to-understand manner. The foundation for this is the 'closest unvisited city heuristic'. The route is generated by selection at each stage of the nearest customer who has not yet been visited. Applying this to data in Figure 10.14, the solution is Harrogate–Knaresborough–Wetherby–Tadcaster–York–Selby–Malton–Pickering–Ripon–Harrogate. In this the service engineer travels 209 kilometres. This solution could be used as it stands, or it could be examined for possible improvements (for example, instead of the sub-route Tadcaster to York to Selby to Malton, would it be shorter to follow Tadcaster to Selby to York to Malton?).

What is missing from the above analysis is any consideration of factors other than cost. It could be argued that there are several other factors which should be taken into account in determining the route that the service engineer should follow. These could relate to the type of contract (priority to those with an agreement), type of service (priority to emergencies), extent of dependence on the service (for example, does the broken cooker provide the sole means of cooking, or does the request come from an 'at risk' consumer, e.g. someone with young children, or a disabled or elderly person). Thus there might be a hierarchy of priorities. Clearly, what is important is establishing the ranking of these priorities. This process ensures that the organization approaches the route planning from a customer focus in a fair and consistent manner rather than being driven simply by operational efficiency. Applying this to the above example, it could be argued that the first call should be to Malton to the established customer with a boiler breakdown (which is the sole form of heating the customer has), followed by Wetherby to the 'casual' customer with the broken gas fire. After that, all calls could be considered equally, as they are routine services (without distinction between types of contract), and the route could be planned using the closest unvisited customer rule. This results in the following route: Harrogate–Malton–Wetherby–Tadcaster–York–Selby–Knaresborough–Ripon–Pickering–Harrogate, which covers 336 kilometres. Thus, while the route is longer, it is more customer focused in its consideration of their requirements.

Vehicle scheduling and routing

The travelling salesman problem, described in the previous section, can be considered to be a simple case of a vehicle routing problem. A number of retail outlets are served by a single warehouse and one vehicle. The decision is over the route for the vehicle which minimizes the distance travelled. Provided the vehicle has the capacity to carry the requirements of all the retail outlets, then the decision can be viewed as a travelling salesman problem, and the heuristic covered earlier can be used; or alternatively, if the benefits justify the increased computational effort, one of the optimizing procedures can be adopted.

If a single vehicle does not have the required capacity, then at least two options are available: to make two trips or to purchase/obtain a second vehicle. In either case, the problem has become more complex as it is necessary to develop two separate routes, to associate each outlet with either the first or second trip/vehicle. The problem grows in complexity as a second and subsequent warehouse is added, as now it becomes necessary to decide which warehouse should serve each outlet or customer. This complexity is illustrated in Figure 10.15.

It is clear that there are a variety of different forms of vehicle routing problem with different constraints. There is no completely general problem and associated solution

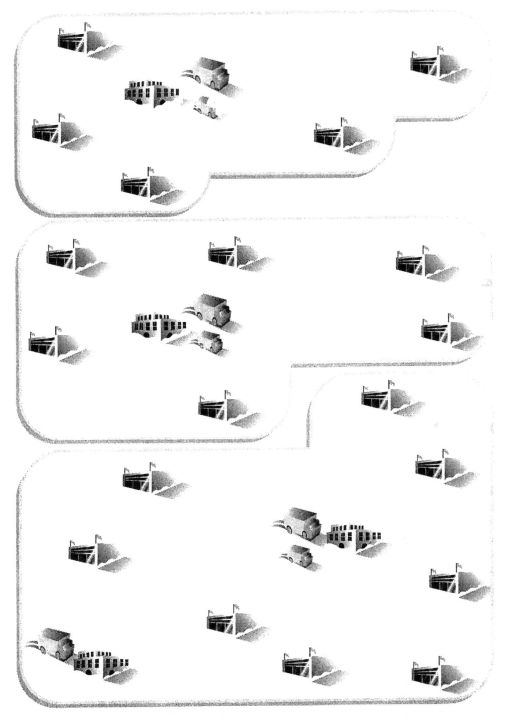

Figure 10.15 Characteristics of a range of vehicle routing problems

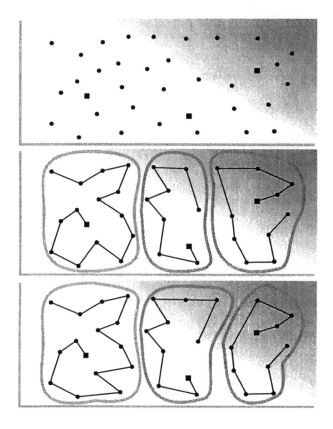

Figure 10.16 Illustration of the vehicle routing development and improvement process

procedure, particularly one which guarantees to give the best performance with respect to some objective. However, a variety of heuristic approaches have been developed for a range of more specific problems. Frequently, these adopt an approach based around generating an initial good solution fairly rapidly. This first step might include clustering customers around their 'nearest' distribution centre, and then for each centre solving several travelling salesman problems for each of the vehicles at the centre. At this stage, vehicle capacities could be taken into account by, for example, prioritizing customers by order size.

The next stage might be to look at the possibilities for improving the solution (or simply removing the infeasibility if vehicle capacities have been exceeded). This is often achieved by considering minor changes to the solution. These can be achieved at the macro level by considering changing the distribution centre to which a customer is allocated (at the 'edge' of a cluster) or at a micro level by changing the sequence of two successive visits (for example, A–B–C–D becomes A–C–B–D). The selection of the customers to change is frequently determined by the estimation of potential savings if the change (either in the centre to which they are allocated or between successive customers in the route) is implemented. Normally a restricted search takes place over possible changes until no potential improvement is predicted. Figure 10.16 illustrates the process, showing the three

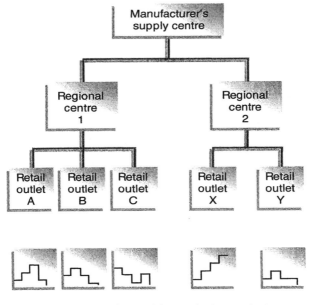

Forecast demand for particular product

Figure 10.17 Illustrative distribution network

centres and customers, an allocation of customers to centres and a possible route (based on one vehicle), and finally a potential improvement in modifying the first route, together with a potential improvement in changing the centre serving a customer.

A number of authors have developed more complex heuristics to tackle a variety of the specific cases. A frequently encountered situation is that the customers have 'time windows' – specific periods during the day during which they wish the 'delivery' to occur. Balakrishnan (1993) presents some simple heuristics which can be used when these can be violated on payment of a penalty. Other approaches have involved integrating the vehicle routing problem with other associated decisions. Bohoris and Thomas (1995) consider a specific vehicle routing and depot staffing problem. This differs from traditional problems in that it involves emptying vending machines, and when a certain limit has been reached, this must be taken to a bank. Salhi *et al.* (1992) consider models which look at the combined vehicle routing and vehicle fleet composition problem.

Distribution resource planning

Distribution resource planning (DRP) is a process which can be used in a complex supply chain system (for example, manufacturers' supply centres feeding retailers' regional centres, feeding retailers' local supply centres, feeding retailers' outlets). It can be used to plan movements through the chain to meet anticipated consumers' demand, taking account of factors such as minimum pack sizes and minimum shipment constraints.

Consider the simplified example presented in Figure 10.17, consisting of a single manufacturer's supply centre supplying two regional centres (RCs), each supplying a number

OUTLET A					OUTLET B				
Lead time = 1 week					Lead time = 1 week				
Safety stock = 5 units					Safety stock = 10 units				
Current stock = 120 units					Current stock = 150 units				
In-transit = 10 units					In-transit = 20 units				

Week	1	2	3	4	Week	1	2	3	4
Gross requirement	50	60	50	60	Gross requirement	80	60	70	70
Nett requirement	–	–	35	60	Nett requirement	–	–	50	70
Planned dispatch	–	35	60		Planned dispatch	–	50	70	

OUTLET C					REGIONAL CENTRE 1				
Lead time = 2 weeks					Lead time = 1 week				
Safety stock = 10 units					Safety stock = 0 units				
Current stock = 100 units					Current stock = 100 units				
In-transit = 10 units					In-transit = 50 units				

Week	1	2	3	4	Week	1	2	3	4
Gross requirement	40	50	40	40	Gross requirement	30	125	130	
Nett requirement	–	–	30	40	Nett requirement	–	5	130	
Planned dispatch	30	40			Planned dispatch	5	130		

OUTLET X					OUTLET Y				
Lead time = 1 week					Lead time = 2 weeks				
Safety stock = 5 units					Safety stock = 0 units				
Current stock = 80 units					Current stock = 100 units				
In-transit = 25 units					In-transit = 20 units				

Week	1	2	3	4	Week	1	2	3	4
Gross requirement	30	40	40	40	Gross requirement	50	60	60	60
Nett requirement	–	–	10	40	Nett requirement	–	–	50	60
Planned dispatch	–	10	40		Planned dispatch	50	60	–	

REGIONAL CENTRE 2					MANUFACTURER'S SUPPLY CENTRE				
Lead time = 1 week									
Safety stock = 0 units									
Current stock = 170 units									
In-transit = 40 units									

Week	1	2	3	4	Week	1	2	3	4
Gross requirement	50	70	40		Gross requirement	15	170		
Nett requirement	–	10	40						
Planned dispatch	10	40							

Figure 10.18 Specimen distribution requirements planning calculations

of retail outlets. The driving force behind the DRP process is the set of forecast requirements for each product at the retail outlet. The logic behind DRP involves taking this gross requirement at each outlet and adjusting it to take account of existing stock, stock in transit from the regional centre and any safety stock (to allow for the various uncertainties in the system – demand, lead times), resulting in a nett requirement. This nett requirement is then 'offset' by the appropriate distribution lead time between the outlet and the RC (these might be different for different outlets) to generate a planned dispatch quantity – a gross requirement at the RC from that outlet. At the RC, the total gross requirements for an item are generated by summing the appropriate planned dispatch quantities resulting from each individual outlet. The process then repeats with the calculation of the nett requirement at the RCs and back up the chain to the manufacturer's supply centre. The planned dispatch figures can be adjusted to take account of any minimum pack or shipping quantities.

An example set of DRP calculations is shown in Figure 10.18. All of the lead times, safety stock, current stock and in-transit figures will be known at the start of the process, as will the gross requirements at the five retail outlets. The remaining figures can all then be calculated.

Thus at outlet X, the gross requirement can be met initially by the current stock plus in-transit stock minus safety stock: that is, $80 + 25 - 5 = 100$. Deducting this leaves the nett requirement of 10 in week 3 and 40 in week 4. Offsetting this by the distribution lead time (1 week) results in planned dispatches on RC2 of 10 in week 2 and 40 in week 3. A similar process applies at outlet Y with the gross requirement met by $100 + 20 - 0 = 120$, resulting in the planned dispatches on RC2 of 50 in week 1 and 60 in week 2 (note that the lead time was 2 weeks). Combining these two sets of planned dispatches gives the gross requirement on RC2: 50 in week 1, 70 in week 2 and 40 in week 3. A similar process applies to outlets A, B and C to generate the gross requirements for RC1, and finally the process is applied to RC1 and RC2 to generate the gross requirement for the supply centre.

This is a simplification of a full DRP system, but it captures the essential features. It has been argued that DRP adds flexibility and that it provides the opportunity to manage change (in that the process can be rerun if demand forecasts alter). It adds a time dimension to planning, looking at the entire period up to the end of the planning horizon, rather than looking simply at the next planning period. More detailed discussion can be found in Martin (1993) and Martin (1994).

Subcontracting the distribution process

In recent years it has become increasingly popular with organizations to contract out all, or part, of the distribution function. Moore (1991) discusses this move in the context of grocery distribution in the UK, pointing out that the major benefits are in the areas of finance (avoiding the set-up costs of a distribution network), personnel (buying in the expertise and experience), technology (access to the most up-to-date physical and information technology) and flexibility (the ability to avoid the impact of industrial unrest). Indeed, this is being seen as a major growth service sector. Major names in the area include Excel, Christian Salvesen, TNT and BOC. Davies (1995) describes the role of these key players in more detail, identifying some of their major clients, and also examining the different forms the relationships between distribution contractor and retailer might take, which include both dedicated and network distribution services.

Cooper *et al.* (1994) analyze suppliers of logistics services in some detail, providing a useful ten-category classification scheme, including dedicated contracted distribution, shared contract transport, express and general haulage. This can be very useful to organizations in identifying those aspects of the overall logistics function which they feel it would be advantageous to contract out. There can be a danger in contracting out the entire process. Sainsbury still keeps around 35 per cent in-house. This gives the organization the necessary knowledge of costs and feasible efficiency levels that it needs in order to benchmark the performance of outside contractors (Brown, 1994).

The contribution of information technology to distribution

Cooper *et al.* (1994) put information technology (IT) applications into four categories: transaction systems; operations planning systems; controlling systems; and directive information systems.

Transaction systems

These are systems which handle the organization's daily 'transactions'. This is one area where IT has made a significant impact, in handling some of the data associated with distribution systems. Electronic data interchange (EDI) is having an important effect on speed and accuracy of transmission of a whole range of transaction data, from schedules to invoices. Bamfield (1994) provides comprehensive coverage of the adoption of EDI by retailers, identifying the major benefits as being cost and productivity savings and a reconfiguration of the value chain in part through faster response. Electronic funds transfer (EFT) is speeding up payment processes and eliminating associated clerical functions.

Operations planning systems

It is probably in this area that the majority of software development has taken place. Using the classification presented in Slater (1986), this covers such applications as fleet management, operations (materials handling), route networks, routing and scheduling, stock location and rotation. Stenger *et al.* (1993) report a comprehensive survey of commercially available software for integrated logistics management which included 880 packages. However, these did include some very broadly based packages. Using the classification in the paper, which included inventory control and order processing, 159 packages included distribution requirement planning, 205 included transportation, 174 included routing and 135 supported electronic data interchange. There were 16 freestanding routing packages.

Controlling systems

These systems are primarily intended to support the measurement and control of the key parameters required by management, including costs, income, productivity and performance generally. Cooper *et al.* (1994) cite such illustrations as automatic monitoring of locations of vehicles, on-line tracing of cargoes, electronic tachographs and tachograph analysis programmes.

Directive information systems

These systems support the strategic distribution planning process. An area which has been developing rapidly is the support for this process provided by simulation models. These allow the manager to predict the consequences of major decisions through the examination of alternative scenarios. Thus it would be possible to look at the impact of changing vehicle mixes in fleet configurations, staffing patterns and so on. Although there are some specific simulation packages available for the distribution industry, advances in software tools are making it increasingly easy for the in-house specialist to develop models tailored specifically to the organization's environment, and to allow the manager to interact visually with the models in use.

Software in use

Canen and Scott (1995) present the results of some work which they carried out in comparing the theory and practice of vehicle routing problems, stating that 'there is now a wide availability in the market place of commercial routing and scheduling software packages' (p. 1). Although only based on a small sample of companies in Scotland, their work seemed to suggest that in a number of cases software was being used to support decisions rather than to make decisions ('routing is done manually. The package is used only to sort the route into sequence for delivery.' 'Use a commercial software package. This is seen as an aid to route planning as the routes are finalised manually' (p. 6)).

Discussion

Transportation and distribution problems arise in a variety of service situations, as well as being a major service area in their own right. The range of situations means that there is no one generic problem and solution. However, it is frequently possible to classify a problem as belonging to a particular group which has a formal method, model or heuristic which can be used as the basis of a methodology to support the decision-making processes. Some of these models have been outlined in this chapter. Use of these can produce quite significant benefits for the organisation: for example, Wunderlich *et al.* (1992) reported projected annual benefits of almost $850 000 from the implementation of software to route and schedule gas meter readers in Southern California.

References

Ackoff, R.L. and M.W. Sasiene (1968) *Fundamentals of Operations Research*, John Wiley, New York.
Balakrishnan, N. (1993) 'Simple heuristics for the vehicle routing problem with soft time windows', *Journal of the Operational Research Society*, vol. 44, no. 3, pp. 279–87.
Bamfield, J. (1994) 'The adoption of electronic data interchange by retailers', *International Journal of Retail and Distribution Management*, vol. 22, no. 2, pp. 3–11.
Bessen, J. (1993) 'Riding the marketing information wave', *Harvard Business Review*, vol. 71, no. 5, pp. 150–60.

Bohoris, G.A. and J.M. Thomas (1995) 'A heuristic for vehicle routing and depot staffing', *Journal of the Operational Research Society*, vol. 46, no. 10, pp. 1184–91.

Bristow, D. (1990) 'The cool chain: the role of the distributor', *International Journal of Retail and Distribution Management*, vol. 18, no. 6, pp. 10–16.

Brown, M. (1994) 'Sainsbury's star act', *Management Today*, April, pp. 79–83.

Canen, A. and L. Scott (1995) 'Bridging theory and practice in VRP', *Journal of the Operational Research Society*, vol. 46, no. 1, pp. 1–8.

Cooper, J., M. Brown and M. Peters (1994) *European Logistics*, Blackwell, London.

Davies, M. (1995) 'Distribution – special report', *Director*, September, pp. 61–77.

Evans, J. (1993) *Applied Production and Operations Management*, West Publishing, New York.

Fernie, J. and A. McKinnon (1991) 'The impact of changes in retail distribution on a peripheral region: the case of Scotland', *International Journal of Retail and Distribution Management*, vol. 19, no. 7, pp. 25–32.

Martin, A.J. (1993) *Distribution Resource Planning*, Oliver Wight, Essex Junction, VT.

Martin, A.J. (1994) *Infopartnering*, Omneo, Essex Junction, VT.

Moore, E.J. (1991) 'Grocery distribution in the WR: recent changes and future prospects', *International Journal of Retail and Distribution Management*, vol. 19, no. 7, pp. 18–24.

Salhi, S., M. Sari, D. Saidi and N.A.C. Tonati (1992) 'Adaptation of some vehicle fleet mix heuristics', *Omega*, vol. 20, no. 5/6, p. 653–60.

Slater, A. (1986) *Handbook of Physical Distribution Software*, Kogan Page, London.

Stenger, A.J., S.C. Dunn and R.R. Young (1993) 'Commercially available software for integrated logistics management', *International Journal of Logistics Management*, vol. 4, no. 2, pp. 61–74.

Sussams, J.E. (1991) 'The impact of logistics on retailing and physical distribution', *International Journal of Retail and Distribution Management*, vol. 19, no. 7, pp. 4–9.

Wilsher, P. (1994) 'Where Britain leads the world', *Management Today*, June, pp. 70–4.

Wunderlich, J., M. Collette, L. Levy and L. Bodin (1992) 'Scheduling meter readers for Southern California Gas Company', *Interfaces*, vol. 22, no. 3, pp. 22–30.

Discussion topics/exercises

1. An organization operates a chain of do-it-yourself (DIY) stores which are serviced by a series of regional distribution centres (RDCs) run by one of the major suppliers. Goods are shipped in standard-sized containers, both from the RDCs to the stores, and also from the manufacturers to the RDCs. The RDCs are limited in the number of containers they can handle. The relative locations of the stores and the RDCs have resulted in different delivered unit costs. The sales at the stores have resulted in different requirements. All of these data are presented below.

store	V	W	X	Y	Z	available
A	17	29	33	36	17	100
RDC: B	32	18	15	25	37	85
C	38	30	22	10	17	145
required	85	90	50	65	40	

How should the RDCs meet the requirements of the stores?

Describe how the above model could be used to support a range of associated transportation decision-making scenarios.

2. Use practical examples and illustrations to explain the following:
   (a) Distribution resource planning
   (b) Transhipment problem
   (c) Vehicle scheduling.

3. You have just taken over as operations manager for the service department of an electrical retailer. Your organization sells a wide range of electrical appliances, and includes extended warranties of up to five years. For larger items (fridges, cookers, dishwashers and so on) any service requirement is handled in the consumer's home. You have a team of six service engineers, and from your base in Exeter, you are responsible for an area extending from Penzance to a line drawn between Bristol and Brighton.

   Currently there is no real system for allocating work to the service engineers. As they arrive for work, they each select the repair requests that they think they can handle that day (on a sort of first-come, first-served basis), normally leaving at least one, and usually two engineers in the workshop to handle the small warranty/repair work which has been posted or brought in.

   You are struck by the apparent chaos that this lack of system has resulted in, particularly from the customers' perspective. Your office receives frequent phone calls concerning progress being made with repairs and for estimates of when a service engineer is likely to call.

   You decide that a more formalized approach is required, and sit down to think about the information you will need, the major decision areas, and how these might be tackled.

4. Describe three different service situations which can be viewed as examples of the 'travelling salesman problem', and in each case outline an appropriate heuristic which could be used to develop a good solution.

Chapter 11

Process design and improvement

Chapter outline

☆ The context and scope of process design decisions
☆ Equipment selection
☆ Work design
     Macro level
     Micro level
☆ Service blue printing
☆ Layout
☆ Benchmarking

The context and scope of process design decisions

We focused earlier on issues associated with identifying customers' requirements, using these as part of the input into the process of specifying the range of services to be provided and finally establishing the key parameters in the specification. This chapter develops this discussion further and presents facets of the process involved in designing the service delivery system: that is, establishing the best (or at least a good) way of providing the customer with the service which has been specified. In terms of the Parasuraman, Zeithaml, Berry (PZB) model of service quality, it is about ensuring the match between service delivery and service quality specifications, eliminating gap 3. In this there is the recognition that the situation changes over time (for example, expectations alter, new technologies emerge, new materials are developed). Thus while there is the need to design initially a very good (the best?) delivery system, there is also the requirement to seek constant improvement in order to maintain and develop advantage over competitors.

In a greenfield situation (a new organization starting to deliver a totally new service in a specific location), there is the advantage of starting from a zero base and making a range of decisions relating to the design of the service delivery system. Initially, these relate to investment in the necessary equipment and infrastructure, and investment in people (skills and competences); these can often be thought of as the strategic-level decisions and are frequently closely related. (In some sense, the location decision can also be thought of as part of the service delivery design process, although it was considered separately earlier.) The next stage relates to considerations surrounding the way work is organized, at a macro level, looking broadly at different work areas. The split between front office (the area with the direct customer contact) and the back room can be important in this context. At the next level, the determination of the best way for the individual to perform the task can be significant. It is crucial to measure performance and to use this internally to drive a process of improvement, but also externally to compare with best practice in the sector – competitive benchmarking. This process is shown diagramatically in Figure 11.1. As an illustration consider the following scenario.

A partnership of three general medical practitioners (GPs) has been providing a medical care service for part of a large town. This has grown from the practice of the father of one of the GPs, which operated from the ground floor of a large Victorian house. At the other side of the town, there is a second GP practice operated by a husband and wife team who plan to retire in three months. The partnership decided to take over this practice and establish a new centrally based GP medical centre. In designing the service delivery system for this new centre, they will be faced with a variety of decisions. Initially, it will be necessary to determine the new staffing requirements: these are likely to fall into around three categories, medical, paramedical (nursing, etc.) and support (clerical, reception, etc.). Issues associated with these decisions are within the human resources sphere and will be dealt with in Chapter 14. Linked to this is the selection of the equipment required for the new medical centre. This will range from medical related to support (for example, a network of personal computers). It will be necessary to look at how the work will be organized among the medical staff, the paramedical and support staff in terms of both patient contact and 'behind-the-scenes' activity. In some areas, it will be necessary to lay down procedures to handle certain (repetitive) activities like handling enquiries, booking appointments and home visits by the GPs. It will also be critical to look at the layout of some of the work areas in some detail.

The presence of customers in the system and their participation in the service delivery adds a further dimension of complexity to the decisions involved in the process outlined in Figure 11.1. Some of the equipment selected will actually be used by the customer, so that because of the relative infrequency of use it might be selected for the ease with which it can be used, rather than the efficiency with which it performs the desired task. In some ways, a 'lowest possible denominator' approach might be adopted, assuming a zero level of familiarity.

Additionally, organization of work can be approached from a variety of perspectives. This can design for the 'convenience' of the service deliverer or for the convenience of the 'customer', and frequently these two do not match up. We are told in stores 'you can't pay for that here, you must pay at that counter over there' (where there always seems to be a queue). We arrive to find signs like 'Office only open 10.00 to 12.00 and 2.30 to 4.00', when we (the customer) are only free at lunchtime. We have to wait at home all morning because we are told that the meter reader will arrive sometime between 8.30 a.m. and 1.00 p.m.

Clearly, we must be realistic in terms of our expectations, and equally organizations must be clear in how they perceive that they compete in the market place (there is a clear difference between competing on cost and competing by offering a highly customized

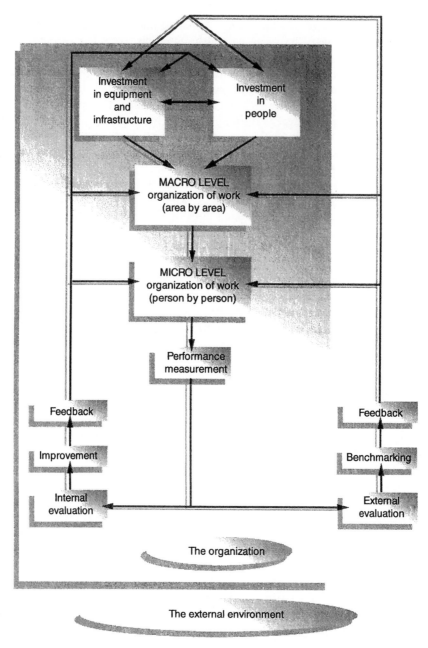

Figure 11.1 The service delivery design and improvement process

personal service). Passengers in the economy section of an aircraft have different expectations from those in the first-class section. In part, this will be reflected in the service delivery systems developed.

In the following sections of this chapter, the various facets of the design of the service delivery system will be covered in more detail. There will be an examination of the key issues which surround the selection of equipment, followed by a discussion of work organization at both the macro and micro levels, including the use of some techniques to support this process. This will be linked to layout, and the technique of service blueprinting. Finally, benchmarking will be presented as part of the continuous improvement process.

Selection of equipment

One of the difficulties in the design of a new service delivery system is the identification of the correct point at which to start and the sequence for the other decisions that follow. In practice, the various different 'activities' (select equipment, select and recruit staff, macro-level organization of work, micro-level organization of work and so on) will go on in parellel, with emphasis and intensity varying over time, and decisions made when all the appropriate information is at hand.

A starting point is the specification of the service designed to meet the requirements of the target group of customers. An early decision which has to be made is the equipment to support this service delivery. Linked to this are issues associated with the way the equipment is to be used, and the layout of the 'area' in which it is to be used. Thus the bus company about to launch a new local service will need to examine the types of route to be covered, the state of the road network (which could influence the possible dimensions and manoeuvrability of the buses) and, the types of customer.

However, we are not always faced with a 'greenfield' situation. It might be that there has been an upturn in demand for a particular service: the management consultancy has seen a doubling of the number of clients and has taken on new consultants; the restaurant has expanded into the building next door in order to satisfy the demands of potential diners. It might be that the existing equipment has become technologically obsolete or uneconomical to maintain. This can be particularly true of equipment based on computers, and is especially important when the equipment is used directly by the consumer. Bank cards where the information is held on a chip are more flexible than those which have the information stored on a magnetic strip. Some international ATM systems can determine the nationality of the customer from the card and display the instructions in an appropriate language.

It is important to understand the context of the equipment selection decision. At the centre is the *use* that it is planned to make of the equipment: this can be either by the employee (regular) or by the customer (casual) or both. In some environments this will be determined by location, as back room equipment is generally available only to employees, while that in the front office can be accessible to either group. Availability relates to when the organization hopes to take delivery of the equipment, and is crucial for planning purposes. The costs considered should be the total lifetime costs, rather than simply the purchase cost. Finally, it is necessary to recognize that the entire decision-making process is surrounded by a degree of uncertainty and to take account of this, as far as is possible and realistic. Each of these aspects will now be considered in turn.

Availability

Some items of equipment are standard and may be available off-the-shelf, so clearly availability should not be a major issue. This also facilitates the selection process, since it allows the organization to view the equipment in use prior to purchase, and possibly talk to existing users (in non-competitive organizations). The college considering replacing its major photocopier might be able to see the model that it is considering purchasing in use in the local authority administration department. Accurate delivery estimates are important for planning purposes if the phasing out of the existing equipment is being co-ordinated with the purchase. This can be more problematical if the equipment will have to be specially designed or customized. Included in this category are items like computer software, where it can be more difficult to predict development time, and there can be the temptation to use the software commercially (to 'go live') before it has been properly tested if the commissioning date has been reached. Computer software systems can be used to support a whole range of services, including providing insurance quotations and documentation, controlling the operations of ATMs in banks, dealing with catalogue enquiries and book issues in libraries, reserving seats on aircraft, processing marks for examinations in colleges, handling tax records for the Inland Revenue, and recording registration details for motor vehicles.

Analysis of use

This is a key factor in the selection process, although it is often tempting to consider cost first. However, if the equipment does not provide the required functionality, then purchase should not be considered. Within the analysis of use, there are a whole range of operational issues which need to be considered. Prior to this analysis, however, it is necessary to determine the required capacity of the equipment over its lifetime: this normally means forecasting the level of activity which generates the required usage. Thus for the photocopier to be purchased by the college, if this was to be used primarily to copy student handouts, then it would be necessary to forecast student numbers over its life, together with the usage of copies per student. This should clearly be within the capacity of the copier.

There are a number of key features which should be examined as part of the use analysis. There are considered in more detail below.

Functionality

Under the heading of functionality, it is important to distinguish between essential functions and desirable functions. Thus we may require our copier to collate (say, up to 50 copies), copy on to card, staple, reduce, enlarge and prepare overhead transparencies; although we might decide that the ability to decide the actual number and position of the staples is only a desirable factor. A key decision can be between general purpose and special purpose equipment. With general purpose equipment, the initial investment is lower and there is less risk of obsolescence. However, the quality can sometimes be rather variable. With special purpose equipment, the efficiency in use is higher, but often a wider range of skills are used. Thus if the reprographic department were staffed by dedicated personnel, it might be decided to purchase a copier and a separate machine to make overhead transparencies. If it were open to all (that is, if the customers could use the equipment), a general purpose copier which also made transparencies might be selected. Often general purpose equipment is attractive for the front office area, where the customer is present and flexibility is at a premium, whereas special purpose equipment is more suited to the back room, where higher levels of efficiency are sought. Flexibility is also important: will it be possible, if necessary, to increase the collating facility to handle 100 copies? Another consideration is the state of development of the equipment: those at the frontiers of technology can offer advantages over the competition, but not without the risk associated with any new product in terms of the lack of a proven track record in use (although the reputation of the manufacturer can be relevant).

Compatibility

Compatibility can be important in the front office if the equipment is to be used by the customer. This is particularly true in a self-service environment. For example, the method of use of the new hot meal dispenser might be very similar to that of the existing hot drinks machine. If there is a lack of compatibility, this can have significant implications for training and require a change in work methods. Consider, for example, the impact of the new computer system at the insurance broker's office, which not only gives quotations, but will also confirm cover and issue documentation, instead of having to send the handwritten proposal form to the insurance company head office for processing.

Ease of use

A key feature is the ease of use, which is naturally even more significant if customer usage is involved, because of the potential irregularity of this use. Thus the microwave oven available to customers in the self-service restaurant to reheat meals will probably need to be easier to use than the microwave used by the kitchen staff to prepare the meals. Equally, safety is an important consideration: potential problems due to misuse are likely to be greater in the front office area than the back room because tighter control can normally be exercised over employees than customers.

Technical/organizational issues

Technical or organizational considerations include such aspects as the installation of the equipment. How long will it take, and how complex will it be? Can the service be offered during the transfer, or will operations cease? No copying can be carried out next Monday and Tuesday while the existing copier is removed and the new copier installed. It will also be necessary to know about the quality of the after-sales service (an engineer on-site to respond to a callout within 4 hours – guaranteed), and linked to this the reliability (likelihood of breakdown) of the equipment. Although maintenance can extend the working life, excessive maintenance is expensive both in terms of direct cost and reduced availability. A planned maintenance schedule is important.

Cost aspects

The important issue here is to recognize that cost implies more than simply the initial purchase price and normally refers to the total life cycle cost, which includes all the attributable costs over the life of the equipment. A piece of equipment might be cheap to purchase yet expensive to run, and this is often more attractive to an organization than one which is slightly more expensive to purchase, but significantly cheaper to run. This is because organizations often distort the evaluation by paying for the equipment out of two separate budgets. The initial purchase comes from a capital budget, but this budget is often very 'constrained' and all departments in the organization make bids for expenditure against this. The running costs, however, might typically come out of an operating budget, under the direct control of the department, over the life of the equipment. This offers more flexibility, especially further into the future.

It is important to 'capture' all of the costs involved in using a certain piece of equipment. The initial costs include the purchase price but also any set-up/installation-related costs. The running costs are those which vary with the extent of usage, and include labour, materials, power and maintenance. This again emphasizes the importance of having forecasts of activity over the life of the equipment in order to be able to estimate running costs. Fixed costs are incurred irrespective of usage, and include elements like insurance. Often there will be positive benefits which can be quantified and need including in the analysis. These include the trade-in value of existing equipment and the sale of redundant spare parts.

It is frequently necessary to take account of the 'time value' of money in this financial analysis, especially if the life of the equipment is long. This process of discounting, involving the calculation of the net present value of the stream of expenditure into the future, allows the estimation of a single current financial equivalent. More details of this can be found in most accounting texts.

Increasingly, there are more varied approaches to the financing of capital expenditure. These range across a variety of different rental, hiring, leasing and contracting options, which may include maintenance or other associated running costs. Some schemes even include provision of operators for the equipment. Evaluation of these can be quite a complex process and should be approached with care.

Uncertainty

Most decisions are taken in an environment which has a degree of uncertainty surrounding it, and it is important that this is recognized. Equipment selection is no exception. A number of steps can be taken, however, to reduce the impact of this and to improve the 'quality' of the decision being made. Existing users of proposed equipment in other organizations can often provide information about the performance of suppliers in areas which are key to the decision. Thus for the copier illustration used earlier, it might be possible to build up a picture of the delivery performance (of the ten customers spoken to, six had the copier delivered on schedule, one a week early, two one week late and one two weeks late), reliability (only two callouts for emergency repairs over a combined 20 years of usage), and response times to callout (both within 4 hours – in fact, maximum response times could also be 'written' into the contract along with penalties for non-achievement).

Frequently, there is uncertainty in the various quantitative parameters surrounding the decision. The organization might find it difficult to forecast accurately the demand for the service (especially further into the future), some of the cost parameters involved, and the price the customer is prepared to pay. These can all have an impact on the relative attractiveness of alternative choices in terms of equipment. It is possible to carry out a sensitivity analysis: that is, to look at how sensitive the decision is to changes in these key parameters. Thus, in choosing between two copiers, it will be possible to estimate the total cost per copy, at different levels of activity. An example of this analysis is given in Figure

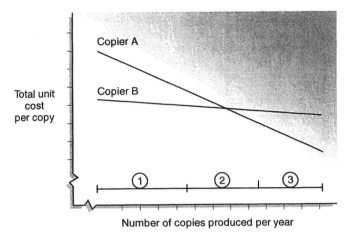

Number of copies produced per year

Figure 11.2 Sensitivity analysis by output level

11.2. It can be seen that if the number of copies required per annum falls within region 1, then copier B is clearly preferable to copier A. Similarly, in region 3, A is preferable to B. However, in region 2, the situation is less clear, and perhaps if usage is likely to be in this region, attempts should be made to obtain better estimates of usage (use of questionnaires or market research in general and so on). This sensitivity analysis can be relatively easy to carry out, and can be completed for any of the parameters over which there is a degree of uncertainty.

Macro-level organization of work

Project, job, batch and flow

There are a number of different suggested structures for a generic framework for the macro-level organization of work. Probably the most common classification puts this organization into four broad categories:

- Project.
- Job.
- Batch.
- Flow.

At one end of the scale, 'project' is used to describe a relatively major and complex undertaking which typically involves a (large) number of related tasks with complex interrelationships. It has a distinct beginning and end. Examples are organizing a major event like an international conference, the launch of a new service (which could include phased market research) and a major management consultancy project. A small illustration is given in Figure 11.3. This is part of a project which involves the organization of a conference. The relationships among the individual activities or tasks which make up the

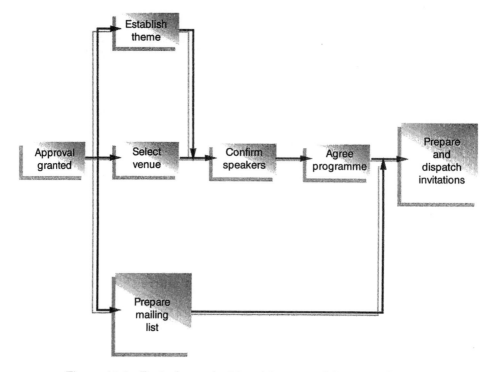

Figure 11.3   Part of a project involving organizing a conference

project are shown by lines. Thus 'confirming speakers' cannot start until the venue has been selected and the theme has been established. The invitations cannot be prepared and dispatched until the programme has been agreed and a mailing list of potential attendees has been prepared.

Provided estimates are available for the durations of the individual activities, the network representation can be used to support a variety of analyses relating to such issues as the likely duration of the project, and the identification of those activities which cannot be delayed without delaying the entire project. This can also be linked into questions surrounding the allocation of resources, when the numbers of people required for each task are known and there is a limit on the overall availability. There are also a number of organizational issues which should be considered which relate to the way the people who work on the individual activities are managed and co-ordinated. These and other related aspects are covered in Lockyer and Gordon (1996).

'Job' is often considered as a smaller-scale 'project', when the entire service is delivered by a single person (or possibly a group of people). Examples are the hairdresser who advises the customer on the style, then cuts, washes and dries the hair; the TV repair person who diagnoses the fault, repairs the set and sends you the invoice for payment (and finally deposits your cheque in the bank); and the weather forecaster who uses a microcomputer to access and analyze the data from the meteorology office, prepares the forecasts, develops the graphics to present them, writes the script to accompany them, and then stands in

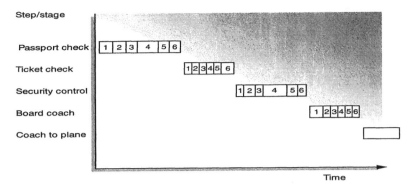

Step/stage

Passport check
Ticket check
Security control
Board coach
Coach to plane

Time

Figure 11.4 Batch processing of passengers boarding a plane

front of a self-activated camera to broadcast them. This approach to organizing work can be popular in high-contact services, as the presence of the customer frequently results in requests for 'customization', which can be handled more easily in the one-to-one situation. However it can require a diversity of skills, as with the weather forecaster just described. It can also result in low utilization of equipment. While this does not matter with low-value equipment, the potentially underused studio in the weather forecasting illustration could be more of a concern. There is a high level of visibility in terms of what is happening, so planning and control are easier. Normally the service is being provided continuously once started, so from the customers' perspective, value is being added all the time.

Handling in 'batches' attempts to gain efficiencies in terms of processing. At each step, the process is carried out on each customer in the batch before the batch proceeds to the next step. Thus a group of passengers flying from Leeds to Paris will queue to have their passports checked one at a time, will queue to have their tickets checked, will have to go through the security check (X-ray hand luggage and body check), will queue to get on to the coach, will be driven to the plane, will queue to get on the plane and will be flown to Paris, after which the reverse process will take place. Part of the process is shown diagramatically in Figure 11.4. Documents are also frequently processed in batches. A set of examination papers might go first to Dr Smith to mark questions 2 and 3; when this is complete, to Professor Brown to mark question 1; and when this is finished to Mr White to mark questions 4, 5 and 6. Finally, Dr Smith will calculate total marks and averages for all students.

As there is a queue for the server, this allows for high levels of efficiency, but is not very attractive from the customer's perspective. It also allows the servers to specialize, and this can be important if they 'belong' to different organizations: for example, immigration (passport control), security and airline (ticketing) in Figure 11.4. The queues also extend the period that the customer spends in the system, which can be a cause for dissatisfaction. Another illustration of a type of batch processing is the manner in which groups of customers are processed simultaneously in lectures, guided tours and so on. In general, the larger the batch, the less the opportunity for interaction (and, therefore, customization) and possibly the less 'satisfactory' the delivered service.

Examining Figure 11.4, it is possible to ask why the traveller cannot go immediately to the next step after finishing the current step. There may be a legitimate reason: for security purposes, the passengers must move together from the airport building to the

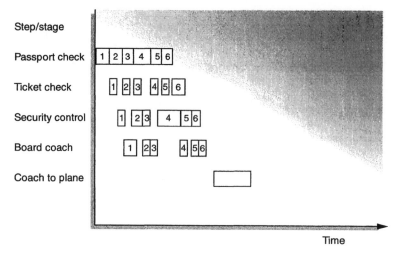

Figure 11.5   Partial flow processing of passengers boarding a plane

coach. Alternatively, more rapid moving on may be a possibility, with passengers moving directly to the next step. The effect on the first three stages is shown in Figure 11.5. It can be seen that, while this 'speeds up' the throughput time, there is still some queuing. This is because the steps are not balanced. If it were possible to ensure that each passenger spent the same time at each step, then they could flow through the system with no waiting. The nature of this process is such that this is unlikely to be possible: some passports will need more detailed examination than others, some passengers' hand baggage will need examination after X-ray, but not all. However, it is sometimes possible to set up a system so that the customer flows through. An example is the electric buggies which some museums use to convey visitors along a prescribed route around exhibits at a predetermined speed. Documents can also sometimes be processed in a flow manner.

In order to study and develop any of the above ways of organizing work, it is necessary to ensure that the method is correct, and to know how long the different steps in processing will take. These aspects will be examined in more detail later in the chapter.

In practice, a hybrid of the above categories is frequently used which has features which follow the dominant type (like the batch processing of patients at a hospital, four arriving each with an appointment at 9.00 a.m. to see the single consultant). Equally, where the service can be divided into front office and back room, in the high-contact area a job-type service can be provided, whereas in the back office, more efficient batch or flow processes might be used. In a restaurant, the waiter service would be carried out on a job basis, while the meals might be prepared and cooked in batches. In the loan office, the assistant will deal directly with the applicant, whereas behind the scenes, the application documentation might be dealt with as a flow process.

An alternative classification

It has been argued (Silvestro *et al.*, 1992) that the following six dimensions should be used as a basis for classifying service processes:

- Whether focus in the delivery system is on the contribution of equipment (e.g. a transportation system) or people (e.g. a hairdresser).
- The length of the customer contact time (short and spasmodic to continuous throughout the service).
- The degree of customization (each individual treated differently, French restaurant; all treated the same, coach tour).
- The extent to which customer contact personnel can exercise judgement in meeting customer needs (ranging from the service offered by a solicitor to that provided by a water company).
- The source of the added value, the front office or the back office (the cinema to an insurance company).
- The product or process focus (electricity supply to an education service).

They base their categorization on a systematic analysis of a variety of different classification systems presented by a range of authors, more details of which can be found in the article. They present a set of formal definitions of these classifications, which are reproduced in Figure 11.6.

They then applied these definitions to eleven for-profit service organizations. From their analysis they concluded that there were three types of service process, professional service, service shop and mass, based on these six characteristics. These are shown in Figure 11.7. By categorizing any particular service along these dimensions, and identifying the dominant process, it is possible to determine the key features in the design of the service delivery system.

The impact of technology on process design

Technology can have a major impact on the design of the service delivery process, in terms of both the macro- and micro-level organization of work. Electronic point of sale (EPOS) systems have improved customer handling at supermarket checkouts by speeding up the process of preparing the bill. In the 'back office' they have had a significant impact too, as price changes (increases!) can be effected more readily and less obviously to the customer (no removal or oversticking with a new price label, simply alter the price allocated to the bar code on the computer database). There is the added (and perhaps less apparent) benefit for the consumer that the system, by capturing information on all sales, can monitor stock levels and thus trigger replenishment for items before stockout occurs. The negative side includes the impact of human error: a price label misread by the checkout operator using manual methods results in one customer being wrongly charged, while an incorrectly recorded price on the database results with EPOS in every consumer purchasing that item being wrongly charged. It is sometimes necessary to spell out the benefits of technology to consumers, as these are often felt to be focused on operational efficiency rather than customer service.

Computerized reservation systems have had a major impact on the hospitality, travel and leisure industries generally, altering methods of working and even office layouts. Consider the typical travel agencies with the computer monitors on the assistants' desks. The level of information on alternatives, availability, and the links between transport and accommodation is remarkable, and have both changed the way staff work and also improved

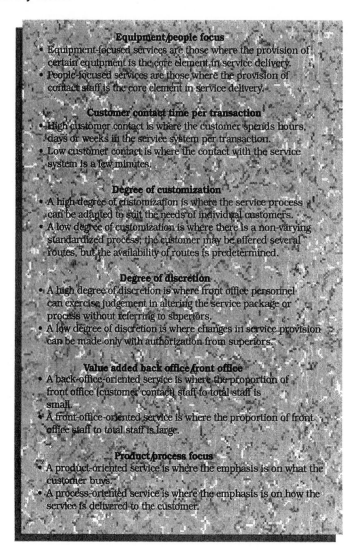

Equipment/people focus
- Equipment-focused services are those where the provision of certain equipment is the core element in service delivery.
- People-focused services are those where the provision of contact staff is the core element in service delivery.

Customer contact time per transaction
- High customer contact is where the customer spends hours, days or weeks in the service system per transaction.
- Low customer contact is where the contact with the service system is a few minutes.

Degree of customization
- A high degree of customization is where the service process can be adapted to suit the needs of individual customers.
- A low degree of customization is where there is a non-varying standardized process; the customer may be offered several routes, but the availability of routes is predetermined.

Degree of discretion
- A high degree of discretion is where front office personnel can exercise judgement in altering the service package or process without referring to superiors.
- A low degree of discretion is where changes in service provision can be made only with authorization from superiors.

Value added back office/front office
- A back-office-oriented service is where the proportion of front office (customer contact) staff to total staff is small.
- A front-office-oriented service is where the proportion of front office staff to total staff is large.

Product/process focus
- A product-oriented service is where the emphasis is on what the customer buys.
- A process-oriented service is where the emphasis is on how the service is delivered to the customer.

Figure 11.6 Definitions of service classifications (Source: Silvestro *et al.*, 1992, p. 67)

the service available to customers. If a departing flight is delayed or cancelled, it is possible to search for alternative routes and check their availability in minutes, thus enabling travel to continue almost on schedule.

The introduction of automated teller machines (ATMs) in banking has had the effect of providing a range of standard banking services, including cash withdrawals, 24 hours a day. At the same time, routine tasks have been taken out of the 'front office' area, allowing greater flexibility and job satisfaction for the counter staff.

A major impact of technology is in either removing some of the more mundane tasks from the front-line staff, or supporting them in performing tasks more efficiently. It is

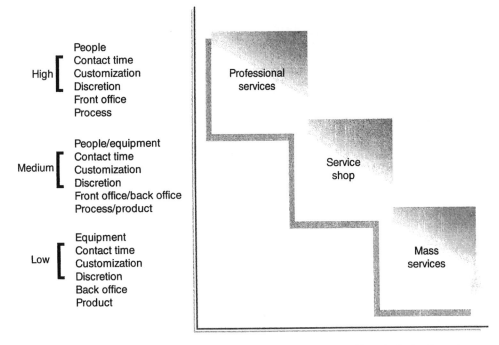

People
Contact time
High   Customization
Discretion
Front office
Process

People/equipment
Contact time
Medium   Customization
Discretion
Front office/back office
Process/product

Equipment
Contact time
Low   Customization
Discretion
Back office
Product

Professional services

Service shop

Mass services

Number of customers processed by a typical unit per day

Figure 11.7   Three types of service process (Source: Silvestro *et al.*, 1992, p. 73)

important, however, to recognize the impact that this might have on the quality of the service as perceived by the consumer. Customers in a variety of service settings value the interaction with the provider of the service, and the introduction of excessive technology can alienate this segment of the market.

Walley and Amin (1994) provide a comprehensive review and analysis of automation in a customer contact environment. They cover a number of issues, including limitations and a conceptual framework. They include case study material from a health care environment, vending machines (ATMs) and petrol pumps.

Micro-level organization of work

A number of approaches can be adopted to examine the micro-level organization of work: that is, at the level of the individual or group of individuals. One approach is frequently referred to as 'organization and methods' when these techniques are applied in a clerical or an administrative context. However, the underlying structure can be applied successfully in a range of service situations. In general terms, it involves an examination of both the way a service is being delivered and techniques for establishing or measuring the time that it should take. Such times are frequently used in capacity management and operations

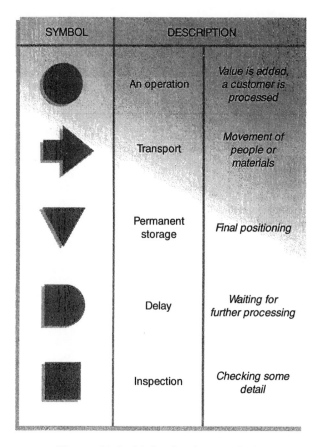

SYMBOL	DESCRIPTION	
	An operation	*Value is added, a customer is processed*
	Transport	*Movement of people or materials*
	Permanent storage	*Final positioning*
	Delay	*Waiting for further processing*
	Inspection	*Checking some detail*

Figure 11.8 Main charting symbols

planning, so these techniques of work measurement will be covered in the next chapter, along with these other issues.

The systematic and structured approach to improving work methods (or method study, as it is sometimes referred to) can be formulated within a six-step process:

1. Select the work to be examined.
2. Record the existing method.
3. Examine the existing method.
4. Develop and define a new and improved approach.
5. Implement the new method.
6. Maintain the new method as standard practice.

Each of these steps will now be considered in more detail.

The selection of appropriate work is the starting point for any such exercise. There are certain factors which indicate that potential benefit might be gained from a method study exercise. These include bottlenecks (there are always queues waiting to use a copier

FLOW PROCESS CHART	●	➡	D	■	▽
Enter shop		●			
Select potential tour companies from display	●				
Walk to counter for missing brochures		●			
Wait to see assistant			●		
Obtain missing brochures	●				
Walk to seating area		●			
Read brochures, select possible holidays	●				
Walk to counter for further information		●			
Wait to see assistant			●		
Enqire about holidays	●				
Assistant logs into system and company database			●		
Examine availabilities, prices, options	●				
Select holiday	●				
Complete booking form and payment	●				
Check all details				●	
Await authorization			●		
Obtain receipt	●				
Leave shop		●			

Figure 11.9 Flow process chart for selecting and booking holidays

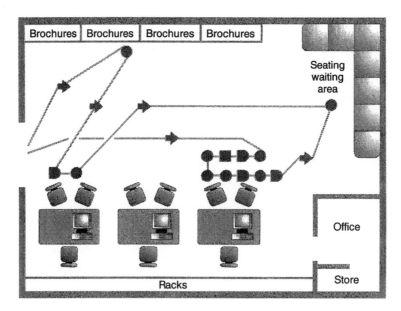

Figure 11.10 Flow diagram for selecting and booking holidays

or computer printer), poor 'quality' (often evidenced by customer complaints about service – 'why haven't I been given a spoon and fork to eat my dessert with?'), idle resources (the checkout operator at the 'baskets only' counter never seems busy) and low morale (often manifesting itself in high absenteeism levels among staff fulfilling a particular role – staff seem to be off sick after three days on the customer enquiry desk, when the 'shift' should last two weeks). Clearly the benefits from the exercise should outweigh its cost. This can mean studying the work involved in those parts of the process which are frequently repeated: for example, table preparation and order taking in a restaurant. It is 'easier' to study work in the back room part of a service organization, where there is little customer contact, although as some of the examples in this chapter show, it is possible in the front office.

The next step is to record the existing method of completing the work. There are a whole range of recording techniques available, depending on the nature of the work. Here two of the major approaches which have been used in a variety of situations will be presented: the flow process chart complemented by the flow diagram. Both of these use five symbols which record the various parts of the process. These, together with their meanings, are shown in Figure 11.8. The flow diagram shows the various parts of the process using these symbols on a representation of the work area, while the flow process chart provides a description of each part, classified according to its type (of the five identified). This is best illustrated with an example.

Consider a couple planning a holiday. They visit their local travel agent. Figure 11.9 describes in detail the process which they go through. It can be seen that they initially look through the brochures to get ideas and then enquire about specific holidays. One of these they finally select and book. The flow process chart in Figure 11.9 is complemented by the flow diagram which shows the process on a diagram of the shop. This is shown in Figure 11.10.

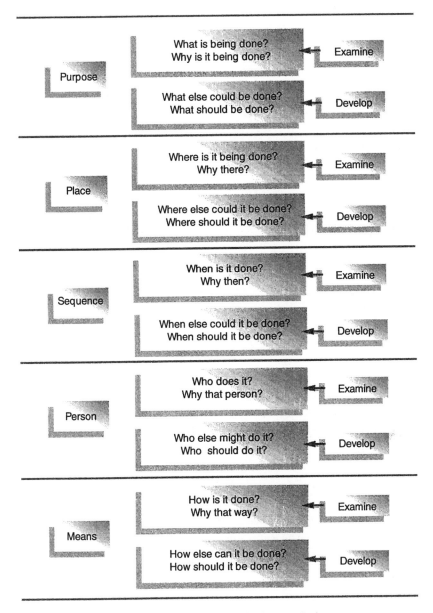

Figure 11.11 The questioning technique

It is worth noting that the record has been viewed from the customers' perspective rather than that of the assistant. Thus for example, authorization is shown as a delay, rather than a transport (assistant walks to the manager's office), wait, inspection, transport (assistant walks back to desk). This recording step is a major part of any study as it can provide great insight into how the service is delivered.

Next, it is necessary to examine critically the record of the way in which the service is being delivered. This can be achieved through a structure called the 'questioning technique'. The format for this is shown in Figure 11.11.

This framework allows both the examination and the development of the improved method to be carried out sequentially. The questions should be posed in the order stated, since if the purpose is challenged, the subsequent activities might disappear. The proposed method can be defined initially using the same recording method, which provides a sensible basis for comparison as part of the implementation process, explaining this to the staff so that they will adopt the new working practice. It is then necessary to take the new method as 'standard operating practice', and maintain its use. This could involve elements of training and ensuring that all new staff are shown the new approach.

Service blueprinting

The rationale behind service blueprinting was developed by Lynn Shostack (see, for example, Shostack, 1982, 1984, 1987). She suggests that blueprinting is an 'extension' of three other basic charts. The flow process diagram (Figure 11.10) and the project network (Figure 11.3, with activity durations added) are 'amalgamated' with elements of the flow diagrams used by designers of computer systems. She uses a simple example of a shoeshine operation to illustrate the approach. The shoes are brushed, polish is applied then buffed off, and finally the money collected. Each activity has a time associated with it: thus brushing the shoes may be estimated to take 30 seconds. Two further concepts make this approach very useful in practice. The first is the recognition of 'fail' points: stages at which things can go wrong and the identification of the remedial action necessary to correct them. The second is the idea of 'line of sight' – some activities can be seen by the customer and others cannot. Thus a fail point could be if the wrong colour of wax were applied and had to be removed, and the process had to be repeated. While the customer could 'see' the shoe-cleaning process, obtaining the materials (polish, etc.) would be outside the line of sight. This is similar to the back room/front office split in some environments.

Shostack identified the key steps in preparing the service blueprint as follows:

1. Identify the activities involved in delivering the service and present these in a diagrammatic form. The level of detail will depend on the complexity and nature of the service.
2. Identify the fail points. These are stages where things might go wrong. The actions necessary to correct these must be determined, and systems and procedures developed to reduce the likelihood of them occurring in the first instance.
3. Set standards against which the performance of the various steps might be measured. Frequently, this is the time taken.
4. Analyze the profitability of the service delivered, in terms of the number of customers served during a period of time.

Consider as an illustration the operations of a small restaurant (the service blueprint is shown in Figure 11.12). Customers arrive and check whether a table is available. They can either have a drink in the bar area and choose their dishes, or go straight through to the restaurant/eating area and order at the table. Decisions are shown in rounded boxes (the

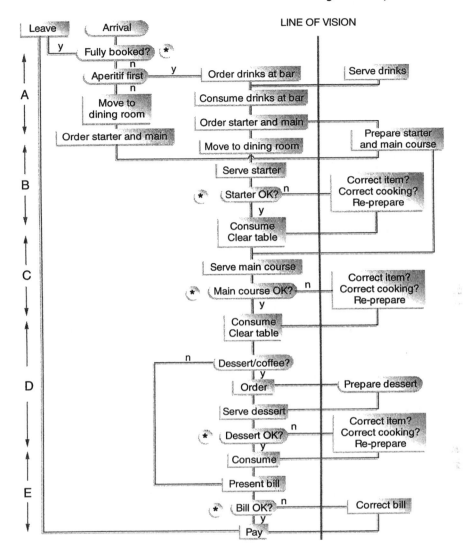

Note: Asterisks mark fail points; decisions are in rounded boxes.

Figure 11.12 Service blueprint for restaurant service

convention in computer flow charts is the use of a diamond). The line of vision is between the restaurant/bar and the preparation areas, and is the interaction between customer and server. One of the first fail points, marked with an asterisk, is if the starter is unsatisfactory. It might 'fail' because it is the incorrect dish or it has been incorrectly cooked. 'Foolproofing' systems to minimize the occurrence of this could include the use of standardized terms for menu items, explanations of cooking styles (rare, medium rare, rose for meat – what do these actually mean?), standard recipes for consistency, procedures to ensure food is ready just as the customer is ready to eat it (or at least ensuring that it can be kept at the correct temperature without drying up or spoiling) and so on. This then repeats for the serving and consumption of the main course. Customers may or may not then take dessert and coffee. The service finishes with the presentation of the bill, and the final fail point. Again, formal procedures in recording the dishes selected, reconciling information from the bar and so on reduce the likelihood of errors here.

The figure also shows the estimated duration of the various stages:

A   5–20 minutes.
B   15–30 minutes.
C   20–40 minutes.
D   0–30 minutes.
E   2–5 minutes.

Thus the entire meal may take between 42 and 125 minutes. Clearly, if desirable these could be broken down into more detail. The variations will be determined in part by the customers (how many drinks do they have at the bar before the meal? how fast do they eat?) and in part by the ratio of staff to clients. However, care is needed (in terms of the design of the system) to ensure the customers are not kept waiting for undue lengths of time, or do not feel that they are being rushed through. Procedures need to be developed to ensure this. The times can be useful as guidelines (how fast can we serve the business group in a hurry?), and to determine profitability (how many diners can be served in one evening with existing staffing levels?).

It is possible to carry out the analysis at a higher level of detail. However, this can then become similar to the method study exercise described earlier. Other illustrations of this approach can be found in Shostack (1987).

Layout

Just as the organization of work can be viewed from both the macro and the micro perspectives, the same is true about layout. In the hospital, it is necessary to consider 'relationships' among the location of reception, the different wards, operating theatres and departments (radiology, pharmacy, pathology and so on). Equally, the layout of the reception area itself must be considered. Where should the reception counter be placed? Where are the entrances and the exits, and what are the traffic flows? Where should the seating and drinks dispenser be located? In the supermarket, how should the different areas be located in relation to each other? Should the bakery products be near to the fresh fruit and vegetables? Within a particular area, how should the different products be positioned (all the apples together? what goes on the bottom shelves?) These examples introduce one of the issues in layout which will be returned to later: how to measure how 'good' the layout is. In the hospital, the concern might be staff convenience or patient convenience; in the supermarket, it could be reducing the distance travelled by customers or exposing them to as many 'purchase opportunities' as possible.

Criteria for layout planning

It is possible to identify a whole range of criteria which should be considered in any situation involving evaluating a layout. The relative importance will clearly vary between different environments. The following list (adapted from Mühlemann *et al.*, 1992) gives some of those key issues:

- *Flexibility*. It should be easy to change the layout if circumstances alter (stores changing layouts for Christmas and Easter).
- *Co-ordination*. It is important that the location of an individual department is viewed in the context of the organization as a whole.
- *Access*. This is particularly important in areas of high customer contact. Consider a small foyer area (3 m × 9 m) in a college building. It has one of the building's two main entrances, doors to two corridors leading to staff and seminar rooms, the only entrance to a 200-seat lecture theatre, a stairway to the first and second floor (no lifts), male and female toilets and a drinks dispenser!
- *Visibility*. It is important that there is a 'transparency of activity' (customers 'forgotten' because they could not be seen waiting, the jar pushed to the back of the bottom shelf in the store).
- *Use of space*. Maximum use should be made of available space (but not to the detriment of accessibility or access). An example is the higher shelves in stores used for storage (rather than selling space).
- *Distance travelled*. Ideally, this should be kept to a minimum both for customers and for staff. However, this is not always the case in supermarkets. Some furniture/household stores are laid out so that customers must walk past all the displays to reach the payment/checkout area.
- *Handling*. It is said that handling adds cost without adding value. This is particularly true in those service environments which involve documents. In supermarkets, products are lifted out of trolleys and scanned, only to be put back into the trolley again.
- *Comfort*. The workplace should be comfortable for both the customer and the staff. This covers such aspects as heating, lighting, noise and so on. This can be particularly difficult in areas where there is a constant throughput of customers.
- *Safety*. All layouts should be inherently safe. This can be particularly problematical in areas where the customer is frequently present. While the behaviour of staff can be influenced by employers, it is more difficult to impose standards on customers since the same 'penalties' do not necessarily exist (for example, passengers walking across the railway line to get to the other side of the platform instead of using the footbridge).
- *Security*. It is necessary to take precautions against theft, fire and so on. This is particularly difficult in environments where there are large numbers of casual, legitimate customers (for example, stores and colleges).
- *Identification*. Working groups identify with and often prefer 'ownership' of their own work area, which can have a significant impact on morale. Consider the personalization of open-plan office areas which frequently takes place.

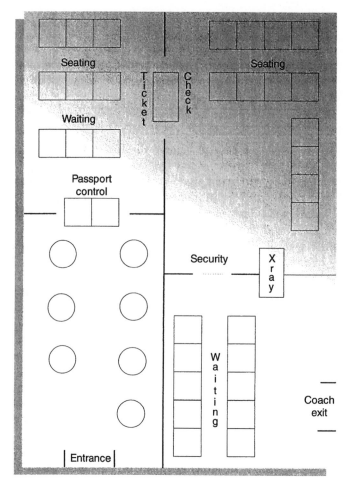

Figure 11.13 Process layout for air passengers

There are a number of approaches to layout problems, and the techniques of method study covered earlier can sometimes be used to examine and improve the layout of a work area. An example is the travel agency described in Figures 11.9 and 11.10.

Process, product and group layouts

The layout at macro level can mirror the way that work is organized: thus batch organization is frequently seen corresponding to layout by process. With this layout, the resources are arranged according to the particular stage in the process that is to be applied to the customer. It reflects a type of 'departmental' structure. A hospital will typically be laid out in this way, with a reception area, pharmacy, radiology department and wards/theatres specializing in particular surgical procedures. A department store is another illustration, with men's wear, ladies' wear, furniture and electrical among the list of departments. Figure 11.13 shows the process layout for the air passengers described earlier in Figure 11.4.

This type of layout is attractive in terms of operational efficiency because the servers need only by provided when the customers arrive, and then there are potentially high levels of utilization because of the queue of customers and the elimination of the idle or non-working times of the servers. It allows the servers to specialize (and possibly become more efficient) at specific tasks. In some cases, the complexity of the process requires this (imagine the radiologist carrying out surgery). Resource shortages with this type of layout need not be too critical. If one of the two staff checking passports in Figure 11.13 is ill, a longer queue forms, *but* processing continues. It is also generally more flexible in that a wide variety of routes might be possible through the resources, and customers can select that which meets their requirements (different patients will visit different departments in the hospital depending on their need: some might require an X-ray, others medication, some both). The disadvantages are primarily from the customers' perspective. The frequency and duration of queuing often mean that customers are in the system longer than they perceive as necessary.

Layout by product or according to the requirements of the service involves identifying the requirements of a specific group of customers and then setting up the resources sequentially so that the customers 'flow' through the system and move from one stage to another until the service is complete. For this flow to be continuous and without delay, each customer must spend approximately the same amount of time at each stage. An example could be a car valeting service. The cars are washed, dried and waxed, the interiors are vacuum cleaned and the upholstery is washed. The correct methods for each of the five processes could be established and each process timed. The correct levels of resources and equipment could then be provided at each stage so that, after initially waiting to start the valeting service, the cars flow through the system without any delays between the individual stages. This layout by product can also be used for processing documents, or in preparing food (often in a fast-food environment).

This approach to layout has the advantage that the customer spends less time in the system than in batch processing because there is little or no queuing, but there are some disadvantages. It assumes that the times spent at each stage are the same for each customer (but the time to wash a large car might be longer than for a small car) and that the stages can be reasonably balanced (resources can be provided so that waxing takes the same time as vacuuming, for example). Moreover, the service has to be standardized, and the customer's presence in the system, interacting with the server, can make this difficult (e.g. a request to clean the inside of the windows again because the customer considers that they are still dirty). There can be initial queuing unless the arrival rate of customers can be managed. If there are problems at any stage (the vacuum cleaner breaks, they run out of wax polish), the entire process halts.

Group layout is a sort of composite of batch and flow, and aims to embrace the advantages of both. The focus is on pulling together resources to meet the requirement of groups of customers with similar needs. Thus a teaching suite might be organized with four small syndicate rooms (each seating fifteen participants) for group work, around a larger lecture room with seats for 80. The motorway cafeteria could have three serving areas instead of just one: the first for hot meals/drinks, the second for cold meals and drinks, and the third for snacks. The insurance office, instead of being organized by process (e.g. renewals, new business, claims), could be grouped by business type: car, personal effects, building. Possibly, even better from the customer's perspective, the organization could be geographical, with a group handling all a customer's requirements (any aspect of any risk), for a specific region (e.g. north-east of England). This approach is generally more customer focused, and is often more satisfying to the employee as it offers a wider variety of possible tasks; stronger links are also built with the customer group.

The use of models

Models can provide an excellent basis for developing and evaluating alternative layouts, and may take a variety of different forms. At a simplistic level, they can consist of no more than a sheet of squared paper, representing, to an appropriate scale, the work area being examined. The resources (people, equipment and so on) can also be represented by cutouts to scale and moved around the work area to different positions. It is then possible to assess the impact of the flow of customers, materials or paperwork through the area. Such a simple two-dimensional model could be used to evaluate different table sizes and the positioning of tables in a restaurant. Here, it would be important to ensure accessibility to all seats at all tables, to the entrances and kitchens, and so on. It is clearly easier to investigate such issues on the model than to move about the actual tables and chairs! A similar type of model could be used to plan out the kitchen area, looking at the interaction between those working in this area. Where height is an important issue, three-dimensional models can be developed, although the effort involved in these is greater.

Earlier in the chapter, flow process charts and flow diagrams were introduced as recording techniques within method study. There are also simple examples of models which can be used to support layout decision making. To these recording techniques can be added the travel or distance chart. This can be useful when the concern is about travel between different locations: for example, offices in an administrative environment, wards in a hospital, lecture/seminar rooms in a college, or departments in a store. This can be viewed from the perspective of either the customer or the staff travelling.

An example is shown in Figure 11.14. This might represent the distance between the various teaching locations (seminar and lecture rooms) in a college and the number of students moving between the locations, during a typical timetabled week. The decision here is to allocate classes to rooms in such a way that the total distance travelled (individual distances multiplied by numbers of students) is kept as low as possible. It can be useful to superimpose the data from a travel chart on to a scale diagram of the locations, by labelling lines joining the locations with the customer (staff) numbers moving between the locations.

This process can be represented in Figure 11.15. This pulls together issues covered earlier in the chapter. The constraints can be 'hard' in that they are conditions which must be satisfied (for example, washroom facilities *must* be next to the entrance), or 'soft' in that they require interpretation (for example, there must be 'good' access). The criteria listed on page 235 can provide a checklist for this part. Frequently, it is possible to measure the 'performance' of a layout, and this can be used for comparison and selection of that which will be adopted. This could be the total distance travelled as a result of the layout, or a composite measure based on a subject assessment against a number of factors (e.g. access, security, flexibility, comfort) and the weighting and summation of these. The search continues with the identification of possible changes (e.g. swapping the locations of pairs of

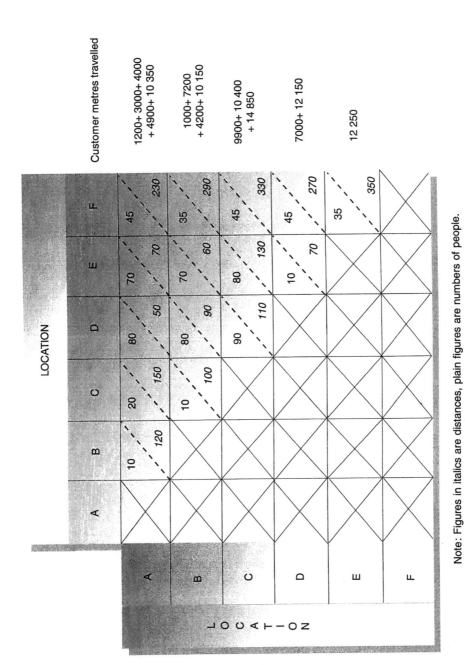

Note: Figures in italics are distances, plain figures are numbers of people.

Figure 11.14 Chart showing distances and travel between locations

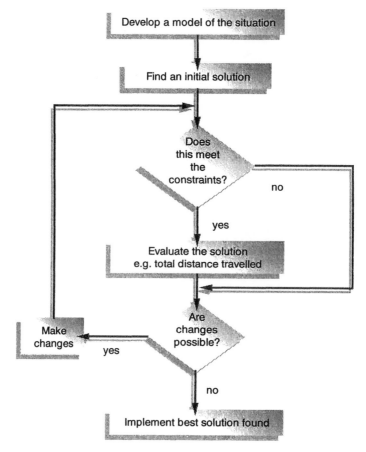

Figure 11.15   Scheme for layout decision making

departments), and the evaluation of the layout resulting from these changes. When no further changes can be considered, the best layout found to date is adopted.

Computers can play a major role in layout situations, particularly when the situation is complex. They can provide the basic pictorial representation in the form of the two- or three-dimensional models described earlier, icons can be used for the individuals and equipment, and various configurations developed and explored interactively very rapidly. In this role, they are supporting the decision-making process. However, software has been developed which goes further, and within a carefully defined environment will handle the entire process shown in Figure 11.15. It will develop a stream of possible 'changes' to an existing layout and systematically evaluate each, finding the best.

Layout in retail environents

Layout in retailing is a key issue: the costs of refitting a shop are quoted as over £1000 per square metre (adjusted from Davies and Rands, 1992). In performance terms, there is

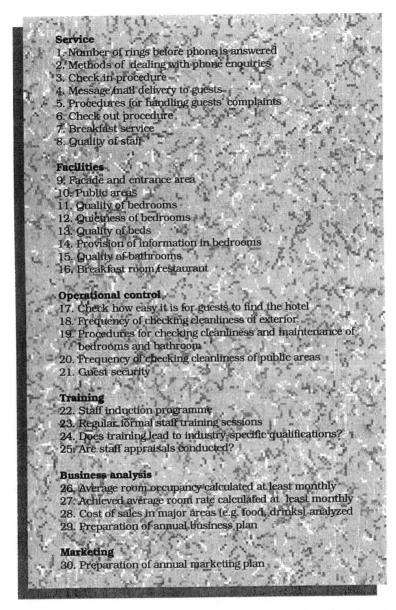

Service
1. Number of rings before phone is answered
2. Methods of dealing with phone enquiries
3. Check in procedure
4. Message/mail delivery to guests
5. Procedures for handling guests' complaints
6. Check out procedure
7. Breakfast service
8. Quality of staff

Facilities
9. Facade and entrance area
10. Public areas
11. Quality of bedrooms
12. Quietness of bedrooms
13. Quality of beds
14. Provision of information in bedrooms
15. Quality of bathrooms
16. Breakfast room/restaurant

Operational control
17. Check how easy it is for guests to find the hotel
18. Frequency of checking cleanliness of exterior
19. Procedures for checking cleanliness and maintenance of bedrooms and bathroom
20. Frequency of checking cleanliness of public areas
21. Guest security

Training
22. Staff induction programme
23. Regular formal staff training sessions
24. Does training lead to industry-specific qualifications?
25. Are staff appraisals conducted?

Business analysis
26. Average room occupancy calculated at least monthly
27. Achieved average room rate calculated at least monthly
28. Cost of sales in major areas (e.g. food, drinks) analyzed
29. Preparation of annual business plan

Marketing
30. Preparation of annual marketing plan

Figure 11.16 Self-assessment areas for smaller hotels (Source: Department of National Heritage, 1996a, pp. 2–7; Crown copyright is reproduced with the permission of the controller of Her Majesty's Stationery Office.)

a somewhat different objective in that the desire is frequently to maximize the customer's exposure to purchasing opportunities. Most retailing texts (see, for example, McGoldrick, 1990) include chapters on layout. Davies and Rands suggest that space allocation in retailing is approached from two standpoints. The first is based on a type of financial modelling: estimating the benefits to be gained from a particular layout or allocation of space. However, this approach is unable to allow for customer behaviour. To balance this quantitative approach, there is the qualitative approach based on the 'designer or social theorist', which, while more customer orientated in so far as it recognizes such issues as aesthetics, colour and lighting, lacks a framework to permit a generic model to be developed to assist in the preparation of a customer-focused layout.

What is striking to the customer is the variability in layouts in retail environments. Consider supermarkets of the same size, both between organizations and within the same organization. Common features arise such as the location of fresh vegetables and fruit products by the entrance, and differences, such as the location of the licensed products sometimes in a separate store within a store. It would not be appropriate here to spend excessive space on this specialist subject. Davies and Rands (1992) include an interesting survey of retail premises. It is important to recognize that many of the ideas in this chapter can also be used to analyze layouts in retail operations.

Benchmarking

Benchmarking is part of the process of continuous improvement. It is defined as measuring the performance of a business against that of the strongest competition in order to establish 'best practice'. Benchmarking can be applied at three levels (Cross and Leonard, 1994). Internal benchmarking can be carried out in the larger organization by way of comparisons between operations units. Thus the supermarket chain might benchmark operations across stores, a financial institution across branches, different hospitals under the same health authority, different colleges under the same education authority. Clearly of paramount importance is how performance is measured, and this has a clear link to the strategy of the organization.

At a second level, competitive benchmarking can be used. This is probably the most frequently quoted use where comparisons are made with directly competitive organizations. This can be achieved relatively easily in some service environments because of the necessity for the customer to participate in the process. As a hotel owner, it is possible to 'sample' the service of a competitor simply by 'posing' as a guest. The airline director can (and probably will anyway) travel on a flight offered by a competitor. Often, however, this is done in an informal manner (Cross and Leonard, 1994). A comparative impression is gained of the service without examining the different facets in a structured way and attempting to measure them.

The third approach is functional or generic benchmarking, which compares specific functions, such as distribution and after-sales service. The advantage here is that information is sometimes easier to obtain than when comparisons are being made with competitors.

Care has to be taken in selecting the dimensions and scales to be used for performance measurement, and in ensuring that due account is taken of all relevant factors. The growth in the use of 'league tables' in the public sector has clouded the issue here. This has been seen in education where, on occasions, there has been a focus on output measures: the number of external examination passes. The concept of 'value added' can sometimes be useful in this situation, examining the difference between output and input. Thus a better

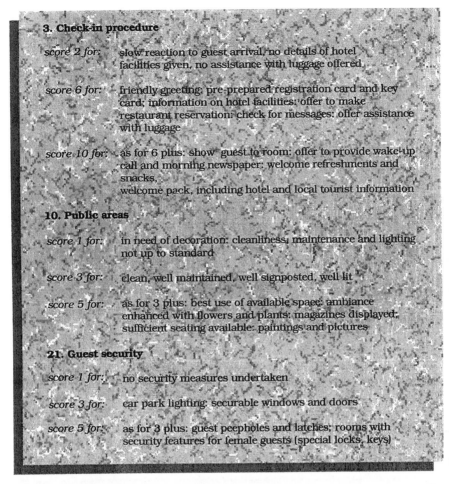

3. Check-in procedure

score 2 for: slow reaction to guest arrival, no details of hotel facilities given, no assistance with luggage offered.

score 6 for: friendly greeting; pre-prepared registration card and key card; information on hotel facilities; offer to make restaurant reservation; check for messages; offer assistance with luggage

score 10 for: as for 6 plus: show guest to room; offer to provide wake-up call and morning newspaper; welcome refreshments and snacks,
welcome pack, including hotel and local tourist information

10. Public areas

score 1 for: in need of decoration: cleanliness, maintenance and lighting not up to standard

score 3 for: clean, well maintained, well signposted, well lit

score 5 for: as for 3 plus: best use of available space; ambiance enhanced with flowers and plants; magazines displayed; sufficient seating available; paintings and pictures

21. Guest security

score 1 for: no security measures undertaken

score 3 for: car park lighting; securable windows and doors

score 5 for: as for 3 plus: guest peepholes and latches; rooms with security features for female guests (special locks, keys)

Figure 11.17 Scoring for check-in procedure, public areas and guest security (Source: Department of National Heritage, 1996a, pp. 2, 4 and 6; Crown copyright is reproduced with the permission of the controller of Her Majesty's Stationery Office.)

performance measure for a school or college could result from attempting to measure the 'ability' of students starting a course, and then repeating the process at the end. The difference would be the 'value added'. Thus it would be possible to compare the performance of different schools (colleges) with different catchment areas (and different inputs).

The Department of National Heritage sponsored a major benchmarking exercise for smaller hotels. This used a self-assessment test which enabled hoteliers to 'measure' their performance across six key areas. Details of these and how they were assessed are given in Figure 11.16. Each of 21 areas are given three descriptions corresponding to scores of 1, 3 and 5; and participants base their score on how they match the descriptions. Illustrations of three of these are given in Figure 11.17. Some of the categories are scored double, and areas 22–30 are simple yes/no. This gives a maximum score of 200 points.

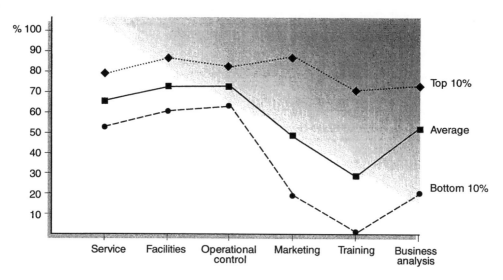

Figure 11.18   Range of performance across the six major areas (Source: Department of National Heritage, 1996b, p. 6; Crown copyright is reproduced with the permission of the controller of Her Majesty's Stationery Office.)

In the benchmarking exercise, 70 hotels were surveyed and the average score was 121. It was suggested that at 130+ a hotel is very efficient and under 110 there is significant scope for improvement. In all cases, scores of 2 or less should be examined. The summarized results are presented in Figure 11.18. These give an organization a clear indication of its relative performance in the six areas.

This case study provides a practical illustration of how a benchmarking exercise could be set up, how the performance could be measured and how it is possible to set in place an action plan for improvement. A generalized scheme is presented in Figure 11.19. The data collection method may be more difficult than that described in the hotel case. Moreover, also in this case, the action plan can be derived more or less directly from the assessment form.

Discussion

This chapter has introduced a range of related issues which are of importance in approaching process design. A set of criteria which are important in selecting the appropriate equipment has been outlined. The various approaches to the organization of work, at both the macro level and micro level have been presented, together with their associated features. This has been linked to the various different approaches to layout. It is thus possible to match the key aspects of the process design to customer requirements. Blueprinting and benchmarking provide frameworks which can be used as part of a process of continuous improvement to ensure that the service delivery system continues to meet customers' requirements.

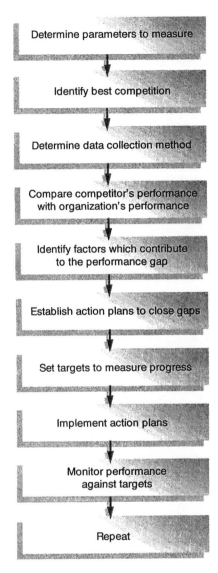

Figure 11.19 The benchmarking process (Source: Adapted from Cross and Leonard, 1994, p. 504)

References

Cross, R. and P. Leonard (1994) 'Benchmarking: a strategic and tactical perspective', in B. Dale (ed.), *Managing Quality*, Prentice Hall, London.

Davies, G. and T. Rands (1992) 'The strategic use of space by retailers: a perspective from operations management', *International Journal of Logistics Management*, vol. 3, no. 2, pp. 63–76.

Department of National Heritage (1996) *Tourism: Competing with the best; benchmarking for smaller hotels*, (a) questionnaire, (b) report, London.

Lockyer, K. and I. Gordon (1996) *Project Management and Project Network Techniques*, Pitman, London.

McGoldrick, P.J. (1990) *Retailing Marketing*, McGraw-Hill, London.

Mühlemann, A.P., J.S. Oakland and K.G. Lockyer (1992) *Production and Operations Management* (6th edn), Pitman, London.

Shostack, G.L. (1982) 'Designing a service', *European Journal of Marketing*, vol. 16, no. 1, pp. 49–63.

Shostack, G.L. (1984) 'Designing services that deliver', *Harvard Business Review*, vol. 62, no. 1, pp. 133–9.

Shostack, G.L. (1987) 'Service positioning through structural change', *Journal of Marketing*, vol. 51, no. 1, pp. 34–43.

Silvestro, R., L. Fitzgerald, R. Johnston and C. Voss (1992) 'Towards a classification of service processess', *International Journal of Service Industry Management*, vol. 3, no. 3, pp. 62–75.

Walley, P. and V. Amin (1994) 'Automation in a customer contact environment', *International Journal of Operations and Production Management*, vol. 14, no. 5, pp. 86–100.

Discussion topics/exercises

1. You have just taken early retirement after 30 years as a lecturer in mathematics at the local college. While not an expert cook, you have always enjoyed experimenting in the kitchen. Additionally, although not completely extrovert, you and your partner enjoy meeting new people.

   About twice a month, you eat out at a local French restaurant. About six months ago the owners purchased a second restaurant in a neighbouring town. However, they seriously overextended themselves and have just gone bankrupt. Both restaurants are now up for sale. You are considering purchasing one. You visit them both, and are very impressed with the location and outlook of your local, although its interior, fitting and equipment look rather 'tired' and dated, especially in the non-customer areas. However, you console yourself with thoughts of your 'lump-sum' and savings, which should more than cover the costs of refurbishing.

   The following weekend, you sit down with your partner to think through what you will need to do if you are to take over the restaurant. In order to plan out when you think it will be possible to reopen, you not only try to map out the major activities, but also try to look in some detail at what will be involved in some of the key decision areas.

2. You are the operations director for an organization which provides a roadside repair and recovery service throughout the mainland United Kingdom. Each year your company replaces approximately one quarter of the vehicles that it uses to support this activity (normally the oldest vehicles).

   Describe how you would approach this process for the current year, paying particular attention to the information required to support the decision and the sources of this information.

3. Select a service delivery system with which you are familiar and prepare flow process charts and flow diagrams when the service is viewed from the perspective of both the customer and the service provider. Identify points where there is a conflict of interest between the two parties.

   Some suggested situations:
   (a) withdrawing cash from the branch of a bank, other than where you hold your account, *without* a cheque guarantee card;
   (b) obtaining insurance cover for your first car, which you are about to purchase;
   (c) the process from checking in for an international flight.

4. Choose a supermarket with which you are familiar. Prepare a plan which shows the layout, and location of the key categories of items.

Prepare a short report and summary which:
(a) evaluates the layout from the customer's perspective;
(b) identifies the features which contribute to the efficiency of the workforce;
(c) suggests and justifies steps which could be taken to improve *both* customer service and store efficiency and effectiveness.

Chapter 12

Resource management and planning

Chapter outline

☆ Resource management and planning decisions
☆ Information requirements
    Forecasting demand
    Establishing the method and resources
☆ Capacity management
    Long-term capacity planning
    Medium-term capacity planning
    Queuing situations
☆ Scheduling and planning
☆ Materials management

Resource management and planning decisions

An organization has to manage a range of different resources. These can be broadly grouped into three categories: physical, human and consumed. All are brought together to deliver a service successfully. Thus the transportation company must have the coach (filled with fuel) and the driver in Leeds to take the passengers to London. The college must have the lecture rooms and teaching staff available in order to take a particular group of students. The hospital must have available beds in wards, operating theatres, drugs, surgeons and nursing staff in order to carry out surgical procedures on potential patients.

The decisions over the management and planning of these resources can be viewed over a range of different time horizons. The long-term decisions are at a strategic level, normally covering years, and relate to major capital and human resource investment decisions: the purchase of new coaches and recruitment of drivers to cover new routes. Medium-term decisions relate to shift patterns and overtime, together with maintenance schedules for coaches over, say, 1–6 months, and the short term concerns the actual allocation of drivers and vehicles to routes (typically, 1 day–1 month). While not all organizations will identify with all these three levels, and certainly the relative timescales will vary considerably from environment to environment, it is important to recognize the importance of planning at these different levels, the objectives of such planning and the information necessary to support the process. This information is key to the planning process, and without it planning would be difficult if not almost impossible. Imagine attempting to establish a timetable for a coach network between major cities before determining the appropriate routes, distances and times. In order to arrange patients' operations, it is necessary to know what each surgical procedure will require in terms of both resources (e.g. nursing and surgical staff) and times (e.g. time needed in the theatre).

Planning is one of the most complex ongoing activities in service organizations (at least in those which practise it!). This is particularly true in those services, or those parts of services, which involve high customer contact. The time to 'process' each customer can vary considerably, and this can cause problems in determining the level of resources to make available. Consider patients arriving for consultations with their general medical practitioner. The first might have a condition that is relatively easy to diagnose and for which there is a readily available medication, while the second might have serious and deep-seated psychological problems which need extensive discussion and counselling to 'tease out'. Both have been 'allowed' the standard five-minute 'interview' with the GP. However, the interaction between the GP and the patient will determine the extent of the time required. Even a more standardized service can suffer from this ('can you cut a little bit more hair off the back please?'; the couple who seem to be spending all evening over their dinner, although there is another booking planned for 9.00 p.m.). Another difficulty in planning is the other side of utilization: spare resources. In the restaurant, if there are spare resources in the kitchen, it might be possible to prepare and store (freeze?) vegetables and other dishes for the next day. However, if no customers arrive and take a table one evening, the potential revenue is lost for ever. Similarly, the empty hotel bed and the empty plane seat are 'lost'. It is not normally possible to 'make for stock'.

Information requirements

Forecasting demand

In order to carry out any serious attempt at planning resources, it is first necessary to have some assessment of the level of activity required of those resources. The better the assessment, the better the quality of the planning. The further into the future, the more difficult this process becomes. However, at the same time, the detail required of the forecasts becomes less. The detail is linked to the planning decisions which are being considered.

In the long term, a tour operator might be attempting to forecast the annual value of holidays sold in order to determine the growth rate, market position and broad-level resource requirements to meet this demand. However, to be of use in planning terms, this would need to be converted into operational units, such as number of holidays sold. Over a shorter timescale, in order to plan the transportation requirements, this would need to be broken down into countries (or at least regions served by major airports). Within each region, it might be possible to break the demand down into specific areas, and within that, specific types of accommodation (luxury, mid-range, economy hotel, self-catering). Figure 12.1 illustrates this hierarchy of detail. As planning drops down through the levels, the realistic forecasting timescale becomes shorter.

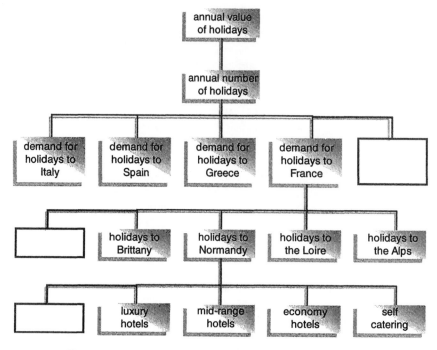

Figure 12.1   Disaggregating the demand for holidays

A variety of approaches are available for forecasting, and a detailed coverage is beyond the scope of this text. Interested readers are referred to Saunders *et al.* (1987) and Wheelwright and Makridakis (1989). Murdick *et al.* (1990) also includes a chapter on forecasting in services. In broad terms, forecasting methods can be thought of as falling into three categories: time-series methods; causal methods; and judgmental methods. Each will be briefly reviewed.

Time-series methods

Time-series analysis at its most naive involves an examination of historical values and the use of these to predict future values. Consider the data in Figure 12.2, which shows the letters handled by a postal agency over a ten-year period, 1987–1996. The simplest estimate for the letters handled in 1997 is the number handled in 1996, 15.94 thousand million. However, if the data are examined in rather more detail, it is possible to refine this somewhat. First, it can be noted that there appears to be a trend in the data. Second, there is likely to be some random variation about the trend. An averaging process (for example, over the last four years' figures) can be used to 'eliminate' the effect of the random variation, while it is possible to look at the percentage growth from one year to the next. These current average and the latest growth estimates can be used for the current forecast. Using this approach, it would have been possible to forecast all of the values from 1991 onwards. Thus in estimating the value for 1997, it would be possible to look at the average deviation between each of the six earlier forecasts and actual values (the mean absolute deviation),

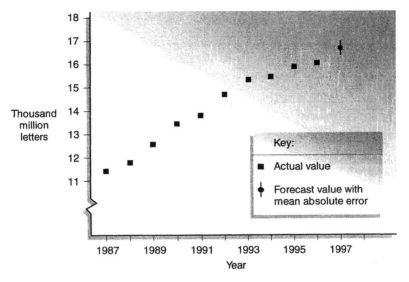

Figure 12.2 Actual and forecast letters handled

and also present this on the chart as the possible error in the 1997 estimate. Knowledge of the possible error in the forecast can be very useful for planning purposes, as it permits the evaluation of worst possible and best possible scenarios.

This simplistic example gives a flavour of the basic time-series approach for forecasting. There are a range of more refined models available which can incorporate more sophisticated trends (for example, various non-linear forms), growth relationships and seasonal factors. There is also a wide range of computer software to support the models, which facilitates analysis and presentation of results.

Causal methods

Causal methods involve identifying the underlying factors which influence the value which is being forecast, and establishing the relationships between these factors and the value. This can be represented as $Y = f(X_1, X_2, X_3 \ldots)$, where Y might be the letters handled by the agency in a particular year, $X_1, X_2, \ldots$ are the values of the causal factors in that year (for example, price charged, number of potential customers) and f is the functional relationship which links them. This is frequently taken to be linear: that is, of the form

$$Y = a_1 X_1 + a_2 X_2 + a_3 X_3 \ldots$$

Historical data are used to estimate the 'best' values of the constant terms a_1, a_2 and so on. This approach has the advantage that it allows different scenarios to be evaluated (what would happen if the values of one of the causal factors changed: for example, a change in price?).

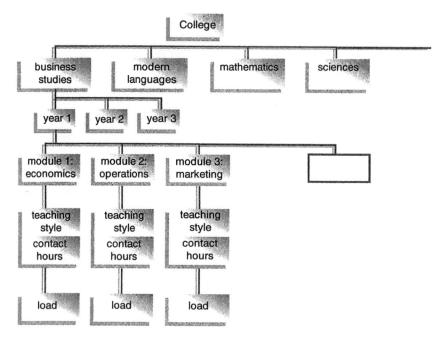

Figure 12.3 Planning resource requirements in a college

Judgemental methods

Judgemental methods are the least precise, in that they involve a group of experienced managers (experts) who have knowledge of the environment in which the forecast is to be made. They review all the available data, and arrive at an 'appropriate' forecast. Various formal and informal structures can be imposed on this process. Murdick *et al.* (1990) reproduce a comprehensive comparison of the different methods of forecasting.

Establishing the method and resources required

In order to complete any realistic planning, it is necessary to have information about how the service is delivered and how long the individual elements of the service delivery process will take. The level of detail will depend on whether the planning is being carried out over the long, medium or short term. For example, in the medium to long term, the planners in a college would be looking at the courses run in each department, the modules attended in each year of the course, and the contact hours required by each module. This could be used to determine the aggregate staffing requirements in each area. Figure 12.3 illustrates a structure for this assessment.

Clearly this is a simplification, assuming, for ease of presentation, one three-year course within each area. There might be interaction between the departments, with students from one department taking modules offered by another department, as well as multiple courses within a single department. It would also be necessary to estimate student numbers on each course and the contact time dictated by the teaching style of each module. These could be converted to staff requirement figures using some accepted aggregate teaching load figure.

In the short term, the planning decisions relate to allocating individual staff members to specific classes in particular rooms. In both cases, information is needed about how the students are taught (mix of large-lecture and small-tutorial contact), the sequence of modules and the times required for each module (year by year or week by week). In a similar manner, an insurance company attempting to set target times to handle claims will need to have a clear picture of the 'approved' (best?) way of processing a claim and the times required in each of the steps of this process. The hotel manager scheduling work for the cleaning staff will need to have established the procedure for preparing a room and the times for the elements of this task.

Chapter 11 described some of the approaches to examining work and determining the best way to complete tasks. Various charting techniques were introduced for presenting them, and these are often incorporated within what is sometimes called a 'standard operating procedure' (SOP) – the approved way of completing a task or series of tasks which comprise delivering a service. While these can be of great use, they should not be so rigid that they preclude the flexibility needed in situations of high customer contact, especially where the customer expects (and deserves?) a degree of personalization/customization in the service. Equally possible fail points should be identified, and steps taken to eliminate these and to 'recover' if they occur. Empowerment of service deliverers to take the steps they perceive as necessary to remedy the situation is also important. These issues were discussed in earlier chapters.

In this section, methods for establishing the times necessary to complete tasks will be examined. These can be grouped into two broad categories: *direct*, involving direct observation of the tasks involved in delivering a service; and *indirect*, studying the 'statement' of the way the service should be delivered. The complete range of techniques is shown in Figure 12.4. The nature of the service will determine the appropriate approach to establishing the times of the tasks.

Time study

This direct method is best suited to repetitive tasks, which are fairly standardized, normally carried out in the back office area of activity. Examples could be the preparation (and cooking) of food in a (fast) food restaurant, document handling in a clerical environment (preparing invoices for payment, etc.), stacking shelves in a supermarket, and preparing a hotel bedroom. Essentially, it involves observing the individual completing the task a number of times, and on each occasion timing how long the task takes. The person completing the task should be following the standard procedure and be properly trained. To allow for the natural variation in effort applied to the task, it is not only timed but also 'rated': that is, the rate of working is compared to the observer's perception of a 'standard', and an appropriate adjustment is made in the final standard time to allow for this. This allows for the natural variation in rates of working. With longer tasks, these can be broken down into a number of elements, which are timed and rated separately, then totalled to give the time for the entire task.

The emphasis should be on the task, rather than on the individual completing the task, and full discussions concerning the process of measurement and the reasons for it should take place with all those involved before the exercise is started. However, time study

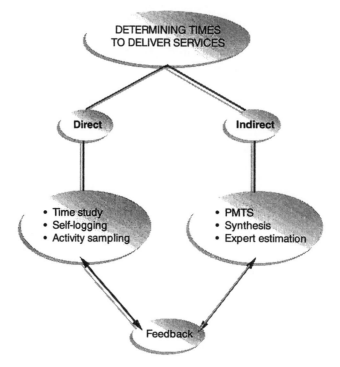

Figure 12.4   Methods for determining times to deliver services

is frequently viewed as a dehumanizing process, with the individuals being observed participating only reluctantly. In spite of this, time study has been effectively used in a number of (back room) service situations, such as banking. It is clearly more acceptable in 'growth' situations where the results might be used to justify extra staffing, rather than in the more frequent 'downsizing' exercises, where the objectives are seen as being 'to get more done with fewer people' and to select those 'to let go'.

Self-logging
As the name suggests, this is where the individual providing the service or completing the task personally records the time taken. This might be broken down into individual components. Before starting, there must be a clear definition of what constitutes the different tasks which comprise the service, and how non-directly productive time might be handled (for example, personal needs – going to the toilet, refreshment breaks). The data need to be recorded and analzed in a standardized format. In some services there is a tradition of self-logging, frequently for costing or pricing purposes: for example in legal and accounting services, where the staff systematically record the times spent on different tasks for different clients (down to the level of detail of telephone calls made, perhaps), and also in management consultancy. Some automated systems can collect this information as a by-product of the system: for example, the electronic point of sale systems used by supermarkets might record the times taken by a checkout operator to serve customers, and link this to the rate at which items are scanned.

Again, a wealth of information can be collected by this approach, although it can be open to abuse, especially if the person is being asked to justify activities for every minute of the day. Care must also be taken to avoid setting up a system which requires an inordinate amount of time and detail in the recording process.

Activity sampling

In general terms, this can be used to establish how a homogeneous group of workers spend their time, by broadly classifying the work into different activities, making a series of random observations of what each person is doing, and then calculating the percentage of the total observations that each activity represents. With care in setting up the study, it is possible to establish standard times for some of the tasks involved. The following example will illustrate the process.

A large city centre hotel has a reception desk and associated back office area, normally staffed by four people. This currently handles 'administration' associated with guests' accounts and a range of 'front office' activities. Increasingly, there are requests from corporate clients for 'clerical support' in such areas as sending/receiving faxes, photocopying and word-processing documents. A problem facing the hotel is the planning of work in reception, and determining the best way to provide the clerical support. A suggestion for this has been to establish a business centre, to provide these and other services.

Activity sampling can be used as a first step to find out more about current activities in the reception area, and to provide data to support the planning process. A first step is to identify and classify all the tasks undertaken, and likely to be observed. A simplified list is shown below:

- Guests checking in (C/I).
- Guests checking out (C/O).
- Sending/receiving faxes (FAX).
- General administration on guests' accounts (A/C).
- Handling telephone enquiries (TEL).
- Making photocopies for guests (CPY).
- Word-processing for guests (W/P).
- Taking reservations for the restaurant (RES).
- Personal time (e.g. lunch or refreshment breaks) (P-T).

This list will result from observations of the work of the reception office, and the objectives of the study. The first stage is to complete a pilot study to ensure that the scope has been correctly determined, to accustom staff to being observed, and to collect some data to use to determine the number of observations in the full study. Normally, around 200 random observations would be made over a representative period of time. Suppose this consists of three days, with a 'normal day' of 0800 to 1800. A typical proforma is shown in Figure 12.5. At the determined random times (obtained using random number tables), the observer notes what each receptionist is doing using the activity codes given in the list. After completing the pilot study, it is possible to calculate the percentage of time spent on each activity. This is simply the number of observations of the activity divided by the total observations made (note that, to make 200 observations, it is only necessary to make 50 tours of observations, since on each tour four receptionists are observed). Suppose these data are as follows:

ACTIVITY SAMPLING STUDY								

ACTIVITY CODES: C/I   FAX   TEL   W/P   P-T
C/O   A/C   CPY   RES   2/3 July

Time of tour	Receptionist				Time of tour	Receptionist			
	1	2	3	4		1	2	3	4
0815	C/O	C/O	C/O	P-T	0809				
0835	C/O	C/O	TEL	C/O	0823				
0911	TEL	C/O	FAX	C/O	0924				
0957	C/O	TEL	CPY	TEL	0952				
1045	P-T	W/P	A/C	FAX	1004				
1052					1039				
1121					1105				
1154					1124				
1212					1207				
1231					1255				
1347					1313				
1359					1358				
1403					1446				
1426					1453				
1538					1503				
1554					1523				
1607					1623				
1640					1624				
1716					1707				
1738					1740				

Figure 12.5 Activity sampling proforma

- C/I   :   34 observations   17%
- C/O   :   16 observations   8%
- FAX   :   12 observations   6%
- A/C   :   42 observations   21%
- TEL   :   24 observations   12%
- CPY   :   14 observations   7%
- W/P   :   18 observations   9%
- RES   :   2 observations   1%
- P-T   :   38 observations   19%

Initially, it is necessary to decide if the 'correct' set of tasks has been identified. Have any been omitted? Should any be further subdivided (for example, split phone calls into incoming and outgoing) or could any be combined (checking in and checking out)? Next, it is necessary to determine the number of observations in the full study. This will be dependent on the desired level of accuracy in the results, and can be found from the following formula:

$$N = \frac{4P(100 - P)}{L^2}$$

where:

N = number of observations in the full study
P = percentage occurrence of key activity
L = required percentage accuracy.

Thus, if P is taken as 21 per cent (percentage of time that general administration of guests' accounts was being carried out) and $L = 2$ per cent (that is, we are 95 per cent certain that the actual value is between 19 and 23 per cent), then $N = 1659$ observations, or around 415 tours of observation are required. Clearly, if greater accuracy is deemed necessary (for example, 1 per cent), then a larger number of observations is necessary. For this type of exercise, a value of 2 per cent is not unreasonable, and a slightly less accurate result (± 3 per cent) might be acceptable.

The next stage is the full study, for which the 415 random tours of observation must be planned over a representative period of time. The results might look as follows:

- C/I : 302 observations 18.2%
- C/O : 85 observations 5.1%
- FAX : 118 observations 7.1%
- A/C : 337 observations 20.3%
- TEL : 217 observations 13.1%
- CPY : 110 observations 6.6%
- W/P : 148 observations 8.9%
- RES : 13 observations 0.8%
- P-T : 330 observations 19.9%

It is possible to rearrange the formula for N to verify that the desired accuracy has been achieved:

$$L^2 = \frac{4P(100 - P)}{N}$$

where $P = 20.3$ and $N = 1660$

So $L = 19.7\%$, as required.

It is possible now to examine the activities associated with the proposed business centre, use of the fax machine, copying and word-processing. In total these occupy 22.6 per cent of the time, so it might be feasible initially to set up the centre staffed by a single person. Moreover, if it is possible to record the number of 'transactions' handled during this period, and the staff available, then it is possible to calculate a standard time for the tasks. Suppose all four staff had been available for the entire period of the study, each from 0800 until 1800, making 10 hours per day, and the study extended over 20 complete days (notice that lunch and other breaks are allowed for within the 'personal time' activity). If, during this time, guests request a total of 803 sheets of documents to be word-processed, the time per sheet can be estimated as follows:

Four people working for 20 days produce $4 \times 20 \times 10 = 800$ hours.
Word-processing occupies 8.9 per cent of the time $= 71.2$ hours, which produces 803 sheets.
Therefore each sheet takes 0.0886 hours, or 5.32 minutes.

Similarly, it is possible to estimate the time taken to check in and check out guests and so on.

Predetermined motion time systems (PMTS)

This is the first of the indirect methods which do not require direct observation. It is suitable for use in similar situations to those where time study might be used: for example, repetitive tasks normally in the back office. The starting point is a standardized classification listing of basic clerical 'activities', together with the standard times associated with each of these. The analyst studies the task to be completed, identifying the basic activities from the listing which make up the complete task. By adding together the predetermined times for these individual activities, it is possible to arrive at an estimated time required for the entire task. Training and experience are required to be able to identify the appropriate predetermined activities. The approach is also limited to tasks which can be seen as comprising these activities. These systems tend to focus on clerical operations with such tasks as preparing and posting off an invoice, and such activities as 'obtain file', 'mail, seal, envelope'. One such system is Predetermined Administrative Data System (PADS), designed by the Methods–Time Measurement (MTM) Association.

Synthesis

This approach is not unlike the predetermined motion time systems outlined in the previous paragraph. Again the task is studied, but instead of having a proprietary set of basic standardized activities (for example, from a system like PADS) from which to select, the analyst draws on previous studies carried out by the organization. Thus an insurance company which had carried out a study to estimate the time taken to handle the documentation on a claim against a house contents policy might use the similar activities within this task to build up a synthetic time to handle the documentation on a claim against a newly developed policy for car contents.

'Expert' estimation

This is probably the most widely used approach to estimating the time a task will take, when such information is absolutely necessary. At worst, it comprises the manager 'working back' from the time that is available. However, this puts the person completing the task or delivering the service under significant time pressure and can compromise quality. Target times must be realistic in terms of what they anticipate staff will be able to do. Statements like 'we have three staff members "serving" and want to handle 30 customers per hour, so each customer must be served in six minutes' are nonsense unless accompanied by some analysis of the task which shows that the customer *can* be served in six minutes. Equally, to expect a team to prepare a training video in 2 weeks without examining the activities involved and the times each will take, together with the composition of the team (numbers, skills and competences) is asking for problems.

Frequently, 'expert estimation' is the only realistic approach to establishing the time for a task, in the short term, in a service environment. However, this should be approached in a structured and systematic manner. The manager should examine in detail the tasks involved in delivering the service. Times for each of these should then be estimated based on the manager's experience, with inputs from as many other reliable sources as possible. This will include experienced staff and other similar exercises which have been completed (self-logging exercises might be of use here). It is important that these times are not seen as 'cast in stone', and that there is a feedback/feed forward system whereby they can be updated in the light of experience (again self-logging can help). In this way, planning using the data will be realistic and the plans prepared will be acceptable to the users.

Capacity management

A starting point with capacity management needs to be a formal definition of 'capacity'. It is important to recognize that this should have a time dimension associated with it. Thus the number of tables (or even chairs) in a restaurant does not measure its capacity; this can be measured as the (maximum) number of meals served per day. In general terms, capacity is measured by the maximum output level (tasks completed, customers served) in a period of time. This maximum value should assumed 'normal' working conditions and not excessive use of overtime and so on. For a hotel it might be beds available per night; for a supermarket, customers served per hour; for an airline, passenger miles per year; and for a college, student teaching hours per semester.

It is important to note that generally it is necessary to express capacity in some 'general' units, particularly when this capacity can and is used to deliver a range of different services. For the college, it is tempting to think of capacity as the maximum number of students on a particular course, whereas this does not portray the true picture, as in reality a mix of courses is offered and different courses have different requirements. Capacity utilization concerns how the capacity is used to satisfy customers. This will be influenced by the mix of different types of customer. The hotel's capacity utilization will depend on the balance between single-, double- and triple-bedded rooms, and how well this matches the number of singles, couples and families staying.

Long-term capacity planning

Long-term capacity planning decisions are generally strategic in nature, normally involving investments in buildings and equipment primarily, and to a lesser extent human resources. They must be made in the knowledge of a range of external factors, some of which were introduced and discussed in some detail in earlier chapters, and include PEST (political, economic, social and technical) analysis. To this should be added consideration of the behaviour of major competitors. Capacity decisions can be to increase capacity, which can be achieved either through one large step increase or through several small step increases, or to reduce capacity, which might come from closing or consolidating 'centres'. Figure 12.6 presents this range of options. Again, forecasting and 'intelligence' in the six key areas which impact on the capacity decisions are of crucial importance.

A major health care provider, with a nationwide network of private hospitals, might be considering an expansion programme. Influences on this might be suggestions that the government plans to allow tax relief on all personal health care insurance plans.

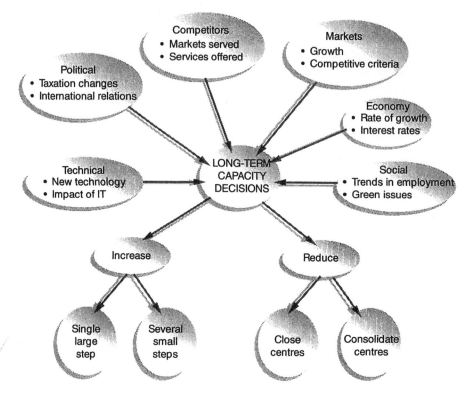

Figure 12.6 Long-term capacity management decisions

Development in technology might mean that it is now possible to screen patients rapidly and cheaply for a whole range of previously undetected illnesses and diseases. Market research might have shown that the 25–40-year-old age group are particularly aware of their vulnerability to stress-related illnesses, yet unhappy at the provision made within the state-run system. Employers are increasingly aware of the impact of stress on their employees, and the effect of long waiting lists and times on employees' productivity. This market might not currently be satisfied by existing providers.

A significant decision for the organization is how to provide the extra capacity. One option would be a major new centre dedicated to the new screening processes. An alternative could be smaller-scale centres attached to a selected set of hospitals within the existing network, introduced over a period of time, at carefully selected centres. Each option has its advantages and disadvantages. Another example is a college facing an expansion in students over the next five years (for example, a doubling in participation rates). Is this best handled with one large increase in capacity, or several smaller increases?

The large increase has the advantage of economies of scale: the change and disturbance caused by the capacity increase last a relatively shorter time. The small increases involve less risk if the predicted demand for the service does not materialize, and when each increase takes place, the latest technology can be used. With the health care illustration, it is also important to recognize that the presence of the customer in the system has an impact on the capacity management decision. If there is likely to be (significant) competition, opening a second centre in a neighbouring location, thus making it 'convenient' for another potential group of customers, rather than doubling the capacity of the existing centre, could be a better strategy. Developments in communication technology have had an impact in this area. For example, capacity management decisions in telephone banking and insurance services are not significantly influenced by the location of the customers, and their location has little impact on increasing capacity.

Medium-term capacity planning

Decisions in this area relate to attempting to match supply of resources and demand, with two broad options being to try and adjust resources to meet demand, or to try to manage demand so that resources do not need to be adjusted. Attempts to manage demand range from the fairly primitive to those which are quite sophisticated. Typical timescales would be weeks and months. However, the following example covers a shorter timescale.

As an illustration, consider the situation in a supermarket. The store manager has to decide on staffing levels at the checkouts, in the shop area (filling shelves) and behind the scenes (in the warehouse). A straightforward approach is to use experience and to try to forecast levels of activity throughout the day and week. This information will be used to establish staffing levels at the checkouts. However, variability and uncertainty in the arrival patterns and service times will make this a very complex process. Typically, these levels could be lower earlier in the day and at the end of the day. As the day progresses and actual customers arrive, during some periods these numbers will significantly exceed the checkout capacity and queues will build up. Later demand might be lower and some of the checkout operators might be idle (they can only work when the customers are available; they cannot work in anticipation of demand – make to stock – as is often possible in manufacturing). This situation is shown in Figure 12.7 (a). This situation is frequently encountered in service environments, with a fixed level of capacity in the short to medium term and little flexibility to alter it. Other examples of fixed capacity levels are the number of rooms available in a hotel and the seats available on an aircraft; an empty bed or seat is a revenue opportunity lost for ever, while the potential guest finding the hotel full will probably stay elsewhere.

However, another possibility is to try to adjust capacity to meet anticipated demand. In general terms, the technology involved in the equipment used to deliver the service, and the flexibility and responsiveness of the workforce, are among the factors which will determine the extent to which this is possible, and the lead time necessary to make the appropriate changes. Thus the supermarket may have additional checkouts and trained staff, and a system whereby, when queues reach a certain level, these are opened, and when they have been 'idle' for a fixed period, they are closed and staff transferred to other duties (for example, shelf filling). This is illustrated in Figure 12.7 (b). Clearly, effective use of this approach needs a system for monitoring the checkout utilization to determine when more should be opened or closed (capacity should be adjusted), and a multiskilled and flexible workforce capable of handling other duties. The speed, responsiveness and lead time in this case are exceptionally short for a service environment. More usually, such capacity adjustments to try to match changes in demand are made day to day or week to week.

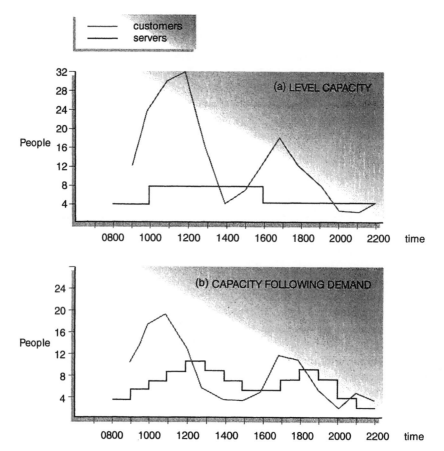

Figure 12.7 Alternative capacity management strategies in a supermarket

In some environments it is important that the service can be 'guaranteed'. Examples are the emergency services (fire, police, ambulance) and also the so-called utilities (gas, electricity and water). For these, it is not unusual to maintain excess capacity, and to develop contingency plans to handle the extremely high levels of demand which can occur very infrequently. Non-urgent, routine tasks are in part used to absorb the excess capacity. This might include maintaining equipment, training and providing advisory services. Within the fire service, plans are drawn up whereby one fire station can have back-up provided by a neighbouring station if levels of 'demand' (fires or other emergencies) are at an extremely high level.

It is sometimes possible to offer an alternative service when capacity limitations are reached within one area. Illustrations are the air passenger upgraded from tourist to club/business class because the tourist section on the flight is full, due to overbooking (in anticipation of no-shows), the holidaymakers offered alternative accommodation because the hotel into which they were originally booked was full, or the diners in the restaurant offered an alternative dish, when the one chosen originally was finished. This process has

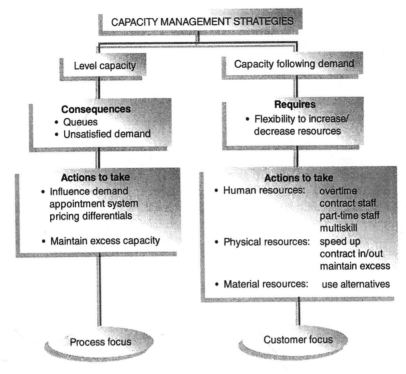

Figure 12.8 Different capacity management strategies

to be handled with care as it can change customers' expectations of the service (the passenger might always expect champagne during the flight!), and it can cause problems with other customers (the other passengers who paid the full club-class fare). On occasions, it is possible to alter the service: for example, at a fairground the rides will tend to be shorter at the weekend and in the evenings as demand gets higher. Again, this can have an impact on the perceived quality of the service.

Two key parameters are the demand from customers and the time required to provide the service. A number of possibilities are available to influence or attempt to manage demand. The most common is the appointment or reservation system. However, this does have the disadvantage that, depending on the consequences, a proportion of customers might not turn up for any given appointment. As a result, organizations can be encouraged to overbook appointments, which can result in either delaying or changing the service. During periods of non-peak demand, different pricing policies are often used to stimulate demand (weekend break offers in hotels, early bird meals in restaurants, happy hours in bars, saver tickets on the rail service). Some of these strategies are summarized in Figure 12.8.

Queuing situations

With the frequent necessity of the presence of the customer in service situations and the inability to hold or make for stocks, queues have an important role to play in service delivery systems and in the management of capacity. There are a number of key parameters in queuing situations: these include the arrival pattern of customers, the service times, the number of servers, the queuing configuration and the queue discipline. These are the parameters which the organization can consider controlling in attempting to manage capacity. In the previous section, some of the alternatives in terms of managing demand were discussed.

Example 1

A small fast-food restaurant has a single service position operated by one person. Studies have shown that customers arrive on average every 4 minutes (at the rate of 15 per hour), and that when a customer arrives does not depend on when the previous customer arrived (normally called random or negative exponential arrivals). It currently takes the server an average of 3 minutes to serve each customer (a rate of 20 per hour), and there is considerable variation in this time. Discussion on the various forms of this variation is outside the scope of this text, but provided it follows certain predetermined forms (for example, negative exponential often occurring in practice: see Page (1972) for more details), it is possible to complete some analysis of the situation.

In general, if the arrival rate is l and the service rate is m, then the utilization:

$$u = \frac{l}{m}$$

It can be shown that the average waiting time:

$$W = \frac{u}{1-u} \times \frac{1}{m} = \frac{us}{1-u}$$

where $1/m$ is the average service time, denoted by s.

Applying these results to the example (given that the arrival intervals and service times are negative exponential):

$$u = \frac{15}{20} = 0.75 \ (\text{or } 75\% \ \text{utilization})$$

It is worth noting that, unless the arrival rate is less than the service rate ($l < m$), the queue will get longer and longer.

The average length of time that a customer will have to wait can be calculated as:

$$W = \frac{0.75}{1 - 0.75} \times 3 \ \text{minutes} = 9 \ \text{minutes}$$

It might be felt that this is unacceptably long. Several options might be possible. The first might be to purchase a more sophisticated cash register which will speed up the payment process and reduce the average service time to $2\frac{1}{2}$ minutes. The effect of this can be evaluated as follows:

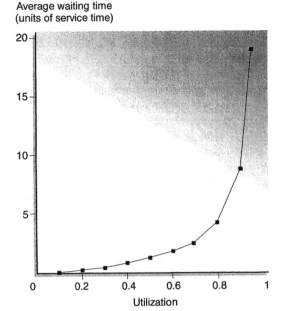

Figure 12.9 Relationship between waiting time and utilization

$$l = 15, \text{ but } m = 24, \text{ so } u = \frac{15}{24} = 0.625$$

$$\text{and } W = \frac{0.625}{1 - 0.625} \times 2.5 \text{ minutes} = 4.2 \text{ minutes}$$

It is interesting to note the relationship between utilization and the average waiting time. This is shown in Figure 12.9, for the single-server queue with negative exponential arrivals and service times. As the organization aims for high levels of utilization, this is at the expense of longer customer waiting times; equally, as shorter waiting times are offered, lower utilization of resources results.

A second option open to the fast-food restaurant would be to employ a second server, and again it would be useful to examine the impact on the average waiting time. The next example will show how this might be achieved. Typically, the decisions open to an organization can be generalized from the above example and frequently expressed in cost terms. This involves balancing the costs associated with customers waiting (customers' lost time, space and so on) and the costs of providing the service (which typically increase as the waiting time decreases). As resources are increased, the cost of providing the service increases, but the cost of waiting reduces. The challenge for management is to determine the resource level which minimizes the total of these two costs. Davis (1991) discusses the entire area of trade-offs in far more detail and raises such issues as the relationship between waiting time and waiting cost, and the links to customer satisfaction.

Example 2

A small medical centre provides a service to the local community. Records show that patients arrive at random at a rate of 9 per hour, and that while there is (random) variation in the consultation time, this has an average of 12 minutes (5 per hour). When patients arrive, they are seen by the first available physician, on a first-come, first-served basis. This illustrates two of the parameters in queuing situations: the type of queue, single or multiple; and the queue discipline, first come, first served. There could be other ways of selecting the next patient from the queue: for example, choosing any children, or older patients, even though they might not have been waiting as long as some of the other patients.

At present there are two physicians, and again attention focuses on the average waiting time. The derivation of this is rather complex (see Page, 1972). However, some appropriate values are given in Table 12.1.

Table 12.1 Tabulated values of the waiting times for a queue with random arrivals and service times

Utilization	Number of servers (*n*)						
	2	3	4	5	6	7	8
0.1	0.0101	0.0014	0.0002	0.0000	0.0000	0.0000	0.0000
0.2	0.0417	0.0103	0.0030	0.0010	0.0003	0.0001	0.0000
0.3	0.0989	0.0333	0.0132	0.0058	0.0027	0.0013	0.0006
0.4	0.1905	0.0784	0.0378	0.0199	0.0111	0.0064	0.0039
0.5	0.3333	0.1579	0.0870	0.0521	0.0330	0.0218	0.0148
0.6	0.5625	0.2956	0.1794	0.1181	0.0819	0.0589	0.0436
0.7	0.9608	0.5470	0.3572	0.2519	0.1867	0.1432	0.1128
0.8	1.7778	1.0787	0.7455	0.5541	0.4315	0.3471	0.2860
0.9	4.2632	2.7235	1.9693	1.5250	1.2335	1.0285	0.8769

$$\text{Utilization} = \frac{\text{Arrival rate}}{n \times \text{Service rate}}$$

Source: Page (1972), p. 152.

Using the notation developed earlier:

$$l = 9 \text{ per hour (arrival rate)}$$
$$m = 5 \text{ per hour (service rate)}$$
$$n = 2 \text{ (number of servers)}$$

Consequently, the utilization:

$$u = \frac{l}{2m} = \frac{9}{2 \times 5} = 0.9$$

Table 12.1 suggests that the average waiting time will be $4.2632 \times 12 = 51$ minutes. There are a number of possibilities for improving the situation from the patients' perspective.

The first is to increase the number of physicians from two to three. The results of this can be assessed as follows. The utilization u drops to:

$$\frac{9}{3 \times 5} = 0.6 \text{ or } 60\%$$

This means that the physicians could be idle (have no patients waiting to see them) for 40 per cent of the time. On the other hand, the tabulated results indicate that the average waiting time will reduce to $0.2956 \times 12 = 3\frac{1}{2}$ minutes. This demonstrates aspects of the trade-off discussed earlier.

An alternative would be to attempt to manage the arrival rate of the patients through some sort of appointment system. To attempt to investigate the effect of this, it would be possible to use one of the alternative queuing models: constant arrival rate and random service times. The average waiting times for this type of system are given in Table 12.2. It can be seen that with this system the theoretical average waiting time is reduced from 51 minutes to $1.933 \times 12 = 23$ minutes.

Table 12.2 Tabulated values of the waiting times for a queue with constant arrivals and random service times

Utilization	Number of servers (n)						
	2	3	4	5	6	7	8
0.1	0.0000	0.0000	0.0000	0.0000	0.0000	0.0000	0.0000
0.2	0.0003	0.0000	0.0000	0.0000	0.0000	0.0000	0.0000
0.3	0.0048	0.0008	0.0002	0.0000	0.0000	0.0000	0.0000
0.4	0.0223	0.0060	0.0019	0.0007	0.0002	0.0001	0.0000
0.5	0.0649	0.0239	0.0103	0.0049	0.0024	0.0013	0.0007
0.6	0.1520	0.0685	0.0360	0.0206	0.0125	0.0079	0.0051
0.7	0.3257	0.1696	0.1020	0.0665	0.0458	0.0327	0.0240
0.8	0.7111	0.4114	0.2725	0.1947	0.1461	0.1134	0.0903
0.9	1.9330	1.2112	0.8612	0.6567	0.5238	0.4310	0.3629

$$\text{Utilization} = \frac{\text{Arrival rate}}{n \times \text{Service rate}}$$

Source: Page (1972), p. 154.

While these models can be very useful in analyzing a range of queuing situations, they do embody certain assumptions about the patterns of arrivals and service rates, queue disciplines and so on. Moreover, they assume that the system has been operating long enough for the queue to have 'settled down' and reached a steady stable state. An alternative approach which can offer the analyst more flexibility is the use of simulation. This involves building a computer model of the situation, and evaluating the effects of different decisions. There are a number of software systems which support this development in a user-friendly environment, providing graphics and visual interaction. However, this approach is more time consuming.

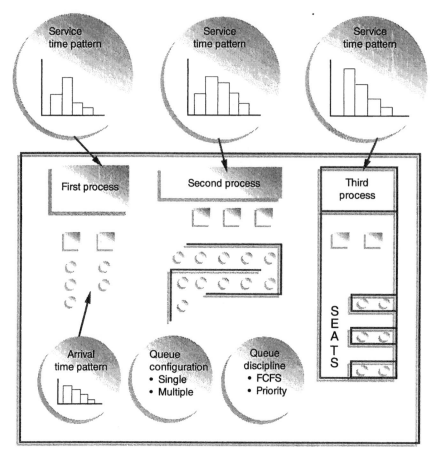

Figure 12.10   Queuing in service delivery systems

General discussion

Queues frequently occur in service environments, and Figure 12.10 illustrates some of the key parameters that are of importance in analyzing them. As the examples in the previous section indicated, it is the uncertainty in some of these parameters which causes some of the capacity management difficulties. In some environments, uncertainty in arrival times can be overcome by appointment systems. Service time variability can be reduced by standardizing the service or possibly by automating parts of it. However, care must be taken so that these steps do not conflict with the organization's strategies towards meeting customer service targets.

Some queuing in services is inevitable given the uncertainty surrounding the presence of customers in the system, and their interaction with the service delivery process. A variety of ideas have been adopted to facilitate this 'experience'. These range from single queues controlled by barriers and lights to indicate the next free server, used by some post offices and banks, to the 'take a number' favoured by in-store delicatessens. At the other end of the scale are the steps taken in the 'softer' areas associated with the queuing experience (providing entertainment and so on). These are covered in Chapter 8, and also in Davies and Heineke (1994).

Scheduling and planning

Scheduling and planning are generally carried out over a relatively short timescale, typically hours, days or weeks, depending on the environment, at the level of detail of the smallest (or at least a smaller) unit of resource. A variety of different terms are used to describe the process in different services. In education, 'timetabling' is commonly used, work rostas are frequently referred to, and the term 'work scheduling' is sometimes employed. It is important to distinguish between the method used to present the plan and the process by which the plan is produced, although the presentation method can significantly assist the planning process. Normally underlying this is a figure which shows what the resources, or group of resources, are doing against a timescale. This can also be viewed from the perspective of a customer.

Figure 12.11 shows a blank timetable for a college. This could be completed to show what a particular group of students were doing (first-year undergraduates in business studies), or a member (or group) of staff (the marketing group), or a composite could show everything. Clearly, the information in this final option becomes more difficult to interpret, as the number of student groups and staff members gets large. This form of presentation could easily be adapted to cover a range of situations: for example, staffing the different areas in a fast-food restaurant.

When the focus is on the customer, and the 'processing time' can vary considerably, then a form of bar chart can be used to represent the manner in which the customers are being served. Figure 12.12 shows a bar chart for patients arriving (at random) to see one of three physicians. They join a common queue and wait to see the first one who becomes free.

Finally, Figure 12.13 presents a rather more complex situation in which patients arrive at a medical centre, and go through a variety of procedures after reception. The first patient sees the physician, and has an X-ray; the second sees the physician, then visits the drug dispensary, and finally sees the nurse; the third goes to see the nurse for some treatment; the fourth sees the physician and then goes to the dispensary, and so on.

Most scheduling takes place 'forwards' in time, from when the customer is likely to enter the system, or from when the resource is available. However, there are some situations where planning 'backwards' can be appropriate. This tends to be the case when a particular task is due for completion by a particular time and a number of activities are to be completed sequentially before this can be achieved. An example could be planning a rail route from Leeds to be in Truro by 6.30 p.m., or planning a meal (purchasing the ingredients, preparing them, cooking them and finally serving for a reception at 12.30).

There are two basic difficulties in the process (as opposed to the presentation) of scheduling. The first is the number of possibilities which are open to the planner in preparing a schedule of work. At a simple level, a radiographer with a queue of ten X-rays to take could do these in any one of 3 628 800 different orders ($10 \times 9 \times 8 \times 7 \times \ldots$). We would prefer that ours was done first (or at least, to be fair, the one which had been waiting

	Monday	Tuesday	Wednesday	Thursday	Friday
0900 to 1000					
1000 to 1100					
1100 to 1200					
1200 to 1300					
1300 to 1400					
1400 to 1500					
1500 to 1600					
1600 to 1700					

Figure 12.11 Specimen timetable

longest was done first). The radiographer might prefer to put them together in 'batches' which are similar, so that the minimum number of changes have to be made to the equipment settings, so that they could all be done as efficiently as possible.

This raises the second difficulty, that of selecting the criterion by which the performance of the schedule should be measured. This can be viewed from a range of perspectives: from that of the customer – meeting their requirements on timing (frequently as soon as possible!); from that of the organization – maximum efficiency/profitability; from that of the employee – job satisfaction (variety in work). Clearly, not all can be achieved simultaneously and compromises must be made. The nature of these will depend on the organization. In preparing the timetable, the college might decide to extend the working day or working week in order to accommodate a particular set of modules chosen by a student. Alternatively, it might decide to block certain modules together, thus reducing the opportunity to combine modules from different blocks, and the choices available, but fitting all within the existing time available.

Much of short-term scheduling involves handling queues of customers or tasks, and the selection of which to process next. Frequently, this selection process can be handled

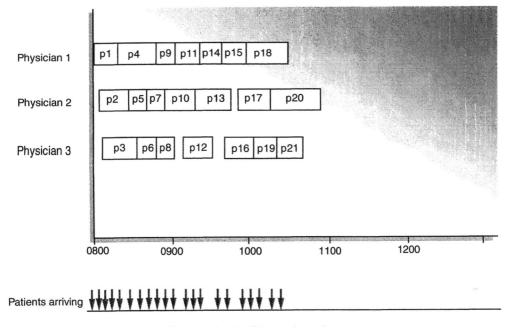

Figure 12.12 Simple bar chart

by a simple heuristic rule which involves looking at the characteristics of the tasks/customers waiting. Here it can be beneficial to consider the distinction between the front office and the back room. When developing rules to handle queues in the front office where the customer is present, these often need to have a customer focus and need to be seen to be 'fair'. Hence the popularity of 'first come, first served'. When this is not followed, it helps if other waiting customers can see (and sympathize with) the reason for deviating from this. In the back room, it is possible to use a wider range of rules which can reflect a broader range of concerns to the organization, to look at costs and efficiencies in doing tasks in different orders, and to build these into the scheduling process.

Focusing on bottleneck resources can also help simplify the scheduling process. It is often found in organizations that not all resources are equally 'important'. Thus not all need be given the same attention in the preparation of a schedule. Some inefficiencies or underutilization can be acceptable for the non-bottleneck resources. For example, in preparing the timetables for the first semester in a business studies department, the bottleneck might be identified as the two large lecture theatres. Thus the use of these could be scheduled first for the large groups which require them. Afterwards the smaller group lectures and all the tutorials which used the smaller rooms could be timetabled around them. It is important to recognize that the bottleneck resources might change over time. Thus in the second semester, when all the postgraduate students are following their chosen electives, the bottleneck might change and become seminar rooms which are capable of seating around 30 students.

It is clear from some of the earlier discussions that there is a difference between the planning function in the back office area of a service organization and that in the front

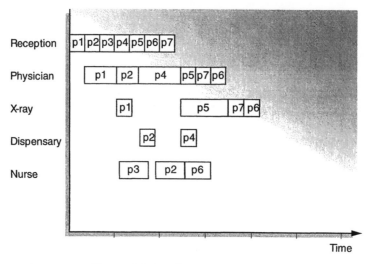

Figure 12.13   Complex bar chart

office, caused by the presence of the customer in the latter. This has lead to the identification of the role of despatcher or receptionist (described in detail in Voss *et al.*, 1985) acting at the interface between the customer and the service provision system (and often part of it). There are a number of facets to this role, which varies from organization to organization. It is important to recognize these facets so that the individual is able to carry out the associated responsibilities.

This person is frequently the first point of contact for the customer, so that interpersonal skills and a knowledge of the organization are crucial. This role can also involve acting as a 'filter' for a scarce resource (the secretary to a hospital consultant), so again interpersonal skills and an ability to determine appropriate responses are important. The role in some organizations involves initial diagnoses, so that appropriate resources can be allocated (repair/servicing). This has implications for technical knowledge. There can also be an element of scheduling in terms of determining the priority of the customers for service (the despatcher for the roadside breakdown service). Finally, the contact with the customer provides selling opportunities (the bank employee, providing foreign exchange, has the chance to ask if the customer needs holiday insurance). It is important that these roles be recognized and exploited, and that they complement the planning and scheduling functions in the back office.

A final responsibility which those who carry out the planning process frequently have is the provision of information on the status of the tasks in hand. This responsibility is frequently not formally recognized, and the information is difficult to come by. Consider the person phoning the hospital to find out how his relative is after a major operation, or the customer who wants to know when she will receive her cheque for a car insurance claim. There are two major problems in providing the information: the volume of data involved, and ensuring the status information is up to date and accurate. Frequently the solution can be to provide the information on a computer database.

Materials management

Materials are characterized by the fact that they are consumed (or used) as part of the process of delivering a service (or maintaining the service delivery system), or contributing to the tangible component of a service. They clearly have a key role to play as part of the planning process, since their non-availability may prevent the service being delivered in the required manner. The responsibilities of materials management can be divided into two:

- Assessing requirements and acquiring.
- Receiving, storing and issuing.

The first of these is most closely linked to the planning function. However, before focusing attention on this, it is worth highlighting some of the issues raised by the second.

The processes of receiving, storing and issuing materials are largely a clerical or administrative responsibility. There are implications for quality, in that the 'materials' supplied should be to the agreed standard, and complaints often need to be registered on receipt rather than on use. The restaurant will have to be happy with the quality of the vegetables delivered, and these will need to be stored correctly to ensure maximum life. Increasingly, organizations are developing long-term relationships with key suppliers which result in an environment of trust, and confidence in the supplier's ability to deliver to the required standard. The issue of materials can be crucial in some environments: for example, in a hospital a careful control and traceback needs to be in place to ensure the correct issue of drugs to patients. Often a record needs to be kept for costing or pricing purposes (for example, car servicing and repair). Even if materials are not directly charged, records often need to be kept to establish the cost in order to provide an input to the pricing process.

Most attention is normally paid to the assessment of the requirements for and the acquisition of materials. Many organizations have large numbers of different types of material under their control, and managers do not want to spend large amounts of their time trying to control these. An initial approach is to use a Pareto analysis (as described in detail in Chapter 13) to determine the degree of control required. The materials can be ranked by the value of their annual usage. Frequently, it is found that about 20 per cent of the items generate around 80 per cent of the total value of the annual usage: these are normally referred to as the class A items. The next 30 per cent generate 15 per cent (B items) of this value, and the final 50 per cent generate 5 per cent (C items).

Major benefits can result from a tight control of the A items, trying to forecast accurately potential usage and other relevant factors. Class B and C items do not require so much management time, and a simpler approach can be adopted. This can come through the use of a reorder level, reorder quantity (ROL/ROQ) system. A recorder level is established, and when the stock reaches this level, an order is placed for the reorder quantity. Provided there is general confidence in these parameters, the materials management decisions can be delegated to the person directly using the materials. The following example illustrates the approach to estimating these values.

A large hotel uses soap at the rate of 1000 bars per week, at a cost of 10p per bar. Currently, it takes 2 weeks between posting an order to the hotel's supplier and the soap's arrival at the hotel. It is estimated that handling the administration/paperwork associated with ordering a delivery of soap costs £10 in staff time (this is irrespective of the size of the order). Holding stocks of materials of any description costs money. There is the capital tied up in the stock, the space it takes up, and so on. A common way of costing this is to express it as a percentage of the average value of the stock held. In this case it is estimated to be 15 per cent. Based on this information, it is possible to calculate the values for the ROL and ROQ.

The rate of usage is 1000 bars per week, and the delivery lead time is 2 weeks, so the ROL should be such that it covers the requirement during the lead time. It should therefore be no less than 2000 bars.

The ROQ is normally based on an analysis of the costs involved. If this quantity is represented by Q, then ideally the new order should arrive just as the stock runs out, taking the level from zero back to Q and this pattern will repeat. Thus the average stock level is $\frac{1}{2}Q$. The annual usage is 1000×52 (assuming 52 weeks per year, and a weekly usage of 1000). Thus if Q are ordered at a time then $1000 \times 52/Q$ orders are placed per year.

The total annual cost can therefore be expressed as:

$$\text{Annual stockholding cost} + \text{Annual order cost}$$

or:

$$\frac{1}{2}Q \times 0.10 \times 0.15 + \frac{1000 \times 52}{Q} \times 10$$

To find the minimum value of this, it is necessary to differentiate it with respect to Q (or note that the minimum value is when the two cost components are equal). This gives:

$$Q = \sqrt{\frac{1000 \times 52 \times 10}{0.10 \times 0.15 \times 0.5}} = 8326.664$$

One problem with this approach is that the square root in the equation almost guarantees that the result will not be a whole number, which initially causes concern. However, examination of the total cost curve (see Figure 12.14) indicates that this is fairly shallow around the minimum value, so it is quite realistic to round this quantity. Thus a quantity of 8000 is ordered, every 8 weeks.

This broad approach can be extended in a number of directions. In practice, it is not unusual for quantity discounts to be offered by suppliers. Thus the supplier of soap might offer to drop the price to 9p if a quantity of 9000 bars or more is ordered. This situation can be evaluated by calculating the total cost (including the cost of the soap itself) based on the normal cost and an order quantity of 8000, and comparing this to the cost of purchasing 9000 at the discount price of 9p.

There is frequently uncertainty both in the usage rates and the lead times. In this case it is important to collect data so that the extent of this uncertainty can be estimated. Forecasting methods can sometimes then be used to arrive at a more accurate estimate of the current usage and lead times. These can be used in the formulae for ROQ and ROL. The ROL can be redefined as the forecast usage in the forecast lead time plus a safety stock to take account of this uncertainty and to reduce the chance of stockout. The higher

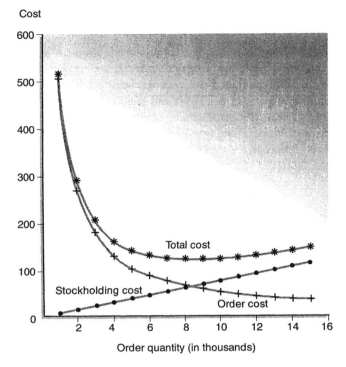

Figure 12.14 Total cost curve for reorder quantity calculation

the safety stock, then the lower will be the likelihood of running out of stock. However this will increase the average stock level and the costs associated with it. Knowledge of the error in the forecast can aid the evaluation of this trade-off. More details can be found in Arnold (1996).

This approach is particularly suited to computerization, and many organizations now have computer systems to support the materials management function. However, a number of issues are of importance in this context. The system should have credibility in the eyes of the user, so order quantities should be in realistic 'pack' sizes: the user should not be instructed to order 8326.664 bars of soap. The output is only as good as the input, so all the key parameters should be accurate and up to date. This is particularly true in terms of the current stock position. Nothing damages a system more rapidly than the user being told that there is stock of an item, only to find the shelf empty. Procedures must be in place to ensure that all usage is recorded on the computer system, and there should be a systematic checking of recorded stock levels against actual stock levels.

Sometimes the requirements for materials are better estimated indirectly by looking at the forecast levels of activity which generate that requirement. Thus in a hospital, usage of certain drugs will depend on the number of certain types of surgical procedure that the medical staff plan to undertake. Requirements for disposable bed linen will depend on the number of patients and the length of the stays. A clear understanding of all the aspects of the process can help with the overall process of materials management.

Discussion

A range of organizations have claimed significant benefits obtained by adopting systematic approaches to the planning functions. Work in educational environments has been reported on course registrations (Graves *et al.*, 1993), course scheduling (Ferland and Fleurent, 1994), examination scheduling (Carter *et al.*, 1994) and class scheduling (Sampson *et al.*, 1995). Love and Hoey (1990) discuss the development and use of a microcomputer-based employee scheduling system used in fast-food operations. Various aspects of scheduling in airline operations have been reported at American Airlines (Vasquez-Marquez, 1991; Anbil *et al.*, 1991) and at Pan American World Airlines (Schindler and Semel, 1993).

References

Anbil, R., E. Gelman, B. Patty and R. Tanga (1991) 'Recent advances in crew pairing optimisation at American Airlines', *Interfaces*, vol. 21, no. 1, pp. 62–74.

Arnold, J.R. (1996) *Introduction to Materials Management* (2nd edn), Prentice Hall, Englewood Cliffs, NJ.

Carter, M., G. Laporte and J. Chinneck (1994) 'A general examination scheduling system', *Interfaces*, vol. 24, no. 3, pp. 109–20.

Davies, M. and J. Heineke (1994) 'Understanding the roles of the customer and the operation for better queue management', *International Journal of Operations and Production Management*, vol. 14, no. 5, pp. 21–34.

Davis, M. (1991) 'How long should a customer wait for service?', *Decision Sciences*, vol. 22, no. 1, pp. 421–34.

Ferland, J. and C. Fleurent (1994) 'SAPHIR: a decision support system for course scheduling', *Interfaces*, vol. 24, no. 2, pp. 105–15.

Graves, R., L. Schrage and J. Sankaran (1993) 'An auction method for course registration', *Interfaces*, vol. 23, no. 5, pp. 81–92.

Love, R. and J. Hoey (1990) 'Management science improves fast food operations', *Interfaces*, vol. 20, no. 2, pp. 21–9.

Murdick, R.G., B. Render and R. Russel (1990) *Service Operations Management*, Allyn and Bacon, London.

Page, E. (1972) *Queuing Theory in OR*, Butterworths, London.

Sampson, S., J. Freeland and E. Weiss (1995) 'Class scheduling to maximise participant satisfaction', *Interfaces*, vol. 25, no. 3, pp. 30–41.

Saunders, J.A., J.A. Sharp and S.F. Witt (1987) *Practical Business Forecasting*, Gower, London.

Schindler, S. and T. Semel (1993) 'Station staffing at Pan American World Airlines', *Interfaces*, vol. 23, no. 3, pp. 91–8.

Vasquez-Marquez, A. (1991) 'American Airlines arrival slot allocation system', *Interfaces*, vol. 21, no. 1, pp. 42–61.

Voss, C.A., C. Armistead, B. Johnston and B. Morris (1985) *Operations Management in Service Industries and the Public Sector*, Wiley, New York.

Wheelwright, S.C. and S. Makridakis (1989) *Forecasting Methods for Management*, Wiley, New York.

Discussion topics/exercises

1. Identify three different actual service environments and describe the planning processes in each. Outline how the characteristics of service contribute to the complexity of these processes.

2. Select a major service market (for example, international air travel, city centre hotel chains, fast-food outlets, supermarkets) and identify some of the key factors which influence long-term capacity management decisions faced by an organization in this market.

    Describe how such an organization might approach reducing the risk associated with the decisions.

    Outline and justify the steps the organization might take either to increase or to decrease capacity as appropriate.

3. Select and describe two actual service situations, one in which the predominant short/medium-term capacity management strategy is to have level capacity, and the second where attempts are made to adjust capacity to meet demand. Identify the reasons for this strategy and the practical consequences of it. Determine steps which the organization might take to improve its overall performance, by alterations/modifications to its approach to capacity management.

4. You are the administrative director of a large hotel in a European capital city. You are concerned at what appears to you to be an excessive annual bill for the purchase of all consumable items used within the hotel. You decide that one approach would be to appoint a 'materials manager' to be responsible for all aspects of the management of these consumable items.

    You sit down to think through what might be the job specification. This takes you into trying to identify the different types of 'material', who else might be involved in this management process, what information would be needed, where it would come from, and how the management process might be approached.

Chapter 13

Performance measurement

Chapter outline

Introduction

Two characteristics of services in particular, *intangibility* and *heterogeneity*, cause problems of measurement and specification. Chapter 8 addressed the problems associated with specification of the product. This chapter focuses on the measurement problems associated with monitoring the delivery of the product:

- Are we producing a quality product?
- How well are we using our resources to produce the product?

Quality measurement

In Chapter 6, issues relating to service quality were discussed. The discussion focused on just what service quality means, and how to identify customer requirements. In particular, some of the seminal work of Parasuraman, Berry and Zeithaml was examined. In this chapter, the use of the SERVQUAL instrument to measure service quality will be discussed, together with some alternative approaches.

SERVQUAL instrument

The revised (1991) version of the SERVQUAL questionnaire is presented in Figure 13.1. The first section of the questionnaire asks questions relating to expectations of the service. The second section repeats the same questions, but instead of eliciting responses about expectations, the perceptions of actual service received are sought. A final section seeks information regarding relative importance of the dimensions.

This revised version differs from the original in a number of ways. Two of the questions, one relating to the assurance dimension and one to the tangible dimension, were changed. Questions were also added relating to 'materials associated with the service' and 'employees in excellent ... will have the knowledge to answer customer questions'. In the original version, some questions were negatively worded. In the revised version, all questions are positively worded. The *should* terminology was replaced with questions in the form 'Excellent ... companies *will* insist on ...'. The cusum section asking respondents to allocate 100 points for relative importance was also added.

These refinements address many of the criticisms which have been levied at the original version of the questionnaire. However, before considering the limitations of the instrument, attention will be paid to *how* the questionnaire may be used.

Parasuraman, Berry and Zeithaml originally claimed that this questionnaire could be used in the form presented, across all service settings. The idea was that all that was required was the insertion of the type of organization: for example, 'Excellent *business schools* will ...'. There are few supporters of this claim regarding the generic nature of the questionnaire, as discussed in Chapter 6.

An analysis of subsequent studies adds support to the viewpoint that the five underlying dimensions of quality proposed by Parasuraman, Zeithaml and Berry are not generic across all services. The studies where the use of the unchanged SERVQUAL questionnaire have been relatively successful are those conducted in situations characterized by low contact, low customization and little need for the use of professional judgement. In other situations, factor analysis of the responses has not identified the original five dimensions. For example, Babakus and Boller (1992) could identify only two factors. In their study, however, some of the questions were still negatively worded, and the factors identified did seem to depend on the form of the wording.

Since the original SERVQUAL questionnaire was published, it has been tested by many researchers in different contexts. What many have done is adapt the questionnaire. A common approach is, first, to hold focus groups to try and identify any missing underlying factors of service quality which will need to be included in a revised questionnaire. These are small groups of users of the service who are asked to participate in a type of brainstorming

EXPECTATIONS SECTION

Directions: Based on your experiences as a customer of telephone repair services, please think about the kind of telephone company that would deliver excellent quality of repair service. Think about the kind of telephone company with which you would be pleased to do business. Please show the extent to which you think such a telephone company would possess the features described by each statement. If you feel a feature is *not at all essential* for excellent telephone companies such as the one you have in mind, circle the number '1'. If you feel a feature is *absolutely essential* for excellent telephone companies, circle '7'. If your feelings are less strong, circle one of the numbers in the middle. There are no right or wrong answers – all we are interested in is a number that truly reflects your feelings regarding telephone companies that would deliver excellent quality of service.

Note: Each of the statements was accompanied by a 7-point scale anchored at the end by the labels 'Strongly Disagree' (=1) and 'Strongly Agree' (=7). Intermediate scale points were not labelled. Also, the headings (TANGIBLES, RELIABILITY, etc.), shown here to indicate which statements fall under each dimension, were not included in the actual questionnaire.

Tangibles
E1. Excellent telephone companies will have modern-looking equipment.
E2. The physical facilities at excellent telephone companies will be visually appealing.
E3. Employees of excellent telephone companies will be neat-appearing.
E4. Materials associated with the service (such as pamphlets or statements) will be visually appealing in an excellent telephone company.

Reliability
E5. When excellent telephone companies promise to do something by a certain time, they will do it.
E6. When customers have a problem, excellent telephone companies will show a sincere interest in solving it.
E7. Excellent telephone companies will perform the service right the first time.
E8. Excellent telephone companies will provide their services at the time they promise to do so.
E9. Excellent telephone companies will insist on error-free records.

Responsiveness
E10. Employees of excellent telephone companies will tell customers exactly when services will be performed.
E11. Employees of excellent telephone companies will give prompt service to customers.
E12. Employees of excellent telephone companies will always be willing to help customers.
E13. Employees of excellent companies will never be too busy to respond to customer requests.

Assurance
E14. The behaviour of employees of excellent telephone companies will instill confidence in customers.
E15. Customers of excellent telephone companies will feel safe in their transactions.
E16. Employees of excellent telephone companies will be consistently courteous with customers.
E17. Employees of excellent telephone companies will have the knowledge to answer customer questions.

Empathy
E18. Excellent telephone companies will give customers individual attention.
E19. Excellent telephone companies will have operating hours convenient to all their customers.
E20. Excellent telephone companies will have employees who give customers personal attention.
E21. Excellent telephone companies will have the customers' best interests at heart.
E22. The employees of excellent telephone companies will understand the specific needs of their customers.

PERCEPTIONS SECTION

Directions: The following set of statements relate to your feelings about XYZ Telephone Company's repair service. For each statement, please show the extent to which you believe XYZ has the feature described by the statement. Once again, circling a '1' means that you strongly disagree that XYZ had that feature, and circling a '7' means that you strongly agree. You may circle any of the numbers in the middle to show how strong your feelings are. There are no right or wrong answers – all we are interested in is a number that best shows your perceptions about XYZ's repair service.

Tangibles
P1. XYZ has modern-looking equipment.
P2. XYZ's physical facilities are visually appealing.
P3. XYZ's employees are neat-appearing.
P4. Materials associated with the service (such as pamphlets or statements) are visually appealing at XYZ.

Reliability
P5. When XYZ promises to do something by a certain time, it does so.
P6. When you have a problem, XYZ shows a sincere interest in solving it.
P7. XYZ performs the service right the first time.
P8. XYZ provides its services at the time it promises to do so.
P9. XYZ insists on error-free records.

Responsiveness
P10. Employees of XYZ tell you exactly when services will be performed.
P11. Employees of XYZ give you prompt service.
P12. Employees of XYZ are always willing to help you.
P13. Employees of XYZ are never too busy to respond to your requests.

Assurance
P14. The behaviour of employees of XYZ instils confidence in customers.
P15. You feel safe in your transactions with XYZ.
P16. Employees at XYZ are consistently courteous with you.
P17. Employees of XYZ have the knowledge to answer your questions.

Empathy
P18. XYZ gives you individual attention.
P19. XYZ has operations hours convenient to all its customers.
P20. XYZ has employees who give you personal attention.
P21. XYZ has your best interests at heart.
P22. Employees of XYZ understand your specific needs.

POINT-ALLOCATION QUESTION

Directions: Listed below are five features pertaining to telephone companies and the repair services they offer. We would like to know how important each of these features is to *you* when you evaluate a telephone company's quality of repair service. Please allocate a total of 100 points among the five features *according to how important each feature is to you* – the more important a feature is to you, the more points you should allocate to it. Please ensure that the points you allocate to the five features add up to 100.

1. The appearance of the telephone company's physical facilities, equipment, personnel and communications materials	_____ points
2. The ability of the telephone company to perform the promised service dependably and accurately	_____ points
3. The willingness of the telephone company to help customers and provide prompt service	_____ points
4. The knowledge and courtesy of the telephone company's employees and their ability to convey trust and confidence	_____ points
5. The caring, individualized attention the telephone company provides its customers	_____ points
Total points allocated	100 points

Figure 13.1 SERVQUAL questionnaire (Source: Parasuraman, et al., 1991, pp. 420–50)

session. These sessions are often tape-recorded to aid subsequent analysis. If it is felt that the original SERVQUAL questionnaire needs adaptation, then the second step is usually the piloting of the revised questionnaire. Any problems which then arise due to ambiguous or confusing questions can be dealt with before a final version is used on the full sample of clients or customers chosen to take part in the survey. The responses are then analyzed, using some form of factor analysis to confirm the existence of discrete underlying dimensions, and the gap score (i.e. the difference between customer expectations of the service and their perceptions of the actual service delivered) is calculated to identify areas needing attention.

It is clear that characteristics of service, such as a high level of contact with the customer, have additional associated underlying factors which influence a customer's perception of quality. So far, no generic framework has been presented which links dimensions to service characteristics successfully. One of the problems is the lack of any commonly accepted terminology. In Table 6.1, the list of dimensions identified in the various studies illustrates this problem. Each researcher has identified a 'new' dimension and thought up what seems to be an appropriate label for the factor. In some cases the same label is used by different researchers in two different studies. This can be misleading because an examination of the factors often reveals that they are clearly not the same factor. The converse is also true. What appears from the description in the studies to be the same factor is often given two different labels.

Another problem facing researchers is the lack of common methodology in conducting the studies. The wording of the questionnaires differs: some include negatively worded questions, which, as seen in the Babakus and Boller study (1992), may distort the results. Another variant already mentioned relates to the phrasing of the expectation set of questions: is the word 'should' used? One of the problems associated with the use of the word 'should' is that respondents simply go down all the questions circling the maximum score in all cases. When there are so many variables involved, it is never clear which aspect is influencing the results.

It appears that, unless the service being examined is one which is very similar to the four used in the original Parasuraman, Zeithaml and Berry study, adaptations to the SERVQUAL questionnaire will be necessary. A starting point will be an analysis of the characteristics of the particular service in question. Here the Haywood-Farmer cube may be of help. Then an attempt should be made to identify studies which have been used in situations with a similar profile of service characteristics. These can be used as a basis for the development of appropriate revisions to the standard SERVQUAL questionnaire. If feasible, focus groups should be held to help identify aspects which will need coverage in the questionnaire.

The refined version of the SERVQUAL questionnaire presented in Figure 13.1 does appear to have overcome some of the problems highlighted in the replication studies of the earlier version, and therefore is the preferred version for use as a basis.

Having administered the questionnaire, a confirmatory factor analysis should be carried out. This is done to check whether the dimensions identified prior to the exercise are in fact discrete factors. The expectation scores are then subtracted from the perception scores for each question. So, for example, if a 7-point scale has been used, and the expectation score is 6 and the perception score is 5, a score of -1 is obtained. The scores across all the questionnaires are summed and averaged to find the score for each question. The results

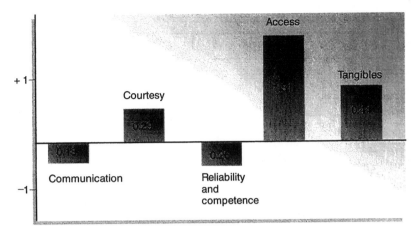

Figure 13.2 Illustration of results across five dimensions (Source: Based on Stewart, 1992)

of the questions within each dimension are then averaged to obtain a score for each dimension. The summary results may be presented as a bar chart, as illustrated in Figure 13.2. These particular results are based on a study of service in the context of firms of solicitors by Stewart (1992).

In this study, an adapted version of the SERVQUAL instrument was used, and the five dimensions were labelled: communication; courtesy; reliability and competence; access; and tangibles. The results in Figure 13.2 show that this particular firm was seen to perform relatively well. Only on two of the dimensions did customers perceive the service to fall below expectations: communication, and reliability and competence. In this case the firm of solicitors now knows where attention is needed in its delivery of the service provided.

The SERVQUAL instrument, whether in the original or in an adapted form, is not only useful for highlighting what is expected from the firm across the dimensions and how customers rate current performance, but it may also be used over time to track movements in customer expectations. It is also possible to ask customers to rate competitors, thus providing a benchmark against which to compare a firm's own performance. Gap 1 in Parasuraman *et al.*'s (1985) model can also be measured by administering the questionnaire to management.

Table 13.1 presents results from the Stewart study of the responses of the solicitors and compares them with those of their customers. The solicitors can be seen to overestimate what the clients expected along all dimensions except communication, and in terms of the perceptions of the service received, they can be seen to overestimate how well they were delivering along the dimensions reliability and competence, and tangibles. The major problem highlighted in this example, however, lies with communication. A negative gap occurred along this dimension for customers, whereas the solicitors themselves thought they were doing better than the customers expected.

Table 13.1 Scores of solicitors vs customers

Dimension	CE	PE	CP	PP	CG[a]	PG[a]
Communication	6.26	6.02	6.13	6.06	−0.13	+0.04
Courtesy	5.11	5.39	5.40	4.96	+0.29	−0.43
Reliability and competence	5.53	6.03	5.27	5.75	−0.26	−0.28
Access	4.49	4.79	5.80	5.45	+1.31	+0.66
Tangibles	5.57	6.01	6.01	6.13	+0.44	+0.12

Notes: [a]A positive score indicates perceptions exceeding expectations.
CE = customers' expectations; PE = professionals' opinion of customer expectations; CP = customers' perceptions; PP = professionals' opinion of customer perceptions; CG = gap between customers' perceptions and expectations; PG = professional's view of the gap between customer perceptions and expectations.
Source: Based on Stewart (1992).

The questionnaire also includes the importance of the relative dimensions. Respondents are asked to allocate points, which sum to 100, across the dimensions. The results can then be used to weight the scores of each dimension and produce an overall service quality score for the service. This is shown in Table 13.2.

Table 13.2 Illustration of calculation of overall service quality score

Dimension	Points	Weight	Score (P − E)	Weight x Score (P − E)
Tangibles	15	0.15	+1.2	+0.18
Assurance	22	0.22	−1.5	−0.33
Reliability	25	0.25	−2.0	−0.5
Responsiveness	20	0.20	−1.3	−0.26
Empathy	18	0.18	−1.0	−0.18
Overall score				−1.09

The importance scores also allow managers to focus attention where it is likely to have most impact. In the above example, reliability was not only the most important dimension, but the gap was also greater for this dimension than for any other. Clearly, in this example, attention should be paid to issues affecting the reliability aspects of the service, before considering the other dimensions.

In the example given in Table 13.2, the importance weights and gap scores can be seen to be related. As importance has become greater, the gap score has become more negative. This relationship is often found. Customers are often most critical of those factors which are most important to them. If some aspect of the service matters a great deal, then any shortcomings will be noticed and subsequently remembered. Problems which arise, but which are not deemed important, may be overlooked and easily forgotten. For example, if the speed of service, i.e. responsiveness, is important because a customer has a tight schedule, then delay in being served will be noticed. Perhaps a customer in a catering facility on a railway station has a train to catch in 5 minutes' time. That customer will be very sensitive to delays in service, because even a short wait may mean that a train is missed. If, on the other hand, responsiveness is not an important factor in the encounter, perhaps because the traveller has to wait an hour for a connecting train, then a short delay may not even be noticed. The actual responsiveness of the server may be much worse than in the first situation, but because this factor is not important in the second scenario, any subsequent scoring of this factor may be more positive.

Conversely, sometimes factors which, beforehand, are not considered important may assume importance when things go wrong. Aspects of a service which are taken for granted may fall into this category. Often the relative importance of the tangibles dimension in services is low. Students may not initially rank tangibles as of great importance, but if the seating in the lecture theatre is particularly uncomfortable and the heating system fails, then this aspect of the service may assume extraordinary importance.

When interpreting feedback from customers, therefore, care has to be taken. Isolated incidents may distort results and consequently be misleading. However, if the questionnaire has been administered to a large enough sample of clients, the results should present an accurate picture of how customers view the service. If a particular factor is very important, then recognition of the fact will allow managers to concentrate effort in areas of the service which are likely to have greatest impact. Marketing can also use this knowledge very profitably. Highlighting features of service in advertisements which are not deemed important by customers is not likely to be a very effective form of promotion.

Limitations of the SERVQUAL instrument
Although the SERVQUAL instrument can provide some extremely useful information, recognition of its limitations is important.

The first set of problems are related to the implementation of the questionnaire. When should the questionnaire be administered and how? Usually both parts are answered at the same time. If service quality is seen as an attitude towards a service which has developed over time, and is not transaction specific, then it could be argued that this poses no problems. General expectations are elicited from informed clients who have already had experience of the service on a number of occasions, and therefore their expectations are probably realistic as opposed to idealistic. The perceptions of the service will have become an overall impression of the service, and should not be unduly distorted either positively or negatively by a single encounter.

One of the problems with administering a questionnaire to repeat customers only is that the views of those customers that have been lost after a first encounter will not be tapped. If the customers who do not come back do not fit the profile of the type of customer that a service is trying to attract, this may not be a problem. However, it costs far more to attract a new customer than it does to retain customers, and consequently, it is usually important to know why an organization is not successful in meeting the requirements of customers during that first transaction.

Another problem with administering both parts of the questionnaire after the event, is that customers may not remember what they expected beforehand. If the service in question was very expensive, they may also rationalize to prevent cognitive dissonance; they do not like to admit to themselves that they made a poor choice of service provider.

If the expectations part of the questionnaire is administered beforehand, two problems arise. First, expectations may be raised by the questions asked, making it more difficult for the service provider to meet those expectations subsequently. Second, although, because the results of the questionnaire are summed and the average score is calculated, the first and second parts of the questionnaire do not need to be matched, it is important that only questionnaires where *both* parts have been completed by an individual are used. Administratively, this adds complexity to the exercise. From a customer's viewpoint it can become tiresome to have to fill in a questionnaire on two occasions, even if the total task is exactly the same.

Other criticisms of the questionnaire include the following:

- Length.
- Repetitiveness.
- Lack of clarity of the questions, particularly when negative forms of questions are used.
- The tendency in the first part, i.e. on expectations of respondents, to circle 'very important' for all aspects.

One factor which does seem to affect the results from the SERVQUAL questionnaire is the educational levels of the customers. Babakus *et al.* (1993) found that higher levels of education were associated with high expectations and more variance of responses, i.e. the more highly educated customers were more discriminating and more critical.

Where service provision is continuous, as is the case with utilities (i.e. water, electricity, gas), Babakus *et al.* (1993) suggest that, because of the low involvement, attitudes may exist as an inactive construct without a complex factorial structure: they may not be multi-dimensional. Similarly, Babakus and Boller (1992) could find only two underlying quality dimensions in a study of an electricity and gas utility company.

Another problem which arises is when the beneficiary of the service is not even aware that the service has taken place. Dalrymple *et al.* (1995) considered the applicability of the SERVQUAL approach in the context of a Food Safety Regulatory Service. As is often the case in services provided by local government, the actual service involved action taken to protect the local community. In this particular case, catering establishments were inspected to ensure that adequate hygiene measures were taken to prevent health risks to consumers. The only time the consumer (the local taxpayer) was aware of the service being provided was when establishments were closed down. The question here is: to whom should the SERVQUAL questionnaire be administered? In their study, Dalrymple *et al.* surveyed organizations which had recently been visited by the service inspectors rather than the end user of the service, i.e. the protected taxpayer.

One final problem with measuring service quality as the difference between perceptions and expectations of a service has been highlighted by Teas (1993). When a service exceeds expectations, it is assumed that the level of service quality rises. This equates with the idea that more of a factor is better. However, consider courtesy: as receptionists are more friendly and courteous, then generally speaking the level of customer satisfaction will increase. But there may come a point where the receptionist becomes too friendly and the level of attention and courtesy becomes excessive and intrusive, and actually detracts from the level of service.

Parasuraman *et al.* (1994) agree with Teas and present the three scenarios illustrated in Figure 13.3. In case A, more of an attribute adds to service quality and the following equation holds:

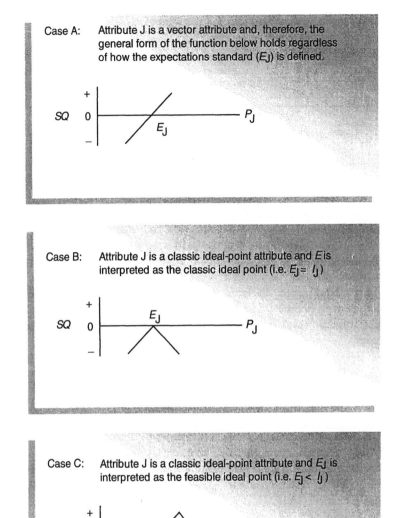

Figure 13.3 Three views of perceptions, expectations and service quality: functional relationship between perceived performance (P_J) and service quality (SQ) (Source: Parasuraman *et al.*, 1994, p. 117)

$$\text{Level of service quality} = \text{Perceptions} - \text{Expectations}$$

In case B, an ideal level of an attribute exists, after which the level of service quality decreases, as was the case in the example of the overfriendly receptionist. In this case the above equation holds only until the ideal point has been reached, after which the relevant equation would be:

$$\text{Level of service quality} = -(\text{Perceptions} - \text{Expectations})$$

Case C takes feasibility into account. There is still an ideal point beyond which a customer will consider that more of the attribute will lead to a reduction in the level of service quality. However, the customer will also consider the feasibility of providing the particular attribute and will be perfectly happy with a level of service which falls short of the ideal point. For example, a client of a solicitor may want to be kept informed of events. He may be happy with a weekly update of progress, and consider that expecting the solicitor to report daily is infeasible, although ideal. If the solicitor then phones two or three times a day to report trivial matters, such as letting the client know that she has phoned the court, but that the person she wanted to speak to was unavailable and she will try again in an hour, then the client is likely to find this excessive communication. In this scenario, the standard level of quality equation will hold up to the ideal point. After the ideal point, the equation becomes:

$$SQ = (\text{Ideal point} - \text{Expectations}) - (\text{Perceptions} - \text{Ideal point})$$

The practical implications of this are likely to be minimal. In most cases, service provision will be below the ideal point and therefore the standard equation and interpretation of the equation will be as originally suggested. However, some thought does need to be given to the possibility that more of an attribute may lead to customer dissatisfaction, and a resultant lowering of customers' perception of an organization's level of service quality.

SERVPERF

Much of the work which has been conducted in the area of the measurement of service quality has been carried out by researchers from the marketing discipline. The links among customer satisfaction, service quality and future intentions to buy have been studied closely. Customers have often been asked to give an overall score of the level of service quality. Correlations between the results obtained when estimating the level of service quality as the difference between expectations and perceptions, and this overall score have been compared with correlations between customers' perception scores only, i.e. ignoring expectations. Cronin and Taylor (1992) claim that: 'A performance-based measure of service quality may be an improved means of measuring the service quality construct' (p. 55).

This approach overcomes some of the problems raised regarding the SERVQUAL approach: raising expectations, administration of the two parts (separately or together), etc. Arguments have also raged over some of the claims by Parasuraman, Zeithaml and Berry in respect of validity and reliability of the SERVQUAL instrument. Many of these have focused on the statistical properties of difference scores. Taking a single measure of service performance (SERVPERF) is also seen to circumvent this issue. However, in terms of operations management, much useful information is lost when only measures of actual performance are taken.

Consider the example presented in Table 13.3. Following the SERVQUAL approach, it can clearly be seen that reliability is the dimension which is furthest from meeting customer expectations, followed by assurance, empathy and responsiveness. From an operations management viewpoint, this information highlights where attention should be directed. What can also be seen here is that reliability has the highest expectations score. As observed earlier in this chapter, this often reflects the fact that it is also the most important dimension, which is another good reason for trying to close this gap first. If performance measures only were considered, then the order would change and attention would first be directed at assurance and then empathy. Reliability would only be third in line, which is very misleading. The benefits of the additional information gained from using the SERVQUAL approach therefore probably outweigh the advantages of using performance (SERVPERF) scores alone.

Table 13.3 SERVQUAL scores

Dimension	Perceptions	Expectations	Difference
Tangibles	6.3	6.0	0.3
Assurance	5.0	6.2	−1.2
Reliability	5.3	6.8	−1.5
Responsiveness	5.8	6.5	−0.7
Empathy	5.2	6.1	−0.9

Disconfirmation

A third approach to measuring service quality has been suggested (Bolton and Drew, 1991a, 1991b; Babakus and Boller 1992; Brown *et al.*, 1993, Peter *et al.*, 1993). This approach, disconfirmation, uses a similar questionnaire to the two approaches taken above, but as with the SERVPERF approach, only one set of questions are asked. For each question, respondents are asked to indicate how they perceived the service when compared to prior expectations. So the scale used takes the form 'greatly exceeds expectations' at one extreme and 'greatly falls short of expectations' at the other extreme. The gap is being measured directly. This is clearly useful for an operations manager, but once again, some information gained when using the SERVQUAL approach is lost.

If one considers the example of Table 13.3 again, the results using disconfirmation should equate with the difference score. What cannot be seen are the relative scores either for expectations or for perceptions. However, if the cusum technique is also used, where, for example, customers are asked to allocate 100 points among the dimensions according to importance, an operations manager, armed with information regarding both relative importance and size of gap, can make a sensible judgement in respect of where attention should initially be directed to remove those gaps which cause the greatest negative impact on a customer's perception of service quality.

Critical incident technique

Another approach which can be very helpful in establishing what leads to both satisfied and dissatisfied customers is critical incident technique (CIT). Customers are approached and asked to recall an incident which caused either satisfaction or dissatisfaction with the service in question.

Bitner *et al.* (1990, p. 74) asked the following questions in a study of customer encounters with service personnel in airlines, restaurants and hotels:

- Think of a time when, as a customer, you had a particularly satisfying (dissatisfying) interaction with an employee of an airline, hotel or restaurant.
- When did it happen?
- What specific circumstances led up to the situation?
- Exactly what did the employee say or do?
- What resulted that made you feel the interaction was satisfying (dissatisfying)?

The responses were analyzed and three groups of responses, based on type of situation, were identified:

- Group 1: Employee response to service delivery system failures.
- Group 2: Employee response to customer needs and requests.
- Group 3: Unprompted and unsolicited employee actions.

Analysis showed that, where a failure in providing a core element of the service occurs, the incident may actually cause satisfation, if handled well by the service provider. Positive responses to special requests also frequently led to satisfaction. However, in over 40 per cent of the incidents, unprompted and unsolicited employee actions led to either satisfaction or dissatisfaction. In this latter category, an example of a satisfactory incident was 'The waiter treated me like royalty. He really showed he cared about me' (p. 78). An example of a dissatisfactory incident was 'I needed a few more minutes to decide on a dinner. The waitress said, "If you would read the menu and not the road map, you would know what you want to order"' (p. 78). Edvardsson (1992) used the technique in the context of an airline, but only looked at negative incidents.

This technique is useful in two respects. First, it facilitates identification of specific aspects of service which have a significant impact. The very fact that customers highlight the particular critical incident indicates the importance of that particular encounter to the overall impression gained of the service by the customer. These critical incidents are usually outside the zone of tolerance. The effect of positive or negative incidents outside the zone of tolerance was discussed in Chapter 6.

Second, these incidents having been identified, systems can be designed to try and prevent the occurrence of negative incidents and to facilitate positive handling by service personnel of such incidents. For example, what was highlighted in the Bitner *et al.* (1990) study was the potential for delays to cause either satisfaction or dissatisfaction. Where personnel kept passengers informed and, if appropriate, compensated them in some way, the failure to provide the core service was remembered positively. If procedures and guidelines are developed for the handling of delays, the front-line staff will know how to deal with the situation. Clearly, they will need to be trained in the systems and procedures, and rewarded for appropriate behaviour, but the risk of such situations being handled badly will have been significantly reduced.

The critical incident technique can also be applied to staff, asking them to remember critical incidents. What this often highlights is that staff do not always perceive incidents in the same light as the customer. Unless misconceptions of staff are eliminated, incidents are unlikely to be handled to the satisfaction of the customer.

All the above approaches have attempted to establish/measure just what a customer may want. They are essential when trying to ensure *quality of design* and when assessing performance of the service from a customer perspective.

Tools of TQM

The techniques which will be examined in this section are concerned with ensuring that the process is capable of delivering according to the service specification, and will thus influence the degree to which an organization can achieve *quality of conformance*: that is, the ability to provide consistently what has been identified as a quality service. The Japanese guru Ishikawa has identified seven basic tools which facilitate this task:

- Process flow charting.
- Tally charts.
- Histograms.
- Scatter diagrams.
- Pareto analysis.
- Ishikawa/cause and effect fishbone diagrams.
- Statistical process control.

The above techniques are all to do with collecting information or data, and analyzing that data to identify: what is done and how often, with what variation, the major problems and the causes of these problems, the relationships between factors, and finally, when action needs to be taken.

Process flow charting

This technique was covered in Chapter 11. There are various forms of charting, but basically it involves the recording of what is done, the order in which it is done, and the relationships with other parts of the process. The major use of this exercise is when examining *how* to perform tasks – what should be done, by whom, in what order, where and how – as part of a method study exercise to determine the best mode of operation. As a diagnostic tool, it helps the analyst identify reasons for poor performance. For example, process charts using pictorial representations of the layout in a hospital may highlight a point of congestion which causes delays and potential confusion for staff and patients. Rerouting either staff or patients may be a simple solution which is not obvious from a description of the situation alone.

Process charts of the type commonly used in computing may highlight a missing information link which precludes excellent service. For example, many organizations are set up to capture initial information on customers which is disseminated to various

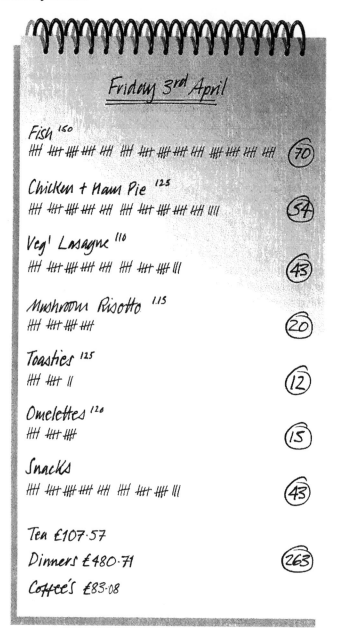

Figure 13.4   A tally chart: recording the number of different types of meal in the refectory

departments, all of which need such details as the address of the customer. If the customer then changes address and informs one of the departments only, are these systems in place to pass back that information to all the other departments, so that they too can update their records? Database systems overcome this type of problem because the basic data on a customer are only stored in one place, and all departments access that information. Once information is updated, it is updated for all users. Whatever the solution adopted, the process chart provides a useful tool for systematically recording what is happening to facilitate subsequent analysis.

Tally charts

This is probably the simplest recording method available. An example is given in Figure 13.4. In this example, the server in a refectory is recording the number of different types of meal that students are buying. As each student pays for his or her meal, a mark is made against the appropriate category. When someone is the fifth student to buy a particular type of meal, a diagonal strike is made through the previous four marks. This makes totalling the scores extremely easy. In this situation, at the end of the lunch period, a record of demand is immediately available. This is particularly useful for planning purposes and helps the staff to ensure that they provide appropriate quantities of the various alternatives for the customers in future. What this would not capture on its own would be shortfalls of particular dishes (e.g. late comers might have preferred the tuna risotto had there been any left). Additional information would have to be gathered regarding the final position – which dishes sold out and which were left.

The same technique may be used in countless other situations. Sometimes types of query at an information desk may be recorded. These may highlight shortcomings in the information given to customers. Records of types of request may indicate the potential for a new type of service. In the context of ensuring that the service provided meets customer requirements, tally charts may be used to record types of complaint or problem. In all cases, tally charts provide a quick and easy way of capturing raw data.

What is particularly important is that tally charts help to quantify the scale of problems. They help to take subjectivity out of the picture. What often happens is that front-line personnel form an impression of preferences or problems, the relative importance of which is distorted by the vociferousness of a handful of customers. A problem may seem more significant because the customer who complained was tenacious and articulate.

Histograms

Histograms give a visual representation of data. Numbers presented in a table may contain exactly the same information, and actually form the basis of the information contained in the histogram, but a pictorial representation of information is much easier to assimilate. The information collected in Figure 13.4 is represented as a histogram in Figure 13.5.

Scatter diagrams

Another simple pictorial technique is the scatter diagram, which can be used to identify a relationship between two variables. Statistical techniques, such as regression analysis, can of course be used to estimate the strength of the relationship between two variables, but plotting the points on a scatter diagram may be sufficient.

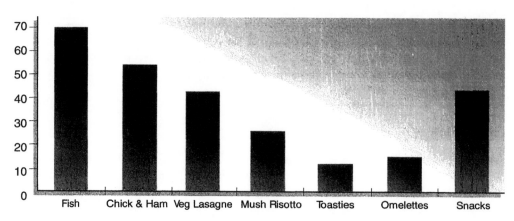

Figure 13.5 A histogram: showing different types of meal recorded in the tally chart

Figure 13.6 is a scatter diagram illustrating the relationship between time spent in a queue and customer satisfaction. The relationship shown is not linear. In this example, until a certain queue length is reached, customer satisfaction is not particularly sensitive. However, when time spent in the queue reaches 5 minutes, additional time spent queuing has a disproportionate impact on customer satisfaction. Monitoring the situation allows service providers to estimate the impact that providing an extra server will have on customer satisfaction, and thus allows them to establish optimal service levels.

Care has to be taken not to mistake correlation and causation. A scatter diagram may show that as temperature rises, demand in a refectory decreases. There may be a direct relationship between the two, but the major reason for the drop in demand is the fact that undergraduate term ends at the end of June, and during the hot months of July, August and September very few students are at the university. Just because two variables follow similar patterns does not mean that one causes the other. However, identifying a relationship may be the first step towards identifying an underlying cause. For example, a scatter diagram may highlight a relationship between complaints and Fridays. The question to ask then will be: 'What happens on a Friday which does not happen on any other day?' It could be that demand is greater on a Friday, all staff are overstretched and performance generally falls; or it could be that because demand is greater on a Friday, part-time staff are employed who are less well trained.

Pareto analysis

This technique is used to analyze data which have already been gathered. It is named after an Italian economist who observed that 80 per cent of the wealth of the population was held by only 20 per cent of the population. This 80/20 relationship has been seen to hold in numerous situations, and analysis to identify the 20 per cent which have such a large impact allows managers to concentrate effort where it in turn will have most impact. But 20 per cent of what? Problems, complaints, errors, delays, customers, sales – all are examples of contexts in which Pareto analysis can be used. For example, an analysis of problems

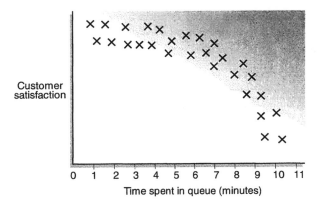

Figure 13.6 A scatter diagram: customer satisfaction and queue length

may show that 20 per cent of types of problem account for 80 per cent of time spent dealing with those problems. Therefore, by concentrating on finding ways of preventing those 20 per cent of problem types, 80 per cent of non-productive time (i.e. problem rectifying) can be saved.

Figure 13.7 illustrates the steps to take when carrying out a Pareto analysis. In this example, Fred, a computer officer in a university department, in addition to his primary responsibility for ensuring that the computing facilities are operating with minimum down-time, is continually interrupted by members of academic and administrative staff, and students who have computing problems. Fred is finding it increasingly difficult to fulfil his prime tasks, and there are ten computers which were delivered three weeks ago which he has not been able to find time to set up. One solution would be to employ another computer officer. However, the university has frozen all new posts at present, and therefore, in the short term, this option is not viable. An alternative approach has been suggested: is it possible to identify common problems which take up a disproportionate amount of Fred's time, which could be pre-empted by some other means: for example, the production of 'an idiot's guide to using e-mail'?

As a first step, data have been gathered on the types of problem which occur, the frequency of these problems and the average time taken to solve them. The second step involves calculating total time per type of problem. In the third step, the problems are ranked in descending order of total time taken and cumulative time is calculated. Cumulative percentage time spent on the problems is also calculated. The final step involves plotting cumulative percentage time against cumulative percentage problem types. These steps are illustrated in Figure 13.7.

The 80/20 rule will not always hold true – it is not always applicable. It is also unlikely that exactly 20 per cent of one factor will account for exactly 80 per cent of another. However, the general principle that a critical few will have a disproportionate effect does hold true in a surprising number of cases.

In this example, 22 per cent of the problems (i.e. the first five) account for 75 per cent of the total time spent dealing with problems. If these problems are considered initially, great savings of time may be made. The problem at the top of the list in this case is a

Step 1 Collect data on problems

Type of problem	No. of problems	Time taken to solve problems (min)
Queries regarding software:		
Works	8	20
Word	20	30
Harvard Graphics	3	15
Powerpoint	8	15
SPSS	2	50
Other packages	7	25
E-mail:		
Sending messages	6	20
Receiving messages	30	30
Attaching files	3	25
Viruses	8	75
Queries relating to hardware:		
Breakdowns:		
Screens	3	40
Keyboards/mice	2	30
Base units	2	80
Last-minute requests for hardware	20	120
Printers:		
Misuse		
Breakdowns	2	40
Paperjams	100	15
Miscellaneous		
Access problems	5	15
Change	130	10
General advice	6	15
Thefts	1	80
Open doors	6	10
Cover for computer services assistant	140	15

Step 2 Calculation of total time per problem

Type of problem	No. of problems	Time taken to solve problems (mins)	Total time (hrs)
Queries regarding software:			
Works	8	20	2.67
Word	2	30	10.00
Harvard Graphics	3	15	0.75
Powerpoint	8	15	2.00
SPSS	2	50	1.67
Other packages	7	25	2.92
E-mail:			
Sending messages	6	20	2.00
Receiving messages	30	30	15.00
Attaching files	3	25	1.25
Viruses	8	75	10.00
Queries relating to hardware:			
Breakdowns:			
Screens	3	40	2.00
Keyboards/mice	2	30	1.00
Base units	2	80	2.67
Last-minute requests for hardware	20	120	40.00
Printers:			
Breakdowns	2	40	1.33
Paperjams	100	15	25.00
Miscellaneous			
Access problems	5	15	1.25
Change	130	10	21.67
General advice	6	15	1.50
Thefts	1	80	1.33
Open doors	6	10	1.00
Cover for computer services assistant	140	15	35.00

Step 3 Rank in descending order, sum time and calculate cumulative % time

Type of problem	Total time (hours)	Cum. time (hours)	Cum % time
Last-minute requests for hardware	40.00	40.00	21.98
Cover for computer assistant	35.00	75.00	41.21
Printer paperjams	25.00	100.00	54.95
Change (money)	21.67	121.67	66.85
E-mail: receiving messages	15.00	136.67	75.09
Software: word	10.00	146.67	80.59
Viruses	10.00	156.67	86.08
Software: other packages	2.92	159.59	87.68
works	2.67	162.26	89.15
Breakdowns: base units	2.67	164.93	90.61
Software: powerpoint	2.00	166.93	91.71
E-mail: sending messages	2.00	168.93	92.81
Breakdowns: screens	2.00	170.93	93.91
Software: SPSS	1.67	172.60	94.83
General advice	1.50	174.10	95.65
Thefts	1.33	175.43	96.38
Breakdowns: printers	1.33	176.76	97.12
E-mail: attaching files	1.25	178.01	97.80
Access problems	1.25	179.26	98.49
Breakdowns: keyboards and mice	1.00	180.26	99.04
Open doors	1.00	181.26	99.59
Software: Harvard Graphics	0.75	182.01	100.00

Cumulative percentage time is plotted along the vertical axis against cumulative percentage types of problem along the horizontal axis.

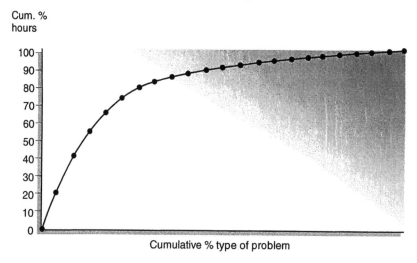

Figure 13.7   Pareto analysis of interruptions

legitimate request made in an incorrect manner. This analysis has highlighted the magnitude of frequency of disruptions to Fred's schedule. This evidence may be used to support a move insisting that no last-minute requests for hardware should be dealt with. The analysis also shows that a considerable amount of time has actually been spent covering for the computer assistant. Questions should be asked whether Fred should provide this cover. The same question could be asked in relation to the fourth problem. Staff and students often need change for the coffee machine and know that there is always a supply of change in the computer services office because of the sale of flexicards, etc. This is hardly a 'core' service of computer services and does take up a considerable amount of time. The extent of the third problem may be due to the use of cheap paper which does not meet the specification for the printer – a common problem caused when purchasing departments buy cheap supplies without giving due consideration to the true costs.

An actual example of this technique used in the context of an airline showed that the major reason for late departures was flights being held for late passenger arrivals. Once this had been realized, a decision was taken that in future, if passengers were late, they missed the flight. Although it was recognized that a few passengers could consequently by upset, it was felt that a reputation for on-time departures was more important for the majority of passengers. What the airline experienced was a dramatic improvement in its performance in terms of timeliness, and as passengers became aware of the strict enforcement of the rule of not holding up flights for late comers, late arrivals became rare (Wyckoff, 1984).

The examples given above illustrate the use of Pareto analysis to identify those negative aspects of service which need attention. The technique is equally useful in helping to identify those factors which have the greatest positive impact on customers, or identifying which services account for the majority of sales revenue or profit contribution. This information can help in deciding which services to expand, which to drop and so on.

Ishikawa/cause and effect/fishbone diagrams

Having identified problems or errors within the process, the next step is the analysis of those problems in an attempt to pinpoint the cause or causes. Ishikawa is the first person credited with using the approach illustrated in Figure 13.8, hence this diagram is often referred to as an 'Ishikawa diagram'. As the diagram also looks somewhat like the skeleton of a fish, another name is a 'fishbone diagram'. The purpose of the diagram is to try and identify the cause of problems and the effects of actions, hence yet another name by which this technique is known: 'cause and effect diagram'. Whichever name is used, the approach is exactly the same.

For any problem, which in the diagram is the *effect*, the potential causes are identified. What inputs in the form of, for example, procedures, equipment and plant, materials, information or people contribute to the final effect? Brainstorming is a technique which is often used in this context. A small group who meet to solve the problem will use the framework to explore ideas. An important element of brainstorming is the atmosphere in which it takes place: all suggestions should be initially accepted without ridicule – the most absurd idea may prove to be the answer.

Pareto analysis may also be used to analyze which of the *causes* identified contribute most to the *effect*.

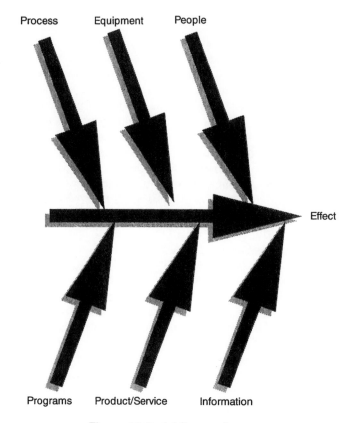

Figure 13.8 Ishikawa diagram

Statistical process control

Statistical process control (SPC) is concerned with ensuring that the process is operating within acceptable parameters, according to specification. It relies on understanding the probability of an occurrence, given the nature of the distribution of the process. Charts may then be designed to monitor the process, which will indicate when there has been a shift away from the desired performance levels. These charts are extensively used in manufacturing to monitor the performance of machines.

For example, a machine may have been set up to make a paracetamol tablet of a certain weight. The weight specification will not be exact – there will be tolerances (i.e. the weight will be specified plus or minus a small amount). Every half-hour a sample of tablets will be taken and weighed. The weights will be plotted on a control chart. On the chart will be warning and action lines. If the weights exceed the 'warning lines', another sample will be taken, as, although there is a 1 in 40 chance that this will occur, it may mean that the machine settings have slipped and the process is 'out of control', i.e. not producing according to specification. If the second sample also plots outside the warning lines, or if the initial sample had been outside the 'action lines', then the process is stopped and

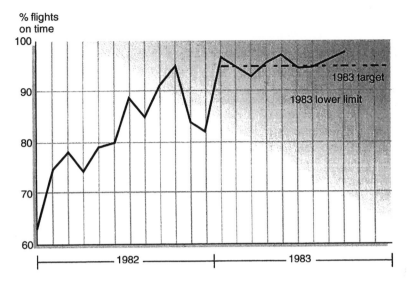

Figure 13.9   Control chart: Midway Airlines departure delays; reprinted by permission of Elsevier Science Inc., from 'New tools of achieving service quality' by D.D. Wyckoff, *Cornell Hotel and Restaurant Administration Quarterly*, vol. 25, no. 3, p.87. Copyright © 1984 by Cornell University

adjusted. The action and warning lines will have been estimated based on the statistical properties of the normal distribution.

There are a whole range of process control charts which may be used in different situations. Most are appropriate for use only when a physical product is involved, and therefore in a service context their usefulness is limited. As a consequence, little attention will be devoted to statistical process control here. A text which comprehensively covers the techniques is Oakland and Followell (1990).

An example of a control chart used in a service context is presented in Figure 13.9. This illustrates a control chart which Midway Airlines used to monitor departure delays.

Other contexts which would be suitable for statistical process control include: the number of errors in invoices, the number of complaints received from customers, and the percentage of trains which arrive late.

Productivity measurement

This final section considers ways in which performance of people and systems may be assessed.

Objectives of measurement

In very general terms, productivity is the ratio of outputs to inputs. The aim is either to obtain more output from a given level of inputs or to obtain the same level of output with reduced inputs. Either approach will improve productivity. Inputs, of course, come in many forms: labour, supporting facilities, facilitating goods, etc. Often, partial productivity ratios are calculated to indicate the performance in terms of output of any one factor of production: for example, the ratio of output to labour. A productivity measure of interest to investors is return on capital employed (ROCE) – the output is the profit, the input is the funds invested. Thus productivity measures can give an indication of how well an organization is operating.

Productivity measures may also be used to monitor the performance of divisions, departments, sections, teams and/or individuals within organizations. They may be used for benchmarking, as targets or for appraisal. It is therefore extremely important that appropriate forms of productivity measure are used. Are they providing useful information along dimensions of relevance? If used as targets which are linked to rewards, or for appraisal purposes in general, the form of measure used will influence performance. For example, rewarding an employee on a helpdesk for the number of queries handled in a given time period will encourage speed of delivery of the service. However, the quality of delivery may suffer as a consequence.

Often what is measured is what is easy to measure. Hence, in the above example, the number of queries dealt with is easy to count. What should be measured is the number of queries dealt with to the satisfaction of the customer. The latter information is much more difficult to capture, and therefore surrogate measures must be used. Some ways of tackling this problem are considered later in this chapter.

Ultimately, measurement for the sake of measurement is pointless. Productivity measurement should take place only when some benefit to the organization will be gained. The objective of productivity measurement must be to help an organization become more successful at whatever it is doing. The way to do this will be to link performance measurement and the use of any measures to critical success factors. As a consequence, the first step must be to identify these critical success factors. Morris and Davis (1992) analyzed the performance of a number of firms and found that those with a customer service focus had higher sales growth rates and increased profit. Thus, a critical success factor could be customer focus. Only when critical success factors have been identified can performance measures be designed.

Care has to be taken to develop a suite of measures, all related to each other, but which take account of the fact that a critical success factor identified at corporate level will have to be dissected into component sub-goals which can be related to at all the different levels within the organization. For example, Azzone *et al.* (1991) discuss timeliness as a potential critical success factor. Value may be added to a service which is delivered quickly. Technicians fulfilling a supportive role may not be aware of this success factor, and even if they are, they may not see how it relates to their task. The majority of their work may be preventative maintenance and they may be reluctant to drop everything in the middle of a complicated repair to respond to an equipment failure at the front-desk. The importance of their quick response to such incidents must be made clear through a clear job specification linked to an appropriate measure of performance.

Care also has to be taken when seeking higher rates of productivity on an individual basis. Multiskilling and flexibility of staff – in other words, a movement away from specialization – has been seen to improve overall performance even though individual tasks may take longer. Employees who are empowered and as a result have a more interesting

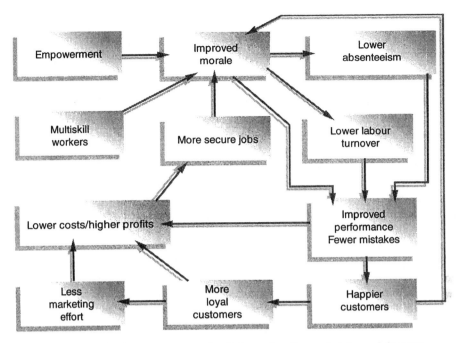

Figure 13.10 Long-term productivity gains through job enrichment

job are likely to have higher morale, leading to lower absenteeism and lower labour turnover. In addition, mistakes and errors are likely to fall, customers are going to be happier because they only have to deal with one employee – who is happier and therefore friendlier and more helpful – and therefore customer loyalty increases. As a result, less marketing effort is required, and overall the organization is more productive. This is illustrated in Figure 13.10.

The initial costs of additional training and the drop in individual productivity rates are more than compensated for by the subsequent gains.

Efficiency, effectiveness, utilization or productivity?

Efficiency relates to the manner in which inputs are used to produce outputs. When a service is produced without wasted effort or resources, i.e. making the maximum use of resources, then the service may be described as efficient. Changes in the layout of a hospital ward may minimize the distance nurses have to walk, thereby making them work more efficiently.

Effectiveness relates more to the outcome of the process. When the objective of the service is met, then the process can be seen to have been effective. Changes in the layout of a hospital ward so that patients have the maximum distance possible between themselves and fellow patients may improve the recovery rate, thereby making the service more effective.

Utilization refers to the percentage of time that resources are employed. If schedules are improved, bed occupancy in a hospital ward may increase and thus utilization of this resource has clearly risen.

Productivity is the ratio or relationship between inputs and outputs. Improvements in productivity, as discussed earlier, may be achieved either by reducing the amount of input for a given output, or by obtaining more output from a given amount of input.

The link between productivity and utilization and efficiency is therefore immediately apparent. If resources are used more efficiently, output will increase and therefore productivity will have increased. Higher utilization of one resource may lead to lower utilization of another, in which case overall productivity may not change, but usually higher utilization of a resource will lead to higher productivity. However, consider the examples given for efficiency and effectiveness. An increase in the efficiency of the nurses due to a layout which minimized the distance between beds may have a negative impact on the outcome of the service. Trying to sleep in a ward when the patient in the next bed is moaning or snoring is difficult. Sleep helps recovery. Thus recovery in a crowded ward will take longer. Improvements in efficiency often lead to a reduction in the quality of the service being provided. Thus care has to be taken when trying to improve productivity.

Utilization of cashiers in a bank may be increased by allowing queues to form. As queues become longer, utilization of cashiers will increase. If long enough queues are permitted, it may be possible to keep the cashier occupied nearly 100 per cent of the time. What impact does this have on the customer? Customers become annoyed and dissatisfied with the service and leave the bank. There is clearly a direct trade-off here between utilization and customer satisfaction.

If the word 'output' in the definition of productivity is replaced by *outcome* (i.e. the resulting output of the process is precisely specified), then any efforts to improve productivity will be beneficial.

When comparing the productivity of workers, problems sometimes occur because the difference between outputs and outcomes is not recognized. If the partial productivity ratio labour/annual accommodation sales is used, and comparisons are made between a two-star hotel and a five-star hotel, the five-star hotel may appear to be performing very badly. However, the service provided by these two categories of hotel is quite different. One would expect the five-star hotel to provide a much more labour-intensive service than the two-star hotel, and so labour productivity ratios will reflect this.

One of the reasons why productivity in services is low in comparison to the manufacturing sector is that, generally, services are labour intensive. It is sometimes possible to automate a service, as is the case with automated teller machines. Self-service is another way of reducing labour intensity. Examples of this range from self-service supermarkets, to self-service petrol stations, to self-service buffet-style meals in hotels. In all these cases, however, the outcome has changed. Elderly people often prefer being personally served by a cashier, as it gives them the opportunity to talk to someone. However, for other customers 24-hour access to cash may be seen as a great improvement to the service. Marketing has often been used to sell a change to self-service as an improvement to the service. Buffet-style breakfasts may be described as 'allowing customers to get *exactly* what they want'.

With either self-service or automation, the customer is being used as an unpaid resource. The result of either stratagem is an increased ratio of output to input. As long as the customer is happy with the new outcome, there is no problem. However, in many services it will not be possible to reduce significantly the level of labour intensity required to provide a service, and consequently labour productivity ratios will always be low in comparison

Reward systems

- *Reward/positive reinforcement*: must be linked to desired outcomes
- *Profit-based accounting measures*: effect of pursing short-term gains must be considered
- *Empowerment/job enrichment*: a form of reward - often leads to improved overall productivity

Job design

- *Labour turnover*: replacement employees take longer; may affect fellow team workers negatively
- *Absenteeism*: often the result of poor job designs - has a negative impact on productivity
- *Heterogeneity*: makes standardization difficult - has a negative impact on productivity

Task support

- *Climate of trust*: encourages openness and problem solving rather than cover-ups of errors
- *Training/education*: has a positive impact on productivity
- *Labour intensity/technology*: generally, higher automation leads to improvements in productivity

Process design

- *Customer involvement/self-service*: usually leads to productivity gains - **Warning** - watch quality
- *Method study*: outcomes must be clear, but will lead to improved productivity

Figure 13.11 Factors affecting performance

to the manufacturing sector. One positive aspect of this, however, is in terms of jobs created, especially in times of high unemployment.

One last factor to consider is specialization. Specialization usually allows employees to become expert in the task they perform, resulting in greater efficiency. The consequence of this may be to lower consumers' perception of the quality of the service provided. This is particularly the case where customers have to pass from one server to the next – multi-stop shopping rather than one-point service. Additionally, as discussed earlier, overspecialization may, in the longer term, have a lowering effect on employee morale, leading to absenteeism and high labour turnover. Once again, efficiency *per se* can be seen to be potentially dysfunctional.

Factors affecting performance

This whole book considers ways of improving performance. Human resource management texts concentrate on managing human resources with a view to maximizing performance. In this section the objective is simply to remind the reader of the range of factors which will impinge on productivity. Productivity measures, when used to monitor performance, can signal both positive and negative changes in performance. When performance deteriorates, further analysis is required to understand why. Any of the factors presented in Figure 13.11 may be identified as being responsible for the deterioration, and appropriate action should be taken to remedy the situation. What is of particular concern in this chapter is the effect that performance measurement itself has on the actual performance which is being measured.

Gummesson (1993) points out that cultural factors will influence productivity. Japanese and German consumers are more likely to read instructions than Americans! Where the customer is involved in the process, Gummesson suggests that the same behaviour may be transferable to the reading of signs and instructions within the service operation.

Rewards, in terms of money, promotion, etc., must be linked to the desired level of performance. Far too often rewards are linked to the volume of work completed without consideration for the quality of the output. This has been commonplace in financial advisory services and the life assurance industry. Commission paid for volume, and minimum volume target levels, have had the effect of encouraging sales staff to have a short-term outlook. Giving the best advice, which may be that no extra insurance coverage is needed at present, may not result in an immediate return, but the customer is much more likely to form a lasting impression that this sales person has the customer's best interest at heart, and in future he or she will certainly return for advice.

This problem is often linked to the short-term profit motive. Equipment is often selected on the basis of lowest price without regard to lifetime costs. Equipment of inferior specification, which is cheaper to buy, may have low reliability and break down frequently. The disruption caused by inadequate and unreliable equipment has immediate effects on productivity. In addition, there are hidden costs arising from a lowering of morale of the workforce. Working with equipment which seems to hinder rather than help you to do a good job can be extremely frustrating.

The use of partial productivity measures, focusing on just one factor of production (e.g. labour or plant), can also be detrimental. Labour productivity may be increased by reorganizing work and providing each employee with his or her own equipment. For example, a photocopying machine may be provided for each employee because previously time had been spent unproductively waiting for the machine to be free. Labour productivity would rise, but as the utilization of the photocopying machine would be low, productivity figures relating to equipment would fall and overall productivity could well drop. The relative costs associated with both labour and plant would need balancing to find an optimal mix of the two, always bearing in mind any effect on the quality of the service provided.

Finally, individual rewards for employees working in teams are likely to cause friction and be counterproductive.

Methods of measurement

Measures of performance should be very closely linked to service specifications. The problems of specifying the service have already been discussed in Chapter 8. If a service can be easily defined, then it can usually, but not always, be fairly easily measured. In particular, measuring effectiveness is a problem. At universities, increasing numbers of students are being processed by fewer lecturers. The number of graduates has increased.

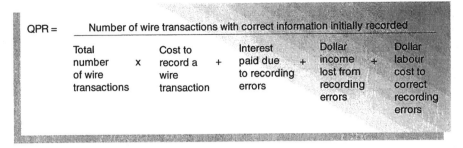

Figure 13.12 Quality productivity ratio (Source: Adam *et al.*, 1981, p. 185)

Productivity could be said to have improved quite dramatically. But has there been an impact on the quality of graduates? Considering the average degree classifications obtained by the students, the evidence would suggest that quality has also risen. However, what may have happened is that standards have fallen and marking has become more generous. Academics and academic institutions are rewarded for the number of students processed, and are ranked by results. The reward system may therefore have encouraged this lowering of standards. On the other hand, academics may just have become much more effective!

In the first section of this chapter, approaches to the measurement of service quality were discussed. Whether SERVQUAL, SERVPERF or disconfirmation techniques have been used, the outcome of the service process, along the various dimensions, is being measured by customers. If the results of these surveys can be linked to individuals or teams, a measure of the effectiveness of those individuals or teams exists. However, even with these instruments, because over time expectations rise, static performance on the part of the service provider will appear gradually to deteriorate. Unfortunately for the service provider, this is a fact of life, and what is good enough today is unlikely to be good enough tomorrow. This will have to be reflected in both service specification and performance measurement.

Adam *et al.* (1981) suggest that measures of productivity be designed with the help of the workforce. In line with the critical success factor approach discussed earlier, employees analyze the service process and identify critical points in the process. Measures are then considered which monitor the outcome at these critical points. Control is not excessive because only the critical stages are monitored. The measures used must take into account the quality of the output. An example of such a measure in the context of the transfer of funds function in a commercial bank is presented in Figure 13.12.

What is particularly useful about involving the workforce in designing measures of performance is that the measures will be seen to be relevant and their input will be valued. If targets are set simultaneously, these are more likely to be seen as realistic and not to prove demotivating, which overambitious targets often are. It is important that overall sight of the critical success factors for the organization is not lost. If, however, help is enlisted to formulate goals in line with company objectives, this exercise should heighten awareness of the workers' role within the organization and additionally promote co-operation as opposed to departmental rivalry.

As what is being measured and how it is measured can affect performance, appropriate measures must be used, as has already been discussed. Various frameworks to aid the

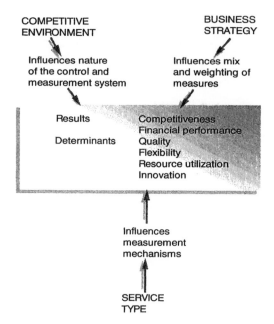

Figure 13.13 Factors which determine the performance measurement system (Source: Fitzgerald *et al.*, 1991, *Performance Measurement in Service Businesses*, CIMA, p. 117)

process of analyzing the type of service have been devised: for example, Haywood-Farmer's cube using customer contact interaction, customization and labour intensity was described in Chapter 7. Dependent upon where an organization is positioned within the cube, the balance between processes, personal behaviour and professional judgement must be adapted, to identify where in the Haywood-Farmer model of service quality (see Figure 7.4) the organization should be positioned. Figure 7.4 also illustrates some of the problems which occur when the wrong mix is chosen.

The first set of problems presented result when the designed system and performance measures used are too rigid and do not allow for differing needs of the customers. Linking rewards to volume rather than quality of outcome is likely to lead to this problem.

The second set of problems may be the result of a lack of any quantitative measures of performance, accompanied by few systems and little training in the 'technical' aspects of the job.

Studies have shown (Prais *et al.*, 1989) that training and qualifications are generally much higher in the rest of Europe than in the UK. Continental employees are encouraged to acquire additional relevant qualifications which enhance their performance at work, and are rewarded for doing so. The waitress who has studied wines and can advise customers will command a higher salary than one who is 'just friendly'. Since the study carried out by Prais *et al.*, National Vocational Qualifications (NVQs) have been introduced into the UK. These encourage the development of relevant skills. At the time of writing, what is not yet clear is how successful these qualifications have been in raising performance at work, but in principle, they should act as a measure of potential performance.

The final set of problems often arise because too much emphasis is placed on qualifications. Solicitors and doctors who have passed all the relevant examinations, and have survived the prescribed period of supervised practice, are not subsequently judged or rewarded for their interpersonal skills.

Fitzgerald *et al.* (1991) suggest an approach which links types of measure, to dimensions of performance, to either results or determinants, which are linked in turn to the factors which determine the desired results and determinants. This is illustrated in Table 13.4 and Figure 13.13.

Table 13.4 Performance measurement across six dimensions

Dimensions of performance	Types of measure
Results	
Competitiveness	Relative market share and position
	Sales growth
	Measure of the customer base
Financial performance	Profitability
	Liquidity
	Capital structure
	Market ratios
Determinants	
Quality of service	Reliability
	Responsiveness
	Aesthetics/appearance
	Cleanliness/tidiness
	Comfort
	Friendliness
	Communication
	Courtesy
	Competence
	Access
	Availability
	Security
Flexibility	Volume flexibility
	Delivery speed flexibility
	Specification flexibility
Resource utilization	Productivity
	Efficiency
Innovation	Performance of the innovation process
	Performance of individual innovations

Source: Fitzgerald *et al.* (1991), *Performance Measurement in Service Businesses*, CIMA, p. 8.

Fitzgerald *et al.* use a two-dimensional classification scheme: number of customers processed by a typical unit per day, versus contact time/customization/discretion/people–equipment focus/front–back office orientation/process–product orientation. Services which rate highly on contact time/customization, etc. and process a low number of customers per day are classed as *professional services*. At the other extreme lie *mass services*. Those organizations lying in between the two are labelled *service shops*. This is illustrated in Figure 11.7.

Tables 13.5 and 13.6 present illustrations of measures in the two extreme situations: professional services and mass services.

Table 13.5 Performance measurement in professional services

Key issues	Performance dimension	Examples of measures
Ability to win new customers Customer loyalty	Competitiveness	% success in tendering % repeat business Market share relative to key competitors
Control of staff costs Trading of labour hours to individual jobs to aid pricing decisions	Financial performance	Staff costs Debtor and creditor days Value of work in progress Profit per service
Relationship building between customer and individual staff Negotiation of project specification with customer Measurement of customer satisfaction; use of unstructured, informal methods	Quality	Investment in training % non-chargeable: chargeable hours Adherence to project specification and delivery promise Customer satisfaction with various aspects of service
Management of short-term volume, specification and delivery speed flexibility Provision of flexibility through job scheduling, multiskilling, job rotation and staff discretion in dealing with customers	Flexibility	% orders lost due to late delivery Staff skill mix % hours bought in from other offices Customer satisfaction with delivery speed
Control of front office staff time	Resource utilisation	Ratio of hours chargeable to client and non-chargeable hours Ratio of supervisors to staff
Measurement of the success of the innovation process and the innovation itself	Innovation	Number of new services New service introduction lead times % training spend invested in new services

Source: Fitzgerald *et al.* (1991), *Performance Measurement in Service Businesses*, CIMA, p. 121.

Table 13.6 Performance measurement in mass services

Key issues	Performance dimension	Examples of measures

Ability to win new customers
Customer loyalty
	Competitiveness	No. of customers
		Market share
		Comparison of competitor
		   prices and product
		   ranges

Asset Turnover
Control of labour and
   capital costs
Costs difficult to trace
   to services due to high
   degree of cost allocation
Profit per service
   difficult to measure
	Financial
	performance
		Return on net assets
		Working capital
		Profit per market segment

Relationship between
   customer and
   organisation
Setting of clear
   customer expectations
Measurement of customer
   satisfaction: use of
   formal, structured,
   sample-based methods
	Quality	Equipment availability
		Product range
		Customer processing time
		Customer satisfaction
		   with various aspects
		   of service

Building volume, delivery
   speed and specification
   flexibility into the service
   design in the long term
Use of level capacity
   strategies
Employment of part-time
   and floating staff
Use of price and promotion
   strategies to smooth
   demand
	Flexibility	Monitoring of queue length
		No. of part time and floating
		   staff
		Customer satisfaction with
		   service availability

Utilisation of facilities,
   equipment and staff
	Resource
	utilisation
		Costs per customer
		Revenue per customer
		Occupation ratios
		   (e.g. % hotel rooms
		   occupied)

Measurement of the success
   of the innovation process
   and the innovation itself
	Innovation	% new: existing products
		   and services
		R & D costs

Source: Fitzgerald *et al.* (1991) *Performance Measurement in Service Businesses*, CIMA, p. 122.

Earlier illustrations in this chapter showed how individual factors may become more productive *per se* at the expense of overall productivity. One technique which has been used to try and assess the contribution of individual variables to overall productivity is multiple regression. Mayo *et al.* (1984) studied the productivity of school food services. They studied the effect that twelve variables (e.g. employee skills, rate of absenteeism, number of employees, facility layout) had on productivity. They used six different measures of productivity: meals produced per labour hour, meals served per labour hour, servings produced per labour hour, payroll cost per meal produced, payroll cost per meal served and payroll cost per serving. Half of these productivity measures are related to labour productivity; the other measures are financial. Stepwise regression was used to build six models, each using a different measure of productivity as the dependent variable. The models were generally consistent and indicated which variables had a positive and which had a negative effect on productivity. Such analysis can help to identify variables which have the largest impact on productivity, and the relative costs and benefits of different actions taken to improve productivity can then be assessed. Again, it must be stressed that measures of productivity must be made with care. In the Mayo *et al.* study, the authors pointed out that using meals served per day could be misleading, as a meal could comprise two, three or more menu items. Servings per day gave a more accurate picture of the changes in output level.

Conclusion

Performance measurement is critical for control, assessment and associated rewards. The most critical point to remember is that sight must never be lost of the ultimate goals of the organization in question, and any performance measures *must* encourage behaviour which will facilitate the achievement of these goals.

References

Adam, Jr, E.E., J.C. Hershauer and W.A. Ruch (1981) 'Measurement as a basis for improvement', in *Productivity and Quality*, Prentice Hall, Englewood Cliffs, NJ.

Azzone, G., C. Masella and U. Bertele (1991) 'Design of performance measures for time-based companies', *International Journal of Operations and Production Management*, vol. 11, no. 3, pp. 77–85.

Babakus, E. and G.W. Boller (1992) 'An empirical assessment of the SERVQUAL scale', *Journal of Business Research*, vol. 24, no. 3, pp. 253–68.

Babakus, E., D.L. Pedrick and M. Inhofe (1993) 'Empirical examination of a direct measure of perceived service quality using "SERVQUAL" items', in *AMA Educators' Proceedings: Enhancing knowledge development in marketing*, vol. 4, Chicago, IL.

Bitner, M.J., B.H. Booms and M.S. Tetreault (1990) 'The service encounter: diagnosing favorable and unfavorable incidents', *Journal of Marketing*, vol. 54, no. 1, pp. 71–84.

Bolton, R.N. and J.H. Drew (1991a) 'A longitudinal analysis of the impact of service changes on customer attitudes', *Journal of Marketing*, vol. 55, no. 1, pp. 1–9.

Bolton, R.N. and J.H. Drew (1991b) 'A multistage model of customers' assessments of service quality and value', *Journal of Consumer Research*, vol. 17, no. 4, pp. 375–84.

Brown, T.J., G.A. Churchill, Jr, and J.P. Peter (1993) 'Improving the measurement of service quality', *Journal of Retailing*, vol. 69, no. 1, pp. 127–39.

Cronin, Jr, J.J. and S.A. Taylor (1992) 'Measuring service quality: a reexamination and extension', *Journal of Marketing*, vol. 56, no. 3, pp. 55–68.

Dalrymple, J.F., M. Donnelly, A.C. Curry and M.K. Wisniewski (1995) 'Assessing the quality of local government service provision using the SERVQUAL scale', in R. Teare and C. Armistead (eds.), *Services Management: New direction, new perspectives*, Cassell, London.

Edvardsson, B. (1992) 'Service breakdowns: a study of critical incidents in an airline', *International Journal of Service Industry Management*, vol. 3, no. 4, pp. 17–29.

Fitzgerald, L., R. Johnston, S. Brignall, R. Silvestro and C. Voss (1991) *Performance Measurement in Service Businesses*, CIMA, London.

Gummesson, E. (1993) 'Service productivity, service quality and profitability', paper presented at the 8th International Conference of the Operations Management Association, 25–6 May, Warwick.

Haywood-Farmer, J. (1988) 'A conceptual model of service quality', *International Journal of Operations and Production Management*, vol. 8, no. 6, pp. 19–29.

Mayo, C.R., M.D. Olsen and R.B. Frary (1984) 'Variables that affect productivity in school foodservices', *The American Dietetic Association*, vol. 84, no. 2, pp. 187–93.

Morris, M.H. and D.L. Davis (1992) 'Measuring and managing customer service in industrial firms', *Industrial Marketing Management*, vol. 21, no. 4, pp. 343–53.

Oakland, J.S. and R.F. Followell (1990) *Statistical Process Control* (2nd edn), Butterworth-Heinemann, Oxford.

Parasuraman, A., L.L. Berry and V.A. Zeithaml (1991) 'Refinement and reassessment of the SERVQUAL scale', *Journal of Retailing*, vol. 67, no. 4, pp. 420–50.

Parasuraman, A., V.A. Zeithaml and L.L. Berry (1985) 'A conceptual model of service quality and its implications for future research', *Journal of Marketing*, vol. 49, no. 4, pp. 41–50.

Parasuraman, A., V.A. Zeithaml and L.L. Berry (1994) 'Reassessment of expectations as a comparison standard in measuring service quality: implications for further research', *Journal of Marketing*, vol. 58, no. 1, pp. 111–24.

Peter, J.P., G.A. Churchill, Jr, and T.J. Brown (1993) 'Caution in the use of difference scores in consumer research', *Journal of Consumer Research*, vol. 19, no. 4, pp. 655–62.

Prais, S.J., V. Jarvis and K. Wagner (1989) 'Productivity and vocational skills in services in Britain and Germany: hotels', *National Institute Economic Review*, November, pp. 52–74.

Stewart, H.M. (1992) 'A measurement of service quality in the legal profession', MBA project, University of Bradford.

Teas, R.K. (1993) 'Expectations, performance evaluation and consumers' perceptions of quality', *Journal of Marketing*, vol. 57, no. 4, pp.18–34.

Wyckoff, D.D. (1984) 'New tools for achieving service quality', *Cornell HRA Quarterly*, vol. 25, no. 3, pp. 78–91.

Discussion topics/exercises

1. Discuss the concept of productivity and, using examples of your own choice illustrate how, in service, productivity may be measured.

2. The performance of service delivery systems is frequently judged in terms of efficiency and productivity.

   Increasingly service organizations are claiming to have a customer focussed strategy.

   Use examples to discuss the implications of these two statements.

3. Discuss the problems associated with the SERVQUAL approach. When and how should it be used? What should be done before adopting such an approach?

4. What is the difference between quality of design and quality of conformance? How can each be measured?

Chapter 14

Human resource management

Chapter outline

☆ Selection
    Job analysis
    Personnel specification
    Attracting a field of candidates
    Selection among candidates
    Establishing the utility of selection
☆ Training
☆ Corporate culture, intercultural issues and empowerment
☆ Performance/rewards/motivation
☆ Conclusion

Introduction

One of the main characteristics of services is the high level of contact between the organization and the customer. The form and the extent of this contact will vary. As was seen in Table 2.1, contact may occur in person: that is, the customer is actually physically present throughout the transformation process. The contact may be between one individual and a number of employees. At the other extreme, customers may be served *en masse* (batched up, in manufacturing terms) and be physically present only at the beginning and end of the transformation process. The actual manner of contact will impact on the transformation process in different ways. However, whatever the extent of this contact, the operations manager needs to manage the encounter consciously. In this chapter, the implications of failure to recognize the impact of this facet on operations management will be explored, and ways of capitalizing on successful human resource management examined.

No matter how well an operations manager designs and manages the supporting facilities and facilitating goods, or designs the processes and procedures, the actual manner of delivery of the service is crucial. An employee who is rude or intolerant or impatient or slovenly or ill-informed may totally ruin the experience of the customer, whatever the situation. Front-line employees need excellent interpersonal skills in addition to any technical skills required to do the job effectively. Take, for example, a university lecturer. The lecturer may be at the forefront of knowledge in his or her particular field and may even be able to present the subject matter relatively well, but unless students find the lecturer approachable and helpful, they may not feel able to ask for points of clarification or help, and the service provided will have failed to meet customer requirements.

Unfortunately, or perhaps fortunately, people are not like machines, and cannot be programmed to behave in a particular way. So, what can an operations manager do to ensure successful delivery of the product? A first step must be the recruitment of suitable employees, who will not only be able to do the technical side of the job, but possess good interpersonal skills. Training in interpersonal skills is possible, but research indicates that there are 'service types' of people who are predisposed to serve (Hogan *et al.*, 1984). Having chosen staff, the issues of training and motivation, and the development of an environment within which good practice can take place, need to be addressed. The design of the processes must help, not hinder the front-line staff to deliver the service effectively. In this chapter, some human resource management aspects will be considered, paying particular attention to areas which are especially important in a service setting.

Selection

The selection of front-line staff in services all too often fails to get the attention it deserves. Receptionists, bar staff, waiters/waitresses, holiday resort reps, shop assistants, etc. are often the first or only contact a customer has with an organization, but often these employees are the lowest-paid workers within the organization, chosen with the minimum of effort and forethought. Complexity and sophistication of selection procedures is usually positively correlated with the seniority of the post and level of salary paid. This is not surprising, but the importance to any service company of the quality of its front-line staff needs to be reflected in the selection procedures for these staff. Poor procedures result in the selection of inappropriate staff. This in turn leads to dissatisfied customers, which may lead not only to the loss of future custom from the dissatisfied customer, but also to the loss of other potential customers.

Other staff who are good often find themselves overladen because they end up 'carrying' the poor performers, thus causing resentment and ill-feeling within the ranks, which in turn may lead to absenteeism and high staff turnover. The inappropriately selected staff member who finds the job 'dreadful because of all those troublesome customers who never let you get on with the job' may also decide to leave. That may be no bad thing in terms of the organization, but it is a costly way of operating. The costs associated with wasted training, lost custom and poor morale resulting from the appointment of inappropriate staff must be considered when the selection process is being chosen or developed.

In any selection process, there are basically five steps as shown in Figure 14.1. The time spent on each of these steps will vary depending on the nature of the job. However, all of the steps *should* take place whatever the job. For instance, unless the job is analyzed in the first place, how can any organization possibly hope to find an appropriate person to fill the post? Yet all too often this first step is completely omitted for these front-line employees who actually come into contact with the customer. Even if the technical aspects of the job are analyzed, the customer contact aspects are often neglected.

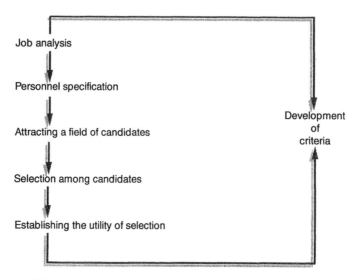

Figure 14.1   Five steps of any selection procedure

Each of these steps will be briefly considered below. For a more in-depth discussion, see Smith (1991) and Molander (1989).

Job analysis

Many service firms are small, with few employees. The owner may have done, at one time, all the jobs, or at least feel that he or she knows what each job involves. Things will, however, change as an organization grows. At one time, the front-line contact person will not have needed to know about the systems operating in the back office, or who does what, because they will often have done most of the tasks themselves. It is tempting, therefore, to think that a job analysis need not be done. However, the results of the analysis will often be surprising. Another aspect of this is that the job may just have 'grown' as the business has grown. Is this the case, or has the job been designed to fit into the transformation process? There is little point in doing a job analysis and subsequently finding a person capable of doing the job, as described, if the tasks analyzed were defunct.

An operations manager should be in an ideal position to conduct or advise personnel in the task of job analysis. Method study, discussed in Chapter 11, is a technique which may already have been used to make sure that the job design was appropriate and effective. The questioning technique will have started by asking the question: 'What is the purpose of this task?' Documentation should already exist which describes and analyzes the tasks done. This can be the starting point of the job analysis to be used in the selection process. Jobs should not be allowed just to grow. If the situation and requirements change, then these should be studied and the job redesigned and rerecorded.

The first step where there is documentation describing the job is to check that things have not changed, and that the analysis is correct and complete. If things have not changed, and the existing documentation is complete, then in effect the job analysis has already been prepared. If a method study has not been carried out, it is usually a good idea to conduct one before employing replacement or additional staff. What often happens is that, as firms get busier, managers put in requests for additional staff. A method study may identify that what is actually needed is not more staff, but more computer terminals; or maybe the computer system needs upgrading to reduce response time, as a high proportion of staff time may have been spent waiting for access to the computer.

Typical approaches to job analysis include the use of: questionnaires, checklists, individual interviews, observation interviews, group interviews, technical conference methods, diaries, work participation and critical incident identification.

Personnel specification

Having established the tasks which need to be done, the question must then be asked: 'What skills are needed to be able to carry out the task successfully?', and a specification of requirements needed by the applicant to do the job must be developed, forming the basis of the job description. It is here that the interpersonal skills and characteristics required for dealing with customers are very often neglected. Lecturers are chosen on the basis of their publication record (can they do research?), lifeguards at a swimming pool on their lifesaving certificates (can they swim strongly enough to save lives?). Clearly, these skills are important, if not essential, but in addition, the lecturer and the lifeguard have to deal with *people*.

This leads on to the categorization of characteristics and skills into those which are absolutely essential for the successful fulfilment of the required roles, desirable skills which will aid performance, undesirable skills which will positively detract, and acquirable skills which may be taught. Thomas Cook, for example, believes that knowledge of the travel industry is not essential when selecting personnel for its travel shops as this knowledge can be learnt: evidence of selling ability, however, is deemed far more important at the selection stage. The specification would therefore list selling skills as essential, and travel trade knowledge as desirable.

A personnel specification should cover more than just technical skills, to ensure a good job/organization–employee fit. Not only will certain attributes be necessary to be able to do the job, but an employee will need to work within the framework of the organization and its culture. Rogers' seven-point plan (see Figure 14.2) provides a helpful framework to ensure that no aspects are overlooked in a personnel specification.

Attracting a field of candidates

The personnel specification and job description having been developed, the search for potential applicants can begin. There are various ways in which this can be done, but factors which will influence the choice of method include the following:

- Cost.
- Access to likely candidates (do doctors read farming magazines for job advertisements?!).
- Speed.
- Catchment area.

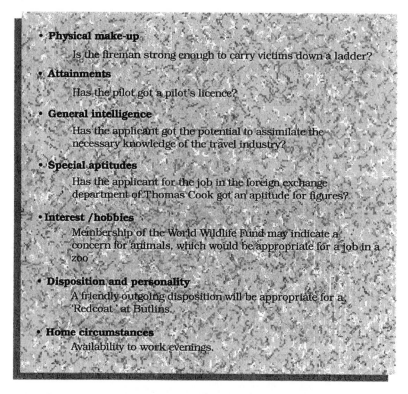

- **Physical make-up**

    Is the fireman strong enough to carry victims down a ladder?

- **Attainments**

    Has the pilot got a pilot's licence?

- **General intelligence**

    Has the applicant got the potential to assimilate the necessary knowledge of the travel industry?

- **Special aptitudes**

    Has the applicant for the job in the foreign exchange department of Thomas Cook got an aptitude for figures?

- **Interest /hobbies**

    Membership of the World Wildlife Fund may indicate a concern for animals, which would be appropriate for a job in a zoo

- **Disposition and personality**

    A friendly outgoing disposition will be appropriate for a 'Redcoat' at Butlins.

- **Home circumstances**

    Availability to work evenings.

Figure 14.2 Rogers' seven-point plan (Source: Adapted from Smith, 1991, p. 30)

Employers do not want to have too many or too few applications. Similarly, they do not want unsuitable applications, or to overlook a promising pool of applicants. However, whichever method is chosen (see Figure 14.3), inequality of opportunity must not be introduced. For example, recruiting family and friends of existing employees where the workforce within an organization is all white, but the local population is mixed, will probably lead to no change in the ethnic mix within the organization, and in effect will act as a barrier to entry for non-white members of the community.

Selection among candidates

There are four requirements of any selection method:

- Practicality.
- Sensitivity.
- Reliability.
- Validity.

Practicality refers to the cost, flexibility, time taken to undertake and convenience of the method.

- Advertising within the organization
- Vacancies boards outside premises
- Files of application forms from previous vacancies
- Government employment agencies
- Private employment agencies
- Headhunters
- Unions and professional organizations
- Universities (milk round)
- Careers conventions
- National newspapers
- Local newspapers
- Trade publications
- Electronic media such as teletext and the internet

Figure 14.3 Methods of attracting candidates

Sensitivity refers to the ability of the method to discriminate between different candidates (i.e. do they get different 'scores' from the 'tests'?).

Reliability refers to the consistency of outcome. If an applicant took a 'test' on two successive days, would he or she get the same score?

Validity refers to the ability actually to identify suitable workers. Is the method effective?

This last attribute of a selection method is clearly very important and reflects the very purpose of the selection process. However, evidence suggests that many methods in common usage are not particularly valid predictors. Figure 14.4 shows the ability of some selection methods to predict.

Cran (1994) states:

Service orientation is a set of basic individual predispositions and an inclination to provide service, to be courteous and helpful in dealing with customers and associates. Service orientation affects the quality of the service interaction in any organizational setting. (p. 36)

He examines the validity of personality tests to identify service orientation constructs which act as effective predictors of required behaviour in service contexts. In particular, he compares the work of Hogan *et al.* (1984), who derived a Service Orientation Index (SOI) using a 92-item scale to measure service orientation, with that of Dale and Wooler (1991), who incorporated service orientation into their model of service characteristics.

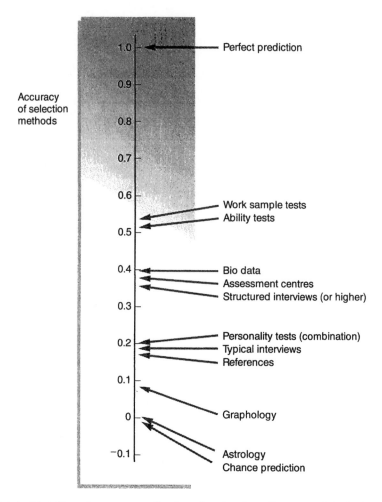

Figure 14.4 Validity of some methods of selection (Source: M. Smith, *Analysing Organizational Behaviour*, Macmillan Press Ltd)

Hogan *et al.* (1984) conducted a study in the USA of nursing aides. Performance of these aides was scored by their supervisors, and their scores were correlated with responses the aides had made to the full Hogan Personality Inventory (HPI). The SOI was derived from those items on the HPI which were highly correlated with the performance of the aides.

A further four studies were conducted in different situations to test the SOI. Finally the scores on the SOI were compared with scores on three other previously well-validated measures: the California Psychological Inventory (Gough, 1975), the Self-Directed Search (Holland, 1972) and the Armed Services Vocational Aptitude Battery (US Department of Defense, 1980). On the whole, the results obtained were as predicted.

Dale and Wooler (1991) found sociability, technical curiosity about how things work (a fix-it mentality), following rules when appropriate, likeability, and good adjustment (coping normally with life) to be personality traits which indicate service orientation.

From an operations manager's perspective, an awareness of such tests is important. However, these tests should not be used by the untrained, whether personnel or operations managers.

Establishing the utility of selection

Once candidates have been selected, subsequent performance should be monitored. Do selected candidates remain for a long period of time with the organization, or was there a mismatch? Comparing methods of attracting and selecting candidates, which approach seems to have been most reliable and cost effective in selecting subsequently successful employees? Feedback from the results of this analysis should be fed back into the process and used to amend/develop selection criteria.

Training

Having selected a candidate for a job, often the next step will be training of some kind. At the most basic level, this may take the form of induction, to familiarize the new employee with the structure of the organization, who does what, and where to find things. This may be informal and may not even last half a day! Even highly skilled, competent and experienced workers will require some kind of orientation to a new organization, and yet this is often overlooked. New members of teaching staff at a university are rarely briefed, being expected to be able just to do the job. But even though, to a certain extent, this is a reasonable expectation, knowledge of even basic information such as where to get stationery, and where and how to get copying done, can lead, at the very least, to inefficient use of time.

What is of more concern is the impact on the customer. How many times have you tried to get help in a shop, restaurant or library, or indeed in any context, and been told 'Sorry, I can't help you, I'm new on the job today.' What can be even more infuriating is when a new employee does not even admit to not knowing, but gives incorrect information or advice. This clearly has potentially serious negative impacts on the image of the organization, and should be avoided at all cost.

Training may be in technical skills, interpersonal skills or, as discussed above, the ways of the organization. Training may be needed because an employee is new to the job, or it may be used to develop skills and competences of existing staff. Markets change over time – some more quickly than others – and to match these changes staff may need to acquire new knowledge or skills. Employees may also expect to progress through an organization, and development training programmes may be needed. Whatever stage the training takes place, and whatever the level of the training, there should be three stages involved in the process, as illustrated in Figure 14.5.

This may seem very obvious, but again it does not always take place. Assumptions are often made regarding the types of training required, and courses are developed based on these assumptions. In some cases, lack of skills may not be the problem and, consequently, training may not be the answer. Poor past performance may be caused by lack of equipment, or poor working conditions. Whatever the situation, the first necessity is to analyze the situation and assess the training needs. From these needs, the requirements of the training should be identified, and an appropriate form of training developed, bearing in mind

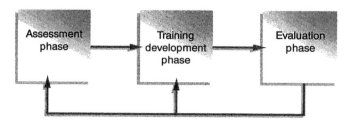

Figure 14.5 The three phases of a systematic approach to training (Source: Taylor, 1989, p. 153)

feasibility and cost. Having delivered a course of training, its effectiveness should be evaluated: were the aims of the course met? is the employee now in a position to do his or her job as required?

Clearly, this last stage is not always easy to do, as the performance of any employee is affected not only by skill levels, but also by motivation, supporting facilities and so on. For example, consider a secretary who is failing to meet deadlines. The cause is identified as problems which arose when the word-processing package was updated to the latest version using Windows. The secretary has been losing a great deal of time struggling to come to terms with the package. A clear training need is identified for familiarization with the package. This may be successfully delivered to the extent that the secretary becomes fully conversant with the new package. But on returning to the job, after having completed the course, the secretary still fails to meet deadlines, and the boss gives feedback to the training department that the training has not been effective. What has happened, however, is that the word-processor was linked to a computer network which has been experiencing technical problems, resulting in down-time for three hours a day while technicians endeavour to correct the fault. In this case the training has actually been very effective. However, it would be easy to draw the wrong conclusions. Care must be taken when evaluating the success of a course, to consider other factors affecting performance.

Training is often seen as an overhead expense – an evil to be minimized. This is a very short-sighted view, but unfortunately a prevalent one in the UK. Comparative studies of attitudes towards training have shown that successful countries like Japan and Germany invest far more heavily in training and have a far more positive approach to it than the UK. For example, Prais *et al.* (1989) compared the productivity of workers in hotels, and found that a major factor leading to improved productivity in Germany was the training of the workforce. In the UK, workers were given the minimum amount of training possible, thereby limiting their ability to be flexible and reactive to situations. The housekeepers in the German hotels were far better qualified and as a consequence were able to take on more of the tasks typically done by management in the UK, thereby releasing management to do what they were supposed to do – manage and take a more proactive role in making the hotel a success, rather than spending time fire-fighting and sorting out relatively trivial matters.

Training is clearly important in all situations, whether manufacturing or services. A structured approach to training in all cases is also equally important. However, what is different in services is the importance of interpersonal skills training. In any organization, staff interact with other staff to varying degrees. A team which works well together is almost certainly going to achieve more than a team in which there is conflict. Managers who interact well with their staff, who can interview well, whether for career development or staff appraisal, and who can motivate their staff will be more successful than managers lacking in interpersonal skills. However, all these interactions are internal to the firm.

In services, front-line staff have to interact with the customer. In some cases, customers are present in the 'production process' all the time (e.g. a patient in a hospital). In such situations, the interpersonal skills of staff directly affect the experience of the customer, and hence the perceived quality of the service. Poor interpersonal skills on the part of the receptionist, waitress, nurse, etc. may lead to lost custom, and at the extreme may cause the failure of the business. It is therefore imperative that interpersonal skills training is provided where necessary. Service organizations do seem to have recognized this fact. Taylor (1989) refers to a study carried out by Coopers and Lybrand and states: 'Companies which did possess a positive attitude towards training tended to be those for whom the impact of *not* training showed up rapidly, for example in the service sector where customer –staff contact influences customer loyalty' (p. 145).

Interpersonal skills training, however, is more difficult than training in technical skills. The most successful way of training people in this high-level skill is labour intensive, requiring skilled tutors working with small groups (typically, three or four people). Role plays which may be video recorded are commonly used. The tutor will identify the most important behavioural acts which need changing, and give feedback and guidance on how to change. The skill needed to be able to do this is at an even higher level than the interpersonal skills being taught. The tutor needs to attend closely to identify exactly where an encounter went wrong, whether it was an appraisal interview or a counselling interview. Having identified the most important issue, the tutor then skilfully leads the trainee to 'discover' it for themselves, thus encouraging commitment and ownership of the solution, or a new way of behaving. Trainees need to internalize and truly accept this new approach, otherwise they are likely to lapse back into their old ways before too long. This can be time consuming. Often because of time constraints it is necessary to tell trainees what they need to do better. Unlike the rogerian approach, often used in counselling, guidance usually needs to be given. It is not enough to get the trainee to recognize the problem, help is usually needed to reach a solution. For a fuller explanation of interpersonal skills training using this approach, see Taylor and Wright (1988).

Training videos are often used to illustrate good and bad approaches to dealing with customers. These are often accompanied by training packs which include exercises for the trainees to try. One of the problems with this approach is knowing where to 'pitch' the video in terms of sophistication. Many service situations are characterized by a mixture of types of employee, often part-time and/or temporary. University students often work in pubs and bars at night to augment their income. Some of these students may be business studies students who have completed marketing, human resource management and operations management courses, and are fully aware of the importance of good employee/ customer relations. Others may have left school at the earliest possible opportunity, have very limited academic abilities, have very limited experience of the world and feel that the world owes them a living. They may see the customer as a nuisance, getting in the way of them doing a 'good job', or making their life difficult by changing the drinks order. With the latter category of employees it will be necessary to 'sell' the importance of customer care to them. With the former category, care will have to be taken not to make the video patronizing. Clearly, these are two extremes, but they show that communicating effectively through a video to a mixed audience is difficult.

The importance of training cannot be overemphasized. It should be thought of as an investment. Training should be viewed in the same way as money spent on improving conditions, or upgrading machinery and equipment, is viewed – as investment, necessary for success in a competitive environment. When developing a corporate strategy, the core skills and competences of the workforce need to be considered (see Chapter 3). Training can enhance the skills of the workforce and give the organization a competitive edge, particularly in service situations.

Advantages to a company which trains its workforce effectively include the following:

- Increased motivation.
- Increased flexibility.
- Reduced turnover.
- Recruitment of good staff.
- Improved performance of workforce.
- Decreased supervision.
- Improved morale.
- Pool of loyal successors.
- Customer goodwill.

Employees who feel they are doing a good job are likely to be happier, gaining more intrinsically from performing well, which in turn leads to an increase in motivation and morale. Being happier in the job also reduces the likelihood of employees wanting to leave, so turnover is decreased. Marriott believes (Hostage, 1975) that happy employees make happy customers. If employees are in a good mood, it shows, and the way customers are handled will undoubtedly be an improvement on interactions with unhappy members of staff.

As mentioned earlier, training increases the scope of tasks that employees can do. This not only means that staff can cover for absent colleagues on holiday or on sick leave, but variety decreases boredom, yet again improving morale and motivation. A further advantage is that staff will also improve their suitability for promotion. Increased chances of development in the job and progress up the managerial ladder not only lead to increased loyalty and motivation, but also make recruitment of good staff easier, as applicants can see the potential in the job offered.

Because the workforce is better trained, it will also need less supervision. This in itself is more efficient and lends itself to a much better experience for the customer, who may be saved a delay while the front-line staff member 'just checks' with the supervisor. It also leads to a freeing up of managerial time. A secretary who is better trained, and who can be relied upon to do a job competently, requires less supervision, allowing the boss to be more productive too.

It can be seen from all the above that a good training programme can be a very worthwhile investment. The returns may not always be immediately apparent, but in the longer term, training can mean the difference between success and failure of a firm.

Corporate culture, intercultural issues and empowerment

Corporate culture

Just as different groups of people throughout the world have different cultures, within which they live by a set of norms and expected ways of behaving, so too do organizations have a 'corporate culture', i.e. a set of perceived common practices. Associated with a culture will be *symbols*, *heroes* and *rituals* (Hofstede, 1991, p. 197). According to Peters and Waterman (1982), 'strong' cultures are more effective than 'weak' ones. This idea has been challenged: what does seem to be important is that the *appropriate* culture is adopted for the situation.

Hofstede reports the results of the IRIC cross-organizational study, which identified six dimensions of perceived practice:

1. *Process oriented vs results oriented*: a concern with means as opposed to goals.
2. *Employee oriented vs job oriented*: a concern for people as opposed to a concern for completing the job.
3. *Parochial vs professional*: employees derive their identity largely from the organization as opposed to the professional end of the dimension in which people identify with their type of job.
4. *Open system vs closed system*: an environment open or welcoming to newcomers as opposed to one in which it takes a long time to 'fit'.
5. *Loose control vs tight control*: refers to the internal structuring of the organization. In a 'loose' setting, time keeping for attending meetings etc. would not be a must and looser cost controls would be the norm. In a 'tight' setting, meeting times are kept punctually, and strict cost controls are in place.
6. *Normative vs pragmatic*: following the rule book without exception as opposed to allowing flexibility to match market demands (e.g. a customer orientation).

The studies upon which these findings were based came from only organizational units in two north-west European countries, and did not cover all types of organization (e.g. organizations in health and welfare, and government sectors were excluded). However, Hofstede believes that it is most likely that these six dimensions would be similar, if not identical, to underlying dimensions of common practices in any organization anywhere in the world.

Successful service units have been seen to position themselves appropriately along these cultural dimensions of operating practices to obtain competitive advantage. In particular, on the process vs results dimension, successful firms were seen to be positioned towards the results end of the dimension. This is not surprising. In a manufacturing unit where there is a high degree of homogeneity in both the product and the customer, focus on the process, to reproduce identical articles repeatedly, is to be expected. In situations where the customers are heterogeneous, more freedom to react is necessary. This particular requirement of services will be explored in more detail when empowerment of employees is discussed.

Some external situational contraints may exist which preclude certain dimensional positioning strategies. For example, units may be subject to regulatory bodies which stipulate procedural exactitude. In such cases, firms or units would have to take a normative as opposed to a pragmatic position along the sixth dimension.

The IRIC study went on to consider quantifiable organizational characteristics, such as labour/capital intensity. It then analyzed correlations between the characteristics and the dimensions. From a service sector point of view, certain correlations prove interesting: 'If an operation is labor intensive, the effort of people, by definition, plays an important role in its results. This appears more likely to breed a results-oriented culture' (Hofstede, 1991, p. 194). Other correlations with a results orientation were with lower absenteeism and flatter organizational structures, which have been seen as giving a competitive advantage in services.

What cannot be emphasized too much is the need to match the culture to the situation, which may change over time. It may be that a service organization would ideally be situated at the results end of dimension 1, the employee end of dimension 2, the parochial end of dimension 3, in an open system with loose control at the pragmatic end of dimension 6. The above profile mirrors fairly closely that of SAS in the IRIC study, the difference being that SAS scored tight rather than loose control.

The logical consequence of this need for a match is either that organizations need to change their existing culture to a suitable one, given the environment in which they wish to be, or that organizations must realize that, given their culture, certain strategies are almost doomed to failure, and alternative options must be considered. 'Cultural constraints determine which strategies are feasible for an organization and which are not. For example, if a culture is strongly normative, a strategy for competing on customer service does not have much chance of success' (Hofstede, 1991, p. 199). But culture change within any organization is not easy and does not take place overnight. Figure 14.6 outlines the necessary steps involved in such a change.

Finally, sub-cultures may exist within any organization. For example, a pathology laboratory within a hospital is likely to be positioned at the process end of dimension 1 as opposed to a children's ward positioned towards the results end.

Intercultural issues

International boundaries will introduce societal cultural differences. These can cause problems for organizations in a number of ways, from problems in negotiating sales, to operating in a foreign environment. For an operations manager, it is the latter which is of concern. The problems can be classified as those arising because of contact with customers from other cultures, and those arising because our employees come from another culture. In both cases differences in things like humour, formalities (e.g. manner of greeting people, or terms of address) and personal space requirements are time bombs just waiting to explode. Joking with customers may be misconstrued. When asked in an Austrian restaurant whether the meal had been satisfactory, an English customer replied not really, the meal had been too salty, to which the waiter replied, 'Oh, the chef's in love!' This seemed to the customer to be rather a strange way to respond, and he was rather offended at this off-hand treatment. Things escalated, with both sides becoming more irate. Later, back home, when the encounter was recounted to a German friend, the remark was explained: there was a standing joke that people in love oversalted food, and the waiter had clearly only been making a standard joke. Both customer and waiter had not realized the

Managing (with) organizational culture
Is a task of top management which cannot be delegated
Demands both power and expertise
Should start with a cultural map of the orgaization
Demands a culture diagnosis

Demands strategic choices
- Is present culture matched with strategy?
- If not, can strategy be adapted?
- If not, what change of culture is needed?
- Is this change feasible – do we have the people?
- What will be the costs in terms of management attention and money?
- Do the expected benefits outweigh these costs?
- What is a realistic time span for the changes?
- If in doubt, better change strategy anyway
- Different subcultures may demand different approaches

Create a network of change agents in the organization
- Some key people at all levels
- If key people start, others will follow
- Can resisters be circumvented?

Design necessary structural changes
- Opening or closing departments
- Merging or splitting departments or tasks
- Moving groups or individuals?
- Are tasks matched with talents?

Design necessary process changes
- Eliminating or establishing controls
- Automation or disautomation
- Establishing or cutting communication links
- Replace control of inputs by control of outputs?

Revise personnel policies
- Reconsider cirteria for hiring
- Reconsider criteria for promotion
- Is personnel management up to its new task?
- Design timely job rotation
- Be suspicious of plans to train others; need for training has to be
  felt by trainees themselves

Continue monitoring development of organizational culture
- Sustained attention, persistence
- Periodically repeat culture diagnosis

Figure 14.6 Key steps and considerations regarding organizational culture (Source:
Hofstede, 1991, p. 202)

misunderstanding of the situation on both sides – they had not realized this intercultural difference.

Humour is a particularly sensitive area and needs a very deep understanding of the other culture in order to be sure of not being misunderstood and causing offence. This particular problem of differences in humour can make the building of successful teams from employees from different cultures difficult. In some cultures the hurling of insults reflects acceptance of others into the close circle of friends, politeness being reserved for those who are not quite accepted. But this can take quite a bit of explaining to someone who comes from a culture where insulting another is a very serious matter. Quite apart from the possible offence caused, lack of humour in the workplace can be negative. A study in the USA found the effects of humour in the workplace to be: a more productive and creative workforce, greater job satisfaction, reduced stress and reduced absenteeism (Matthes, 1993). How universal these findings are, however, is unknown.

Informality can be seen as a lack of respect. Students from the Far East often have a problem calling lecturers by their first name, as this makes them feel uncomfortable. Prompt service in a hotel in the Caribbean may mean 'sometime today' as opposed to within the next half hour, even when it's only the bulb in the room that needs changing! On holiday in Crete, one of the authors was becoming increasingly exasperated by being told that the promised tennis court would be finished in the next two days. At first it seemed rather impressive that Cretan workmen would be able to complete the task so quickly, and the offer of the resort rep to try and find other alternative accommodation where there was an existing tennis court seemed unnecessary. However, by the end of the two-week stay, it had become apparent from this and other incidents that it seemed impossible for the Cretans to tell the truth if they thought the tourist wanted to hear something else!

These problems need careful consideration. Communication skills need enhancing by training. An awareness not only of the other culture, but of one's own culture, is necessary to be able to understand potential friction. Specific knowledge of the other culture is first required, followed by acquired skill to fit into the other culture. This training is particularly important for recruitment of staff and in respect of staff development. Employees will be needed within international organizations who can communicate effectively with units abroad, not just by being bilingual, but by thoroughly understanding the other culture and its norms.

Team building, working procedures, power structures, work layout, customer care progammes, etc. will all need to take cultural differences into account.

Empowerment

Empowerment is giving employees the power to make decisions as they think appropriate to enable them to serve the customer. This is particularly appropriate in a service setting where customers are heterogeneous, and where flexibility to react quickly to their needs is important. There are costs and benefits associated with empowerment. Costs include additional training costs necessary to enable the employee to make informed judgements; costs of providing 'additional' service, such as free drinks to compensate for delays in take-off when a plane has had to wait for the late arrival of the pilot who forgot he was flying (as experienced recently by one of the authors of this book); and costs of making the wrong decision, which may be the perhaps excessive costs of the hotel porter taking the next flight across the world to return a suitcase to a customer who had accidentally mislaid it, or legal costs arising from a decision of a front-line employee who had unknowingly broken some regulations which resulted in legal action and fines to the company. Some customers may also be unhappy because they perceive inequity of treatment, as some other customer seems to be getting preferential treatment, or perhaps waiting time in the queue is greater because standardized and quick procedures are not followed.

Some of these costs may be controlled to a reasonable level. For example, in the study of productivity in hotels in Germany and the UK (Prais *et al.*, 1989), the housekeepers in Germany had a higher level of training than their counterparts in the UK. They were given budgets within their control and were able to make decisions (empowerment), so long as they did not exceed budget. This was seen to free up their managers, but at the same time was not risky in the sense that the freedom to exercise judgement was limited.

The benefits of empowerment include the following:

- Happier customers who are treated as individuals.
- Happier customers who have had a problem resolved quickly.
- A more loyal customer base as a consequence of the above.
- Reduced costs in getting new customers.
- Happier employees who feel valued.
- Happier employees who feel able to do a good job.
- More variety and more interesting jobs.
- Increased loyalty to the firm by employees.
- Less absenteeism.
- Lower turnover.
- Reduced hiring costs.
- Reduced training of new employee costs.
- Managers with more time to plan as opposed to directing/problem solving for subordinates.

What goes hand in hand with empowerment is a flatter organizational structure as much less time is spent referring decisions upwards, and spans of control can be wider. This happened to SAS when Carlzon took over the organization (Leirvaag, 1988).

Many organizations have gone down this route very successfully and have gained a competitive advantage by being seen as concerned with the customer. Marriott hotels (Hostage, 1975) and Delta Airlines (Labich, 1991) are just two examples of this kind of approach. However, empowerment is not always appropriate. If an organization is trying to provide a low-cost, high-volume service, a production-line approach where the delivery systems are standardized, as in McDonald's, meets the requirements of the business. Where differentiation and customization are required for a small market segment with customers who will pay accordingly higher prices, empowerment is essential.

Corporate strategy and the target market are only two issues to consider when deciding whether or not empowerment of employees is appropriate. Is the product or service such that customers are likely to return and a long-term relationship is likely to develop? What kind of technology is involved in delivering the service: simple and routine, or highly complex and variable? The environment within which the service takes place may be predictable or not. The existing workforce may be resistant to added responsibility – they like reduced uncertainty and pressure, knowing *exactly* what is expected of them and no more.

Bowen and Lawler (1992) present a methodology to help decide whether or not to empower. This is reproduced in Table 14.1. Organizations need to consider the five contingencies according to their own situation. High scores indicate that empowerment is appropriate.

Table 14.1 The contingencies of empowerment

Contingency	Production-line approach		Empowerment
Basic business strategy	Low cost, high volume	1 2 3 4 5	Differentiation, customized, personalized
Tie to customer	Transaction, short time period	1 2 3 4 5	Relationship, long time period
Technology	Routine, simple	1 2 3 4 5	Non-routine, complex
Business environment	Predictable, few surprises	1 2 3 4 5	Unpredictable, many surprises
Types of people	Theory X managers, employees with low growth needs, low social needs and weak interpersonal skills	1 2 3 4 5	Theory Y managers, employees with high growth needs, high social needs and strong interpersonal skills

The term 'empowerment' has been used here to mean empowering employees to make decisions which often have direct financial implications for the company, without the opportunity for management to intervene, because the decision and behaviour are simultaneous. Other levels of empowerment exist which involve people working in teams, perhaps in quality circles, and being given additional responsibility and involvement in the decision-making process. These have some of the benefits of fully fledged empowerment: for example, increased motivation due to a feeling of being valued and having one's ideas listened to, and having some say in the direction of the unit or firm, without the associated risk of precipitous action, i.e. the manager still has the opportunity to say yes or no to the suggestions.

At a lower level still, suggestion boxes also give employees a limited input in the direction the company may take, or its methods of operation. Suggestions from staff at McDonald's have been adopted and have led to new products such as the Big Mac.

Empowerment can give an organization the flexibility it needs to meet customer requirements. However, the associated costs need to be balanced against the associated benefits before going down the road of empowerment, and the environment carefully considered to make sure empowerment is an appropriate policy to adopt.

1. What is the problem in behavioural terms? What precisely is the individual doing or not doing which is adversely influencing his or her performance?

2. Is the problem *really* serious enough to spend time and effort on?

3. What reasons might there be for the performance problems (see column 1)?

4. What actions might be taken to improve the situation (see column 2)?

POSSIBLE REASONS FOR PERFORMANCE PROBLEM	POSSIBLE SOLUTIONS
Goal clarity. Is the person fully aware of the job requirements?	Give guidance concerning expected goals and standards. Set targets, MBO
Ability. Does the person have the capacity to do the job well.	Provide formal training, on the job coaching, practice, secondment, etc.
Task difficulty. Does the person find the task too demanding?	Simplify task, reduce workload, reduce time pressures, etc.
Intrinsic motivation. Does the person find the task rewarding in itself?	Redesign job to match job-holder's needs.
Extrinsic motivation. Is good performance rewarded by others?	Arrange positive consequences for good performance and zero or negative consequences for poor performance.
Feedback. Does the person receive adequate feedback about his/her performance?	Provide or arrange feedback.
Working conditions. Do working conditions, physical or social, interfere with performance?	Improve light, noise, heat, layout, remove distractions, etc., as appropriate.
Personal problems. e.g. stress, substance abuse, family problems, etc.	Provide counselling if sufficiently skilled. Call in specialist helper.

5. Do you have sufficient information to select the most appropriate solution(s)? If not, collect the information required, e.g. consult records, observe work behaviour, talk to person concerned

6. Select most appropriate solution(s).

7. Is the solution worthwhile in cost–benefit terms?
   (a) If so, implement it.
   (b) If not, work through the checklist again, *or* relocate the individual, *or* reorganize the department organization, *or* live with the problem.

8. Could you have handled the problem better? If so, review own performance. If not, and the problem is solved, reward yourself and tackle the next problem.

Figure 14.7 Checklist for improving work performance (Source: Wright and Taylor, 1989, p. 127)

Performance/rewards/motivation

Performance, rewards and motivation are inextricably linked, and are all areas of human resource management about which much has been written (Armstrong, 1991; Cowling and Mailer, 1990; Molander, 1989). Rewards, both extrinsic (e.g. monetary rewards) and intrinsic (e.g. job satisfaction) are one factor which motivates people to improve performance at work. At the end of the day, the operations manager is concerned about the performance of the workforce – how diligently, effectively and efficiently they work. Wright and Taylor (1989) developed a checklist for improving work performance, presented here in Figure 14.7.

What is of critical importance to the operations manager is that the rewards encourage the desired behaviour. There is a danger in a service setting, where it is difficult to measure performance, that the surrogate measures used to monitor performance actually encourage undesirable behaviour. For example, if an employee, maybe at an information desk, is rewarded for the number of customers *seen*, as opposed to the number of customers served who went away *happy*, an abrupt manner may be the outcome, leading to a rapid turnover in customers, who go away unhappy.

Conclusion

In this chapter, some of the issues of human resource management have been briefly considered. It is important that operations managers do not distance themselves from any of these issues on the grounds that they are outside their remit. Figure 14.8 illustrates how getting human resource management right can lead to greater efficiency, larger profits and, ultimately, continued success.

The aim is to select and retain appropriate people for the organization. Helping people to do the job well by training and giving support when needed, empowerment of employees – which not only makes them feel valued, but makes the job more interesting and often means that they can help customers better, which in turn leads to implicit rewards – together with appropriate explicit rewards, all lead to happier employees, who are much more likely to stay within the organization. A happy workforce with lower turnover reduces the cost of recruitment, training and termination costs. A happier more experienced workforce will be more productive, through increased efficiency, effectiveness and flexibility, which will all lead to increased profits.

Being in a job for a sustained period allows relationships to be built up between the customer and the employee. This has a twofold effect. From an employee's point of view, knowing the customers and their requirements enables them to deliver a better service, which leads to more job satisfaction. From the customers' point of view, having their needs known without having to go into long explanations time and time again increases their satisfaction. The net result is loyal customers who come back again and again. It costs far less to retain a customer than it does to attract a new customer in the first place. There are therefore not only operational cost savings in performing more cost effectively, but also marketing cost savings in reduced costs incurred in attracting customers in the first place. Yet a third cost saving comes in the form of lower customer training costs – if they are repeat buyers, they know the system, and less time is needed to deliver the service. All

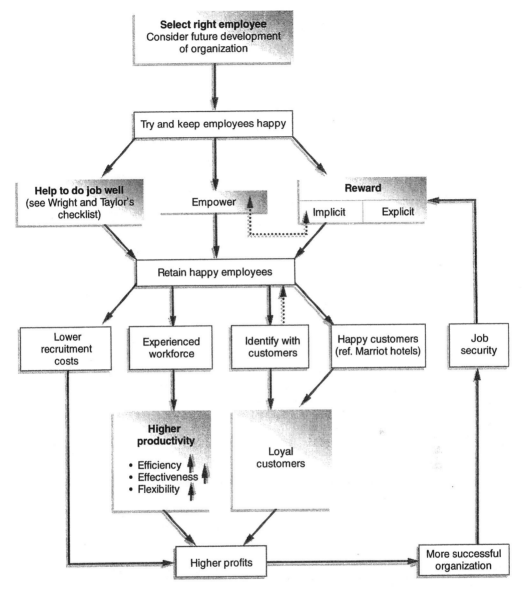

Figure 14.8 The relationship between human resource management and success

these factors lead to a more profitable and successful organization, which in turn leads to increased job security. This acts as a reward, which helps in the retention of employees.

A critical factor in the above is the recruitment of *suitable* employees in the first place. Unsuitable employees can have very negative effects, not only on the employee–customer interface, but also on other employees. If employees who are good at their job keep having to deal with problems caused by colleagues who are not good at their job, frustration and resentment can result.

The actual importance or strength of the link between a stable effective workforce and the customer base will in part depend upon the nature of the business – is the building up of a loyal set of customers a feasible option? For example, catering facilities in an airport do not rely on repeat purchases from the same set of customers.

A frequent argument against the above schema is that an experienced, long-standing, more flexible workforce will cost more in terms of pay and rewards. This is, of course, true. However, the overall costs will in most cases be less, once the additional costs of recruitment, training and marketing caused by higher labour turnover are taken into consideration.

In a service industry where labour intensity is high, and interaction of personnel with the customer has a major impact on the customer's perceptions of the service itself, an understanding of the importance of good human resource management is critical.

References

Armstrong, M. (1991) *A Handbook of Personnel Management Practice* (4th edn), Kogan Page, London.

Bowen, D.E. and E.E. Lawler III (1992) 'The empowerment of service workers', *Sloan Management Review*, vol. 33, no. 3, pp. 31–9.

Cowling, A. and C. Mailer (1990) *Managing Human Resources*, Edward Arnold, London.

Cran, D.J. (1994) 'Towards validation of the service orientation construct', *Service Industries Journal*, vol. 14, no. 1, pp. 34–44.

Dale, A. and S. Wooler (1991) 'Strategy and organization for service', in S.W. Brown, E. Gummesson and B.O. Gustavsson (eds.), *Service Quality: Multidisciplinary and multinational perspectives*, D.C. Heath/Lexington Books, Lexington, MA.

Gough, H.G. (1975) *Manual for the California Psychological Inventory*, Consulting Psychologists Press, Palo Alto, CA.

Hofstede, G. (1991) *Software of the Mind*, McGraw-Hill, London.

Hogan, J., R. Hogan and C.M. Busch (1984) 'How to measure service orientation', *Journal of Applied Psychology*, vol. 69, no. 1, pp. 167–73.

Holland, J.L. (1972) *Professional Manual for the Self-Directed Search*, Consulting Psychologists Press, Palo Alto, CA.

Hostage, G.M. (1975) 'Quality control in a service business', *Harvard Business Review*, vol. 53, no. 4, pp. 98–106.

Labich, K. (1991) 'Delta aims for a higher altitude', *Fortune*, 16 December, pp. 52–3.

Leirvaag, S.O. (1988) 'The human factor or how do we organize SAS in the future?', SAS, Oslo.

Matthes, K. (1993) 'Lighten up! Humor has its place at work', *HR Focus*, February, p. 3.

Molander, C. (ed.) (1989) *Human Resource Management*, Chartwell-Bratt, Bromley, Kent.

Peters, T.J. and R.H. Waterman (1982) *In Search of Excellence*, Harper Row, New York.

Prais, J.J., V. Jarvis and K. Wagner (1989) 'Productivity and vocational skills in services in Britain and Germany: hotels', *National Institute Economic Review*, November, pp. 52–74.

Smith, M. (ed.) (1991) *Analyzing Organizational Behaviour*, Macmillan, London.

Taylor, D.S. (1989) 'Training', in C. Molander (ed.), *Human Resource Management*, Chartwell-Bratt, Bromley, Kent.

Taylor, D.S. and P.L. Wright (1988) *Developing Interpersonal Skills Through Tutored Practice*, Prentice Hall, Hemel Hempstead.

US Department of Defense (1980) *Armed Services Vocational Aptitude Battery (ASVAB) Counselors Guide*, Military Enlistment Processing Command, Ft Sheridan, IL.

Wright, P.L. and D.S. Taylor (1989) 'Managing unsatisfactory performance', in C. Molander (ed.), *Human Resource Management*, Chartwell-Bratt, Bromley, Kent.

Discussion topics/exercises

1. Discuss the importance of front-line staff in a service organization characterized by high contact with the customer. What staff-related issues should an operations manager be aware of?

2. Why is training and selection of staff in services more difficult than in a manufacturing context?

3. What does empowerment really mean? What implications does it have for an organization? Should there be any limits to the empowerment of staff?

4. How can rewards be dysfunctional? Discuss the situations in which you think rewards have been inappropriate and then think of suitable ways of rewarding performance in those situations.

Index